MODERN SUPERMARKET OPERATIONS

MODERN SUPERMARKET OPERATIONS

Third Edition

Dr. Faye Gold
Instructional Program Management Specialist, Marketing Education
Bureau of Business and Marketing Education
Board of Education of the City of New York

Dr. Alfred E. Berkowitz
Professor
Program Director, Retail Business Management and Food Marketing
Kingsborough Community College

Milton M. Kushins
Executive Vice-President
Associated Food Stores, Inc.

Based on previous edition by Dr. Edward A. Brand

Fairchild Publications
New York

Designed by Janet Solgaard

Third Edition, © 1981 by Fairchild Publications
Division of Capital Cities Media, Inc.

Previous editions, © 1965, 1963 by Fairchild Publications, Inc.

Standard Book Number: 87005-263-2

Library of Congress Card Catalog Number: 80-70882

Printed in the United States of America

TABLE OF CONTENTS

Since its initial publication, *Modern Supermarket Operations* has served as a very valuable reference work and textbook for a most vital and important industry—food retailing, the nation's largest business. This book has proven most useful to employees who wish to advance to managerial positions and to students, trainees, and others interested in careers in food merchandising.

The food retailing industry is a dynamic field; both practitioners and those who aspire to careers in it must constantly be alert to new and emerging developments so that they can better adopt them or utilize them as points of departure for creative problem solving in their places of business. This revised and updated edition reflects the many changes in food retailing and distribution that have occurred during the past two decades. Also, in order to better understand these changes, an overview of the history of food retailing has been greatly expanded.

Modern Supermarket Operations provides an in-depth study of current practices and procedures in the food industry as well as offering insights into emerging trends and developments in the field. Its purpose is to provide a clear understanding of operations, functions, and services involved in successful food store management. Examined in detail are: merchandising, management, and operation of each of the product-based departments, including the grocery, meat, produce, dairy, frozen foods, delicatessen, bakery and general merchandise departments; functions of personnel at all levels; buying, pricing, ordering, receiving and stock-keeping procedures; customer service operations; sales promotion, advertising, and display techniques; store sanitation, maintenance, and security; storewide management control and personnel techniques; store location, layout, and equipment; and food distribution centers. Also, a checklist has been included to summarize many of the pointers for more efficient operations made throughout this work.

To provide a more comprehensive presentation of past, current and emerging practices in the industry, the contents have been reorganized and updated. In addition, new chapters have been added to provide more complete coverage of the industry. These include new chapters concerned with checkout management and control, general merchandise, the delicatessen/appetizing department (and other service departments discussed within other chapters), and consumerism and government regulatory agencies.

An entirely new feature included in the third edition is a glossary of terms commonly used in the supermarket industry. Also, the bibliography has been updated in order to enhance its usefulness.

The new chapters, as well as other revised material, reflect the many technological changes that have occurred since the publication of the last edition. These changes include, for example, the tremendous advances in electronic data processing for inventory and sales procedures, and in new equipment, especially in the area of checkout management and control.

Also, these changes are related to recent political, economic and social trends in our society. Among these are the efforts of the consumer to exercise more control in the marketplace, the pressures of inflation, and a growing concern over the relationship between health and the foods we eat. These developments have resulted in an increasing presence by government in the regulation of the food industry and in a strong consumer movement.

There have been, in addition, powerful changes in the role of women in society and the concept of the conventional family. Examples are the growth in divorce rates, single-parent households, working mothers, people living alone, and shrinking family size.

In response to these and other forces, during the past two decades, the food industry has experienced many advances and innovations. And, the next two decades surely will witness further change. Constructive growth must be based on a knowledge and understanding of the past as well as the current practices described in this book.

The information, statistics, and data in this revised, updated edition were gathered from many sources: government publications and agencies; trade associations; trade publications; reports of trade meetings; and from the personal knowledge of successful, prominent practitioners of supermarket operations and management throughout the United States, who so generously shared their expertise and experience in the intricacies of the industry.

The authors wish to acknowledge the following individuals for their cooperation and aid in the preparation of this book: Dan Burry, security consultant; Martin H. Jacobs, director of personnel, Times Square Stores Corporation; Alfred Leffel, vice-president, frozen foods, Waldbaum's Supermarkets; Bernard Paroly, president, Pathmark Division, Supermarkets General Corporation; Walter Reed, vice-president, Markland Advertising; Jules Rose, president, Sloan's Supermarkets; Charles Thaler, consultant, sanitation and safety; Howard B Tisch, executive director, Greater New York Metropolitan Food Council and former deputy commissioner of consumer affairs for the City of New York; Milton Widerman, director, store planning, Supermarkets General Corporation; Jim Zellner, United States Department of Agriculture; and Sidney Zukerman, vice-president, advertising, Waldbaum's Supermarkets.

We also wish to acknowledge Nick Benizi, Stanley Dubrow, Dennis Hart, Charles Heft, David Karin, Howard Kaye, Alan A. Meredith, Leonard Rapoport, Tony Spetz, John Walsh, and the Executive Committee of the Eastern Produce Council.

A special thanks to Dick Topus, assistant professor, Hofstra University.

1

Food distribution plays a vital role in the economy of the United States and in the well-being of its citizens. It is the nation's largest business, with annual sales reaching an all-time peak each year. Total annual retail food store sales are currently over $200 billion. Food stores account for an estimated 22 percent of *total retail sales*. Grocery stores and supermarkets (defined as food markets with minimum sales of $2 million) account for 93 percent and 65 percent of total food store sales, respectively. The following is a brief background history of how supermarkets achieved this dominant position in American food distribution.

The retailing of food can be traced to antiquity. The earliest written records and relics of Carthage, Athens, and Rome reveal the existence of both a wholesale and retail food trade.

In the United States, in the 1600's, trading posts were established at the headwaters of navigable streams and at the intersections of Indian trails. Many cities, such as Detroit, Chicago, St. Louis, and Des Moines, were originally trading posts established for traders who came to barter with the Indians. The early 1700's to the late 1850's was the period of greatest growth for the general store. Storekeepers sold bulk food and necessary items which people did not grow or produce for themselves, such as sacks of flour, barrels of lard, and slabs of soap. Although the general stores usually carried fewer than one hundred food items, it was the one-stop shopping center for the surrounding area.

During the late 1860's, most communities and towns grew and flourished. The Industrial Revolution brought men and women to work in factories in towns where the population growth and density left little space for people to produce their own food. The great variety of merchandise carried by the general store made it difficult for these stores to offer a wide selection within each class of merchandise. As a result, the specialty store came into existence; in food retailing: the butcher, the baker, the grocery store, and in some areas, the greengrocer and fish market.

The small, specialized retailer soon learned that the limited lines stocked also limited expansion and profit potential. Combining of similar lines, such as groceries, produce, and meats, into one store was economically desirable. This was accomplished by forming partnerships, or the grocer or butcher simply began stocking other food lines. The grocery store became a complete food store. This is not to imply that the specialty store was eliminated; some of them continue to operate. Some aggressive operators developed complete stores, while a few developed chains of butcher shops, bakery shops, and so forth. "Creaming" the merchandise of specialty retailers became a food store practice. It refers to selecting the traffic or volume items that most people buy frequently and stocking them, leaving the handling of the complete line to the specialty store. Creaming permits the store to stock added lines without changing the basic risk pattern, and to gain sales and profits without changing the basic pattern of operation.

Expansion of merchandise lines was followed by expansion of stores, and the chain store system evolved. Local retailers resisted the expansion of chain competition. This opposition took many forms, but the enactment of special per-store taxes, in an attempt to make chain stores unprofitable, received the greatest effort. "Support local merchants" and "Keep the money in the community" promotions did not deter shoppers. The more efficient retailers survived, and the opposition subsided. Many chain store taxes have been repealed, and the chains are now an integral part of the food marketing scene.

A significant advance in food store operations was the development of the self-service supermarket. In 1980, the supermarket industry celebrated its fiftieth anniversary. The Food Marketing Institute credited King Kullen of Westbury, New York, with the establishment in 1930, on Long Island, of the first supermarket. Others have attributed the start of the supermarket to the advent of the first self-service grocery store—started in 1916 by Clarence Saunders in Memphis, Tennessee. Big Bear stores (same name, but different ownerships) opened in Elizabeth, New Jersey, and Columbus, Ohio, in the early 1930's. FMI acknowledged the Saunders operations, but felt that the King Kullen operation was closer to the supermarket as we know it today, and thus 1930 is officially designated as the birthyear of the supermarket.

Supermarkets had their beginnings during the

Photo courtesy of The Great Atlantic & Pacific Tea Company.

As long ago as 1890, A&P, then a modest chain, was already tying food sales to promotions. In this Newark, New Jersey location, featuring tea, coffee, and dairy products, A&P offered premiums—dishes, lamps, vases—along shelves seen at left.

depression of the 1930's. Available buildings, such as garages and warehouses, were equipped with crude fixtures, and opened cases of merchandise were stacked on the floor. The concepts of reduced costs, high turnover rates, variable margins based on "cents" margin rather than "percent" margins were supermarket innovations.

The early supermarket was simply a food store, often starting as a grocery operation with leased specialty departments. However, costs increased, stores became more luxurious, leased departments were absorbed, competition increased, and profits decreased.

This situation again activated the expansion cycle, and supermarket operators began to cream health and beauty aid items from the drug store, household items and housewares from hardware and variety stores, and so forth. Thus sales and profits were increased without changing the basic risk pattern. (Much in the way of retail merchandising is a two-edged sword.

Today, many drug, variety and discount stores use food items as loss leaders.)

As the supermarket expanded the number of departments it contained, the number and variety of lines it carried, and the services and conveniences it offered, costs rose. The modern, glamorous supermarkets hardly resembled the original bare-bones stores.

A number of European operators of food stores, with the onset of an inflation that preceded that in the United States, decided to return to the basics of food retailing and started to open "no-frills" types of operations which much more closely resembled the early U.S. supermarkets. As inflation spread to this country, the concept returned to the United States in the form of limited-assortment and warehouse-type stores. However, they did not immediately succeed.

Among the first firms to experiment with the limited-assortment store in the United States was Pathmark, which tried several in New York City without success. The warehouse concept was attempted in the early 1970's when Food Fair, Hills, and A&P all started such stores in New Jersey, also without success. The A&P venture, which started as Warehouse Economy Outlet stores, soon was shifted to WEO (Where Economy Originated) and touched off a number of regional price wars when the program was shifted to all existing A&P stores as a price reduction move in order to recapture a portion of the market that A&P had been losing over the years.

Aggressive supermarket operators in the 1930's and 1940's, looking for expansion opportunities, moved their stores to suburban areas. During the early years of the expansion to suburbia, the supermarket was usually the first store to open in an area. As the population of suburbia increased and the problems of getting downtown multiplied, other retailers became interested in expanding; the shopping center concept became a reality. During recent years, nearly every major trading area has experienced the development of at least one shopping center.

During this period, supermarkets began offering more nonfoods. Two factors made this expansion attractive: the first suburban stores found a need for an outlet for nonfood volume items, and the cost-profit squeeze forced the stocking of high-margin nonfood items. Thus, the expansion by supermarkets into nonfoods was encouraged by shoppers and, at the same time, needed by operators.

Some supermarket operators have gone all the way into full-line department store operations built around a basic, large supermarket. One of the pioneers in this concept was Fred Meijer, who owns a chain of Thriftiacre stores in Michigan. Another was the late Fred Meyer in the Pacific Northwest, who founded a chain bearing his name. John Schwegmann, in the New Orleans area, also experimented with this idea. (Although many people think the hypermarket concept originated in France, the idea was developed by the above-named and refined into the concept that swept Europe and South America.)

Most American supermarket operators, however, have been much more cautious and have taken on only selected general merchandise lines. In the past decade or so, however, there has been a marked trend toward combination stores and superstores, which have plunged much more heavily into general merchandise selling.

Increased competition between shopping centers forced planners to devise new ways of providing greater shopping convenience in order to compete advantageously with older centers. One such development is the enclosed, air-conditioned mall that permits consumers to shop the various stores without going "outdoors." Shoppers are now able to shop the entire center as easily as the various departments of a larger store.

The discounter movement, which started after World War II, saw nonfood retailers begin to cut prices (discount) on big-ticket items, such as washing machines, refrigerators, and other such "white goods." The advent of the original television boom brought "brown goods" into the fold. However, the discounter needed heavy traffic in the stores to build volume for the items they specialized in—hard goods.

Two Guys (originally Two Guys from Harrison) and Korvettes tested the ideas of opening their own (Two Guys) or leased (Korvettes) supermarkets in or adjacent to the discount operation to build traffic. This was successful for nearly twenty years. But as supermarket competition increased, the discounter-supermarket began to operate at a disadvantage compared with other supermarkets. The discounter generally restricted the use of general merchandise items in the food operations (which the regular supermarket could carry and discount) for fear of hurting the departments that carried such merchandise in the discount stores. As competition in food departments increased, many supermarkets began to rely more heavily on profits from nonfoods departments, a course not available to discounter-tied or owned supermarkets. Thus, the supermarket operations in these stores began to lose money. Many firms that had ties with discounters either abandoned them (those associated with Korvettes) or went bankrupt (Allied supermarkets in its ties with K-Marts), or owned-by-discounter markets (Two Guys) began to lose money and were selectively closed. On the other hand, Fred Meyer, Lucky and Fred Meijer stores continue to thrive, and FedMart stores on the West Coast are adding food departments to stores that do not already have them.

Some visible changes that have been taking place in supermarkets include: the closing of smaller and less profitable supermarkets; longer hours of operation, including Sunday openings; more sales promotions; and openings of combination and larger stores.

Productivity has been a sore point in the supermarket in recent years. Virtually all statistics have shown a decrease in productivity, despite the increase in the use of scanners at the checkout, which speed up the checkout process as well as providing all sorts of useful data. (At the warehouse level, productivity has been aided by fully-automated order selection systems as well as batch-pick section, computerized slotting, and determination of order selection.)

One of the primary reasons for the decline in productivity has been the proliferation of service departments and other areas that are being instituted to build traffic in the store. An ever-growing, heated

Photo courtesy of The Southland Corporation.

So-called convenience stores were actually pioneered by this unassuming frame building in Oak Cliff, Texas. In the late 1920's, Southland Ice Co. cleverly deduced that ice customers might also buy milk, bread, and eggs—the basics. They were right.

Forerunner of the modern supermarket is this food operation whose signage indicates it was "Store #11" in the Skaggs United Stores chain. Of special interest is the meat department at right and the display of merchandise up front. Store likely pre-1930.

debate continues between the merchandising and productivity-oriented segments of the industry.

The merchandisers say service departments, such as scratch bakeries or bake-off departments, service delis, etc., build traffic and total sales and profits. Those oriented toward productivity point out that every time another service function is added, the productivity level declines. With labor costs the largest individual cost item at the supermarket, this is an important factor.

It is this latter factor, according to many close to the supermarket industry, that has led to the spread of various types of "box" stores—warehouse stores and limited-assortment stores—which cut the service levels to almost nil, reduce the number of items carried, and sell food at discounted prices.

Statistics indicate that the typical American family spent approximately 16 percent of its disposable income for food, and the percentage remained relatively constant for many years. However, in recent years, more people live alone, more women have joined the labor force, and an increased percentage of the food dollar is paying for meals fully or partly prepared away from home and consumed either at home or away from home (although this fluctuates with inflation and the economy), thereby reducing the share of income spent in the food store. Also reflecting these sociological trends, an increasing volume of expenditure in the food store is for prepared, ready-to-eat, packaged, canned and frozen "convenience" foods. The people who manage and work in today's supermarkets must be aware of trends such as these in order to maintain their dominant role in food distribution.

Today, supermarkets (defined as complete, full-line, self-service food markets with a minimum volume of $2 million per year) account for 65.2 percent of total food store sales. The balance is shared by superettes ($500,000 to $2 million), 7.8 percent; other grocery stores (convenience stores and other small grocery operations under $500,000), 20.2 percent; and specialty food stores (meat, seafood, fruit and vegetable, confectionery and bakery stores), 6.8 percent.

To achieve this commanding position in food distribution, the modern supermarket must be run efficiently. The supermarket is a complex operation depending for its efficiency on the smooth workings of a host of interrelated parts. But of all the factors that work together to achieve an efficient, low cost, high turnover operation, undoubtedly the single and most important factor is the people who manage and work in the markets.

In large chain organizations, there are over 200 job classifications involving most types of managerial and technical skills. The most ingenious mechanical equipment, the most attractive and appetite-appealing package, the most interesting store design and architecture would have little importance in the food distribution pattern were it not for the legions of store managers, assistant managers, department managers, and other employees responsible for daily operation.

2

THE MODERN SUPERMARKET

The story of the supermarket is, in a very real sense, the story of America. The food distribution industry is not great because of any unified power or monopolistic control, nor has it attained its greatness through government aid. It is great because of the pioneering spirit and the leadership of its owners and operators, and because it answers a need—the low cost merchandising of food.

Of all the major industries in the Unites States, the food distribution industry is the most decentralized. Although there are many large chains, there is not one that is truly nationwide. In spite of the large chains, the industry still is dominated by independent operators of one to five stores. Even among the chains, most of them are regional.

The supermarket of today represents the last word in the modernization of the nation's largest industry—food distribution. It is generally housed in a modern building designed and erected especially for the efficient operation of a supermarket. The doors are fully automatic; entrance doors open to welcome shoppers, and the exit doors allow customers carrying packages to leave with greater ease. The interior layout accents the food store's major potential for inducing maximum sales, including promotional displays for impulse buying.

A great deal of refrigeration and electrical equipment is installed for the convenience of customers and for the preservation and display of foods. Meat, dairy and produce cases are refrigerated. Frozen-foods cases house convenience foods which include frozen vegetables, fruits, juices, bakery products, dinners, and specialty items. Fluorescent lighting and spotlights illuminate the store to a pleasant brilliance and increase the merchandise appeal. Scanner-equipped cash registers with special checkstand conveyor equipment speed the customer out of the store with an accuracy unmatched in history.

No effort is spared to keep products fresh, to display them in more accessible and appealing ways, and to provide convenience for the customer. The average supermarket opened today has a total area of about 29,700 sq. ft., a selling area of 21,300 sq. ft., costs nearly $1 million to build, and requires an overall investment of approximately $2 million. The overall investment averages over $65 per square foot, including land, building, leasehold improvements, store equipment, and fixtures, but excludes opening inventory and opening expenses. There is considerable variation in these cost figures between companies and localities.

With retrenchment, caused by rising overhead and declining sales, many chains, including A&P, Krogers, and Safeway, have sold stores that provided little or no return (and frequently a loss) on investments. Others have combined by means of acquisition and merger with other food chains and have concentrated on expanding and enlarging more profitable units of the chain. Some of these stores have been acquired by independents or by retailer-owned warehouses.

Between 1975 and 1980, nearly 2,000 A&P's of about 3,600 chain outlets went through this process. Closings, not nearly so drastic, took place at Kroger, Safeway, and virtually every major chain. Small stores that could not be expanded and made profitable were closed, and often one large store replaced two, three or even four smaller outlets.

The advantage of acquiring an existing store is that the cost is one-fifth to one-quarter of the amount needed to build a new store. The most important considerations in planning an acquisition, say those who have successfully managed them, are the current or past sales and the potential for increasing the volume.

But just because a large chain cannot operate these stores successfully does not mean that they cannot be operated successfully by smaller chains or single entrepreneurs. In Kansas City, Kansas, several years ago, Kroger sold about fifty-five stores in the area. The entire package was bought by Associated Wholesale Grocers, a cooperative, which is owned by independently run supermarkets and small chains. The purchased Kroger stores were offered to the individual members of the co-op, and those not sold to the members became the nucleus of a successful, small, regional chain.

There are a variety of reasons why these stores could be made successful under new managements:

1. Sometimes, when the volume at the distribution facility falls below a certain level, even stores that in themselves are profitable are pulled down because of the inordinately high burden of the cost of running the reduced-volume warehouse.
2. Sometimes, the owner-operator is more innovative or has much greater leeway in promotional activity to stay competitive and attractive to the consumer than a manager whose hands are tied by policy of a large chain.
3. Often, union contracts with a large chain and seniority rules were more restrictive on the large chain than on the independent—and quite often the independent has no union contract at all.

In recent years, more than half of the new supermarkets opened in the United States were in neighborhood shopping centers—a planned center with more than one store, but dominated by the supermarket. About three of every ten units opened were in community shopping centers—a planned center dominated by a large department or discount store.

Some of the trends in supermarket operating results appear in Table 1.

Store inventories average two to three times weekly sales. A store with $130,000 in weekly sales needs at least $270,000 worth of merchandise to produce anticipated sales.

Although supermarket sales have increased steadily over the years, it is predicted that sales will increase at no more than 2 percent annually through the 1980's, as against an annual 3.5 percent increase through the 1960's and early 1970's. The decline in sales growth is attributed in part to the fact that more people live alone, more women work, and more food money is being spent in fast-food shops and restaurants. A slowdown in population growth is exacerbating the problem. The supermarkets are battling against higher prices and operating costs and searching for new merchandising methods.

In recent years, the so-called superstore has evolved, an extra-large supermarket that offers convenience "one-stop" shopping by featuring almost as many nonfood items as food. Superstores already account for one-third of all supermarket sales and are expected to approach 50 percent by the end of the decade. In an Alpha Beta store in San Diego, California, more than a third of the floor space is devoted to nonfood items, including a "style aisle" of clothing racks next to the bakery department. On Long Island, a Pathmark "supercenter" offers not only food, but also auto supplies, linens, hardware, and a pharmacy; store officials expect most of their profit to come from nonfood items. In the Denver area, Kings Soopers has what may be the ultimate supermarket—a superstore with a fast-food unit that advertises "Buck a Bag"

TABLE 1
TRENDS IN SUPERMARKET OPERATING RESULTS, 1974-1979*

	1979	1978	1977	1976	1975	1974
Gross Profit With Warehouse (% of Sales)	22.3%	22.6%	22.0%	22.2%	22.3%	20.9%
Gross Profit Without Warehouse (% of Sales)	20.5%	21.0%	19.7%	20.0%	19.3%	19.0%
Sales Per Man-hour	$76.77	$71.00	$59.62	$57.40	$54.06	$47.70
Sales Per Square Foot	$ 6.49	$ 6.17	$ 5.80	$ 5.50	$ 5.33	$ 5.09
Sales Per Customer Transaction	$11.60	$10.28	$ 9.85	$ 9.39	$ 8.75	$ 8.23
Average Hourly Labor Cost#	$ 5.92	$ 5.36	$ 4.91	$ 4.53	$ 4.25	$ 3.69
Store Labor Expense	8.3%	8.5%	8.4%	8.3%	8.1%	8.1%
Fringe Benefit Expense	1.8%	2.0%	1.7%	1.5%	1.4%	1.4%
Net Profit (Before Taxes)	1.9%	1.7%	1.4%	1.3%	1.5%	1.8%
Grocery Department Shrink	0.6%	0.5%	0.5%	0.6%	0.6%	0.8%

*Food Marketing Institute, "FMI Speaks, 1980."
#Excluding fringe benefits

Many modern supermarkets, located in suburban shopping centers, house their operations in buildings they hope will help draw traffic. Among the enticements: easy car loading and parking, convenient hours, attractive frontages, homey atmosphere. Four that operate in suburbia are: National, Piggly Wiggly, Pathmark, and Kroger.

lunches and offers to "fry your chicken while you shop." Elsewhere in the country, other unusual devices are being employed to attract shoppers into the supermarket.

Just as the nation's supermarkets have expanded into nonfoods for additional volume and profit, so other segments of retailing have begun to edge into the food field. Discount houses, drug chains, service stations, department stores, and variety stores are turning to food items as customer traffic-builders. A few are offering a complete supermarket stock, while others are using selected items to attract customers and build traffic. Some discount stores sell a handful of grocery items at below operating cost as a traffic builder. All of this competition represents a new trend in retailing and presents yet another challenge to supermarket operators. But supermarket operators used these same tactics to win customers originally.

Supermarkets increased the struggle for customers on the price front in the early 1980's. A growing trend, shown here, is warehouse selling. The message is clear: We save on fixturing, cut out middlemen, pass along savings to our customers.

An important challenge to supermarkets is meeting specialty food tastes of a very diverse population. Signage, fixtures, marketing considerations all play a role. Here, clockwise from upper left: health foods section, fixture with caviar, "family size" packaging, and section with imported items and foods with a "foreign flavor."

3 _____ STORE ORGANIZATION

The purpose of store organization is to establish relationships and lines of communication that will provide a pattern of authority and responsibility for the purpose of guiding personnel in their efforts to achieve the objectives of the business. Whenever responsibility is assigned, the necessary authority commensurate with the responsibility must be delegated. The organization plan establishes clearly defined lines of communication which flow from top management to the beginning worker, and which permit information to flow back again to management. Every individual employee must be made aware of his responsibilities and must know to whom he is responsible. Store organization is an effective tool for controlling the operation; and if the established organization is not effective, it must be changed to effect greater efficiency of operation.

To say a store is well-organized is not the same as saying it is well-managed. Organization is not management. Store organization provides the plan, the structure, the suggested format by which the store should be operated. Store organization provides the plans, and management executes them.

PRINCIPLES OF STORE ORGANIZATION

Good organization is achieved when the employee image of the company, store, customer, and fellow worker is favorable and conducive to doing a good job. The store becomes an efficient operating unit when the store manager delegates responsibility and the necessary authority to competent department heads, who in turn delegate both responsibility and authority to their employees.

The following principles should serve to establish a more effective organization:

1. Establish objectives and policies that are clear to all employees.
2. Prepare an organization chart designed to accomplish the objectives and in consonance with established policies.
3. Develop job specifications for each job.
4. Select, train (where necessary), and assign qualified personnel to fill each designated job slot. All personnel should be thoroughly familiar with the organization, its objectives and policies.
5. Establish lines of authority and responsibility.
6. Change, when advisable: objectives, policies, organization, job specifications, lines of authority, and channels of communication. All changes should be communicated to and made clear to all personnel.

DIRECTION AND SUPERVISION IN STORE ORGANIZATION

At the store level, the big problem is direction and supervision. To say that the objective is to increase sales and profits while reducing expenses means nothing without proper directive planning. Directive planning points the individuals within the organization toward the desired goals. It sets down methods to be used for reaching the desired goals and provides for instruction.

The store manager strives to ease the task of accomplishing the necessary work by the use of established practices and specific instruction for each employee. By having instructions written and posted in the store, every employee knows what is to be done and by whom. This eliminates duplication of effort and friction that could arise between employees. It also provides for a system of fixing responsibility when a job is not done right. Morale is higher if employees know their work assignments and the established performance standards.

But there are disadvantages to written instructions, which should be avoided. Sometimes, written instructions limit flexibility. Employees think they are fulfilling their obligations when they do only what is written and no more. Written instructions, supplemented with oral instructions, must establish the basic patterns of action, yet provide flexibility to meet the exceptions.

The making of decisions, an important part of direction, requires the gathering of facts. The manager or department head must delegate routine matters while devoting time to gathering and evaluating facts in order to decide important matters intelligently.

Decisions should be made at the level at which the problem arises. If the head of the meat department has a problem within the department, the head of the meat department should make the decision. In a well-organized operation, decisions are made at the lowest level at which the problem can be resolved.

An East Coast small chain recently bought a number of stores from two other chains and quadrupled its size. In converting ownership and attempting to establish the new chains of command, a problem-solving team was established. The team consisted of a number of operational executives. The original concept was that this team would meet about once a week and in an hour or two handle whatever problems might arise during the transition period.

From the outset of the program, the team was swamped with problems, so much so that they were spending every hour of their regular work week plus many more just solving problems—and not getting any of their regular work accomplished. With the number of problems submitted to the team growing daily and the team falling further and further behind, the directive of the team changed from "give us your problems" to "please tell us how you solved your problems so that we can share your solutions with other stores in the chain. Submit problems for solution to the team only if you cannot solve them."

In a very short period, the number of problems to be solved was reduced to a manageable level and the number of problems solved at store or district level swelled. As a result, those stores or districts that had incompetent management and those that had people deserving promotion were identifiable.

Soon, only two types of problems were being presented to the team: those that required capital expenditures for solution, which only the team was authorized to commit, and those that required approval from top management to permit changes beyond the authorization of the individual department, store manager, or district supervisor.

Good direction in store organization also means being sensitive to suggestions from all levels. If new ideas are of value and are used, the person(s) responsible should be given proper credit and recognition. This is what was lacking in the example cited above. When it was corrected, the situation improved.

In order to implement directive planning, supervision is necessary to see that each person within the store does the assigned work. Supervision is not merely restrictive, it is also constructive. It helps individuals perform effectively within the organization while also minimizing deviations from established practices and instructions.

Productivity in the supermarket industry has been declining. Yet, one of the best methods of achieving better productivity and providing improved employee morale has been taking place in Japan since the end of World War II. It started with American industrial experts who were sent to Japan in 1945 and 1946 to help reestablish Japan as a world industrial power.

The name of the program is Quality Control Circles, and it entails employees in a given department who meet on a regular basis to attempt to solve problems that arise and to improve the quality of work or working conditions. In recent years, the program has been reintroduced in the United States. Tested at several General Motors plants throughout the nation, the programs have brought results that were extremely satisfying to the employer, the employee, and unions. The results have been better quality, fewer problems, and higher productivity.

In the food field, one of the first to experiment with the program was General Foods. When management at the plant employing the program changed, the program was scrapped. However, another General Foods plan is contemplating reentry into a QCC program. Several other food manufacturing, retailing and wholesaling firms are looking at the program with an eye toward adopting QCC or some version of it for their firms.

PATTERNS OF STORE ORGANIZATION

Supermarket chain organizations follow many different patterns. But basic to all is that a store has one overall manager. The manager generally reports to a line supervisor and works with district departmental supervisors to run the store's various departments. Many supermarkets are divided into three departments, while other companies may use as many as ten. Yet, as long as the manager is successful and knows his neighborhood, he often has the final word. Each company develops a unique pattern of store organization adapted to its own needs and circumstances.

This form of organization claims many advantages. One is that it pinpoints responsibility and centralizes authority in the person of the store manager, which is in consonance with the basic precept of organization—the centralization of authority and responsibility.

The fundamental substance of centralized executive control provides the establishment of definite lines of supervision and authority from the store manager through department heads to their subordinates. Many functions, such as planning, buying, merchan-

PATTERNS OF STORE ORGANIZATION

FIGURE 1

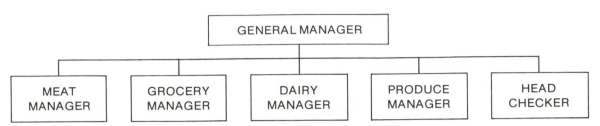

Figure 1 depicts a basic organization chart in which the store manager is responsible for the overall operation. The store has been subdivided into five departments, and they are subordinate to the general manager in a direct line of authority. None of the department heads is subordinate to any other department head. The store manager normally designates the grocery manager (many companies term this position "assistant manager") to assume command of the store when he or she is absent. Any of the other department heads also may be chosen to perform this temporary function.

FIGURE 2

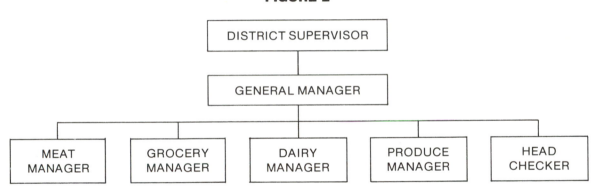

Figure 2 represents the organization chart of a supermarket that is supervised by a district supervisor. The district supervisor has line authority and is directly responsible for the success of the overall store operation. The district supervisor may supervise all department heads, but usually works through the store manager.

FIGURE 3

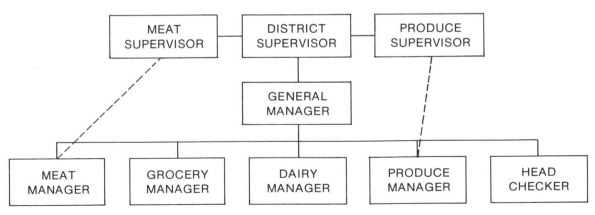

Figure 3 illustrates an organization chart similar to the one depicted in Figure 2. The main difference between the two is that the district supervisor has two staff assistants to help in the performance of his or her responsibilities. These specialists offer staff assistance to the produce and meat departments and are responsible to the district supervisor in a direct line of command.

FIGURE 4

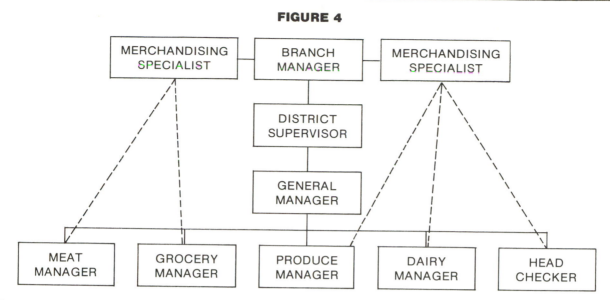

Figure 4 illustrates the organizational situation in which the district supervisor is still the line supervisor for the store. The store receives staff assistance from merchandising specialists who report to the next level of authority above the district supervisor.

dising, and accounting, are performed in central, corporate headquarters. Operating under these conditions, many companies feel that they must have at least one executive at the store level who can plan, merchandise, direct, and coordinate all the store's operations.

Another advantage is that it organizes the store in a manner that frees the store manager from much of the detail work. The store is divided into departments, and the details of these departmental operations are supervised by department managers. The store manager has more time to plan, direct, coordinate, and

supervise the overall operation and is in a better position to pinpoint areas of operational weaknesses. There is more time to assist in the operation of any department that is having operational problems. The manager should allow his subordinates to operate all routine activities as long as they perform satisfactorily. When they fail to do so, the manager should be free to step in and apply corrective action.

A great deal of responsibility is placed on the shoulders of one person. To alleviate this situation, assistant managers and bookkeepers are assigned to assist the store manager.

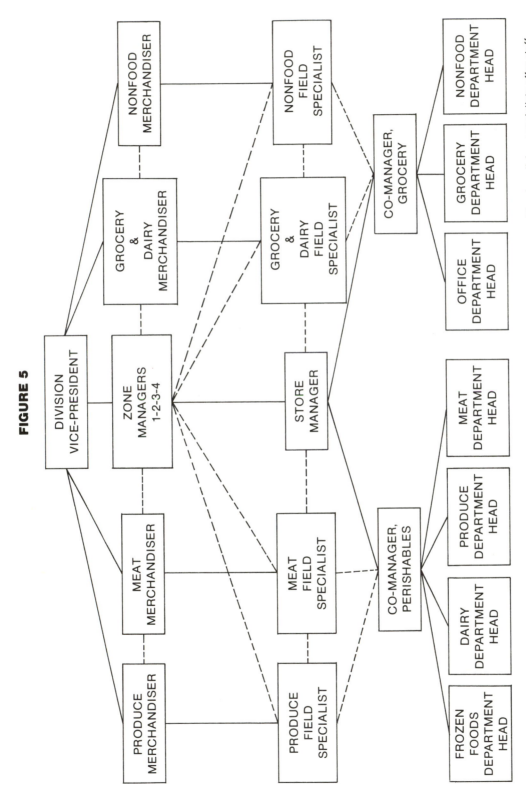

FIGURE 5

Figure 5 illustrates a chain store organization plan in which the store manager reports to a zone manager. Merchandising specialists offer staff assistance to the store manager. This form of organization plan increases in effectiveness as the number of store units increases.

4

THE GROCERY DEPARTMENT

The single largest department in a supermarket is the grocery department. Groceries are usually defined as nonperishable processed foods. However, depending on the size and organization of a store, products included in the sales of the grocery department may include general merchandise, general household items, and other edible and nonedible items. In some of the smaller supermarkets, dairy and/or frozen food may be included in grocery sales totals at the checkout counter. However, with electronic cash registers, most stores tend toward more rather than fewer breakdowns by category. Generally, the grocery department does not handle items that require special storing facilities, such as freezing, moisture, or heated storage.

Dry groceries alone account for approximately 27 percent of total supermarket sales. When dry groceries are totaled with nonfood sales, the grocery department accounts for approximately 50 percent of total supermarket sales.

THE IMPORTANCE OF
THE GROCERY DEPARTMENT

The grocery department handles the largest inventory, has the greatest volume of sales, and occupies the largest amount of floor space in a supermarket. The gross profit margin of the grocery department is the lowest of all of the departments, yet its large volume enables the department to contribute a moderate dollar profit to the organization.

Products in the grocery department do not usually contribute to building the store image and do not offer competitive advantage for the supermarket operation, unless cut-price policies are the rule. (In such cases, the traffic-building potential becomes more important than profit, which may drop to nil or even a loss.) Actually, the brand-name cans and packages stocked in one supermarket are much the same as products carried in another. Other than private labels and generic, second-generation generic and packer brands, most supermarkets carry the same national brands and the same varieties of canned and packaged groceries. Hence, the prevalence of grocery items as objects of price wars.

In the past few years, generic (no-frills), second-generation generic (store-confined label, lowest price line) and packer brands have been attracting an ever-growing consumer clientele. Thus, the grocery departments of many stores have begun to take on a character of their own and differ from competitors' grocery departments in some ways other than price.

But even the price picture changes from one chain to another, if the store is large enough to carry a well-accepted private-label line plus price-attracting lines (generics, etc.). Since the profit margins of private-label lines generally are somewhat better than nationally branded lines, a difference in sales mix from one store to another can substantially alter its pricing structure for the branded items.

The higher margins on private-label items, if the volume is great enough, can permit the retailer to cut the margin of the branded items and still keep the department's gross margin equal to competitors' even when the branded items are sold at reduced margins. Although the product sales mix keeps the total margin for the department equal to the competitors', the fact that the branded items are lower priced creates the image in the minds of customers that the store is lower priced than competitors.

Supermarkets account for over 75 percent of all sales of groceries; the annual per capita consumption of dry grocery products is approximately 440 pounds. Therefore, supermarket operators should continue to anticipate volume and profit from the largest department in the store—the grocery department.

THE RELATIVE COST OF
GROCERY DEPARTMENT OPERATIONS

Despite intensive competition in grocery item sales, the relatively low operating expense structure of grocery department operations still enables it to provide moderate profits for the supermarket operator. The gross profit of a department depends, in part, upon: processing required for the products, display and storage equipment required, spoilage, shrinkage, and supplies needed.

In the grocery department, products are preprocessed, need no special storage equipment, and require relatively low dollar investment and maintenance for basic display gondolas and shelves. Since there is an insignificant amount of spoilage, shrinkage is relatively low. Also, merchandise is prepackaged so that special supplies are not required in the handling of grocery products.

In addition, space in a grocery department can be used more efficiently than in other departments; merchandise can be displayed in depth from the floor to the top of shelves, and there is no wasted space between categories of merchandise. Also, since technically trained personnel are not needed to stock shelves or to preserve or process merchandise, the labor costs for the department are lower than in departments where specially trained personnel are needed.

Other factors that contribute to the low operating cost of the grocery department and enable it to operate profitably with a lower gross margin than needed in other departments include:

- Displays and signs supplied by the manufacturer
- The stocking of shelves and displays by distributor's representative (when permitted by the union)
- The availability of manufacturer's special promotions
- Coupons or premiums
- Other manufacturer/distributor promotions, cooperation, and assistance.

NEW ITEMS

New items are any product the store is not currently stocking on the shelf—a new label, a new package size, new packaging for an established product, or a totally new item. A supermarket that stocks as many as 15,000 items may have a grocery department with at least 7,000 items. The items stocked are not static. New items are offered continuously to the buyers of any large supermarket operation. Products introduced during the past twenty years are responsible for at least 70 percent of the grocery department sales. The new item problem is important in terms of store space and store image.

While food items tend to be considered static by the consumer in terms of processing, packaging, and convenience, more than half the items stocked today did not exist ten years ago. Projecting into the future, if the same conditions exist (although retail resistance is growing), ten years from now, over half of the items stocked in supermarkets will be new, although they are unknown today. Methods of preserving, processing, and packaging are changing rapidly.

A major issue facing buyers is deciding which items will sell in sufficient quantity to pay for the shelf space they will occupy. Factors to be considered in new item selection include the following:

- Reputation of the source
- Promotion of the item by the supplier
- Product research conducted in developing the item
- Market research conducted by the supplier
- Product quality
- Price and margin
- Package design
- Items in stock that fill the same customer wants
- Item or items that can be eliminated if new item is stocked.

Reputable companies spend the time and money needed to develop a new item and establish the extent of consumer acceptance through market research. This does not guarantee success in all areas; however, a well-planned and researched item backed by a substantial promotional campaign will be successful in most market areas. The organization with a past record of successful new items will continue to market successful new products. This is not to imply that small operators or newcomers in the field cannot produce successful new items. However, the buyer must exercise care and skill in selecting the items to be accepted.

GROCERY DEPARTMENT PACKAGING

The can and carton continue to be standard containers for many grocery department items. For the manufacturer, these packages are easily produced at high speed with fully automatic equipment. Attractive labels provide sales appeal on the supermarket shelf. The customer is accustomed to using canned and packaged foods.

Despite the many advances in packaging technology, the round can is still very widely used for many food items, even though space is wasted in packing cases and on store shelves.

There is a continued need for packaging that will provide the consumer with greater convenience and that will preserve the consistency and freshness of contents which may be kept in original containers after they are opened in the home. Easy-to-open containers improve the opening and resealing performance of covers and caps. Cans of dry products, such as coffee and nuts, have been provided with plastic covers so that cans can be closed after the lid is removed. Plastic containers have replaced glass and tin for liquid detergents, bleach, household cleaners, beauty aids, and other liquid products. General merchandise items are packed in protective, pilfer-proof, plastic blister packages. The packaging industry is continuing to devise packaging materials that will better protect the product and serve the consumer.

Two revolutionary packaging concepts—the retort pouch and aseptic packaging—are on the horizon for the supermarket. Both already have proven themselves practical and are growing in use.

The retort pouch is a hermetically sealed package of aluminum and plastic laminated layers. The pouch generally is packed inside a flat cardboard container. From the standpoint of stocking the package on shelves, there is absolutely no waste space as exists with cans, jars, or bottles.

But much more important is the fact that the package is absolutely air-tight. Prepackaged items, even gourmet meals that now require freezing to insure freshness, can be stored on a shelf with no refrigeration or special care and have a shelf life as long as any canned items.

When ready for serving, the package can then be heated, opened (or opened and then heated), and a dish as fresh and wholesome as one just prepared from scratch is available. To date, the one drawback to the retort pouch is the fact that it must be opened and put into a new container before being heated in a microwave oven. However, the makers of the pouch are working to correct that problem, if it be a problem.

The other development is aseptic packaging, which has been available in Europe and Israel for more than a decade and in much of the rest of the world (except for the United States) for somewhat less time. Aseptically packed milk, juices, and other perishables are packed in an environment away from air (actually in a "sea" of the product itself) and sealed in an airtight package. Each package, if not punctured, has a shelf life, without refrigeration, of six months to a year. Once opened, however, the product must be refrigerated and has the same life expectancy as if it were bottled conventionally. Currently, the Food and Drug Administration is still testing the process for acceptance in the United States.

Both these developments hold out the promise of a supermarket of the future that requires no freezers and a sharply reduced amount of refrigeration for display cases and storage. (Freezer and refrigerator fixtures are the major equipment costs and biggest energy users in any supermarket.)

STORE IMAGE

In the supermarket, it is meat, produce, and perishables that are the prime creators of a favorable store image. It is important to note that image is a total concept. The grocery department, despite its rela-

tively small competitive advantage, must be included in any consideration of the total store image.

The grocery department image-building factors include the:

- Quality of the items stocked
- Variety
- Condition of the shelf stock

TABLE 2
VALUE OF FOOD USED IN A WEEK BY HOUSEHOLDS[1], SPRING 1977-WINTER 1978*

	Total	At home	Away from home
	DOLLARS PER CAPITA		
All households	$20.26	$15.36	$4.90
Region:			
Northeast	22.82	17.06	5.76
North Central	19.45	14.93	4.52
South	18.60	14.41	4.19
West	21.31	15.56	5.75
Urbanization:			
Central City	21.27	16.08	5.19
Surburban	21.22	15.52	5.70
Nonmetropolitan ..	18.50	14.65	3.85
Income (1976) before taxes:			
Under $5,000	16.88	14.77	2.11
$5,000–$9,999	18.18	14.84	3.34
$10,000–$14,999 ...	19.23	14.83	4.40
$15,000–$19,999 ...	20.47	15.27	5.20
$20,000 and over ..	23.87	16 43	7.44
Income Not Reported	20.18	15.38	4.80
People living in household:			
One...............	28.59	19.66	8.93
Two	24.44	18.12	6.32
Three	21.19	16.03	5.16
Four	18.82	14.39	4.43
Five...............	17.59	13.57	4.02
Six or more	15.45	12.62	2.83
Race			
White	20.89	15.60	5.29
Nonwhite	16.81	13.80	3.01

*USDA, 1977–78 Nationwide Food Consumption Survey, 48 Contiguous States, Spring 1977–Winter 1978.
[1]Includes value of food used by household members and guests which was bought, home produced, and received as gift or pay. Value of food received without direct expense by household is based on the average price per pound paid for that food by survey households in the same region.

TABLE 3
CIVILIAN PER CAPITA CONSUMPTION OF MAJOR FOOD COMMODITIES (RETAIL WEIGHT)[1]*
POUNDS

	1970	1972	1973	1974	1975	1976	1977	1978[2]	1979[3]
Meats	151.4	153.5	142.6	152.5	145.4	155.3	154.6	149.3	147.7
Beef	84.1	85.9	81.1	86.4	88.9	95.7	93.2	88.9	79.9
Veal	2.4	1.8	1.5	1.9	3.5	3.3	3.2	2.5	1.6
Lamb and mutton	2.9	2.9	2.4	2.0	1.8	1.7	1.5	1.4	1.4
Pork	62.0	62.9	57.6	62.2	51.2	54.6	56.7	56.5	64.8
Fish (edible weight)	11.8	12.5	12.9	12.2	12.3	13.0	12.3	13.4	13.4
Poultry products									
Eggs	39.5	39.1	37.3	36.6	35.4	34.8	34.5	35.2	35.8
Chicken (ready-to-cook)	40.5	42.0	40.7	41.1	40.6	43.3	44.9	47.7	51.8
Turkey (ready-to-cook)	8.0	9.0	8.5	8.9	8.6	9.2	9.2	9.4	10.2
Dairy products									
Cheese	11.5	13.2	13.7	14.6	14.5	15.8	16.4	17.3	17.9
Condensed and evaporated milk	7.1	6.4	6.0	5.6	5.0	5.0	4.5	4.2	4.4
Fluid milk and cream (product weight)	296.0	298.0	293.0	288.0	291.1	292.0	288.4	285.9	284.2
Ice cream (product weight)	17.7	17.4	17.5	17.5	18.7	18.1	17.7	17.8	17.7
Fats and Oils—Total fat content	53.0	54.3	54.3	53.2	53.4	56.1	54.4	55.6	57.6
Butter (actual weight)	5.3	4.9	4.8	4.6	4.8	4.4	4.4	4.5	4.5
Margarine (actual weight)	11.0	11.3	11.3	11.3	11.2	12.2	11.6	11.4	11.6
Lard	4.7	3.8	3.4	3.2	3.0	2.7	2.3	2.2	2.3
Shortening	17.3	17.7	17.3	17.0	17.3	18.1	17.6	18.2	19.2
Other edible fats and oils	18.2	19.8	20.8	20.3	20.3	22.0	21.6	22.6	23.4
Fruits									
Fresh	79.3	74.8	74.2	76.9	81.3	83.7	79.6	81.6	80.5
Citrus	28.1	26.7	26.9	27.1	28.7	28.5	25.2	26.3	24.3
Noncitrus	51.2	48.1	47.3	49.8	52.6	55.2	54.4	55.3	56.2
Processed									
Canned fruit	23.3	21.4	21.3	19.6	19.3	19.2	19.9	19.0	18.0
Canned juice	14.6	15.5	15.9	14.7	16.2	16.2	15.4	17.4	17.5
Frozen (including juices)	9.8	10.4	11.2	11.3	12.6	12.2	11.9	11.3	11.8
Chilled citrus juices	4.7	5.2	5.3	5.2	5.7	6.2	5.8	6.2	6.4
Dried	2.7	2.0	2.6	2.4	3.0	2.6	2.5	2.0	2.3
Vegetables									
Fresh[4]	91.0	91.6	93.0	95.0	94.1	94.2	91.8	93.3	97.2
Canned	53.0	55.2	57.7	56.9	55.1	55.7	56.2	54.1	55.0
Frozen (excluding potatoes)	9.6	9.9	10.6	10.1	9.6	10.2	10.3	10.8	11.1
Potatoes[5]	115.3	116.9	114.4	112.3	120.3	114.4	119.8	122.9	123.0
Sweet potatoes[5]	5.2	4.6	4.6	4.9	5.0	4.9	4.5	5.0	5.0
Grains									
Wheat flour[6]	110	109	112	110	113	118	114	114	112
Rice	6.7	7.0	7.0	7.6	7.7	7.2	7.6	5.8	8.9
Other									
Coffee	10.4	10.5	10.1	9.5	9.0	9.4	6.7	7.9	7.8
Tea	.7	.8	.8	.8	.8	.8	.9	.7	.7
Cocoa	3.1	3.5	3.4	3.0	2.6	3.0	2.7	2.7	2.7
Peanuts (shelled)	5.9	6.2	6.6	6.4	6.5	6.3	6.6	6.6	6.6
Dry edible beans	5.9	6.3	6.4	6.7	6.5	6.3	6.1	5.9	5.9
Melons	21.2	19.9	19.8	17.1	17.3	18.6	19.3	20.1	18.9
Sugar (refined)	101.8	102.8	101.5	96.6	90.2	94.7	95.7	93.1	91.6

*National Food Review, United States Department of Agriculture, Fall 1979.

[1] Quantity in pounds, retail weight unless otherwise shown. Data on calendar year basis except for dried fruits, fresh citrus fruits, peanuts, and rice which are on a crop-year basis.

[2] Preliminary.

[3] Forecast.

[4] Commercial production for sale as fresh produce.

[5] Including fresh equivalent of processed.

[6] White, whole wheat, and semolina flour including use in bakery products.

Note: Historical consumption and supply-utilization data for food may be found in Food Consumption, Prices, and Expenditures, Ag. Econ. Report 138 and annual supplements, ESCS, USDA.

TABLE 4
CONSUMER BEHAVIOR

SALES BY DAY OF WEEK*

Supermarkets Open Sunday

Monday	9.4%
Tuesday	9.3%
Wednesday	12.8%
Thursday	15.1%
Friday	19.9%
Saturday	23.2%
Sunday	11.5%

Supermarkets Closed Sunday

Monday	9.6%
Tuesday	10.4%
Wednesday	15.0%
Thursday	17.0%
Friday	22.6%
Saturday	25.7%

*Food Marketing Institute, "FMI Speaks," 1979.

- Labels stocked—well-known, distributor, or controlled
- New items stocked
- Store layout
- Special features
- Convenience of shopping in the store.

THE CUSTOMER

In a recent *Progressive Grocer* magazine study, it is reported that knowledge about the store's customers is of prime importance in merchandising to them, and they note differences in shopping patterns of the following customer types among others: upper income customers, apartment dwellers, young family customers, blue-collar customers, small town customers, discount shoppers, etc. Additional customer characteristics may be taken into consideration by the merchandiser, such as: ethnicity of the population, number of persons per household, shopping patterns (days, hours), age of population, and the like.

A knowledge of consumer behavior is important to the food merchandiser. Average weekly expenditures per capita for food used by households are given in Table 2. Table 3 lists the major food purchases, indicating per capita consumption in pounds. Table 4 gives supermarket sales by day of the week.

THE EFFECT OF "OUT-OF-STOCK" ON GROCERY DEPARTMENT PROFITABILITY

Profits depend, in part, on having the items customers want on the shelves. "Out-of-stock" is a cause of lost sales; some customers will wait until the next shopping trip; others will go to another store; and some will substitute an available item, although many shoppers will not accept substitutes. The degree to which substitutes are acceptable depends upon the type of item and the use to be made of it. The individual preparing food for guests is likely to insist on a particular label, but may accept a substitute for family use.

Empty spaces on the grocery department shelves create an unfavorable impression. The fact that items are not available is irritating, even when the out-of-stock item is not on the shopping list. Full stocks are an important image-building factor.

Controlling out-of-stocks requires cooperation on the part of the buyers, the warehouse, and the store. Store over-ordering drains warehouse stocks, while under-ordering reduces warehouse movement and delays reorders. Store ordering determines the rate of movement and reorder points; it is the key to successful, in-stock conditions in the warehouse and store.

Out-of-stocks and how much, if any, is acceptable has been a subject of debate in the supermarket industry since its beginning. On one side of the debate is the cost of stocking slow-moving items, the cost of the money tied up in stocks of such items, and the fact that such money could be much more productive when put to other uses. This side argues that it does not pay to carry slow movers in the stores or warehouse. It not only ties up capital, they say, but also valuable space.

The other side of the argument is that many merchandisers feel that an out-of-stock can create a bad image and can often result in the loss of a valuable customer to a store that carries the item in question. The story (apocryphal, perhaps) is told of a supermarket chain that lost the patronage of a $150-a-week customer when it stopped carrying guava jelly in one of its stores.

Is the store justified in making the decision to continue or discontinue a slow mover in the face of the potential loss of customers or the increased cost of doing business, particularly when there is the knowledge that if the desired product is discontinued in one store, it probably will not be at the competitor's?

Please refer to pages 88-93 for a further discussion of grocery receiving, storing, stocking and price marking.

5

The individual planning a meal usually thinks first about the main dish, which frequently is meat. Meat may be the most expensive single item in a meal, and most meats do not carry a brand name other than the store price label. Therefore, the meat department is a strong image-building factor in supermarket operations. A customer who is consistently satisfied with meat purchases in a market will be a loyal customer of that market.

Products carried in most meat departments of a store include:

- Beef and veal
- Pork
- Lamb
- Poultry
- Organ meats
- Seafood
- Processed meats
- Meat cuts and specialties to meet the demand of ethnic group(s) within the trading area.

THE DEVELOPMENT OF THE MEAT DEPARTMENT

The early grocery store stocked and merchandised only grocery items; meat was sold by the butcher shop or meat market. Then a few operators combined grocery and meat stores, either with a leased meat department or as independent operators sharing overhead costs. Gradually, the meat operation was absorbed by the grocer (as were the produce and dairy departments), and the combined food store emerged.

In 1929, only about 30 percent of the grocery stores handled meat. Ten years later, combined stores sold 50 percent of the total meat volume. Larger supermarkets at that time, as well as all new supermarkets, included a meat department. Today, all but the smallest food stores handle meat to some extent, and supermarkets sell 65 percent of all meats sold at retail.

The first supermarket meat departments were the service-type, consisting of one or two refrigerated cases. Merchandising in these service-type depart-

ments was very limited. Impulse buying was negligible due to the lack of available variety. The customer told the butcher the type of meat desired and was sold a particular cut—often with an explanation of the best cooking method. Sales effort was directed to selling additional meat items to complete the weekly menu plan.

Organ meats, as they are known today, were usually the "push items" for the butcher. The direct customer contact in the early meat departments gave the butcher an opportunity to move slow-selling items, high-margin items, and less desirable cuts of meat.

In the service meat department, the personality of the butcher played an important role in the success of the market. Tables of smoked meats were the only displays used. Fresh meats were kept in refrigerated cases, and during warm weather, many smoked meat items were also refrigerated. Ice and dry ice were used prior to mechanical refrigeration. With the advent of government food inspection, the use of refrigerated cases became a requirement.

During the early 1930's, the meat price level started a steady increase. As meat prices advanced, profit margins declined. With prices rising and operating costs increasing, supermarket operators started looking for ways to cut expenses. Experiments were conducted to find ways to reduce the expenses incurred in selling meat.

THE DEVELOPMENT OF THE SELF-SERVICE MEAT DEPARTMENT

As early as 1920, meat department operators had begun experimenting with meat self-service. Cutting and pricing presented no important problems, but wrapping did. Customers would not accept "blind wrapped" meat, and no transparent film was available that was sufficiently durable to be satisfactory. Therefore, precut meat, selected by the customer, had to be wrapped by a clerk; when volume was low, the operation proved more costly than regular meat service.

Another major problem was displaying precut meat. Early experimenters used dairy cases with ice cooling. These cases did not maintain a temperature

Photo courtesy of Safeway Stores, Inc.

A Safeway meat department in the 1930's—note "2 lbs. ground beef, 25¢"—with heavy promotional signage and well-staffed division. Among messages: beef is economical, has lots of protein, is good to eat hot or cold, or even outdoors!

low enough to hold the "bloom"(the attractive, fresh, red look) on the meat. For lack of satisfactory refrigerated display cases and wrapping materials, the advent of self-service meat operations was delayed.

In the late 1920's, the H. C. Bohack Company, in Brooklyn, New York, attempted to service approximately fifty small stores with central, prepackaged meat. These stores were too small to operate service meat units, and the meat was sold from the dairy case by store clerks. This experiment failed. The lack of refrigerated display space and inadequate wrapping materials caused a high percentage of returns to the central plant. Also, grocery clerks failed as meat merchandisers; they displayed meat poorly and exercised inept stock control.

Through the 1930's, the same conditions prevailed. Many operators experimented and gave up their self-service meat operations. Then, the A & P pioneered a self-service meat case. Their engineers converted a fish and delicatessen case into a usable meat case. This breakthrough in self-service meat display increased meat sales in the experimental stores

by about 30 percent without increasing labor costs. The improvised case was modified by refrigeration equipment manufacturers, and the first practical, refrigerated, self-service meat display equipment was put into production.

However, World War II created material shortages and curtailed the manufacture of refrigerated cases. It was not until 1946 that self-service meat cases were again manufactured. By 1949, over 1,000 food stores operated self-service meat departments with refrigerated display cases. Retailers, trying to find ways to reduce costs in the meat department, turned to self-service as rapidly as equipment became available.

Self-service meat merchandising requires a wrapping material that is clear and durable over a wide temperature range. The materials available throughout the 1920's and 1930's became brittle at low temperature and required an over-wrap when the customer made a selection for purchase. Also, the percentage of rewraps was very high.

The development of plastic films made self-service meat practical and economical. A variety of these films are now available in a range of widths, weights, thicknesses, breathing qualities, moisture retaining qualities, and heat-sealing abilities. New processes, such as vacuum wrapping for ham and turkey freezing, soon came into use.

The sale of self-service, sliced, processed meats increased in volume as wrapping materials and techniques improved. Wrappings that are satisfactory for good display, prolonged shelf-life, customer handling, and price marking made complete self-service possible.

Another important advance, the automatic scale, calculates the selling price, allowing for tare (weight of packaging); prints the label with the name of the cut, weight, and selling price; and heat-seals the label to the package.

THE IMPORTANCE OF THE MEAT DEPARTMENT

Despite the fact that the grocery department in the average supermarket provides the greatest volume of sales, the meat department acts as a customer magnet for the store and accounts for anywhere from 12 percent to 35 percent (an average of about 20 percent) of the supermarket's volume. Much of the image of the store is dependent on it. Therefore, it is little wonder that so much attention is paid to this department. The key factor in the department is fresh meat, and primary here is beef.

The per capita consumption of red meat is about 150 pounds per year. Beef accounts for about 59 percent of the total, pork is second with about 38 percent, and veal (young beef) is third with 2 percent. Lamb and mutton (older lamb) are in last place with a total of slightly less than 1 percent. The per capita consumption of chicken is about 50 pounds per year and turkey, 10 pounds.

Supermarket meat department sales, on a national basis, average:

Beef	39%
Pork	9
Veal	2
Lamb	2
Packaged Bacon	6
Cured Ham and Picnics	6
Frankfurters	3
Sausages and Sausage Products	8
Cold Cuts	10
Poultry	11
Fish	4

For specific holidays, other meats may temporarily take the spotlight away from beef (ham at Easter, turkey for Thanksgiving, and turkey and goose at Christmas and New Year's), but on a day-in-day-out basis, it is beef around which the meat department revolves.

THE EVOLUTION OF MEAT PREPARATION FOR SHIPMENT

Until about the early or mid-1960's, virtually all stores had overhead rails leading from the back door into the meat cooler and work areas. Sides of beef were delivered from refrigerated trucks and moved by rail into the store, where the actual "breaking" of the carcass (cutting it into primal cuts which then were cut up into retail cuts as the customer desired) was done. This process entailed shipping the live cattle to a number of slaughterhouses all over the nation for killing, skinning, cleaning, and sectioning prior to shipping out in sides (halves) or quarters.

When the beef sides or quarters were delivered to the stores, they still had to be deboned and trimmed and made into primal cuts. A great deal of time was spent by the store butcher in an assortment of operations preparatory to the offering of meat ready to be shown to the consumer. A great deal of the butcher's time (highly skilled, expensive time) was spent in trivial operations, which, if the volume warranted, could be done by unskilled help.

Another problem was that fat, bones, and waste amassed in such back-room operations were sold to renderers at minimal prices. Such products, when amassed in cutting rooms supervised by the U.S. Department of Agriculture (USDA), could bring four or five times as much as they brought from renderers at the stores. The reason for the differences was that *supervised* wastes could be attested to as fit for human consumption, whereas unsupervised wastes could not; the latter could only be used for soaps or animal consumption. Also, the small renderers and their overheads and profits were eliminated. Few, if any, stores could afford the cost of a USDA inspector to be present in the store cutting room to supervise the operation.

Another major factor was that the individual store butcher was forced to perform a host of duties on the carcass and therefore wasted a great deal of time. Assembly-line types of operational efficiencies and savings were not available.

A number of major chains started central cutting facilities. In the beginning, these were hardly more than a slightly larger back room, where the cutting was done for three or four stores. Later, this evolved into larger, specially-designed facilities which did the cutting for one or more large chains. The efficiencies more than paid for the extra investment in the special facilities. Still, even though all the waste, fat, and bones could now be sold at the higher rates because the central facilities could be USDA supervised, there was still the cost of shipping these unusable products.

Thus, the concept of boxed beef evolved. The boxed-beef concept, to date, is the most efficient system of delivering meat to the store. The beef is reduced to primal cuts at one facility for the entire nation. Since the assembly-line technique is used throughout, the high skill required of the master butcher is eliminated. Each operation is broken down so that unskilled labor is capable of performing it.

The acceptance of boxed beef did not come about easily. There are many blots on the history of the supermarket industry as bloody and corrupt battles took place between the boxed-beef firms, unions, and supermarket managements. In some parts of the nation, to this day, boxed beef is permitted to be sold in the stores only through the practice of featherbedding, bribery, and other devices.

The boxed-beef system is not perfect. Stores still have to fill in with extra amounts of specially desired cuts and sections. However, it is the most efficient system to date.

At some point in the future, perhaps, the public will accept frozen beef and even store cuts that will be made centrally, so that the overwhelming amount of beef sold in the store will be ready for the case when it comes into the store, and only a fraction of the sales will have to be specially cut. To date, however, there is very little acceptance of frozen beef. Even consumers who buy fresh beef and store it in their own freezers, insist on buying it fresh and freezing it themselves.

SELF-SERVICE MEAT DEPARTMENT OPERATIONS

The boxed-beef concept and central cutting facilities have freed the in-store butcher to cut primal cuts into store cuts, which a wrapper then weighs and puts into the self-service case. This has cut the costs of the butcher operation considerably.

Although almost every meat department has facilities for the customer to call the butcher for special service, most of the meat is sold from the case. For the most part, under this system, the butcher is free to do what he or she is trained for—cut meat—and not spend most of his or her time waiting on customers.

To handle the meat tonnage, supermarket back rooms are used for receiving, storing and cutting meat. Power equipment makes the cutting operation efficient and easy. Conveyors, trays, tenderizing ma-

chines, prepackaging scales, and automatic meat chopping machines make mass production possible. The automatic packaging machines put the meat department into high-volume production. To keep up with this high volume and maintain the proper bloom on red meat, temperature-controlled conveyors are used. They permit people to work behind the meat cases, giving the customers the feeling of being in a butcher shop with someone to give service and answer questions.

Better control over the quality and freshness of prepackaged meat is accomplished by controlling the temperature from the back door to, and including, the meat case.

Since 50 to 60 percent of meat selling cost is labor and packaging materials, efficiency and improve-

Supermarkets go to great lengths to create prestige meat departments, and with good reason: Many patrons judge the entire operation on the quality and display of meat. And 20 percent of supermarket volume is generated by meat sales. Here, open and closed meat departments. In both instances, informative signage is included.

ment in these two areas are vital. A reduction of handling costs makes the individual retailer more competitive, lowers retail prices, and increases sales and productivity. The average meat department pays one man-hour of labor for every forty-two pounds of meat handled in the store. (The amount of "central" or "packer packaged" meat stocked affects this figure.) As operational costs rise, efficiency and productivity are increasingly important.

Today, about 85 percent of the total meat volume is moved through self-service departments. In most supermarkets, the meat operation is self-service, with cut-to-order service available for customers who prefer it. However, local conditions and the type of supermarket may justify service meats. Some service and some partial self-service units still operate. In the partial self-service operation, there is a display of prepackaged meat and a service counter where meats are cut-to-order.

A self-service meat department requires:

1. *Production planning*—in quantity and variety of items, in meeting traffic requirements, and utilizing employee time efficiently.
2. *Shelf-life control*—meat is highly perishable and customers buy only fresh-appearing packages. An orderly case is essential to create a favorable image.
3. *Full displays at all times*—a full display does not mean stock for peak traffic, but stock for *reasonable* selection.
4. *Anticipating customer demands*—the cuts, quantity, size of packages, etc., that customers will buy.
5. *Attractive packages*—customers select only neat, clean and well-wrapped packages.
6. *Personalized service*—an employee should be in sight and available to provide service.
7. *Minimizing special orders*—special orders cannot be eliminated totally since some customers want cuts or quantities not available in the case. However, the self-service meats should be promoted and special orders reserved for unusual situations. Some operators offer both service and self-service in the meat department. Inventory control to avoid heavy rewrapping is essential.
8. *Informative labeling*—to conform to the various weights and measures laws as well as the pure food and labeling laws. Packages are subject to inspection by customers and government inspectors.

With the advent of electronic cash registers, scanning, and the greater use of past performance data for stores, many firms now are able to predict quite closely just what the specific meat requirements on any given day and almost at any given time should be. The store knows what the history of the store is in comparable periods with similar specials on meat items and can fairly accurately predict what demand there should be, taking weather and other outside factors into consideration.

Not only is the approximate mix and quantity of meat required predictable, but also just how much labor will be required. In this way, scheduling for the meat department becomes a much more accurate function. With much of the guesswork eliminated, this should cut the labor costs of the meat department considerably.

These butchers are working behind the scenes in a supermarket, cutting, trimming and packaging meat for store display. Their efforts may actually cost the supermarket more than the meat does! But the supermarket's image may hinge greatly on their expertise.

THE COST OF OPERATING A SELF-SERVICE MEAT DEPARTMENT

The cost of materials, labor, and equipment are important factors in the profits returned from the operation of a self-service meat department. The cost of supplies used in self-service meat operations runs approximately 3 percent of meat sales. Supplies for cut-to-order meat cost about 1.2 percent of sales. The average cost of rewrapping is ten cents per package, 30 percent of which is for supplies and 70 percent for labor. Trimming or converting outdated items to other uses adds additional costs and reduces the selling price. Rewraps are costly and must be controlled.

Controls should allow adequate displays for effective merchandising.

Labor cost differentials are difficult to determine since the wage rates and productivity of labor vary for each market. Assuming the same wage rates and efficiency, the main advantage of self-service operations appears to be better work schedules and the use of less-skilled workers. The meat cutters become production-line workers and cut more pounds per hour. Wage rates have increased to compensate the meat cutter for his increased productivity. As a result, the cost of labor as a percentage of sales is almost the same for service and self-service meat departments. Operating efficiencies of the department, whether they offer service or self-service, account for any differences in operating costs.

The cost of equipment is dependent upon the degree of mechanization desired and the amount of refrigerated display space used. Prepackaging requires a work table with space for supplies and heat-sealing equipment, plus conveyors, trays, etc. The cost of equipment for meat department operation is relatively high, depending upon the degree of mechanization desired. If the capital is available, management must determine if daily savings on labor warrant the capital outlay.

Self-service meat departments require more space than service departments; i.e., a self-service meat department needs larger display and work areas than a service department doing the same weekly volume. However, spreading displays over a larger area makes shopping easier and more attractive and should increase sales. Thus, comparisons are difficult, if not impossible, to make.

MEAT DEPARTMENT SANITATION

Bacteria are the scourge of the meat department. Bacteria cause spoilage, reflecting directly on the sales and profits of the department. Furthermore, bacteria make meat turn "gray," reduce the shelf life of the product, and create additional work and expense with the need for retrimming and rewrapping. Off-condition trimmings must be discarded, since they will cause fresh meats mixed with them to turn gray; steaks or roasts that have turned gray cannot be used for stew meat or chopped meat.

Recommended procedures for controlling bacterial growth should double the shelf life for prepackaged fresh meat and reduce rewraps or reprocessing of discolored prepackaged meat by at least 50 percent.

To control bacteria in the meat department, the following measures should be taken:

1. *Proper Refrigeration.* Meats should be kept in the cooler. Move red meats fast; process them first. Keep a constant check of refrigeration in the cooler (28° F.), in the cutting room (40° F.), and in the cases (32 to 35° F. internal).

Never stack meats in the cutting room; stacking more than one high causes meat to bleed and the temperature in the room to rise.

2. *Handle meat as it arrives in the store.* As soon as meat arrives in the store, move it from the truck into the cooler.

3. *Keep equipment clean.* Knives, scrapers, and steels should be washed daily in a detergent solution, rinsed in a bleach solution, and then air dried. Band saws must be broken down daily, washed in an alkali solution to dissolve grease, rinsed in a bleach solution, and then air dried. Blocks must be scraped thoroughly, washed with a bleach solution, and air dried, daily.

The grinder, mixer, and cube steak machine head must be cleaned daily. Component parts must be washed in an alkali solution to cut grease and in a bleach solution to kill bacteria. The head of the grinder and the cube steak machine must be soaked overnight in an alkali solution and rinsed the next morning in a bleach solution. Trays must be washed daily in a bleach solution. A sponge dampened in a bleach solution should be used immediately to remove any bloody spots on trays.

In order to avoid the spread of trichinosis parasites, most local health departments require that all utensils and equipment be washed after working with pork and before working on other meats or poultry.

4. *Keep area clean.* Sweep floor frequently and change absorbing compound used on floor often. Personal cleanliness is extremely important in the meat department. Meat department personnel must wash their hands frequently: before starting the work day, at the end of a break, upon return from lunch, and after going to the restroom. Cuts, sores, or abrasions should be covered at all times. If one's apron becomes bloody, it must be changed. Long hair must be covered with a net. After handling pork, smoked meats, or poultry, hands must be washed.

PRICING MEAT

A definite pricing plan must be followed in meat merchandising to assure the retailer of a gross margin that will cover expenses and provide a satisfactory profit. Market operators consider a gross margin of 25 percent on sales as representative for the industry. (This 25 percent figure is an average.) Current trends seem to indicate the gross margin is on the decline, with current emphasis on competition and volume. It is also common practice for a firm to take a slightly higher markup when meat prices are relatively low and to cut this markup during periods of higher prices.

MERCHANDISING MEAT

Meat merchandising is the process the supermarket operator follows in buying meat from resources and selling the meat to its customers through advertising, display, and the personal efforts of the store department manager or butcher.

The store may order meat from the chain warehouse, its regular wholesaler, a meat broker, or from a packer. Season, weather, and competition play a big role in determining which meats are to be featured.

The reputation of the supermarket often rests with the customer's satisfaction with meat purchases. Traffic flow is of prime importance in meat merchandising, and the following general principles should be carefully considered:

1. Items first in line of customer traffic flow reach more customers. These should be profitable items (generally, not advertised products).
2. Advertised, low-profit-margin items in any category within the meat department should be flanked by profitable items.
3. Loss leader, low-profit items should be displayed in the last line of traffic of a meat family grouping. (However, do not hide these items.)
4. Point-of-sale (POS) signs sell meat. A good sign on an item that is not advertised, but is prominently displayed, creates a "good buy" feeling within the customer and sells merchandise.
5. Post signs at all times.
6. Sales are directly influenced by the number of facings in the display case.

No matter how efficiently the meat department is laid out, during busy periods there is congestion in the department, particularly in sections of the meat display cases where specials and seasonally desirable items are stocked.

A well-run store will make sure that such items not only are in ample supply, but that a replenishment supply is readily available and put into the cases quickly. Unless this is done efficiently, not only will a bottleneck block traffic in the meat department, but disappointed customers may leave the store without making meat purchases and may feel forced to shop at a competitive store.

The package is the "salesman" in a self-service meat department. The critical point of either sale or rejection is reached when the customer picks up the package of meat and looks at it. There is a split second in which the customer either puts it in his or her cart or places it back in the display case. The appearance of the package is an important factor in consumer acceptance of any item.

Factors related to wrapping include: correct wrapping materials for each item, legible labeling, and a visible product.

Quality control must be maintained throughout the meat preparation process, and temperature and humidity control in the display cases are essential factors. Quality control in the display case can be maintained by careful observation of the products and by code-dating each package. (In some localities, the last sale date must appear on the label.)

There are two general methods used in the display of meat products in a supermarket. Meat is separated in the display case either by the method of cooking (broil, roast, etc.) or by the carcass method. Combinations may be used, of course. No one method is best for every meat department. Customer acceptance, as measured by sales, indicates the degree of success achieved.

Displaying by method of cooking entails putting roasts in one section, chops in another section, stews in another, etc., regardless of the meat type. Displaying by carcass, or by the animal that yields the meat, results in sections for beef, pork, lamb, veal, poultry, fish, etc.

Usually, the method of cooking or the carcass method is used with variations. There are, however, some specific display factors that should be considered, including:

- Departmentalization
- Traffic flow
- Ends
- Related items
- Promotions
- Location
- Color.

Departmentalization. Departmentalization of products can be done by the methods previously mentioned, i.e., by mode of cooking or carcass or by a combination of the two methods. Departmentalization is important since most customers want meat for a particular cooking method, or they want beef, pork, lamb, or veal. Very few customers know the exact cut they want. Therefore, departmentalization and complete labeling are extremely important in the merchandising program.

Most stores have stickers that are affixed to the package of meat after wrapping or weighing, which simply say: "London Broil" or "Stew" or "Roast," etc. Such labels are extremely effective and are used as guides by many shoppers.

Other guides for customers and important merchandising aids that make shopping at one store more desirable than shopping at others, are weekly menus and recipe information that tell the shopper how to use certain cuts of meat, fish, and other items to the best advantage. Some stores even keep a home economist on the premises to help the shopper.

A number of years ago, a West Coast chain and manufacturer trained a number of local residents to be available in the store and help shoppers plan their menu for the week. The shopper told the planner what budget was available and the likes and dislikes of household members. The planner then helped plan the menu for the week, taking advantage of items on special. When tests of this system proved highly successful, an attempt to get the government to fund such a program in all disadvantaged areas proved unsuccessful, and the chain and manufacturer terminated it.

Traffic flow. Traffic flow is a prime factor in display case layout. Generally, high-profit items are displayed in "hot spots" where traffic is heavy or where the customer first contacts the display case. Care must be taken to avoid "dead spots" in the case created by building high displays or by using display point-of-purchase material that obstructs the view from the direction of traffic flow. Convenience items provide a higher gross margin than demand items, which are purchased weekly or biweekly by the customer. The proper display of convenience items stimulates sales and meat department profits, which often need balancing because of the adverse effect of specials and loss leaders.

Ends. The ends of the meat case are a common problem. The solution is to devise some method of getting the customer to shop the entire case. Special displays of demand merchandise, such as frankfurters or bacon, will pull the customer to the end of the meat case and expose him or her to the entire meat display case.

Related items. Related-item displays need not be limited to meat department items. Complementary grocery items, or any commonly sold and served with meat, may be used, if feasible. Point-of-purchase material is important in conveying the related-item idea to the customer. Without some message to the customer, a related-item display would be useless.

Promotions. Promotions should be continual. Every day offers an opportunity to promote some items. Promotions should not be limited to advertised items, but should be used in conjunction with a balanced selling program. Change is a very important factor in any meat display, and promotions can supply the necessary change to draw the customer to the meat department. In promoting certain cuts, it is advisable to promote adjacent cuts. If not, one must order supplemental amounts of the items on special at higher costs or face the prospect of adjacent cuts not moving as fast as those being promoted, and thus spoiling.

Location. Location of each item in the case

Pricing combinations and imaginative display techniques play a role in promoting meat sales at the supermarket. At left, Pegnatore's Market uses a blackboard to herald specials. At right, Falley's puts large meat bundles together for family buying.

should be considered in the light of volume as well as gross margin dollars. Locating high-margin, slow-moving items next to fast movers will increase sales and profits. The allocation of space to each item should be determined by the item's turnover and profit.

Color. Color is used to make the meat department attractive. The proper combination and use of color contrast makes a display case more attractive and increases sales.

Inventory control in the meat department is vital to the merchandising program. Too much inventory increases waste and shrink; too little inventory results in a loss of sales. Control is exercised by checking Saturday night inventory. The desired inventory is generally 20 percent of weekly sales, with 25 percent considered satisfactory. Inventory above or below this level normally is considered to be unsatisfactory. The inventory should be balanced—an indication that adequate stocks of all commodity groups will be on display on Monday. Items in short supply should be stocked as early in the week as possible. Merchandise on hand should be balanced at all times.

There is little excuse for overstocking or understocking product in a store that has been open for several years. A well-run store or chain will have records of the movement of all items for any given period of time or even for specific dates. Thus, a department manager should have at his disposal the amount sold for any given item in the comparative period over a span of several years. (With scanners, this information is available even by the hour.)

Also to be taken into consideration should be weather and other determining factors. Thus, for example, if a warm Labor Day weekend is expected, there is little excuse for a department to run out of the most demanded items in that particular store.

In preparing for ordering for the department, the manager should know what items the store will be promoting for the period and check past records for similar movements of such items, taking into account other factors, such as expected weather, etc. After the history is obtained, new factors should be considered (e.g., changes in ethnic makeup of neighborhoods; weather forecasts, easily obtainable from the local weather bureau with a fair degree of accuracy; and other variables, such as economic factors which may have changed in the area).

When all factors are properly weighed, the ordering should take place. If there are available contingency plans, these too should be made. The system should be used not only for ordering, but also for labor scheduling.

The department manager who does such planning may not be accurate every time, but will have a much higher success rate than those who use "seat-of-the-pants" methods. Many of the more successful chains already insist that such planning be done, not only at the individual store and department level, but also at regional and headquarters levels for chains.

Operate the meat department on a "cut and trim to sell" basis and avoid waste. For example, if a high-priced cut, such as a porterhouse steak, does not sell because of the tail, it eventually has to be put into hamburger; it is much more profitable to trim the cut properly and sell it as a steak.

Some important steps to increase sales are:

1. Keep frozen meat cases filled at all times. Have a full variety of frozen meat products available.
2. Early in the week, Monday through Wednesday, meat packages should be stacked no more than two packages high. Keep reserves in the refrigerator.
3. Sale items should be on display every day of the week, with point-of-sales signs over the items—particularly the first hour of the opening day of the sale.
4. Have a variety and selection of meat and meat products on display every day.
5. Be sure that there is a sufficient quantity of sale items in reserve.
6. Keep a full variety of chopped meat and patties available at all times.
7. Maintain a good refrigeration and sanitation program.

Please refer to pages 93-94 for a further discussion of meat receiving, storing, stocking, and price marking.

FIGURE 6

RETAIL CUTS OF BEEF

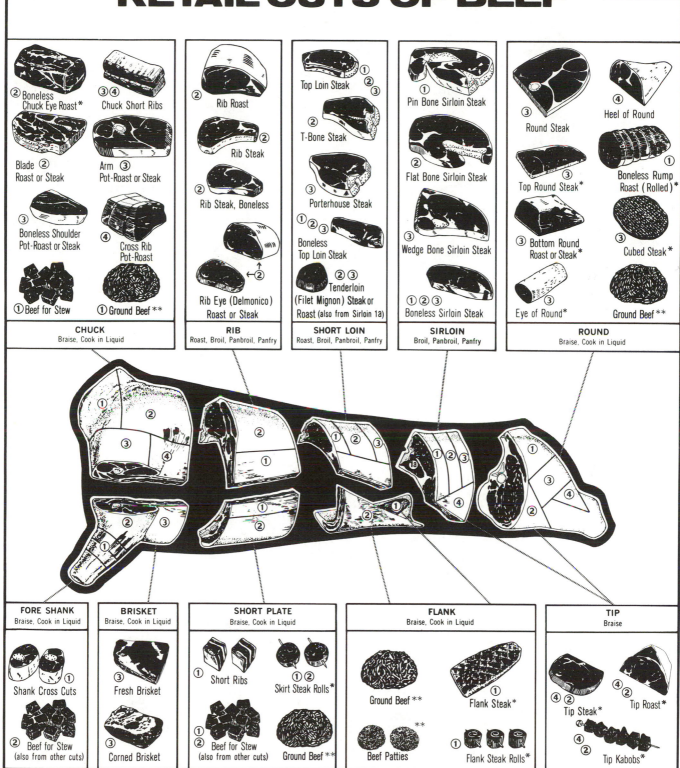

CHUCK
Braise, Cook in Liquid

② Boneless Chuck Eye Roast*
③④ Chuck Short Ribs
Blade ② Roast or Steak
Arm ③ Pot-Roast or Steak
③ Boneless Shoulder Pot-Roast or Steak
④ Cross Rib Pot-Roast
① Beef for Stew
① Ground Beef**

RIB
Roast, Broil, Panbroil, Panfry

② Rib Roast
② Rib Steak
② Rib Steak, Boneless
②→ Rib Eye (Delmonico) Roast or Steak

SHORT LOIN
Roast, Broil, Panbroil, Panfry

① Top Loin Steak ②③
② T-Bone Steak
③ Porterhouse Steak
①②③ Boneless Top Loin Steak
②③ Tenderloin (Filet Mignon) Steak or Roast (also from Sirloin 1a)

SIRLOIN
Broil, Panbroil, Panfry

① Pin Bone Sirloin Steak
② Flat Bone Sirloin Steak
③ Wedge Bone Sirloin Steak
①②③ Boneless Sirloin Steak

ROUND
Braise, Cook in Liquid

③ Round Steak
④ Heel of Round
③ Top Round Steak*
① Boneless Rump Roast (Rolled)*
③ Bottom Round Roast or Steak*
③ Cubed Steak*
③ Eye of Round*
Ground Beef**

FORE SHANK
Braise, Cook in Liquid

① Shank Cross Cuts
② Beef for Stew (also from other cuts)

BRISKET
Braise, Cook in Liquid

③ Fresh Brisket
③ Corned Brisket

SHORT PLATE
Braise, Cook in Liquid

① Short Ribs
①② Skirt Steak Rolls*
①② Beef for Stew (also from other cuts)
①② Ground Beef**

FLANK
Braise, Cook in Liquid

Ground Beef**
① Flank Steak*
Beef Patties**
① Flank Steak Rolls*

TIP
Braise

④② Tip Steak*
④② Tip Roast*
④② Tip Kabobs*

*May be Roasted, Broiled, Panbroiled or Panfried from high quality beef.
**May be Roasted, (Baked), Broiled, Panbroiled or Panfried.

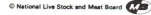 © National Live Stock and Meat Board

FIGURE 7
RETAIL CUTS OF PORK

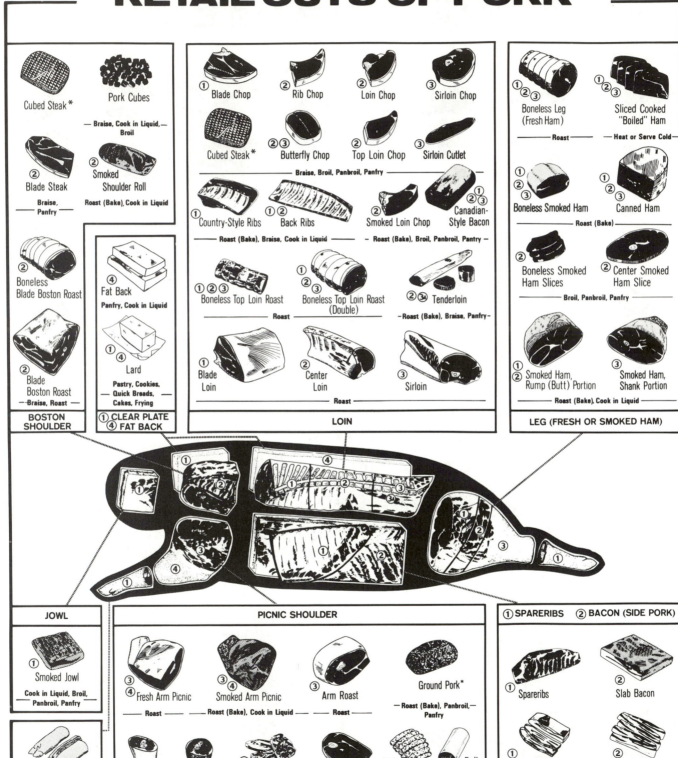

BOSTON SHOULDER

Cubed Steak*

Pork Cubes

— Braise, Cook in Liquid,— Broil

② Blade Steak

② Smoked Shoulder Roll

— Braise, Panfry —

Roast (Bake), Cook in Liquid

② Boneless Blade Boston Roast

② Blade Boston Roast

— Braise, Roast —

① CLEAR PLATE / ④ FAT BACK

④ Fat Back

Panfry, Cook in Liquid

①④ Lard

Pastry, Cookies, Quick Breads, Cakes, Frying

LOIN

② Blade Chop

② Rib Chop

② Loin Chop

③ Sirloin Chop

②③ Cubed Steak*

②③ Butterfly Chop

② Top Loin Chop

③ Sirloin Cutlet

— Braise, Broil, Panbroil, Panfry —

① Country-Style Ribs

①② Back Ribs

Smoked Loin Chop

②③ Canadian-Style Bacon

— Roast (Bake), Braise, Cook in Liquid — — Roast (Bake), Broil, Panbroil, Panfry —

①②③ Boneless Top Loin Roast

①②③ Boneless Top Loin Roast (Double)

②③④ Tenderloin

— Roast — — Roast (Bake), Braise, Panfry —

① Blade Loin

② Center Loin

③ Sirloin

— Roast —

LEG (FRESH OR SMOKED HAM)

①②③ Boneless Leg (Fresh Ham)

①②③ Sliced Cooked "Boiled" Ham

— Roast — — Heat or Serve Cold —

①②③ Boneless Smoked Ham

①②③ Canned Ham

— Roast (Bake) —

② Boneless Smoked Ham Slices

② Center Smoked Ham Slice

— Broil, Panbroil, Panfry —

①② Smoked Ham, Rump (Butt) Portion

③ Smoked Ham, Shank Portion

— Roast (Bake), Cook in Liquid —

JOWL

① Smoked Jowl

Cook in Liquid, Broil, Panbroil, Panfry

① Pig's Feet

— Cook in Liquid, Braise —

PICNIC SHOULDER

④ Fresh Arm Picnic

③④ Smoked Arm Picnic

③ Arm Roast

Ground Pork*

— Roast — — Roast (Bake), Cook in Liquid — — Roast — — Roast (Bake), Panbroil,— Panfry

Fresh Hock

Smoked Hock

②③ Neck Bones

③ Arm Steak

Link / Roll Sausage*

— Braise, Cook in Liquid — — Cook in Liquid — — Braise, Panfry — — Panfry, Braise, Bake —

① SPARERIBS / ② BACON (SIDE PORK)

① Spareribs

② Slab Bacon

① Salt Pork

② Sliced Bacon

— Bake, Broil, Panbroil, Panfry, Cook in Liquid — — Bake, Broil, Panbroil,— Panfry

*May be made from Boston Shoulder, Picnic Shoulder, Loin or Leg.

© National Live Stock and Meat Board

FIGURE 8

RETAIL CUTS OF VEAL

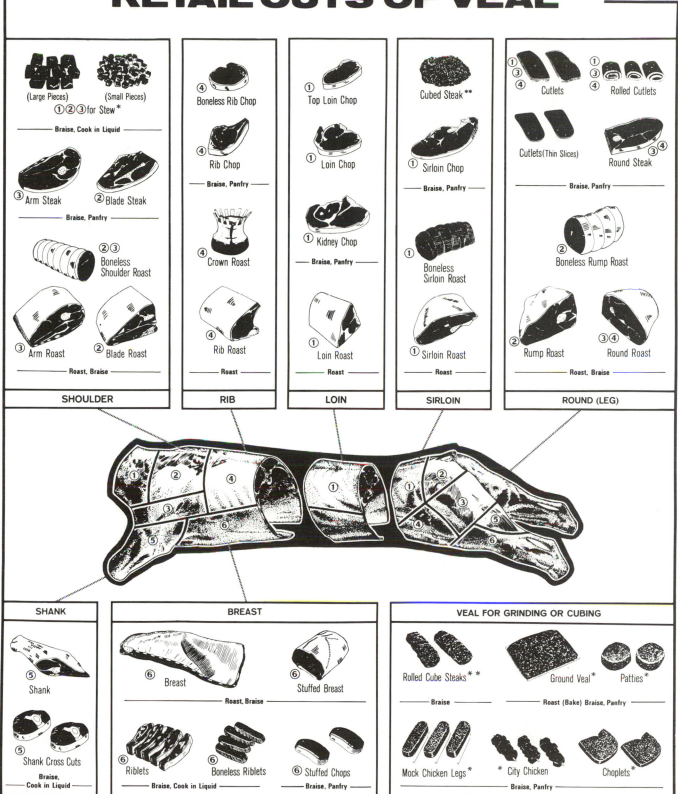

SHOULDER

(Large Pieces) (Small Pieces)

① ② ③ for Stew *

— Braise, Cook in Liquid —

③ Arm Steak   ② Blade Steak

— Braise, Panfry —

② ③ Boneless Shoulder Roast

③ Arm Roast   ② Blade Roast

— Roast, Braise —

RIB

④ Boneless Rib Chop

④ Rib Chop

— Braise, Panfry —

④ Crown Roast

④ Rib Roast

— Roast —

LOIN

① Top Loin Chop

① Loin Chop

① Kidney Chop

— Braise, Panfry —

① Loin Roast

— Roast —

SIRLOIN

Cubed Steak **

① Sirloin Chop

— Braise, Panfry —

① Boneless Sirloin Roast

① Sirloin Roast

— Roast —

ROUND (LEG)

① ③ ④ Cutlets   ① ③ ④ Rolled Cutlets

Cutlets (Thin Slices)   ③ ④ Round Steak

— Braise, Panfry —

② Boneless Rump Roast

② Rump Roast   ③ ④ Round Roast

— Roast, Braise —

SHANK

⑤ Shank

Shank Cross Cuts

Braise, Cook in Liquid

BREAST

⑥ Breast

⑥ Stuffed Breast

— Roast, Braise —

⑥ Riblets

⑥ Boneless Riblets

⑥ Stuffed Chops

— Braise, Cook in Liquid —   — Braise, Panfry —

VEAL FOR GRINDING OR CUBING

Rolled Cube Steaks **

Ground Veal *   Patties *

— Braise —   Roast (Bake) Braise, Panfry

Mock Chicken Legs *   * City Chicken   Choplets *

— Braise, Panfry —

*Veal for stew or grinding may be made from any cut.

**Cube steaks may be made from any thick solid piece of boneless veal.

FIGURE 9
RETAIL CUTS OF LAMB

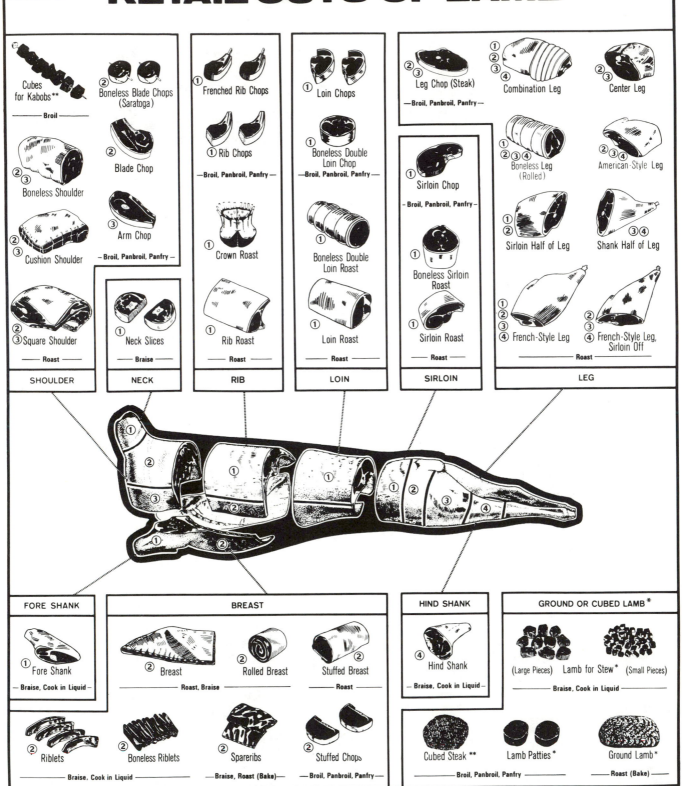

② Boneless Blade Chops (Saratoga)

Cubes for Kabobs**

— Broil —

② Blade Chop

③ Arm Chop

② Boneless Shoulder

②③ Cushion Shoulder

②③ Square Shoulder

— Roast —

SHOULDER

① Neck Slices

— Braise —

NECK

① Frenched Rib Chops

① Rib Chops

— Broil, Panbroil, Panfry —

① Crown Roast

① Rib Roast

— Roast —

RIB

① Loin Chops

① Boneless Double Loin Chop

— Broil, Panbroil, Panfry —

① Boneless Double Loin Roast

① Loin Roast

— Roast —

LOIN

② Leg Chop (Steak)

— Broil, Panbroil, Panfry —

① Sirloin Chop

— Broil, Panbroil, Panfry —

① Boneless Sirloin Roast

① Sirloin Roast

— Roast —

SIRLOIN

②③④ Combination Leg

②③④ Boneless Leg (Rolled)

①② Sirloin Half of Leg

①②③④ French-Style Leg

②③ Center Leg

②③④ American-Style Leg

③④ Shank Half of Leg

②③④ French-Style Leg, Sirloin Off

— Roast —

LEG

FORE SHANK

① Fore Shank

— Braise, Cook in Liquid —

② Riblets

— Braise, Cook in Liquid —

BREAST

② Breast

② Rolled Breast

② Stuffed Breast

— Roast, Braise —   — Roast —

② Boneless Riblets

② Spareribs

② Stuffed Chops

— Braise, Cook in Liquid —   — Braise, Roast (Bake) —   — Broil, Panbroil, Panfry —

HIND SHANK

④ Hind Shank

— Braise, Cook in Liquid —

GROUND OR CUBED LAMB*

(Large Pieces) Lamb for Stew* (Small Pieces)

— Braise, Cook in Liquid —

Cubed Steak **

Lamb Patties *

Ground Lamb *

— Broil, Panbroil, Panfry —   — Roast (Bake) —

* Lamb for stew or grinding may be made from any cut.

**Kabobs or cube steaks may be made from any thick solid piece of boneless Lamb.

6

THE PRODUCE DEPARTMENT

Today's supermarket shopper can select fresh produce from a display of seventy-five to three hundred possible items. Produce items are highly perishable and this makes frequent shopping necessary. Shoppers become loyal customers of supermarkets offering a good variety of fresh produce.

On a national basis, share of sales in the produce department average:

Fruits	39.5%
Vegetables	43.5%
Other	17.0%

Twenty-two items (of the possible seventy-five to three hundred items carried in the produce department) account for 80 to 90 percent of the department's sales (see Table 5), while 10 to 20 percent of sales are from horticultural items, garden supplies, dried fruits, nuts, bulk candy, and other fruits and vegetables not listed in the top twenty-two.

TABLE 5
TWENTY-TWO TOP-SELLING
ITEMS IN PRODUCE DEPARTMENT

Fruits	Percentage of Total Dept. Sales	Vegetables	Percentage of Total Dept. Sales
bananas	10%	potatoes	12%
apples	5	lettuce	9.25
oranges	5	tomatoes	6
grapes	3	onions	3.75
cherries	3	celery	3
grapefruit	3	beans	3
watermelon	2.5	cabbage	2.5
peaches	2	carrots	2
strawberries	2	sweet corn	1
tangerines	2	cucumbers	1
cantaloupe	1		
pears	1		
	39.5%		43.5%

In addition to fruits and vegetables, produce departments in supermarkets may be responsible for selling:

- Dried fruits
- Nuts
- Loose or packaged candy
- Plants, artificial or real; and cut flowers
- Plant support items, including: soil, plant food, flower pots, and the like.

THE IMPORTANCE OF THE PRODUCE DEPARTMENT

The produce department today is second only to the meat department in creating the image of the store and attracting the customer. In a number of cases, it even outshines the meat department.

Until the early 1970's, Gelson's in Los Angeles was regarded as a model of what the most desirable produce department should look like. But a number of progressive supermarket operators around the country refused to accept "but Gelson's is in the produce heart of the nation" as an excuse for their firms not having such departments. Soon it was not uncommon to walk into Byerly's in Minneapolis or a Pathmark in New Jersey or a Price Chopper in upstate New York in midwinter and find colorful, attractive, fully stocked produce departments with a variety of in-season and out-of-season products.

The produce department occupies 8 to 10 percent of the selling area of a supermarket. Nationally, produce sales range from 8 to 20 percent of total sales. Gross margin of the produce department averages 32 percent (11 percent of the store's gross profit) as compared with about 16 to 18 percent for the grocery department, and 22 percent for the entire store.

Annual stock turns in the produce department are the highest for the store:

Department	Number of Stockturns
Entire store	34
Produce	130
Grocery	26
Meat	78

High weekly turnover on a comparatively small investment is the key to the substantial net profit that is possible. Investment in stock, fixtures, and floor space is reasonable in relation to other departments in a store.

About 10 percent of the consumer food dollar is spent for produce items. The customer image created by the produce and meat departments is important to the entire store. Typically, customers shopping one department spend under $4; those shopping two departments average about $8, and those shopping three departments average over $11. The increase in the average sale means increased sales for *each* department, not simply additional purchases in the *other* departments. For example, grocery sales increase from an average of $4 to $5 when shopping only the grocery department to over $7 for groceries spent by customers shopping three departments. Part of this difference is due to the type of shopping—fill-in or major. The figures indicate that meat and produce are essential to attracting major shopping trip customers.

Temperature and humidity controls and a great deal more information on extending the shelf life of produce have made many fruits and vegetables available for much longer periods than only a few decades ago. For example, apples are now virtually a year-round fruit even though the growing season has not been extended. Some varieties of oranges are available the year round. Navel oranges, which only a few decades ago were available for less than two months a year, are now in abundant supply some six to eight months a year.

In addition to storage techniques, improved transportation availability and techniques (such as flying strawberries from coast to coast and even flying field-ripened pineapples to East Coast markets directly from Hawaii) make fruits and vegetables from all corners of the earth available at all times and turn the produce department into a year-round garden spot.

Produce items are among the most colorful in the food store. Unlike displays of processed items, they have a natural beauty that is appealing. The variety of colors and the fact that they are natural adds much to the attractiveness of the store.

Few items afford so great an opportunity for exercising merchandising skill as do fruits and vegetables. Clean, attractive produce displays help pave the way for customer acceptance of the entire store.

BUYING PRODUCE FOR THE SUPERMARKET

Produce is purchased directly through a wholesaler or broker. In recent years, the methods of marketing and the channels through which fruits and vegetables flow from growers to retailers have changed. A major change is the rapid growth of affiliated groups of independent supermarket operators and the growing practice of these buying groups and of supermarket chains to buy directly from the growers. Some large central buying organizations buy direct and ship to their member stores from their own centrally located terminals.

Terminal markets have their place in the marketing system by bringing large groups of big-city buyers and sellers together in a specific area. A recent survey revealed that approximately 70 percent of fresh fruits and vegetables passed through the wholesale market, while 30 percent went directly to chains. The extent of terminal activity can be better understood by the number of carloads unloaded in major cities in a single year as shown in Table 6.

TABLE 6
UNLOADS IN MAJOR
UNITED STATES CITIES
(ANNUALLY)

New York	101,150
Los Angeles	90,900
Chicago	45,500
Philadelphia	39,200
San Francisco	39,150
Boston	36,300
Detroit	31,500
Atlanta	22,600
Cleveland	22,500
Pittsburgh	22,300

ORDERING PRODUCE FOR THE SUPERMARKET

Produce purchases or orders may be made by:

- Chain warehouse
- Buying from a regular wholesaler
- Buying FOB from a shipper
- Buying from a buying broker
- Buying from a shipper's agent
- Buying from a terminal market
- Buying from a fruit auction
- Buying from local farmers.

The produce department will usually sell 50 percent of its volume from Monday through Thursday and 50 percent on Friday and Saturday. Stores open Sunday can expect that Monday to Thursday will account for 47 percent of weekly sales, and Friday,

Saturday, and Sunday will account for 53 percent. (See Table 7.)

TABLE 7
PRODUCE SALES BY DAY OF WEEK

Supermarket Closed Sunday

Monday	10%	
Tuesday	10	
Wednesday	12	50% of sales
Thursday	18	
Friday	24	
Saturday	26	50% of sales

Supermarket Open Sunday

Monday	10%	
Tuesday	10	
Wednesday	12	47% of sales
Thursday	15	
Friday	20	
Saturday	22	53% of sales
Sunday	11	

Although computers play an important part in the distribution of produce, the manager of the produce department has an important role in ordering the items needed for the store. Before writing or phoning an order to headquarters for computerization, the manager should:

1. Consult the produce price list for the following week's business as provided by the buyer, and note seasonal items.
2. Study past order guides, price sheets, sale item inventories, records of past sales and promotions, and bulletins issued by headquarters.
3. Note changes in produce movement, week-to-week and beginning and end of week.
4. Take accurate inventory.
5. Write orders using "planned dollar sales" as a guide.
6. Take into consideration weather conditions; drastic price changes (up or down); seasonality; special promotions; fixed warehouse delivery dates; problems in warehouse or markets.
7. Consider items that are purchased early in the week and those that are "backoffs," such as pineapples (customers rarely repeat purchase during the same week).
8. Phone orders for computerization at designated hours on designated days.

RECEIVING AND STORING PRODUCE

Before the produce truck arrives, the cooler and back room should be prepared for receiving merchandise. Produce items that are store-ripe should be moved to the preparation area and space cleared in the cooler for the new merchandise. The old stock should be positioned for first-out stock rotation.

Incoming merchandise should be checked for quantity and condition. All discrepancies should be reported according to company procedures. Usually the truck driver takes the report back to the warehouse. Movement of incoming produce to controlled temperature and humidity areas is a must since high temperatures wilt produce rapidly. Care in handling is essential to prevent bruising and other damage.

Good storing procedures include:

1. Coding and rotating all items.
2. Storing items at appropriate temperatures. Items that must be kept in the cooler should be limited to less than one hour out of the cooler while production is taking place.
3. Items that are received in a more advanced state of maturity (tomatoes, peaches, canteloupe, lettuce, etc.) may be offered for sale before older stock, if their condition warrants. Some items may require additional conditioning outside the cooler (green or light pink tomatoes) to allow them to "break" color.
4. Items, such as broccoli, bunch radishes, corn, watercress, and parsley, should be stored in the cooler and/or iced down.
5. Items, such as white and Spanish onions, bulk case and packaged garlic, waxed and unwaxed yellow turnips, fresh yams, and fresh sweet potatoes, should be stored in a cool place outside the cooler.
6. "Loosen up" original packages of leafy vegetables, such as escarole, chicory, collards, mustard greens, turnip greens, and romaine, by removing one-third of the original case and placing them in empty cases.

BULK AND PREPACK PRODUCE

Consumers have accepted packaged food items, including fresh meats. Consumer acceptance depends on the degree of quality upon which the consumer can rely. While the completely prepackaged produce department is not common, supermarket operators report that over 60 percent of their tonnage and dollar sales are currently being sold packaged.

Most produce departments display both bulk and packaged items. In many instances, the same item

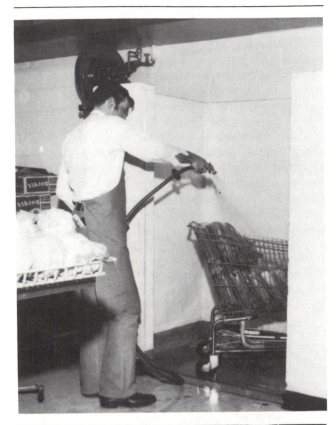

In dealing with bulk produce, supermarkets recognize that customers will usually be able to handle the merchandise. Therefore, in preparing leafy items for display, a thorough hosing is in order (top). Next step (bottom) is to insure you make the most of merchandise display opportunities.

may be sold in both packaged and bulk forms. For example, potatoes are usually packaged by the grower or distributor in five, ten or twenty-pound bags. For customers who want smaller quantities, bulk is available.

Some of the factors to be considered in bulk and prepack are:

Bulk
- Customer can select each item
- Flexible quantities can be bought
- Lower prices
- Easier to mass display
- Mounds of produce are more visually attractive
- More spoilage through handling
- Customers are less likely to complain if they select their own produce.

Prepack
- Customer cannot handle produce
- Cost for packaging
- Fewer accidents caused by loose fruit on floor
- Easier to rotate
- Convenient (shopper does not have to pick)
- Growth in number of one- and two-individual households (such shoppers often buy in much smaller quantities than normal prepack amounts)
- More hygienic.

Shoppers generally accept prepackaged produce whenever quality and freshness control is maintained. Since packaging interferes to some extent with the customer's ability to select items, the retailer must assume the responsibility for quality and establish customer confidence by guaranteeing satisfaction.

Packaging makes feasible the use of brand names. Hard produce items are frequently packaged by the grower or grower-cooperative and carry a brand name; for example, Sunkist for citrus fruits and Diamond for walnuts. Growing area designations are used to differentiate Texas, Florida and California citrus; Idaho, Maine and Long Island potatoes; and so forth.

Cartons or trays are used to package some "soft" items, such as grapes, mushrooms, berries, and corn-on-the-cob. These cartons offer space for brand names. Producer, distributor and store labels are used.

Some basics for successful packaging of produce include the following:

1. Pack only top-quality merchandise. The reputation of the store is at stake in every produce package.
2. Package in an assortment of convenient quantities. It is possible to persuade customers to buy larger quantities by using larger size packages, but if packages are too large, many customers will not buy, and spoilage will increase. Therefore, a variety of package sizes is desirable.

3. Package as close as possible to the time of sale for freshness control. Strict rotation is essential. Code-date packages that have a shelf life of more than one day.
4. Price package produce sensibly. Too high a premium on package produce will reduce sales.

SHRINK

Shrink plays a very important role in produce merchandising. Reduction of shrink adds dollar profits by reducing waste. Shrink in produce inventory may be caused by:

- Dehydration of produce items
- Shortages in receiving
- Overtrimming produce items
- Bruises in produce caused by handling
- Overbuying
- Short weight that is paid for
- Incorrect pricing
- Spoilage due to improper or poor rotation
- Spoilage due to improper temperature control
- Poor merchandise selection
- Poor merchandising of the produce
- Over- or under-displays
- Neglecting to break down the department for the night (or weekend)
- Lack of adequate storage, refrigerators, or coolers
- Failure to read scale properly or to use correct price for item when weighing merchandise.

Incorrect rings at the checkout counter frequently fail to credit the produce department with sales made. This can distort all figures, attribute an inordinate amount of waste, add to the apparent cost, and decrease apparent profitability of the produce department.

PRICING PRODUCE

The produce department pricing plan must assure the supermarket operator of a gross margin that will cover expenses and provide for planned profit. Market operators consider a gross of from 29 to 33 percent of sales as representative of the industry. Current trends indicate the gross margin can be increased slightly with better distribution, more effective use of prepacks, more sophisticated buying, ordering through the use of computer assistance, and with better merchandising techniques. There are many factors that influence the price of produce:

- The supply and demand for specific items
- Competition
- Labor costs (unions, strikes)
- Cost of growing (fertilizers, energy, equipment, etc.)
- Method of transportation
- Acreage planted
- Weather conditions
- Seasonability
- Source (local, import, growing area)
- Consumer boycotts
- Quality or grade.

Prices appearing on prepacks must conform to local, state and federal regulations and bear price labels which include information such as the name of the item or the grade, the price, and the name of the packer.

MERCHANDISING PRODUCE

Every produce merchandiser is a walking merchandising laboratory; week in and week out he or she juggles to achieve required margins; struggles with supply, demand, seasonality, and other product factors; and manipulates the selling techniques of special pricing, display, promotion, and advertising. Some of the information is extrapolated by reading and interpreting computer data, some of the information is committed to memory, and some insights may consist of pencilled notes on a clipboard.

More effective methods of merchandising are constantly being sought. One such project, COSMOS (Computer Optimization and Simulation Modeling for Operating Supermarkets), was conducted for produce departments. Techniques used permit extrapolation of results to products and to combinations of variables other than those tested, which means that the results can be used by merchandisers to determine how various factors affect the sales of items with certain characteristics. It is interesting to note that test results provided few surprises for experienced produce merchandisers who had found these things out for themselves.

In the COSMOS project, test items were selected to secure a cross section of characteristics that were judged to have a strong influence on potential sales; for example, whether the item is a relatively slow or fast mover, low or high in price, or is available all year long or seasonally. Four merchandising and promotional appeals were tested: prime location, doubling display space, reaction of featured items to advertising, and the effect of a 10 percent or more price reduction. Results indicate that price is the least effective of the appeals; increasing display space pays off

Two aspects of a well-merchandised produce department are demonstrated here: signage that draws traffic, and food displays conven-ient to customers. Special assortments enhance the overall effect.

in increased sales in almost every instance; advertising works effectively with hard fruit and cooking vegeta-bles; prime location boosts sales for hard fruit and cooking vegetables, and for both high-volume and nonseasonal soft fruit, but does not affect the sales of salad vegetables and high-priced or low-priced soft fruit.

Displays that sell are planned in advance. An on-paper plan for the display layout takes time, but it is well worth the effort. It helps incorporate good display principles; items can be moved on paper easier than they can be moved physically; and valu-able labor time can be saved by having a paper plan for easy reference when building displays. Frequently, the produce merchandiser at headquarters sends sug-gested plans for produce displays to each produce manager.

The following general principles of good display should be followed:

1. Allot the proper amount of space to each item.
2. Give fast-selling items and advertised items more space than slow movers.

3. Give proper locations to each item. Do not hide advertised items; give them prominent locations. Spot impulse sale items around the high demand items.
4. Place demand items throughout the display area.
5. Group related items.
6. Contrast the natural colors of fresh produce when they are displayed on racks.

In addition to following the above guidelines, the plan must be worked and follow-through must be effective.

In produce merchandising, the following points are frequently cited as assuring customer interest and producing high volume:

1. Use day-to-day promotions of staple items in a neat, clean environment. Customers are influenced in their shopping habits by the impact of the store, particularly its cleanli-ness. Clean stores create a favorable cus-tomer image.

2. Merchandise early-in-season and peak-of-season items. Good quality fresh fruits and vegetables, properly handled and displayed, virtually sell themselves; but the difference between a "good" and an "outstanding" produce department often lies in one word—merchandising. In the North, local fruits and vegetables are available in the spring, summer, and fall. In the winter, fruits and vegetables from the South, California, Puerto Rico, and Mexico are available. One of the most important factors in the promotion of vegetables is timing. For the most part, the produce manager who adheres to the "rights" of merchandising will have a successful produce department.

3. Spring is the time to put additional effort into produce merchandising. With a change in weather, there is a change in living and eating habits. The desire for easy-to-fix, low-calorie meals affects the entire food line. Salad preparations take on more importance along with picnic items.

4. Merchandise for holidays and other special occasions. Use displays and signs for suggested selling.

5. Tie in sales, featuring produce with related items.

6. Emphasize eye appeal by maintaining fresh produce on display, using color contrast and mass appeal.

7. Rotate merchandise.

8. Maintain an adequate variety.

9. Use "talking" signs.

10. Make the department easy to shop.

Whether displayed in open bulk or prepacked, good merchandising practices will sell produce in quantity at a profit. Advertising is a very important aspect of the produce merchandising effort. Items are selected for advertising promotion based on the season, availability, appeal, offerings of competitors, special buying advantages, and consumer demand. Items advertised should be featured in the store by placing them in a good location and by using point-of-purchase (POP) signs and window signs.

In addition to newspapers, stores use other media, including circulars, television, radio, and in-store public address systems. Customer handouts or leaflets attached to produce items can promote the product by including recipes, nutritional information, and popular weight reduction and/or control hints through the use of the produce. Although coupons are used, this is not the most effective method of enticing customers into the produce department.

One of the complaints voiced about many supermarket produce operations is that standardization has reduced the variety and types of vegetables and fruits that used to be available in the older greengrocer stores. Rarely does a supermarket carry more than three or four varieties of apples. The varieties of pears carried by most supermarkets are generally down to two or three. How many supermarkets these days carry rhubarb?

The conversion of shrink or waste into high-profit items often differentiates the top merchandisers of produce from the average. A trip to a number of supermarkets will find that quite a few managers will have a display of ripe produce for quick sale. Often the produce manager will trim away half a melon that is beginning to spoil and put the other half of the melon in this rack.

The real merchandiser, however, will dice up every usable part of the melon and mix it with other fruit that is reaching the stage of being too ripe, even mixing in lesser portions of normal fruits to make a display of fruit salad in jars or plastic containers which bring in better profits than the fruit itself would bring. Similar techniques are used to make tossed salads ready for eating, coleslaw ready for serving, etc.

Here's an added merchandise touch in the heart of a produce section. This supermarket has located a section and islands of plants to supplement its produce volume. Sometimes the plant-loving customer then becomes the store's produce customer.

The alert produce department manager can build a thriving and highly profitable business by advertising and making available fruit baskets which can be ordered for delivery or taken out of the store on short notice.

The more sales-oriented produce manager will spend as much time as possible on the selling floor,

The customer selecting from the fruit bins wants personal service and gets it. Since produce is turned more than any other commodity, many patrons want the option of asking about quality.

helping customers determine the ripeness of melons, distinguish between various salad greens, etc. Not all shoppers know how to select produce items, and nothing drives a customer away from a store faster than a surly or indifferent clerk when the customer needs help in selecting merchandise.

Another high-profit adjunct to the produce department is the flower and plant department which has become popular in supermarkets in recent years. Here, too, the untended department rarely is success-

ful, but one that is properly attended can be one of the most profitable parts of the supermarket.

The manager and at least one clerk should be given the proper training and instruction as more techniques and data become available. Such training will more than pay for itself in a successful, highly profitable section.

Please refer to pages 94-95 for a further discussion of produce receiving, storing, stocking, and price marking.

7   THE DAIRY DEPARTMENT

The dairy section was one of the first areas in supermarkets to use self-service successfully. Packaged eggs, butter, milk, and cheese gave this department the essential ingredients for self-service, and a steady evolution into the modern dairy department took place.

Supermarkets usually list at least three departments in their store organizations: grocery, meat, and produce. At headquarters level, there are provisions for the buying and merchandising functions of the dairy operation, but at store level, operation of the dairy products section is frequently under the aegis of the grocery department manager, with a dairy clerk performing the necessary activities.

In stores with higher volumes, department heads will assume the responsibility for the dairy departments.

Products sold in the dairy department include:

- Milk
- Milk products, such as cheese, butter, cream, and yogurt
- Eggs
- Margarine
- Dips
- Fresh juice
- Refrigerated dough products

Ice cream is usually included with frozen foods.

THE IMPORTANCE OF THE DAIRY DEPARTMENT

The dairy department occupies about 5 percent of the selling space, produces 9.5 percent to 12 percent of the store's volume, with a gross profit percentage of 19.7 percent. The average annual number of turns of dairy products is 64.

The diary department offers an opportunity to create a favorable store image through quality eggs, milk, butter and cheese. Offering variety provides an additional opportunity to attract shoppers.

Few dairy products are eaten by themselves. Customers buying dairy items are in the market for other foods. Dairy items have a partnership with products in other departments—eggs and bacon, or ham; milk and cookies; butter and bread; and cheese and crackers.

Typically, milk, eggs, and butter are purchased at least every week. Dairy customers visit the store frequently and shop other departments.

People are using more snack, party, delicacy and imported foods than ever before. The dairy section stocks many items that satisfy this new demand.

DAIRY DEPARTMENT OPERATIONS

The dairy department, with its prepackaged products and control of perishables, can do well with a headquarters merchandiser controlling in-store inventory, ordering, receiving, stocking, display, and promotion.

Many dairy products are delivered directly to the store by the processor or distributor. For some products, when permitted by the union, delivery is made by driver/salespeople who are assigned specific shelf space in the dairy cases and who service these areas, removing out-of-date products, stacking shelves, and placing reserve stock in the store's dairy cooler. Generally, however, this is a function of a clerk within the store.

Operation of the dairy department can be controlled by standardizing the flow of work of the in-store dairy clerk; by the training and supervision of the dairy clerk by a store department manager or by a field supervisor from headquarters; by sending fliers with instructions for displays, facings, and point-of-purchase signs; and by standardizing procedures to follow in preparing reports and ordering.

Since headquarters merchandising is the mode, input from each store is essential. The dairy clerk must keep weekly sales records by item. This record is used as the basis for ordering dairy items, especially those not under supplier-guaranteed sale and freshness control. For example, items such as milk and cream, when delivered by a dairy, carry a sale guarantee; and in many locales, the dairy is required to print the last sale date on the item. The dairy replaces outdated stock and keeps the case stocked with fresh products. Most

While dairy departments take up only about 5 percent of store space, they can contribute about four times that figure in gross store profit. That's because of heavy traffic and product turn. Vital here is cleanliness, freshness, and quick replacement.

cheese items are not on a guaranteed sale contract; therefore, freshness control is vital and can be achieved by noting the manufacturer's date or the pull date on the product. The limited number of items stocked makes itemized weekly records possible. Controlling the number of facings according to sales and the performance of new items can be achieved.

Sales records are needed to indicate when seasonal items begin to sell, how much inventory is needed, and the best combination or product mix required in each store. By checking the weekly sales records, the merchandiser can determine the best display product mix for each store.

Quality is the one factor in the dairy operation that must be maintained through freshness control. While many dairy section items are guaranteed and returnable, it is the responsibility of the dairy clerk or department head, by rotating stock and adhering to last-date-of-sales markings on products, to assure product freshness control. Consequently, maintaining quality is primarily a supervisory function.

DAIRY DEPARTMENT SANITATION

Dairy products are highly perishable, and deteriorating items produce objectionable odors. Milk cartons tend to leak; eggs may get cracked or broken, and leak. The dairy case must be cleaned daily and must be completely dismantled and scrubbed at least once a week. A clean, odorless dairy department is essential to continued dairy sales.

While rotation of stock is important in all departments, it is essentail in perishables departments. Nowhere in the supermarket is product more apt to be returned for spoilage than in the dairy department.

Many of the most modern supermarkets have facilities for moving milk into the sales area by merely moving loaded carts through a plastic curtain from the storage room directly into the cooler cases. Although such a setup is created to save time and effort in stocking the milk in the cooler, it also demonstrates the need to keep the product in constant refrigeration. An hour out of the cooler can reduce freshness one to three days, depending on the temperature. Sour milk will be returned.

The dairy clerk should be just as alert at all times in moving other dairy products from the back-room cooler into the selling cooler. Depending on the temperature in the store, thirty minutes to an hour of keeping cream, yogurt, and similar products outside the cooler can reduce the freshness of the product by as much as a day or more.

Speed in moving product from the back-room storage cooler into the selling case, stock rotation, and case cleanliness and maintenance are essential in running an efficient dairy department.

A good manager can tell how well the department is run by a regular visual check on the amount of stock, whether it is rotated properly, how clean and fresh-smelling cases are, and whether stock is placed higher than the safety marks in cases. Most important is the record of how much product is returned or has had to be replaced for customers because of spoilage even before expiration dates.

DAIRY DEPARTMENT MERCHANDISING

Techniques of self-service merchandising can be aptly applied to dairy product promotional campaigns. When using dairy items as traffic builders, the dairy merchandiser should be certain that adequate merchandise is available and the higher margin dairy items are placed next to featured items.

Quality fresh eggs can be promoted to attract shoppers and build long-term, regular customer traffic. To maintain adequate supplies of high-quality eggs and to control freshness require control of distribution from farm to store by the retailer.

Dairy products lend themselves to the promotion of related items. Tie-in sales help stimulate greater profits from a promotional effort. Examples of possible tie-in combinations are:

- Eggs with bacon and/or pork sausage
- Milk with cereals, chocolate flavorings, cookies
- Cream with coffee, fruit
- Whipping cream with gelatin desserts, bakery items
- Butter with bread, rolls, waffle and pancake mixes
- Cheese with macaroni, spaghetti, apple pie.

Although the meat manager may prefer to display meat items exclusively and may be opposed to giving up space to nonmeat items, larger quantities of *both* meat items and tie-in dairy items can be sold by placing them together. The same technique can be used in the produce department.

If space is not available for mixed merchandising, results that are almost as good can be achieved with the proper use of pictures over or near the related items. Such pictures should be accompanied by recipes and other nutritional and diet information. Many stores have special alcoves or places in the store where weekly menus, recipes, and other shopper aids for meal preparation are available. Stores and chains that make use of such merchandising techniques rarely lose customers to competitors.

Many dairy products are excellent traffic builders since they are purchased as staples. Price specials on demand items, such as orange juice, cottage cheese, margarine, eggs, and milk, are effective price-image builders. Point-of-purchase signs should be used to call attention to advertised, featured and new items.

8 THE DELICATESSEN/APPETIZING DEPARTMENT

The service delicatessen/appetizing department (usually called deli or sometimes "appy") plays an important role in the mass merchandising approach of supermarkets. This section of the store is devoted to prepared specialty foods. It is a service area designed to attract customers who are looking for international food favorites and who currently may be purchasing these specialties elsewhere. It also attracts customers looking for new ideas for family meals and for entertaining. For the supermarket operator, it may be a drawing card that also stimulates added volume and the sale of items related to the convenience foods. The deli counter can be promoted as an alternative for customers who patronize fast-food establishments, since the shopper can purchase prepared foods and needs only a beverage to serve a complete meal.

Many supermarkets became concerned when they found themselves competing with fast-food operations for the consumer food dollar, and the deli department became their jumping-off place to fight back.

If customers were already buying raw chicken or hamburger meat, it was not too difficult to convert some of those same customers to buying the finished hamburger or fried chicken. In addition to take-out services, many supermarkets have even added sit-down restaurants which use the delis for their kitchen facilities. Many such firms have found that new customers attracted by the fast foods or restaurants have become regular shoppers in the rest of the supermarket. Such dual benefits from a service department are not unique.

The service deli/appetizing department can create satisfied shoppers by offering:

- Maximum service
- A large variety of deli items (cold cuts), smoked fish, bulk or freshly sliced cheeses, salads, condiments, and prepared food items
- Quality products, freshly prepared
- Good value.

Currently, of the chains and supermarket independents in the United States, only 17 percent feature in-store service deli departments. These departments are most frequently found in stores grossing about $50,000 or more weekly or $2.6 million or more annually. Expansion to include deli/appetizing departments has been regional. The extent of total consumer exposure to supermarket service delicatessens is about 66 percent in the area composed of New England, New York, the Mid-Atlantic states, and Chicago; 18 percent in East Central, West Central and Southeast states; and 7 percent in the Southwest and Pacific states. (Note: These figures reflect service deli departments only. Many supermarkets feature prepackaged deli items, such as sliced, smoked meats in the meat department and packaged potato salad in the dairy case.)

Items offered in the service deli department include:

- Sausages/franks
- Luncheon meats
- Hot foods
- Salads
- Cheeses
- Ethnic foods
- Gelatins
- Puddings
- Pickles
- Many other food products.

THE IMPORTANCE OF THE DELI DEPARTMENT

A recent study reveals that 66.9 percent of all shoppers buy in service delicatessens, and only 29.5 percent of delicatessen buyers buy from supermarkets. Regionally, the supermarket share of deli sales and the potential for growth are illustrated in Table 8.

Further, of the 29.5 percent of the households using supermarket delis, 14.3 percent use the deli four or more times a week, 8.1 percent buy two to three times a week, and 1.6 percent buy at least once a week. These statistics would indicate that most of the deli shoppers fall into the "heavy shopper" category, which may be reflected by additional purchases in other departments to supplement purchases made in the deli section. Deli shoppers also spend at a fairly high weekly rate: 19 percent spend more than $6 per

The service delicatessen represents the supermarket's answer to fast-food operations. One key is big selection—of cheeses, as seen here, packaged meats, salads, ethnic dishes. The service "deli" is still in development. Fewer than one in five supermarkets has one.

week; and fully half spend more than $4 per week. Such totals from 29 percent of all customers add up to a substantial dollar gross for a store.

TABLE 8
SUPERMARKET SHARE OF DELI SALES

	East and Chicago	East/West Central and Southeast	Southwest and Pacific
% Households using any deli	76%	61%	68%
% Households using super-market service deli	52	24	13
Growth potential for supermarket deli	46%	154%	423%

On an average, 2.3 percent of total store space is devoted to the deli department, and the yield is 4.07 percent of the annual gross volume of the store. Gross yield in dollars per square foot of space is 77 percent above that realized in total for the average store.

Satisfied customers in the deli department can:

- Generate additional sales and profit
- Enhance the store image
- Provide a competitive advantage over other supermarkets and neighborhood delis
- Develop more loyal customers.

DELI DEPARTMENT OPERATIONS

One of the persistent problems in the operation of a deli department is the difficulty in finding, training, and keeping well-qualified personnel. Since the deli department is a service business and may be the only department in a store where there is consistent personal contact with the customer (other than the cashier-checker), it is important to hire and/or train personnel who know how to cut, weigh, help customers in their selection, keep themselves and the area clean, and who also like to serve people.

It is of extreme importance to know the volume patterns of a particular store. Nationally, deli department sales indicate a somewhat different pattern than those indicated for produce. Sales patterns change with Sunday store openings or closings. (See Table 9.)

TABLE 9
SALES OF DELI DEPT. BY DAY OF WEEK

Supermarket Closed Sunday

Monday	10.3%	
Tuesday	10.8	52.3%
Wednesday	14.3	
Thursday	16.9	
Friday	22.3	47.7%
Saturday	25.4	

Supermarket Open Sunday

Monday	9.2%	
Tuesday	9.6	46.7%
Wednesday	12.8	
Thursday	15.1	
Friday	19.9	
Saturday	22.7	53.3%
Sunday	10.7	

These figures alone, however, do not tell the complete story. In many areas, stores that are open on Sundays find a higher total service deli volume. This, in part, may be due to the fact that the deli picks up some business that might normally be filled by a fast-food operation. Also a factor is the tendency on Sundays to select easy-to-serve meals that require little or no preparation at home.

Supermarkets that have fast-food adjuncts as part of their service delis find that not only do these facilities add sales for the deli departments, but they also draw new customers for other departments of the store. In-store restaurants also serve this same purpose.

The service factor in the deli tends to reduce total store productivity, but many operators feel that the additional traffic such departments build for the rest of the store, much more than compensates for the lowered total store productivity rates.

Because the emphasis in the deli department is on quality and service, most deli departments employ department managers. The major responsibilities of the department manager include: planning, organizing, directing, and training; increasing merchandise turnover; controlling operating expenses; and coordinating the many day-to-day details of operation.

Buying for the deli department of a chain store operation is a function performed at corporate headquarters by a specialist knowledgeable and trained in recognizing the quality of products. Some bulk items carried in the department, such as cheese and candies, may be purchased by the dairy or the produce buyer. Lists of available products and prices are sent to the stores, and ordering for the store is done by the department manager.

The service deli department becomes the place in the store where many high-profit specialty items can be merchandised. It is really the only department in the supermarket (except perhaps for the service bakery) where a salesperson can relate directly with the customer. Here, sales ability, courtesy, and the proper attitude can boost volume tremendously and build traffic for the other departments in the store.

Effective supervision adds to the success of the deli department operation. The deli department is a labor intensive department, marketing highly perishable items, and so must be supervised by the department manager, the store manager, and the headquarters deli specialist. Important supervisory involvement includes:

- Checking for correct prices, fullness of displays, and prominent display of advertised items
- Checking for cleanliness and sanitation
- Checking the handling and control of supplies
- Checking the cooler for proper storage and rotation
- Checking the work schedules
- Reviewing sales planning and ordering
- Checking gross profit and volume reports
- Checking closing procedures
- Reviewing progress of new employees.

MERCHANDISING THE DELI DEPARTMENT

An analysis should be made to project sales. Some factors to consider in this analysis include: ethnic area (proper merchandise to cater to ethnic tastes); seasonal considerations; holidays (e.g., Christmas, New Year, Thanksgiving, ethnic holidays); and review of sales history to eliminate guesswork (last year vs. current year).

Some promotional suggestions include:

- Identify the department with attention-getting signs

The key to successful deli departments is service. Unlike the overall self-service environment of a supermarket, this department requires one-on-one relationships between counterperson and customer. Good service also requires staff teamwork, as shown at right.

- Feature seasonal items
- Use several media for advertising (circulars, newspapers, in-store bag stuffers, etc.)
- Allow customers to sample products
- Arrange for product demonstrations.

Awareness of volume patterns (early in the week, weekends) is critical in determining proper case displays. Personal cleanliness is of prime importance because personnel handle the food being purchased.

Displaying may be done by section within the display case; e.g., salad section, cold cuts section, cheese section. Tops of counters may be used for special promotions or for related items from other departments as well as the deli department.

A store merchandising philosophy and policy should be developed so that the service-deli department does not compete with vac-packed and pre-packed deli merchandise being offered in the meat or dairy department or elsewhere in the store.

9

BAKED GOODS AND THE BAKERY DEPARTMENT

Grain is an ancient and major source of food. A large variety of high-quality, mass-produced baked goods is available at reasonable prices. The annual value of total domestic consumption is approximately $17 billion. It is truly an important segment of the food industry.

In general, baked goods are in two categories in food stores: crackers, cookies, and related baked or toasted products are considered regular grocery items and are displayed in a section of the grocery department; prepared and prepackaged bread, rolls, and sweet goods are considered as perishables and are displayed in a baked goods section.

In baked goods, the latest addition to the supermarket is the service bakery. This can assume a number of forms. In some markets, it is merely a counter and display case where bread, rolls, pastries, and cakes of various sorts that are baked elsewhere (perhaps a tie-in with a local bakery that has a good reputation) are sold. Special-occasion cakes can be ordered or may be on hand and iced and lettered to order.

An even simpler version consists of merely a doughnut machine that makes hot doughnuts throughout the day which can be iced to order. Also alone or in conjunction with the doughnut machine is an automated oven that bakes bread and/or rolls and requires only semi-skilled preparation.

Next in line of complexity is the bake-off operation. Here the preparation and sometimes even partial baking is done at some central point and completion of the baking is done on the store premises. The most complex of the in-store baking operations is the scratch bakery, where all the preparation and baking are done on the store premises.

These last two operations have proven themselves big attractions for customers in many supermarkets in recent years, and the trend to either the bake-off or scratch bakery is growing. Its advantages and potentials are very similar to the service deli.

Most supermarkets have a self-service pre-packaged section for sweet goods. The bakery department depicted here also has a service counter and display case (at left) for fresh bread and rolls.

The cookie and cracker section appeals to the sweet tooth and results in strong impulse buying. Variety and product freshness are key factors.

CRACKERS AND COOKIES

Crackers and cookies account for about $3 billion worth of products each year. Grocery stores sell about 89 percent of the total output. Crackers and cookies account for about 1.7 percent of total store sales. The gross margin is a little higher than the store average, usually about 25 to 30 percent. Supermarkets stock 125 to 175 items.

Variety and freshness control are vital to a profitable cracker and cookie section. The impulse value is high, meaning effective merchandising is essential to high volume and good profit. Point-of-purchase promotion effort is effective, as are special displays and related item promotions.

BREAD AND CAKE VARIETIES

Bread, rolls, and sweet goods account for about $11.8 billion worth of products each year. The grocery store share of the market is about one-half. Eating establishments, home delivery routes, and bakeries sell the other half. The baked goods section accounts for 3 to 6 percent of total store sales and earns a gross margin of 18 to 20 percent.

The range of items stocked in supermarkets is large—a low of about 100 items to a high of about 250 items. It is not uncommon for a supermarket to stock 50 to 60 kinds of breads, 20 to 25 types of rolls, and 100 to 150 sweet-goods items. There is much duplication, since most operators stock the baked goods of several bakeries as well as a store-label line.

Since bread is a demand item, the section layout should force shoppers to walk past the impulse items before coming to the bread. Store-label bread usually gets the lion's share of the space and promotional effort.

Bread and rolls account for about two-thirds of the volume and the sweet goods, one-third. Bread is a good price-image item. Sweet goods are high-impulse items and should be merchandised and promoted to increase total sales. The baked-goods section should be convenient for the fill-in shopper.

CUSTOM QUALITY BAKED GOODS

Several different types of baking operations are used by supermarket operators to supply custom quality baked goods, including:

- In-store or on-premises scratch bakery
- Company-owned central bakery with daily deliveries to retail outlets
- Bake-off operations
- In-store or on-premises operations supplying other nearby stores
- Leased department operations.

In-Store or On-Premises Scratch Bakery Operations

In scratch bakery operations, all the preparation and baking is done on the premises of the supermarket. It is not subject to price competition and builds a quality image for the supermarket, thereby attracting shoppers and increasing store traffic by about 10 percent.

The aroma of baking is enticing; a number of stores pull the bakery aroma into their ventilating systems and circulate it throughout the store. Also, the high-impulse appeal of baked goods is effective.

In middle to high-income areas, it is not uncommon to have 50 percent of the shoppers buy quality baked goods. The average sales ticket for quality baked goods is in the $1.75 to $4.00 range, causing an increase in the average sales ticket.

Many stores that have found the bakery department itself only marginal or potentially less profitable than some other potential departments—even if running at a slight loss—also have found that volume in the rest of the store increases to the extent that they consider the in-store bakery a worthwhile traffic builder.

The in-store bakery can provide assets to the supermarket above and beyond the immediate profitability of the department. Uniqueness of product allows for extra profit margin. The traffic pull can create new store regulars. And, oh, the delicious aroma!

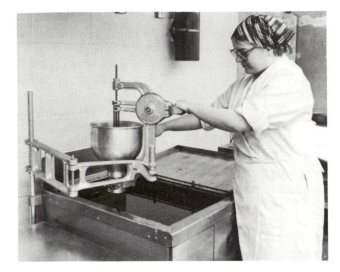

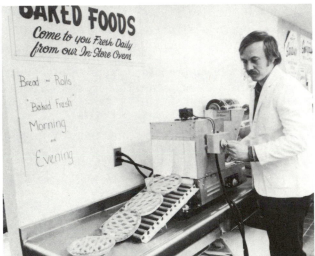

While in-store bakery operations require trained help and an investment in good equipment, it all seems worthwhile when you see the results (lower right). Of course, you need batter or dough (upper left), easily controlled and modern ovens (upper right), and supervisors who check the finished product (lower left) before enticing customers.

Freshly baked goods tend to pull shoppers into the store more times a week. Fill-in shopping is done in the supermarket, making customers more loyal. Promotion of baked goods increases store traffic by inducing customers to shop daily or every other day.

The gross profit for on-premises baked goods is 55 to 75 percent. (This gross profit figure includes only the material or ingredient cost.) Since baking is a production process, other costs should be deducted and an actual gross and net profit figure computed. On a percentage basis, an in-store bakery is very profitable. But since percentages are not a substitute for dollars, it is evident that weekly volume is the major factor determining profitability.

Central Bakery Operations

The major advantages of a central bakery over on-premises bakery units include:

- Lower total investment
- Less store space required
- Less skilled labor required.

A central bakery designed for greater production utilizes more equipment, and much of the production can be automated. Economy results from facilities with great capacity. A central bakery operation saves on the considerable square footage needed by an on-premises bakery unit.

The number of skilled or journeymen bakers needed to operate a central bakery is much lower in a large, mechanized and/or automated unit than in small on-premises units. Labor costs are lower, and the problem of enough journeymen bakers is lessened.

A hot bakery in a supermarket will account for approximately 5 to 6 percent of store sales. A cold bakery section, served by a central bakery, accounts for 4 to 5 percent of store sales. Therefore, a hot bakery is worth 1 percent more of store sales than a cold bakery section serviced from a central bakery—plus the fact that it has built sales in other departments.

Frequent store deliveries, good product mix, good merchandising, and quality control are essential to successful operation.

Bake-Off Operations

The bake-off operation combines the advantages of an on-premises bakery with the economy of a central bakery. The basic product is prepared elsewhere, perhaps in the central bakery owned by the supermarket operator, but may be supplied under contract, and then sent to the supermarket for finishing. The products prepared in the bakery and sent to the store include: prepared dough that is partially baked; frozen dough, etc. The product is finished in the supermarket and placed on display in the selling area.

Major items of equipment needed at the store level include an oven, a proof box, a storage freezer, a work table, and a sink. In addition to the finishing equipment, the usual sales area display shelving is needed. The dairy or produce coolers or frozen foods storage freezers can be used to store unbaked products and to retard proofing.

Labor costs and problems are reduced. Bake-off workers can be trained in a week or two. The labor requirements are simplified, since operators can train unskilled workers to perform all the jobs. Less space is needed for a bake-off operation than for a complete on-premises bakery.

Since most of the baking is done in the store, the customer image and the aroma impulse value is

basically the same as for a complete on-premises bakery.

On-Premises Bakery Supplying Other Nearby Stores

Many supermarket buildings do not have the adequate square footage required for an on-premises bakery to produce a profitable weekly volume. A solution has been to install a larger bakery unit in one supermarket and supply one or more additional stores. Delivery to nearby stores can be frequent and economical. Since the number of baking units is less, fewer skilled bakers and other workers need be employed. Although this may be the best available solution, if there is enough room, a bake-off operation will increase sales of other departments in a store.

Leased Department Operations

Some retail bakeries have established themselves as leased bakery units in high-traffic stores, such as supermarkets. The lease is a contract between the store operator and the bakery. Clauses may vary, but usually the lease is based on a percentage of total bakery sales—in the range of 6 to 8 percent.

The amount of space varies, as does the location, which may be outside the checkout area or in a traffic location in the supermarket shopping area. The supermarket furnishes the space, heat, air conditioning, and light, while the operator is responsible for the energy used for baking. The baker often furnishes the display equipment and the employees to staff the section.

Some leased bakery departments operate their own cash register. A system of sealing the packages and attaching the sales ticket is used. In other leased bakeries, the items are price-marked and checked on a bakery key on the register at the checkouts. The supermarket with a leased quality bakery must still maintain a commercial bakery section. Volume items priced for the mass market must be stocked.

The leased bakery section provides the supermarket with quality baked goods without many of the problems related to performing the baking function.

10 — THE FROZEN FOODS DEPARTMENT

THE HISTORY AND DEVELOPMENT OF THE FROZEN FOODS INDUSTRY

In 1923, while fishing in Labrador, Clarence Birdseye discovered that the sub-zero temperatures quickly froze fresh fish and that the fish retained their natural flavor and texture. As a result of the discovery, Birdseye experimented with freezing, and in 1930, he was issued a patent for the equipment he developed for freezing foods.

In 1930, a group of ten retail food stores in an eastern U.S. city, in cooperation with Birdseye, conducted a carefully planned sales campaign. Frozen meats, vegetables, and berries were promoted and displayed at prices comparable to the best quality fresh items. The experiment succeeded in proving that consumer acceptance could be achieved. The depression of the 1930's delayed the expansion of frozen foods processing and the development of more satisfactory equipment for display and storage.

The subsequent evolution of satisfactory frozen food cases induced many food distributors—including A&P, Grand Union, and Gristede's—to experiment with the sale of frozen foods. Even though the test results were not startling, stores retained their frozen food cabinets, and others added frozen food lines.

During World War II, the frozen foods industry grew rapidly. Fewer ration points were required for frozen foods than for similar canned food items, and many customers tried the new products to save points. The government awarded the frozen foods industry large volume contracts to supply the armed forces. Frozen foods were space-savers in shipment, lasted better than fresh vegetables, and required less scarce metal than canned goods.

The boost given the industry by rationing and government contracts brought many new packers into the frozen foods field. In the scramble for fast profits, some of these firms employed poor handling methods and poor quality control. As a consequence, the reputation of frozen foods fell, bringing a definite slump to the industry following the war.

It was the acceptance of frozen orange concentrate in 1948 that started the boom era for the whole frozen foods industry. Each year, the quality, han-dling methods, sales, and acceptance of new and different frozen varieties have improved and increased.

New techniques for quick-freezing created better preservation of the frozen foods—both in taste and texture. In today's facilities for freezing, the process takes seconds between start and finish. Many fruits and vegetables are frozen in equipment that is brought to the fields so that within minutes after being picked, the product can be packaged and frozen. Similarly, many boats contain freezing equipment by which fish, even complete fish dinners, can be frozen soon after the seafood is caught.

The taste improvement in fresh-frozen products has restored the positive image of frozen foods. Not only are plain fruits, vegetables, fish, and meats available, but the past three decades have seen the tremendous spread of convenience frozen items—complete meals, entrees prepared by gourmet cooks, a variety of complex desserts, baked goods, etc., have become available to the consumer.

Home freezers have become as commonplace as the refrigerator and the oven in many areas. Many homes today carry as much frozen food in the home freezer as the entire grocery store carried just a few decades ago.

A customer flow study of supermarkets reveals the fact that most shoppers buy some frozen food items. The leading prepared frozen food items include juices, meat, prepared dinners, dessert items (especially baked goods), ethnic foods, and specialty foods.

THE IMPORTANCE OF THE FROZEN FOODS DEPARTMENT

By nearly every standard used for grocery industry analysis to measure the performance and potential of supermarket products, frozen foods stand out as one of the most promising sources of continuing growth in food retailing profits. As higher labor and investment costs continue to erode supermarket net profits, supermarket executives seek categories that will insure a steady increase in high-margin sales growth. Frozen foods present the supermarket oper-

Rapidly growing and profitable—that's the way frozen foods departments are described. Up to 2,000 frozen food items are now available. One problem on the horizon: increasing energy costs.

ator with a substantial challenge, that of making a serious commitment to meet the staggering demand that is certain to result from the continued growth of the department.

It is estimated that during the 1980's the volume of frozen foods sales should reach more than $10 billion a year. With better merchandising, space, advertising, and promotion, that figure could easily be surpassed.

Frozen foods return high profits compared to most other departments. For example: a store producing only 6 percent of total sales in frozen foods could very well have returns of 12 to 14 percent of the store's profit. However, an increase in the cost of energy needed to keep foods frozen may reduce the profit margin.

Value is determined by price and quality. Most frozen food products are of the highest quality, since the ingredients of the prepared food are frozen at the peak of freshness—at -40° F. The frozen foods department is truly a gourmet department and a strong image builder for the store.

Frozen foods account for an average of almost 7

percent of total store sales, contribute 24 to 28 percent of the total gross margin, and produce a much higher return per dollar invested than other departments. Turnover averages 45 to 55 annually.

About the only cloud on the horizon of the frozen foods industry at present are the two new forms of packaging noted in Chapter 4, "The Grocery Department," which already are making inroads into the field and which some see as supplanting it.

The first of these is the retort pouch. Because of its shelf-life potential without the need for energy-consuming freezing or expensive fixtures, many see this type of packaging revolutionizing the supermarket. They also predict that such packaging will replace cans and jars because of their space-saving potentials.

The other form of packaging is aseptic packaging, already a major form of marketing in most parts of the world. Since the package is air-tight and bacteria-free, it, too, has an indefinite shelf life (as long as it is not opened or punctured).

Both of these methods have the potential of eliminating the overwhelming amount of freezer or cooling equipment now needed in the food store. Thus, initial investment, maintenance, and spoilage waste could be sharply reduced or eliminated.

FROZEN FOODS DEPARTMENT OPERATIONS

Today, many food distribution centers, both chain and group, supply the frozen foods line to the stores that they service. However, after reviewing costs of storing and distribution, some of the food distribution headquarters have chosen to use frozen food distributors to service their stores.

In the store, a frozen foods clerk, under the supervision of the dairy-frozen foods department manager, and with the additional supervision of a field supervisor, is responsible for ordering from an item list of 300 to some 2,000 varieties of frozen foods available. One of the major problems in the frozen foods department is out-of-stock, which is estimated at about 17 to 22 percent, at a cost to the industry of almost $1 billion in sales and almost $250 million in gross profits. Computerization, careful record-keeping, and proper supervision can reduce the cost of out-of-stock.

Since a clerk or department manager does the actual work, it is important for management to establish routines and procedures that will increase the viability of the department. These routines and procedures may include weekly activities, such as discussing with the store manager the projected sales plan and resulting volume anticipated for the new

Photo courtesy of Harris-Teeter Super Markets, Inc., Charlotte, North Carolina.

A big challenge to the frozen foods manager or the clerk in charge is maintaining inventory. Out-of-stock items in frozen foods sections cost supermarkets an estimated $1 billion in sales. Very careful procedures are essential.

week, and reviewing activities to be accomplished during the week, including feature product ordering, special displays, housekeeping, and the like.

The frozen foods clerk or department manager should be required to keep accurate records of items sold each week. These figures provide input for the computerized order lists. Deliveries of frozen foods are made as needed, depending on the rate of sales and the capacity of the back-room freezer.

The effects of improper handling and stocking of frozen foods in the store are very expensive; food quality can deteriorate, and sales can be lost. The proper handling and stocking of frozen foods is very simple, if the cabinets are maintained in excellent working condition and the foods are kept at 0° F. or below from the time of delivery at the store until they are carried home by customers.

Cabinet maintenance is best described in the operating and maintenance instruction guide supplied by the manufacturer of the cabinets. A responsible person should be trained to follow the manufacturer's instructions to maintain the cabinets.

The following rules for frozen foods and equipment should be followed scrupulously:

1. As soon as a frozen food delivery is made to the store, it should be checked at once for proper temperature and accuracy, and immediately placed under protective refrigeration—either in the walk-in freezer or in the display cases.

2. In taking frozen foods out of the walk-in freezer for restocking cases, take out at any one time only as many frozen foods as can be displayed inside the cases in twenty minutes or less.

3. Open one carton at a time, price mark it, and place the packages in the case immediately.

4. Practice proper stock rotation—place all new packages in back or behind packages of the same item and brand already in the case.

5. Open only one door at a time in a line-up of glass door reach-in cabinets, place the new product in quickly, but rotate the stock and close the door again as soon as possible.

6. Never place even a single package of frozen foods above or in front of the safe-load line marker on all open-type display cases.

7. Never place a frozen food package on or against the front return air flue of any open-type display case.

8. Never leave gaps or low spots inside the frozen food fixture. If product is not available for some reason, then dummy cartons should fill the spaces. Freezer equipment is forced to work much harder to keep empty air space cooled.

9. Freezers should be cleaned and policed regularly. Automatic defrost units should be checked to make sure they are working properly and that drainage vents are not clogged.

10. Many chains use a central alarm system to inform headquarters and store managers when a compressor or freezer system breaks down. Check these periodically to make sure they are working. Whether a central alarm system exists or not, it should be the function of someone in the store to make sure that the total system is functioning at all times and that food in the equipment is being maintained at proper temperature. This is especially true just before store closing time.

11. For stores that are closed for long periods or even a whole day, some method of checking the system regularly must be maintained and covers put in place.

When the above simple rules are made a part of the store's operating policy and diligently carried out, the following benefits can be expected:

- Better, fresher frozen foods on display
- Neater, cleaner packages with no frost and ice accumulation on the packages or in the case
- Better satisfied customers for the store

- Better store image among shoppers for having fresher, cleaner, more neatly displayed frozen foods at all times
- An increase in frozen food acceptance and sales
- Reduction in the store's losses from torn or damaged frozen food packages
- Reduction of cold aisle problem
- 10 to 20 percent lower power consumption (electricity)
- Fewer case failures and lower service and maintenance costs
- Greater net profit from frozen foods for the store
- Elimination of spoilage due to thawing.

FROZEN FOODS MERCHANDISING

Twenty percent of the total frozen food items account for 62 percent of the sales in the department. Failure to give enough space to high-turnover items, while overstocking slow movers, will result in high out-of-stocks on the biggest profit producers.

Space allocations are vital to top profit performance. Space allocation in frozen foods varies because there are simply too many individual variables and unpredictable factors. Therefore, cabinet engineering plays a very important part in assuring supermarket operators the profits they are looking for in frozen foods.

Nationally advertised frozen food brands offer the supermarket operator an established and recognized name plus quality merchandise that is advertised to create consumer demand for the label. Nationally advertised brands are easy to sell, and the advertising bill is paid by the producer.

Regional packers also offer frozen food items to retailers. These labels require advertising and promotion by the retailer. Since the margin is larger, many operators are willing to stock these regional labels. Continuity of label is an important factor; if the retailer spends money to create a demand for the label, the line must be available. Quality is the responsibility of the processor, but the retailer must maintain adequate checks to assure continuity of quality as well as supply.

Distributor and private-label frozen foods are used by most large operators. Some operators use a first and second grade or quality label. Private-label frozen foods carry a higher margin, but the retailer assumes full responsibility for quality, continuity, and advertising. The battle of the brands is as much an issue in frozen foods as in the canned foods field.

11

Supermarkets have traditionally sold nonfood items such as soaps, detergents, cleansers, brooms, and paper goods. The expansion to additional convenience and impulse nonfood items was a natural evolution. Today, all supermarkets sell varieties of general merchandise, including items such as automotive supplies, housewares, hardware, health and beauty aids (including full-line pharmacies), notions, soft goods, hosiery, stationery, magazines and books, photographic supplies, phonograph records, tapes and supplies, greeting cards, sporting goods, appliances, and many other items.

THE DEVELOPMENT OF
GENERAL MERCHANDISE
IN THE SUPERMARKET

The pattern of nonfoods development, as a part of the merchandising structure of a supermarket organization, has followed fairly closely the geographic growth of the supermarket. Southern California and Texas, where supermarkets expanded rapidly, became the spawning areas for nonfoods. These areas were typified by especially rapid growth after World War II. The supermarket was strategically located and, as the first retailer in a new residential section, offered more complete lines of food and nonfood items. After the war years, the move to the suburbs gave new impetus to the supermarket to feature nonfoods; this development was aided by the fact that formerly many nonfood items had been available only in older shopping areas.

Most supermarkets began by offering health and beauty aids (HABA), followed by kitchenware, magazines, books, glassware, hardware, toys, stationery and, finally, soft goods.

Many supermarket operators moved into the nonfood area to gain the higher gross profit margin that nonfoods provided. Nonfood items—at least before the advent of the discount houses—carried a 36 to 50 percent markup in their regular outlets, such as drug, variety and department stores. Supermarket operators, who earned an average gross margin of 17 to 19 percent, very logically calculated that they could merchandise these items at regular prices (often fair traded) or, if necessary, at discount store prices, and still increase net profit.

The next stage in the move into nonfoods came when supermarkets began to face more intense competition from each other. Trading stamps and below-cost selling narrowed the gap between operating costs and selling margins in many areas, causing operators to look even more seriously into high-profit nonfoods. Since the addition of limited stocks of HABA, housewares, magazines, records, pet supplies, and other general merchandise was profitable, supermarket operators expanded the number of items stocked and added new lines. Most soft-goods lines were added with emphasis on children's clothes and hosiery. And hard-goods lines were extended to include electrical goods, hardware, automotive supplies, and other items. This expansion changed the terminology from "nonfoods" to "general merchandise."

More lines and larger stocks required more store space. At first, supermarket operators used aisles for general merchandise. Then, to entice customers to shop the general merchandise, operators changed to displaying these goods next to related food items (where applicable), or they set up "home centers." The home center often was located in the center of the grocery gondola area, and customers had to pass it in order to shop the entire grocery department.

Currently, some supermarket operators are viewing the "superstore" or combination store as the successor to the present-day supermarket. Superstores utilize up to 40 percent of selling space for general merchandise. There are savings in proportion to the size of these superstores: one supermarket selling $200,000 per week is more efficient than two with an equivalent total area each doing $100,000 per week. However, the merchandising of food is far different from the merchandising of those items in the general merchandise category; the gross margin earned from selling general merchandise requires the expertise of individuals trained in general merchandising.

Naturally, everything is not all additional profits, or the supermarket quickly would become a variety or department store. The general merchandise purchased in the supermarket is sold because the traffic created by food shoppers is exposed to the general merchandise items.

The extra profit margins or markup that is afforded by the general merchandise items is balanced by other factors. Since such merchandise moves more slowly than foodstuffs, there is a longer tie-up in cost of merchandise, and the cost of money becomes a factor. Many firms have had to re-evaluate their thinking about general merchandise lines and have had to take into account these factors in evaluating what, how much, and what percentage of the store should be devoted to general merchandise.

The most drastic change in the handling of general merchandise is the type of product handled and the grade of such products. In the earliest additions of general merchandise items in supermarkets, store operators tended to confine themselves to very inexpensive items, feeling that the customer might not be willing to buy the more expensive items in supermarkets. Many stores carried only the lowest-end merchandise—often discontinued lines, seconds, and merchandise often considered shoddy or second-rate.

Some stores started to add better-grade items, but again, they feared that the consumer might not pay full price for these items, so the tendency was to take a smaller markup than the department store or even the discounter was taking on similar items. Since the normal supermarket markup was so much lower than the markup normally taken at department stores or even the discount houses, the prices charged by those supermarkets still were lower than rival outlets, and the supermarket operator was making a better markup than he was used to in foodstuffs.

However, the turnover of general merchandise items was not as fast as with foodstuffs, and although the markups were greater, there was also considerably more capital tied up in these inventories than with foodstuffs. The new crux became not sales per square foot, but profit per square foot, with *all* factors taken into account.

Also, the discounters began to fight back. Divergent schools of thought engulfed the industry. For example, Fred Meyer stores on the West Coast and Fred Meijer stores in Michigan (pronounced the same way, but in no way related) have supermarkets of 30,000 sq. ft. or more within stores that range in size to over 200,000 sq. ft. and that rival full-line department stores in what the stores carry. On the other hand, there are stores that limit their lines to foodstuffs only. Both types of stores do well. And in stages in between are regular supermarkets, superstores, and combination stores.

THE IMPORTANCE OF GENERAL MERCHANDISE IN THE SUPERMARKET

At the outset, the selling of nonfoods in supermarkets was a creaming operation, and operators carried impulse and convenience items. The status and importance of general merchandise sales has changed considerably. In a recent survey of chains and independents, *Supermarket News* found that most supermarket executives (85 percent) felt general merchandise would increasingly be responsible for a larger share of store sales. Supermarket operators especially like the higher gross margins on nonfoods, compared with those available through food products. As a response to already high levels of general merchandise sales, executives in the survey indicated a greater consumer acceptance of supermarkets as the place to buy general merchandise.

Currently, general merchandise occupies between 5 and 10 percent of the total store footage. The *Supermarket News* survey results indicate that 83.6 percent of the chains and independents earn gross margins of from 26 to 50 percent, 55.2 percent earn from 31 to 50 percent gross margins, and 22.4 percent earn from 36 to 50 percent gross margins. (See Table 10.)

TABLE 10
GROSS PROFIT MARGINS FOR GENERAL MERCHANDISE*

Gross Margin	% of Chains and Independents
46–50%	4.5%
41–45	3.0
36–40	14.9
31–35	32.8
26–30	28.4
21–25	13.4
16–20	3.0

(46–50%, 41–45, 36–40 bracketed as 22.4%; those plus 31–35, 26–30 bracketed as 55.2%; total bracketed as 83.6%)

Supermarket News, Market Research Report, January 8, 1979.

General merchandise sales as a percentage of total supermarket sales (for stores allocating between 5 and 10 percent of total footage to general merchandise) were reported in the same survey. (See Table 11.)

More and more, supermarkets are gaining a greater share of the general merchandise market. It is estimated that by the middle of the 1980's, supermarket sales of general merchandise will exceed the $9 billion mark.

A recent study by *Redbook* Magazine, made in cooperation with the Food Marketing Institute reveals that 93 percent of all households have purchased general merchandise in a supermarket, and the median number of items purchased was 5.2. The national average spent in the supermarket for household prod-

General merchandise accounted for 5 to 10 percent of total supermarket space in the early 1980's, with the prospect that this would grow during the decade. Here, clockwise from upper left, are examples of: household supplies; kitchenwares; books and greeting cards; stationery; glassware; and clothing and other soft goods.

TABLE 11
GENERAL MERCHANDISE SALES AS A PERCENTAGE OF TOTAL SUPERMARKET SALES*

% of Total Sales	% of Chains and Independents
1%	6.4%
2	8.1
3	6.5
4	11.3
5	14.5
6	16.1
7	6.5
8	8.1
9	1.6
10	4.8
11–15	6.4
16 and over	9.7

Supermarket News, Market Research Report, January 8, 1979.

ucts, including general merchandise, was $35.39 per month. The study showed that 44 percent of the shoppers reported that they are spending more for nonfoods in the supermarket than they did in the past. And, as supermarkets grow in size, the importance of general merchandise will grow.

GENERAL MERCHANDISE OPERATIONS

Supermarket operators started nonfood lines through the rack jobber. Nonfoods buying and servicing requires specialized knowledge. Availability, delivery time, sources of supply, terms, quantity units, etc., for general merchandise are different than that for the grocery trade. The buying pattern for general merchandise is also different.

The rack jobber operates through driver/salespeople, and the operation is only as good as the supervision and control exercised by management. The store manager must supervise the driver/salesperson either directly or by delegating the supervisory function in order to assure the maintenance of peak volume. The rack jobber assists the merchandiser by offering specials at agreed intervals, which may be included in the weekly ad.

Supermarket operators utilize direct purchasing operations when volume in any category is large enough to permit buying in quantities to obtain maximum discounts and economical shipping quantities, and when warehouse space and trained personnel are available. The warehousing, service, and delivery must be performed at a reasonable cost and at a savings over rack jobber margins.

The following comparison of rack jobber and direct stocking and warehousing of general merchandise should be considered prior to making decisions:

Advantages of Dealing with Rack Jobbers

1. Specialists do the buying and select the assortments.
2. Merchandising knowledge and experience are available. The rack jobber understands the buying patterns, the seasonal factors, and the obsolescence.
3. No investment in inventory—usually the retailer pays for the merchandise sold, not the merchandise stocked.
4. Inventory control is the responsibility of the rack jobber.
5. Stocking is the responsibility of the rack jobber—very little store labor is required.
6. Quality control is handled by specialists.
7. Order is written and placed by jobber.
8. Unsalable and damaged merchandise is removed and replaced by jobber.

Disadvantages of Dealing with Rack Jobbers

1. Lower margin. The rack jobber requires a margin to operate and make a profit.
2. Cost of route drivers is higher than delivery through the warehouse.
3. Store personnel can stock the nonfoods at less cost than a driver/salesperson can.
4. Quality control is in the hands of the rack jobber.
5. Stock control in the hands of a driver/salesperson. He may or may not maintain the inventory at peak selling efficiency. Often, items are stocked even though they are out-of-season.

Advantages of Direct Stocking and Warehousing

1. Quality control is within the company.
2. Items stocked are controlled by the operator.
3. Margins are higher, i.e., margins average 5 percent higher than through the rack jobber. Handling costs are less than the 5 percent.
4. Greater continuity is possible.
5. Greater flexibility available.
6. Wider diversification possible.

Disadvantages of Direct Stocking and Warehousing

1. Capital is required for store and warehouse inventory.
2. Warehouse space is required—many items are small and valuable, requiring special handling in a small-goods room.
3. Merchandising and inventory control are the responsibility of the retailer.
4. Specialists must be hired or developed from within.

Each retail operator must decide which situation will produce the largest volume and profit dollar: using rack jobbers or stocking and warehousing. Some lines, such as records, magazines, stationery, etc., are better handled through rack jobbers. Apparently, the rack jobber is still an important element in general merchandise operations; *Supermarket News* reports that 15 percent of the chains and independents surveyed are either partially or fully supplied by jobbers.

Criteria for stocking general merchandise include:

1. General merchandise should earn at least as many margin dollars per square foot of space as the average for the grocery department, i.e., sufficient volume to warrant the space.
2. Items stocked should generally have universal appeal, i.e., most customers should use the item and it should have high repeat sales. (Some items with a limited appeal are profitable, however.)
3. Pilferage factor must be low, i.e., packaging should be a deterrent to pilferers.
4. Each item stocked should be a value to the customer. General merchandise quality must be consistent with the quality image of the store. Avoid "junk" gadgets and defective merchandise.
5. The package must possess self-sevice sales appeal, i.e., the packaging must conform to mass merchandising techniques.
6. Stock turn must be more than that experienced by the traditional retail outlet for the general merchandise. Stock control must be exercised by the store manager.
7. Evaluate the competitors who sell the same items. Know the type of merchandising and the variety and amount of space needed to compete.
8. Impulse, necessity-type merchandise sells best with the lowest loss through shrinkage, markdowns, returns, seasonal changes, etc.

No set of criteria will guarantee success. Management must exercise judgment, creativity, imagination, and courage. Experimentation should be used to prove or disprove decisions without involving the entire operation. The use of test stores, test promotions, and test situations is strongly recommended.

One-time promotions or short-term projects (known as "in-and-out" merchandise) can be profitable and at the same time add interest and variety for shoppers. Merchandise must be of good quality, and the price should make the item a real consumer value.

Some of the basic principles that should increase the profitability of general merchandise offerings include:

1. *Hire qualified personnel.* Buyers and merchandisers for nonfoods lines, particularly soft goods, must be able to recognize quality and value, must know the markets, and must have a good knowledge of the sources of supply. Too often the assistant grocery buyer or some other available person is expected to handle nonfoods buying as a sideline instead of as a specialist. Competitors use specialists to buy and merchandise these items.

2. *Top management must support the line.* General merchandise must be accepted as an integral part of the organization. General merchandise personnel must be included in all merchandising, advertising, and planning.

3. *Stock good quality merchandise.* Good quality—quality that is a good value for the customer—will maintain the store image and hold customers. Many operators offering Grade A produce, choice quality meats, and well-known brands of groceries offer inferior general merchandise. This policy is not consistent with good retailing practices and does not create a favorable store image.

4. *Have a definite advertising and promotional program.* Too many supermarket operators think that a general merchandise business can be built on existing traffic, but experience shows that customers must be told about these items. Advertising is a necessity. Successful nonfood operators, such as Pathmark, Shop-Rite (Co-op), Kroger, and H.E. Butt, believe the general merchandise deserves special ads for seasonal peaks, such as back-to-school and Christmas, and should carry the main theme of the organization's promotion from time to time.

5. *Use variety store merchandising techniques.* Proper display counters and tables are a necessary part of a nonfoods department. Converted grocery gondolas and makeshift shelving will not do the best job. While pegboards and prepackaging are essential, many customers like to feel the material and inspect soft goods.

6. *Aim for low unit price, fast turnover items.* An exception to this rule may be essential seasonal merchandise, such as lawnmowers, barbecue grills, etc.; many operators have found these "big-ticket" items profitable.

MERCHANDISING GENERAL MERCHANDISE

Each supermarket has a consumer image. In general, this image is built around quality and price. General merchandise must be added in conformity with the existing image. Since consumer store image is a total store concept, nonfoods must be merchandised as aggressively as the other departments. The weekly ad should include general merchandise items. Price specials should be used as well as special displays and merchandising gimmicks.

Balanced selling can be accomplished by using high-markup, high-impulse, value nonfoods as related items in special displays. Signs suggesting uses of the items on display increase the sales of *all* displayed products.

The merchandising of general merchandise must be tailored to fit the supermarket's general, overall operation. Some supermarkets may not fulfill the needs of their customers by adding an extended line of general merchandise. Each store must fit the shopping area that it serves. Many supermarket operators find that some of their locations have a limited nonfoods appeal either because of the neighborhood or existing competition from specialty and variety retailers. If this situation exists, profits will be lost because of the diminution of valuable grocery space within the store. The degree to which a supermarket operator undertakes the stocking and merchandising of nonfoods depends upon the market area, the competition, the space available, the know-how, and the capital and management ability available for the project.

The debate over the proper merchandising technique for general merchandise continues to be tossed about in the industry. However, a *Supermarket News* survey indicates that 65 percent of those questioned preferred the integrated rather than the segregated approach.

The integrated approach entails putting general merchandise items with or near related food items (e.g., coffeemakers, cups, and mugs alongside the coffee; baking equipment in the flour, cake mix and related items department). The segregated department consists of separate aisles or alcoves devoted to only general merchandise items. The combination approach uses both systems, with many firms (if the space is available) duplicating a number of items so they are available both ways.

According to the *Supermarket News* survey, many companies using the integrated approach felt it had been the most effective way of boosting impulse purchases as well as encouraging customers to shop all the aisles. The segregated or departmental technique was defended by supermarket operators as the neatest way to merchandise the category.

However, it was also found that a combination of both methods is often utilized. Supermarket operators indicated that a segregated approach has certain stocking advantages, but a strong tie-in with food products on the gondolas should not be ignored. Seventy percent of the operators who segregate merchandise reported that they use interior aisles.

Some problem areas in merchandising nonfood items include: pilferage, delivery, shelf tidiness, selection of goods, training of personnel, damage, and relations with outside vendors.

Many successful merchants who are doing well with general merchandise warn neophytes not to be blinded by just the extra profit margins available in general merchandise lines. Those that can work into the store image and sell well are assets. Those that cannot, waste capital and valuable store space which could be used for salable items.

General merchandise stores are not sitting idly by, just waiting for the supermarket operator to replace them. They have merchandising techniques as good as those of supermarket firms, and they have competitive skills at their disposal. In recent years, many variety stores, drug store operators, and discount operations have been using grocery items as loss leaders and have used the supermarket operators' own tactics to fight the supermarkets.

12

THE FRONT END—CHECKOUT MANAGEMENT AND CONTROL

The front-end operation does not produce revenue, yet it is a key element in contributing to the profitability of supermarket operations. Included in front-end operations are: checkstands, courtesy booths, record keeping, bookkeeping, and customer services. (See Chapter 18, "Customer Services.")

THE IMPORTANCE OF THE CHECKSTAND

In a typical supermarket, cash in-flow at the checkstands is almost $5 million annually. (This is a national average.) Often, the checkstands are the only areas in which customers have human contact with store personnel. Therefore, the checkstand is important in shaping store image.

At the checkstand, checker-cashiers perform duties which include: ringing sales, handling coupons, bagging, receiving cash or checks, making change,

issuing trading stamps and money orders, weighing produce, and other work.

The checkstand is all too often a bottleneck in a supermarket, and waiting on a checkout line is a source of irritation to customers, but the use of scanners and Universal Price Code (UPC) scannable products (see page 66) are helping to alleviate this. Long lines at checkout counters may cause customers to abandon filled carts and go to another market to shop.

For the supermarket operator, the checkstand can prove to be an expensive drain on gross margin and net dollar profit. A study by the Super Market Institute (now called the Food Marketing Institute) indicates that under rush conditions, ringups run 2 to 3 percent less than the actual value of the order, and that an undercharge of even 1 percent per order can easily represent a loss of thousands of dollars to the supermarket operator. Some of the frequent errors that can result in miscalculating the planning of pur-

No problem at the checkout counters here because it is a relatively slow period in the store. Note that at the most active counters, the cashier-checkers are assisted by baggers.

chases and sales, estimating shrinkage, and determining profits include:

- Ringing items into wrong department key, (e.g., grocery item into meat department)
- Ringing wrong amount due to illegible price marking
- Ringing advertised specials at regular prices
- Failing to ring items
- Miscalculating the cost in multiple-priced items
- Ringing wrong price on unmarked items
- Making change incorrectly.

Studies prove that price-ring errors are overwhelmingly in favor of the customer. The scanner corrects all these mistakes except for deliberate failure to ring or mistakes in making change, although the register tells the cashier what change to give. The scanner speeds the checkout process as much as three or four times and insures an accuracy unattainable by regular checkout methods—even checkstands that are equipped to weigh and price produce.

Many firms have installed electronic scales at the checkout. The extra expense involved in the purchase of such scales is often paid back in a year or less, since such scales charge for every unit of weight, whereas clerks do not, and often cannot, calculate fractions of ounces and, therefore, charge to the next lowest ounce on the scale.

CHECKER TRAINING PROGRAMS

To overcome problems arising from human error, supermarket operators have implemented intensive checker training and retraining programs designed to increase efficiency and to develop better customer relations. *New* checker training programs should cover:

- Company policy and regulations
- Orientation to the store
- Introduction to department managers and employees
- Special training in produce recognition
- Grooming
- Courtesy
- Methods of setting up the register and the checkstand
- Explanation of how to work the various keys of the register
- Register operation, including how to handle overrings, underrings, coupons, refunds, rainchecks, stamps, etc.
- Making change

- Bagging
- Handling customer complaints.

Retraining of *experienced* checkers should include:

- Courtesy
- Key depression techniques
- Underring and overring procedures
- Checking for merchandise placed at bottom of cart
- Handling customer complaints
- Other problems.

Training and retraining programs do help to reduce errors at the checkstand. However, a reduction in errors is directly related to the recency of training. Checkers should undergo retraining periodically.

SCHEDULING FOR OPTIMUM CHECKSTAND UTILIZATION

Checkstand operations account for approximately 20 percent of the total store payroll. Efficient front-end labor scheduling can help reduce the cost of checkstand operations and increase customer satisfaction by reducing waiting time.

Data available from electronic cash register and scanner checkstands make scheduling much more accurate and eliminate the guesswork from the scheduling process. The data available from the registers have been used by many companies for a number of years to tell front-end managers just how

The checkout nightmare is familiar to many supermarket managers and millions of their customers. It can drive patrons to competitors. It also can lead to human error at the cashier level.

many cashiers, baggers, cart retrievers, etc., should be available, at what hours and days.

Since most states have laws that no employee can be brought to work for less than four hours on any given day, this may make scheduling difficult at times. Most front-end managers use a variety of scheduling methods to make the optimum use of personnel.

Primary among these methods is the overlapping of shifts so that the overlapping covers the heaviest shopper hours. If there are gaps between two heavy periods, sometimes lunch hours or breaks can be scheduled to best advantage during such slow periods.

Some stores have combination checker-stock-clerks and use slow periods for stocking shelves, returning abandoned merchandise, and even policing the aisles and gondolas to keep the entire store looking neat and clean, and to make sure there are as few out-of-stocks as possible. One of the problems with the combination of duties is that often it results in mediocre performance by these joint checkers and stock clerks.

If the store is a small or average operation, it may be impossible for all or the majority of the employees to be specialists. However, if the store is a high-volume operation, it becomes much easier to create specialists who are highly skilled at their specialties.

Fill-in help generally is available as part-time help. In many high-volume stores, the number of part-timers can run as high as eight to ten times the number of full-time employees.

One method of increasing checker productivity is to decrease the number of duties that the checker performs. Check verification can be (and in many operations is) done at the courtesy booth; bottle refunds and rainchecks can be handled at the courtesy booth or another designated area; and more express checkout lanes can be opened during rush periods.

Bottle returns, in particular, are becoming a major bottleneck in those states that now have mandatory deposit laws. It becomes impossible for the checkstand to handle the volume of bottle returns, and even the courtesy counter cannot cope with the problems. Therefore, in most stores in such regions, separate bottle-return centers have been set up where returns are accepted, verified, and either vouchers or cash given to those returning the deposit items.

Efficient scheduling consists of planning the hours and work assignments of employees to assure that the right person is doing the right work in the right place at the right time. The supermarket operator will gain more checkout payroll savings and higher checkout productivity from careful scheduling at the checkstand than from any other single move. Many man-hours can be saved, while at the same time improving customer service, by taking the time to follow the procedures suggested below:

1. Determine the hourly production capacity of the checkstand when operated by a checker alone and then by a checker with bagger assistance.
2. Calculate the number of customers, the amount of sales, and the average order size for each hour of each day. Set up an hourly profile for each day of the week.
3. Determine the number of man-hours required for each hour of each day.
4. Construct a schedule assigning people to specific jobs during specific hours.
5. Adjust schedules to allow for rush periods, holidays, bad weather, vacation periods, and the like. The schedule must be *flexible*.

CHECKSTAND STAFFING

By manipulating the number of persons assigned to one checkstand, a supermarket manager can control, to a certain extent, the number of transactions that can be efficiently processed through the stand in a given period of time. There is, however, a direct ratio between transactions handled and labor costs. The problem is to man the checkstand in the best interests of the customer in regard to service and of the store in regard to cost. Costs must be kept to a minimum. Each additional person assigned to the checkout operation should materially increase the efficiency of the operation.

While efficiency and productivity are highly desirable goals, a word of caution must be inserted here. The point of greatest irritation in the supermarket is the checkstand. An inefficient or discourteous checker can undo every bit of effort that goes into attracting the customer to the store. It takes a great deal of intensive effort and expenditure to bring a customer into the store and away from a competitor. Promotions, advertising, quality, and/or price advantages are useless, if the customer leaves the store with a feeling of discontent.

Yet the most pleasant and courteous checker can do little to mollify the customer who has been standing at the checkstand for as much as an hour, while other registers are unmanned. It is difficult to explain to that customer about scheduling and other problems. He or she feels insulted and angry. Often the customer, in disgust, may abandon the loaded shopping cart at the checkstand and depart without having made a purchase.

Balancing the number of people needed for an efficient front-end operation with the customer satis-

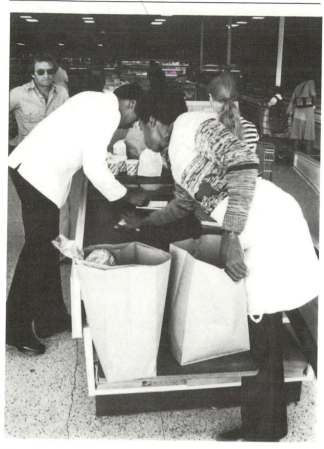

Here, three persons actually work this checkout counter. The man at left is actually a head checker, sometimes rating title of assistant manager. His role: to expedite customer flow. He moves about where he is needed—approving checks, filling out delivery forms, scheduling front-end personnel, etc. The bottleneck is his enemy.

faction accomplished by a fast, courteous trip through the checkout is not an easy task. The higher the volume of the store, the easier it is to accomplish.

Using a standard or change-computing cash register, a one-checker operation is the most efficient in terms of transactions per hour. One person can handle an average of thirty-four transactions per hour. Adding a bagger to the checkstand operations increases the average to fifty-nine transactions. Therefore, if both checker and bagger are receiving the same rate of pay, greater efficiency is achieved by using two separate checkstands, each operated by one employee and together producing an average of sixty-eight transactions per hour. If there is a differential in the rate of pay, however, greater efficiency in terms of cost-per-transaction may result from the checker-bagger combination. Since this is usually true, most store managers use the checker-bagger combination. But

regardless of pay scales, in peak business hours, all posts must be manned in order to get the customer out quickly.

A number of innovative methods have been attempted with varying degrees of success to create more efficiency at the checkout counter. One fairly simple method that is taking hold in many markets, particularly in box stores, where customers do their own bagging, is the use of a sectionalized end of the checkout counter. By means of a wooden bar, which is fastened at a pivot point, the order being checked at the moment can be diverted to one of the sections at the end of the checkstand. (Usually there are only two sections, but some stores have experimented with three.)

Thus, when the first order has been paid for and is being bagged, the next order can be checked out and the merchandise shunted to the other side of the partitioned-off checkstand. Generally, by the time the second order is completed, the first space is free so that the next order can be shunted into that space while the second order is being bagged. Such a system permits three baggers to keep busy at two checkstands and speeds up the checkout. In those stores where the customer must do the bagging, the checker can be working on the next order while the preceding order is being bagged. Again, there is a considerable saving of time for the checker.

Another system, which was started by Grand Bazaar, Jewel Tea's experiment into *hypermarkets (hypermarches)*, was the use of a separate checker and cashier. The order was rung up by a checker, who did not take cash, but gave the register tape to the customer. In those stores, the order was put back into a cart unbagged. The customer then proceeded to a bagging table, where the order was boxed or bagged by the customer. When the bagging was completed, the customer presented the tape to a cashier and paid before leaving the store. One cashier could handle many checkers. However, the system had a number of obvious flaws and was abandoned about a year after its adoption.

Another method of payment has been experimented with in a number of areas. When the checker has totalled the tape, the customer turns over a bank electronic funds transfer card. The card is inserted into the terminal and the amount of the order is transferred from the customer's account into the supermarket's account. The advantages to such a system are obvious, but there are also a number of pitfalls which still have to be worked out before such a system can be put into effect universally. Such a system works best in an area where only one bank dominates the region. Unless all the various banks in the area tie into the system, it is limited.

No visible funds change hands here in a transaction performed with a bank transfer card. A card is inserted in a terminal by a checker, which moves funds from customer's account into the supermarket's. This system works best when one bank dominates community—or when all banks participate.

TECHNOLOGICAL CHANGES IN FRONT-END OPERATIONS

Rapid advancement in electronic technology has led to the development of a variety of point-of-sale (POS) systems which are producing dramatic changes in the supermarket industry. Through use of this technology, customer purchases are automatically checked out at the checkstand faster by means of automatic price look-up and tax computation; and supermarket management can use concurrently and automatically stored information for reordering merchandise, verifying customer credit, scheduling personnel, and analyzing checker performance and department sales, among other things. Use of the technology has a distinct impact on reducing costs of distribution and increasing customer service.

FIGURE 10
EXAMPLE OF UNIVERSAL PRICE CODE (UPC)

The basis for scanning technology of POS systems is the Universal Product Code (UPC) imprinted on supermarket packages by manufacturers, processors, packers, and other suppliers of supermarket goods. The UPC consists of bars and spaces representing ten-digit numbers. The first five digits identify the manufacturer, chain, or group, and the last five digits identify the item. Distribution Codes Incorporated is responsible for UPC management and assigns the first five digits to specific manufacturers, chains, or groups. The manufacturer, chain, or group designates the second five digits which identify the product. By centralizing the assignment of identifying digits, duplicates in codes are made impossible, since more than 100 billion unique UPC combinations are possible.

POINT-OF-SALE (POS) ELECTRONIC CHECKOUT SYSTEMS

POS systems include the hardware, software, and expertise involved in the capturing, display, and effective utilization of data obtained at the point of sale. Equipment may include the following:

- An electronic cash register (ECR) which speedily records the data.
- A point-of-sale terminal in which an ECR interfaces with a mini-computer in an on-line, real-time mode.
- An optical scanner which usually uses laser beams to optically read and decode the UPC symbols. The scanner also checks the digit function and transmits the data to the mini-computer. The transmission is performed at speeds of electronic micro-seconds.
- A computer containing all stored information.

Of course, there are variations of the system, designed by computer engineers, to meet the specific needs of a supermarket. An electronic cash register may be a stand-alone, noncomputer-tied information bank for storing transactions from the register on magnetic tapes, cassettes, or discs, which then can be transmitted over communication lines to an Electronic Data Processing (EDP) Center.

Chains that cannot afford the very high cost of complete installations in each store may utilize a "store-and-forward" device which is a magnetic tape data concentrator designed for use with a complete system. It permits a remotely controlled computer to communicate with the device and triggers a transmission of the ECR stored information. Equipment of this type can be either purchased or rented.

THE SCANNING SYSTEM

For a scanning operation to be economically beneficial, at least 80 to 90 percent of a store's items must be UPC symbol marked, either at the source or in the store. Large supermarkets stock between 10,000 and 15,000 different items. During the early stages of automated checkout system development, a large number of in-store symbol printing and attaching had to be performed. Efficient methods and procedures of printing symbols and marking merchandise must be established, and the various marking systems and equipment available on the market must be evaluated to determine which can best meet the needs of the operation.

The Scanning Operation

In a scanning operation, the checker, after "signing-on" to the system, passes items over a fixed slot scanner (wand scanners are not usually used in supermarket operations). The scanner can read symbols moving across it at speeds up to 100 inches per second; and it can read labels that vary in size from 0.8 inch to 1.5 inches in height with varying widths of lines and spaces (depending on the numbers in the UPC symbol). What the scanner actually reads is the variation or differences in distances between the bars and spaces (dark and light) to determine the Universal Product Code.

The reading process, when passing the label over the scanner, takes microseconds, and the scanner, via laser beam, decodes the UPC and instantly accesses the in-store computer or controller to determine the price. The data then goes back to the terminal which displays a description of the item and its price. Simultaneously stored within the computer's memory is information such as price; description of item; whether or not the product is taxable and/or eligible for food stamps or trading stamps; and other information.

Most scanners can read in any direction, no matter in which direction the UPC symbol is passed over them. However, a damaged or poor printing quality of the UPC symbol cannot be scanned, and must be manually keyed-in in the same way as nonsymbol items.

The controller (or mini-computer) computes automatically, adds taxes, and displays change due to the customer. Customers who pay by check can have checks approved at the terminal by having a courtesy card inserted into the point-of-sale terminal. Any task currently performed on a conventional electric cash register can be performed on an electronic cash register.

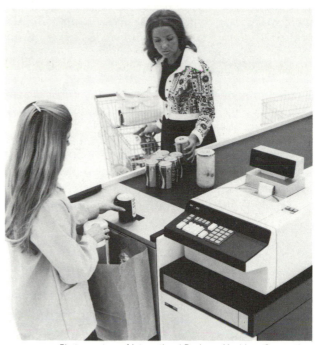

Photo courtesy of International Business Machines Corporation.

Checker (at left) is passing a can over an electronically operated scanner which captures sales data helpful in management decisions, and also relieves checker of most register keying and arithmetic operations.

The Effect of the Scanning System on Supermarket Operations

Upon demand, authorized personnel at the store can ask the system for any information desired, including: statistical information on sales, by item, by time of sale, by totals per sale; dollar value and number of items sold; sales by department; cashier productivity information; cash drawer status; action on specials and advertised items; and other information vital to efficient operation.

Corporate or regional headquarters can contact each store's minicomputer through telecommunication. Selected data can be transmitted to the electronic data processing (EDP) center over telephone lines for further processing.

Information from the computer can be used to make buying decisions, to determine the viability of a new product, to pinpoint busy periods which would be the basis for personnel scheduling, to determine the pulling power of various promotions and advertisements, to determine the pulling power of display areas, to determine item movement, and for numerous other uses.

The scanning system can improve supermarket operations by providing data needed for more efficient ordering, pricing competitively, allocating shelf space, scheduling personnel, and planning and analyzing sales. Scanning can provide the means for:

- Improving service at the checkstand and operating it more efficiently
- Obtaining information about item movement
- Helping bookkeeping, accounting, and cash-control activities
- Reducing errors at the checkstand caused by looking up prices incorrectly, by incorrect calculation of taxes and cost of multiple-priced items, and the like
- Verifying checks prior to accepting them
- Verifying and validating coupons to purchase, and
- Many more applications.

Supermarket management can use data obtained from transactions at the checkstand and from other store operations to accomplish some of the following:

- Automatic ordering of merchandise or to provide the buyer with information needed to buy
- Reduction of out-of-stock conditions
- Monitoring of sales performance at the store
- Analysis of demographics, store by store
- Monitoring stock shrinkage
- Keeping track of new product performance
- Analysis of the effect of promotion and advertising efforts
- Management of delivery to stores
- Allocation of shelf space
- Scheduling of employees
- Cash and accounting controls, and
- Any other information that the operator would like within the capacity of the system.

It is estimated that the food industry will install more than $1 billion of new electronic equipment during the 1980's, equipment with varying degrees of sophistication. Most small stores will install electronic cash registers with capabilities for upgrading; these eventually will be upgraded. Larger stores will use computerized terminal systems, including scanning.

TECHNOLOGICAL INSTALLATIONS AND THE CUSTOMER

The general feeling in the supermarket industry is that the use of available technological equipment will in part counteract rising food prices by speeding deliveries and increasing productivity. Consumer advocates do not necessarily agree with this. They worry that the high initial cost of the systems will be passed along to shoppers, lead to the removal of prices marked on individual items, and that consumer privacy could be threatened if the computerized systems are used to authorize check cashing or credit.

In response to consumer action, many local, city, and state governments have passed ordinances making it mandatory for food stores to continue to stamp the price on each item. Stamping prices on each item is costly to supermarket operators. If customers want each item priced, they will have to continue to pay for this service.

Stores planning a UPC-scanner system installation use some form of pre-installation consumer information system. Supermarkets have used a variety of methods to tell shoppers about new checkout procedures and the UPC symbol—both the manufacturer supplied and in-store versions. Leaflets, bag stuffers, and newspaper advertisements are some of the methods that have been used to inform the shopper. In addition to written explanations, most stores testing equipment have installed a demonstration scanner so that customers can scan items, see the name and price on the display unit as well as on an itemized register tape, and discuss the system with an individual provided by the manufacturer of the equipment or with a trained store employee.

Inevitably, as more and more stores install scanners and some form of electronic point-of-sale equipment, customers will come to accept the new technology. In every store already using scanning, acceptance is almost universal, to the point that many customers now refuse to shop in nonscanner stores.

While most consumers feel that the only problems in setting up a UPC-scanner system consist of whether to price-mark items or not, there are considerably more problems that are burdensome to the supermarket operator, which consumers seldom, if ever, encounter. One of the more frequent problems is the UPC symbol that cannot be scanned. This can result from faulty printing, the lack of contrast between the symbol and the background, or printing in a color that the scanner cannot pick up. The UPC Council has set up a special committee that is weeding out and solving these problems. Hopefully, in a few years such problems will become virtually nonexistent.

The problems with any electronic cash register—or for that matter an electric cash register—is that when the power fails, the entire system is shut down. (However, with an electric register or an ECR, standby battery-operated calculators that have tapes have been used in emergencies.) When the scanner looks up prices based on the UPC and there is no price marking on the items, a power failure or computer failure just about shuts the store down.

Those store operators who have encountered such malfunctions all say they would never again operate without standby generators for power failures and some sort of backstop computer capacity, either in the form of telephone-linked equipment at headquarters or at the wholesaler's establishment or even a second computer.

One firm that had a four-day computer breakdown issued each customer a crayon on arrival at the store and explained the problem. The customers were asked to write the price as it appeared on the shelf label under each item. At the front end, the orders were handled on the ring-up portion of the registers. To compensate the customers for marking their own prices, a certain number of free items were given to them, depending on the size of the order. (The number of mismarked prices were surprisingly few and averaged almost as many overprices as underprices.)

Another retailer who had a total front-end breakdown late on a Friday and was unable to get it fixed until Monday, used another method which was costly but established goodwill and kept the customers contented. A management person stood at each checkstand. Each customer was asked, "How much do you estimate this order would total?" Depending on the amount recited by the customer and the amount of merchandise in the carriage, the official then deducted $5, $10, or $15 from the amount cited as payment for the order and thanked the customer for putting up with the inconvenience.

But even before the first ringup by the scanner, weeks of programming, checking, and testing go into each operation before the system can be put into use. The original price book (file) must be put into the computer so that when the scanner reads the symbol and transmits it to the computer, the proper price comes back. Each scanner then must be checked numerous times with random sample orders which on a number of occasions must call up each item the store carries to make sure the right prices come up whenever that item is scanned.

Similar checks must be made every time a price changes—up or down. Thus, when an item goes on special and when it goes off, the computer must be checked to confirm the prices. A good rule of thumb is to change prices in the computer first and then on the shelves when the prices go down and the reverse when prices go back up, so that customers shopping the store at the time of the change get the benefits and do not feel they are being cheated.

13

The buyer for a supermarket chain or group is a highly skilled, knowledgeable individual responsible for purchasing one classification of goods or a group of related goods. Buyers must know the products they buy, the markets from which goods are obtained, and the customers who will ultimately purchase and use these products. Supermarket organizations employ grocery buyers, produce buyers, meat buyers, general merchandise buyers, and other specialty buyers (including buyers for departments with subspecialties), according to the size of the organization.

Many food buyers have achieved their positions after years of on-the-job training within the industy or may have risen to their positions after specialized college training and on-the-job experience. In some companies, the buying of general merchandise has been added to the duties of the grocery buyer. However, since the advent of the superstore, and with the increased emphasis and expansion of nonfood offerings in the supermarket, astute management has employed the merchandise specialist as the buyer of general merchandise, often individuals recruited from discount or department store organizations.

SOURCES OF MARKET INFORMATION

One of the vital needs of buyers in the food industry today is to keep fully informed on market conditions. Among the more important sources are:

- Government reports
- Trade publications
- Commercial organizations
- Daily consumer newspapers
- Salespeople
- Information from within the organization.

Government Reports. The federal government is a very valuable source of market information which the buyer can use to great advantage. Many agencies, bureaus, and departments of the government publish a variety of useful reports. A guide to federal publications is generally helpful in locating specific types of information. The government publishes a *Distribution Data Guide* which lists the sources and availability of government publications. *Department of Agriculture Reports* are examples of government reports that may prove useful to the buyer. These reports show the current situation of supply, demand, and price and the outlook for such commodities as dairy products, fruits, livestock and meat, and poultry and eggs.

Trade Publications. Trade publications may prove highly beneficial in gathering market information. A great deal of information can be gleaned both from editorial material and vendor advertisements. Information about new products, promotions, and consumer advertising can be found in these sources.

Business publications print detailed information on all categories of merchandise, new products, merchandising and promotion aids, operating ideas, and other material. Information describing the activities of other firms published in various business publications can prove of considerable value to executives. Trade association news and reports often contain ideas that are adaptable and useful.

Commercial Organizations. Some buyers make use of organizations whose primary purpose is to provide market information for a fee. These organizations are able to gather information from producers, manufacturers, dealers, and consumers and to employ specialists to interpret the data obtained.

Daily Consumer Newspapers. Daily newspapers can be an invaluable source of buying information. Many newspapers publish daily market information, such as market prices for butter, eggs, poultry, and livestock. Often, the business columns of these papers will contain useful information about consumers. Most newspapers have sections of interest to householders. Articles contained in these sections often indicate consumer interests that are important to buyers of the items mentioned. Retail food advertising in daily newspapers can provide the buyer with information on competition. Most newspapers publish daily and long-range weather forecasts that may help the buyer in his purchases of seasonal merchandise.

Daily financial and commercial newspapers give extensive coverage of grain, poultry, egg and livestock market quotations. Buyers also can gather in-

FIGURE 11
DAILY NEWSPAPER MARKET INFORMATION

Cash Prices

THURSDAY, APRIL 16

FOODS	Thu.	Wed.
Butter AA Chi lb	1.47	1.47
Broilers Dressed a ny pound	.4756	.4758
Eggs Large white Chi lb	.72½	.72½
Flour Minn per hundredweight	15.95	15.85
Coffee Parana ex-dck, NY cnts pr lb	1.25	1.25
Coffee Medlin ex dock NY cnts pr lb	1.43	1.43
Sugar No. 11	16.50	16.82
Sugar No. 12	18.76	1..84
Orange Juice spot	1.33	1.36
Hogs Ohama 1-2 200-250 lb per lb	40.50	40.50
Steers Joliet choice & prime per lb	63.00	63.00
Beef 600-900 lbs midwest per lb	99.00	89.00
Feeder Cattle 500-600 Okl City	67.75	70.00
Pork Bellies 12-14 lb midwest per lb	48.00	50.00
GRAINS & FEEDS		
Corn No 2 yellow Chi	3.54½	3.51½
Oats No 2 heavy Chi	2.33½	2.29½
Wheat No 2 soft Chi	4.18¾	4.15
Soybeans No 1 yellow Chi	7.64	7.56½
Wheat No 1 dk nthn 14pc-pro Mpls	4.38¾	4.80¼
Wheat No. 2 hard KC	4.45	4.41½
FATS & OILS		
Cottonseedoil crude tk cars NY lb	.28⅛	.28⅛
Coconutoil crude Pac Cst lb	.24½	.24½
Cornoil crude dry mill Chi lb	.25	.25
Peanutoil crude dry southeast lb	.33½	.32⅛
Linseedoil raw tk cars NY lb	.34	.34
Soybeanoil crude tk cars NY lb	.24½	.24⅜
METALS		
Aluminum, Unalloyed ngot 99.5pcf cts	.76	.76

Food prices have to keep up with price changes in the market. Many find helpful information in consumer papers that carry regular reports on primary market trends. Here, a typical report on vital supermarket categories: meat, dairy, grains, and oils.

formation on new items and promotions from these papers. Their articles on trends in business can be useful.

Some newspapers publish periodic reports on the trading area reached by the paper's circulation. These report the findings of research studies and sometimes indicate the percentage of the market total that is accounted for by the various retailers in the area. Similar reports on products list the position of various manufacturer and distributor brands, in terms of extent of distribution in the market area. Buyers can consult the research director of major newspapers in the trading area for this material.

Salespeople. The various salespeople that call on the buyer can also provide market information. Many supplier companies go to great lengths to study consumer buying and consumption patterns. The results of these studies are made available to buyers from the salespeople. As more and more companies gather market information, the salespeople become an increasingly useful source of information.

Information from Within the Organization. Records and reports supplied by department and store managers provide information for the buyer. With increased information available from UPC-scanned, computerized information, the buyer will have better information about demographics, out-of-stocks, purchasing patterns, item acceptance, and other information needed as a basis for buying.

SOURCES OF SUPPLY

A major part of the buying function is the selection of sources of supply, or resources. Each buyer develops a file of information for each resource, noting quality, prices, terms, services, sales record of new items, and promotional support. This information is essential for making buying decisions.

Buying sources include:

- Brokers
- Wholesalers
- Rack jobbers
- Manufacturers and processors.

Sources for buying perishables are somewhat different from those used for buying groceries and general merchandise. Sources for buying produce include:

- Growers and their marketing associations
- Produce markets
- Produce wholesalers
- Group wholesalers.

Sources for buying meat include:

- Cattle ranchers or their marketing organizations ("on-the-hoof")
- Meat brokers
- Boxed beef distributors
- Meat and poultry markets
- Meat and poultry wholesalers
- Group wholesalers
- Meat processors.

Brokers

Many manufacturers use brokers to sell their merchandise. A broker contracts with manufacturers or processors for exclusive sales territories and sells noncompeting products for a number of manufacturers on a commission basis. The broker-salesperson offers territory coverage on a fixed-rate basis regardless of the volume, or on a salary plus commission arrangement. The broker and his sales force must sell merchandise since they operate on commissions earned. Therefore, brokers are anxious to represent companies having well-known products with high volume potential. Brokers do not take title or possession of the merchandise they sell for manufacturers; they negotiate contracts between buyers and sellers.

Photo courtesy of Harris-Teeter Super Markets, Inc., Charlotte, North Carolina.

The central data processing center for a supermarket chain can provide management with important information based on material gathered by its scanners in member stores. Better decisions on pricing, ordering, inventory control are likely.

The bulk of grocery items are bought either through the manufacturer's salesperson or the broker's sales representative. That is, supermarket operators having the facilities and volume buy from manufacturers or brokers; operators lacking the facilities and volume join a voluntary or cooperative wholesaler or merely may be serviced by a wholesaler. Group distribution centers buy on the same basis as chain operators from manufacturers or brokers.

Wholesalers

As chains grew, they were able to effect savings and bulk buying which created efficiencies that threatened the existence of the smaller independent stores. The chains, if they were a danger to the independent store operator, therefore, were also a threat to the wholesalers that supplied such independents.

In a defensive measure to preserve their existence, two new forms of supermarket wholesaling emerged in addition to the standard operation: the voluntary and the co-op. The voluntary sponsors a group of independents (under a common name or banner) and supplies services that replace the headquarters functions of chains, thus bringing the costs of these services into reach of the independent. For this, a fee (or upcharge) is added to the cost of the product. Specific services are charged on a pro-rata or "as used" basis.

The co-op is similar to the voluntary in that the independently owned stores trade under one chosen name or banner. The difference lies in the fact that the co-op members own the warehouse and wholesale facility rather than being customers of it. Whatever profit is normally made by the wholesale arm is returned to the members in the form of rebates based on the amount of goods purchased.

The advantages of the voluntary or co-op can readily be seen in the following example: A chain that has ten stores in a given area served by one newspaper can divide the cost of the ad by ten in allocating the cost per store. An independent with only one store, who must advertise to compete, must pay ten times the advertising cost for the same-size ad. Costs of other headquarters-type functions also are that many times as expensive. If a voluntary or co-op has a number of stores under a common banner in an area, such costs can be divided proportionately and make the stores competitive. Thus, it can be seen that the voluntary or co-op was the salvation of the independent supermarket.

Wholesalers operate on a cost-plus basis and service stores with scheduled deliveries. On a fee-for-services-rendered basis, the following services are available:

- Advertising service: mats, group ads, and group promotions
- Handbills: weekly or for special promotions
- Display materials: sign service and point-of-sale material.

Services offered without an added fee include:

- Retail price lists: suggested retail prices and markup percentages
- Comparison price information: usually only for major competitors in the area
- Merchandising programs: weekly specials are suggested, including retail price and cost
- General market information: price trends, product availability, deals available.

Group Wholesalers. Of the top twenty-five companies in the food retailing business, thirteen are corporate chains and twelve are voluntary or cooperative groups. Group wholesalers have formed federated groups to secure the advantages of larger area coverage and volume for their labels and store names. The federation has greater buying power and can conduct large-scale promotions.

Some of the federated groups have formed wholesale units that own and operate warehouses and supply groceries, meats, produce, and general merchandise, and that offer a complete list of services, from accounting to operational aids, to planning and financing.

Cash-and-Carry Wholesalers. The cash-and-carry wholesaler may be distinguished from other wholesalers by several factors. The retailer must call at the wholesaler's place of business to obtain merchandise, and the transactions between the retailer and the wholesaler are on a cash basis—payment is made at the time of purchase.

The cost of operation for a cash-and-carry wholesaler is low—probably lower than for other types of wholesalers. However, the retailer must add pick-up and delivery costs to merchandise costs. Adding the direct costs usually reduces the cash-and-carry wholesaler to a quick service resource for a limited number of high turnover items since total costs are frequently higher. The cash-and-carry wholesaler is an excellent resource for the small operator and may be used as a fill-in resource for others.

Large retailers rarely use cash-and-carry, and then only to fill in items needed on an emergency basis that are not immediately available from the warehouse. Often, a supermarket may "borrow" from another market belonging to the same multi-store or group unit to fill-in emergency out-of-stocks.

Rack Jobbers

The rack jobber distributes nonfoods, such as health and beauty aids, housewares, hardware, soft goods, stationery, and toys to supermarkets. Usually, the jobber is allotted a specific amount of display space by supermarket operators.

The rack jobber operates on a gross margin on goods sold, guarantees sales, rotates stock, and takes back slow movers. It is advantageous to both the retailer and the rack jobber to merchandise for maximum sales; nevertheless, the store manager must supervise the rack jobber operation and permit only items that are selling to remain on the shelves or racks.

Most chains and wholesalers warehouse nonfoods, thereby eliminating the rack jobber. This is done to achieve better control and earn the margin taken by the rack jobber. Typically, the retailer grosses about 25 to 30 percent on "rack" merchandise. Since the rack jobber grosses 10 to 15 percent, the chain operator performing the warehousing function and assuming the risk of sale increases his gross as well as his costs. Whether the chain operator is able to earn a larger net profit by warehousing nonfoods depends on the skill of the nonfoods buyer and the operational efficiency of the warehouse.

Manufacturers and Processors

The buyer for a large company buys from the manufacturer many of the items that the company stocks. The small, independent, unaffiliated operator cannot usually purchase directly from the manufacturer since the volume does not permit large quantity buying. This makes it necessary for them to buy from wholesalers.

Some food processors and manufacturers depend primarily on their own sales organization to sell their products. Quantities sold must be large enough to permit shipping to the buyer at a reasonable expense ratio. The manufacturer must maintain and stock warehouses throughout the territory to enable prompt delivery to each buyer on a dependable schedule.

The manufacturers' sales representatives cover the territory and products assigned to them, under the supervision and control of the manufacturer. The sales effort is concentrated, the name of the manufacturer is easily recognized, the promotional program is presented, and company policies and interests are promoted.

Direct Store Delivery. A number of supermarket items are serviced by direct store delivery. Typically, baked goods, some dairy products, beverages, cookies, crackers, nut meats, etc., are handled by driver-salespeople. The frequency of delivery as well as freshness control are best handled by direct store delivery.

Buyers arrange the contracts for direct store delivery; that is, the decision regarding how many bakeries, dairies, etc., are to stock the stores and which items are on the basic stock list, is a buying function. The store manager is responsible for receiving, checking the quantity delivered, allocating and controlling shelf space, checking the sales slip, and stock control. Delivery schedules should be established to avoid overcrowding and unnecessary delays for salespeople and to facilitate checking by the store manager or by the person assigned the responsibility.

The direct-store-delivery (d-s-d) system is a costly one—for the producer as well as the retailer and, ultimately, the consumer. It was originated to guarantee freshness (milk, dairy, and bakery) or to eliminate bulky deliveries to and from the warehouse (soda pop). Direct-store-delivery drivers generally work on commissions rather than salaries.

Because of the nature of the operation, direct store deliveries force the retailer to divert one employee or official at each store who must check these deliveries. In a large store, this becomes a full-time occupation.

Human errors, theft, and disappearance of product as well as accounting errors are among the major problems. Even when the store personnel, drivers, and all personnel involved with the delivery are beyond reproach, the additional access to the back door for other employees and/or customers creates another problem area for the retailer.

In regions where distances between stores are great, most such deliveries are handled by the warehouse that normally supplies the store, and the direct store deliveries are eliminated. Retailers in areas where d-s-d are the norm have looked at such regions with envy and on numerous occasions have cited the productivity gains and efficiencies as reasons for adopting such a system nationwide. In the mid-1970's, the National Center for Productivity scheduled a test of a non-direct-store-delivery system for the Tampa area, but pressure from d-s-d driver associations and a lack of funds aborted the test.

In areas where direct store deliveries are rare (because of the distances between stores), the wholesaler or chain uses a truck that is compartmentalized, and dry groceries, perishables, and frozens are carried on the same truck.

Because of the commission payment to drivers, the strongest resistance to the elimination of direct store deliveries has come from their groups. However, many manufacturers feel that d-s-d guarantee freshness and in-stock positions that are beneficial to them.

Another drawback found by many supermarkets occurs when rival-product drivers are permitted to stock their own goods (where unions permit this). Often rival drivers change shelf allocations to favor their own items. Drivers have also been known to damage packages of rival firms to ensure the sales of their own.

Sources for Buying Produce

Sources of supply for produce are the growers and their marketing associations, markets in large cities, and produce and group wholesalers.

Growers and Their Organizations. Growers and their organizations are frequent sources of supply. The buyer may deal directly with the grower, or may buy through a cooperative association of growers. These cooperative agricultural marketing groups include such organizations as the Florida Citrus Commission and the Indian River Vegetable Marketing Cooperative. Although the organization and operational methods of these cooperatives may vary, the underlying principle of each is to assist the farmers or growers in marketing their products.

These grower outlets can be used during the harvest season for each growing area. Unless the growers are in the immediate vicinity of the store or stores, only large operators can use their facilities. For example, the Sunkist Growers Association is an excellent source of supply for California citrus, but it is too distant for all but the largest volume operators.

Some supermarket field buyers contract for supplies with growers. For example, a supermarket field buyer may contract for a specific type of sweet corn with a grower or growers; the contract may include conditions, such as hours of picking, cooling, time of delivery, etc. Thus, the retailer is assured consistent quality and supply of the item under contract—assuming a good growing season.

Produce Markets. Some large cities have produce markets that hold daily sales of the merchandise received since the previous day's sale. Producers, through associations and commission agents, ship by the carload on an open bill of lading. As the cars roll toward market areas, cars are dropped at terminals as the supply and demand appraisals of commission agents indicate. Each morning—at about 4 or 5 A.M.—the produce is sold at auction.

Buyers of volume quantities of produce—whether small of mid-sized chain, group, or independent retailers —attend the auctions and bid on items for their organizations. The market closes when the merchandise has been sold. The buyers arrange delivery, and the market prepares for the next day.

As carloads of produce are received, the merchandise is unloaded and inspected for condition and quality. A number of units are opened for display, and the available quantity is noted. Buyers arrive early and review the available merchandise so that when the bidding begins, they know the supply situation. The demand becomes evident as bidding progresses. Thus, the buyer must know the various items, the current consumer demand, the price the customers will pay, and then bid accordingly.

Usually the multi-store operators, produce wholesalers, and group wholesalers will send produce buyers to the market. The produce market is the prime source of produce throughout the year.

Produce Wholesalers. Supermarket operators who are unable to send buyers to produce markets use the produce wholesaler. The retailer can order by telephone, and the wholesaler will deliver the quantities ordered. Some retailers prefer to send a representative to the wholesale house to select the items to buy. Selection is based on the quality available, appraised in terms of the store clientele and the price they are likely to pay.

Many small retailers do not have produce buyers and depend upon the produce wholesaler to keep them competitive in terms of variety, quality, and price.

Group Wholesalers. Originally, group wholesalers stocked only dry groceries. A few cooperative units were organized to wholesale produce in the same manner that the group handled groceries. These were separate operating units.

Some group wholesalers bought existing produce wholesalers, some merged cooperative produce and grocery wholesale units, while others expanded their operations to include produce.

Most group wholesalers are becoming complete merchandise houses. The availability of produce and other items may be an important factor in selecting a group wholesaler.

FACTORS TO CONSIDER IN SELECTING A RESOURCE

Buyers continually seek new resources for new items or to replace vendors whose products or services are not satisfactory. For most types of merchandise, many resources are available; however, it is impractical and expensive to buy from a large number of suppliers. The buyer, therefore, must select those resources that offer both the products and services needed at a satisfactory price. The following factors are important in resource selection:

- Product factors
- Price factors
- Service factors.

Product Factors. All items stocked must be compatible—in terms of price, quality, and appearance—with the rest of the store. Packaged merchandise must be conducive to self-service merchandising and make for good display. The package must be designed to resist pilfering. Continuity of brand or label is essential in order to develop repeat sales. The product must be acceptable to the clientele of the stores and must be available in sufficient quantity to supply all the stores.

Price Factors. Generally, other factors being equal, the supplier offering the lowest prices and the best terms of sale is selected.

Service Factors. Services offered by resources are an important consideration in selecting sources of supply. Buyers should demand that all resources deliver *dependable* services. Dependability includes consistent quality, delivery on schedule, and service as per agreement. The buyer should be able to rely on receiving the same quality on reorders as was delivered on the initial order. The buyer also should be able to rely on the supplier making delivery on orders as scheduled.

Merchandising services, such as promotions, display materials, point-of-sale supplies, and store demonstration services are essential to the development of sales and to the development of a favorable customer image of the store and the products offered for sale.

RETAILER-SUPPLIER COOPERATION

Good supplier relations develop reliable resources that will give good service, including market and pricing information.

Cooperation between producer, wholesaler, and retailer has accomplished much that has improved the efficiency of the supermarket and benefited the consumer. Chief among these is the Universal Product Code, uniform case marking and a case code system, a computer-to-computer system that links all lines of the process from store through to manufacturer and other yet-to-be completed and instituted efficiencies. (Chief among these probably will be modular packaging.)

Also, out-of-stocks have been reduced through the establishment of uniform reorder procedures and dependable delivery time. Other efficiencies developed by cooperation have been the standardized pallet, standardized contract forms and terms, etc.

In recent years, there has been growing sentiment in favor of the total-systems approach to food distribution from the farmer to the consumer. Such an approach would have all sectors of the pipeline of food distribution meet regularly to discuss problems and set up means of solving them.

Some of the problems that arise regularly come from one sector of the industry not taking other segments into consideration when making decisions. For example, a manufacturer might decide that for certain marketing advantages it might be advisable to change the size or shape of a product's container. Such a decision might well occasion all sorts of problems in shipping, warehousing, and retail stocking of the product. The proliferation of sizes and flavors creates all sorts of retailing headaches. Better sales and greater efficiency are achieved through retailer-supplier cooperation.

BUYING POLICIES

Buying policies are the operating guides for the buyer and determine the type of buying organization used. The functions performed are the same for all types of food retailers. Therefore, the differences are primarily in organization, procedures followed, and the resources used.

The small, unaffiliated independent usually buys from wholesalers, drop shippers, rack jobbers, and cash-and-carry wholesalers, since the small volume places limitations on available resources.

The buying department of a food-chain organization varies from company to company; degree of specialization in the buying function depends on the size of the organization. The buying department determines which items are to be stocked by distribution centers and which are to be available through direct delivery. In multi-unit operations, pricing is a function of the central-office buying department. However, for competitive maneuverability, many chains permit district supervisors and even store managers the right to match prices when competitors stand a chance of gaining an edge, if a particular maneuver is unchallenged.

In voluntary groups, the basic selection of merchandise is delegated to the wholesale unit. Members are free to buy merchandise from other resources, but must buy a specified amount to remain in the group. However, members usually buy the major portion of their stock from the distribution center, which offers them better services, price, and support. New item selection is a group function performed by buyers or a buying committee composed of buyers and representatives of the membership. Most voluntary groups offer an exclusive label.

In a cooperative group—a group of retailers who form an organization for the purpose of operating their own warehouse—experts are hired to do the purchasing. The group formulates policies, and each member buys primarily from the cooperative warehouse according to contract terms.

The basis for all co-op or voluntary cooperation, however, is the agreement to comply with all specials and pricing policies of the group. This does not mean that all stores under the same banner must carry all of the same products at the same prices. Generally, each store will choose a "price zone" for each department of the store and abide by the group-wide specials.

Voluntary and cooperative groups usually operate as efficiently as chain organizations. The major difference is in supervision and control.

BRAND POLICIES

The determination of brand policies is a top-level administrative function. The brand policy adopted affects the buying functions and procedures. The brand owner assumes the responsibility for the quality, size of unit, label, continuity of supply, storage, and financing.

The manufacturer assumes these functional responsibilities for his label and, in addition, creates the consumer demand. The retail buyer evaluates the various labels or brands available, decides which items to stock, and establishes buying arrangements. This accomplished, buying becomes a reorder process. A completely automatic reorder is possible.

On company-owned labels, the buyer assumes the functional responsibilities. Quality control becomes a buying function and is determined by the buyer with or without the help of a research organization. Since quality in growing areas varies, the maintenance of a uniform product often becomes a problem. Labels must be designed and furnished to the packer. Continuity of the label is a buying function—that is, the season's or year's supply must be contracted, financed, and stored. Change in price is an added risk. Capital is required to finance the inventory. Reordering can be automatic or partially automatic as long as the contracted supply lasts.

A modification of the company label is the group label, used by a group of noncompeting companies that form a buying organization. This means that the functions become the responsibility of the buyers for the group. Topco Associates, using the Food Club and Top Frost label, and Staff, using the Staff label, are examples of group buying labels.

Another brand policy may be the purchase of quantities of an item offered by packers of merchandise not sold under an advertised or contracted label. This label has no continuity, but may be available each year in limited quantities.

The use of a franchise label provides the exclusiveness of a company label without increasing the scope of the buying function. Very few food packers offer franchise dealerships. Usually, the packer is relatively small and is able to contract his entire output to a few customers on an "exclusive territory" basis,

Here, A&P dramatically challenges major national brands with its own house brands. Focusing here on cleaning materials and foods, A&P in effect says: We carry the national brands, but we think our brands represent better customer value.

while leading manufacturers are interested in complete market coverage to attain the greatest sales volume.

The newest label is, in effect, a nonlabel—generics. It has replaced the packer label in many cases and has become the basis of the lowest end of the merchandise line. The proliferation of generics is so unique that even stores and chains that have never in the past attempted to compete on a price basis now carry generics lines.

The buyer must have the ability and personnel to buy according to the brand policy established by top management. There are only a very few large operators that do not stock any company labels. Some stock a limited number, while others stock considerably more labels. Thus, the policy decision is usually one of degree.

The retailer is in business to make money by selling consumers the merchandise they want. Volume should be an important factor in the brand policy decision. Any change in brand policy must be followed by a check on sales, item by item, for the period of time required to determine the customers' acceptance of the new labels.

The importance in terms of volume of retailer-owned labels should be a factor in deciding the degree of participation. Any appraisal of private-label merchandise is usually restricted to high-volume items.

The successful merchandising of a private-label line must take into account the size of the store as well as quality and acceptance.

One East Coast co-op (Wakefern, whose stores carry the ShopRite banner) dominates its trading area in New Jersey. Its private label has won wide acceptance. Because so much private label is included in its sales mix, the group has been able to cut the prices of branded items to a smaller markup than many of its competitors. The overall gross is made up by the better markups on the private-label portion of its sales.

A number of years ago, one of Wakefern's members (Foodarama) bought a chain of smaller stores in Queens and Long Island, New York. One of the problems Foodarama faced was that due to the size of the stores (smaller than the average ShopRite) and lack of recognition of the private label, the sales mix differed from the other ShopRite stores. The lower markup on branded goods, which other ShopRites could afford because of the beneficial effects the private-label line gave the total mix, could not be put into effect. The entire merchandising program of the larger stores could not be used for these stores.

The lower prices that can be put on branded merchandise because of the private labels creates the image of the store being the best-priced in the region.

This, in turn, helps the sale of the private labels (if quality standards are maintained), since the consumer feels that if the branded items are good values, so too must be the private-label items.

BUYING WHAT THE CUSTOMER WANTS

The buying function is partly the routine procedure of reordering merchandise included in the basic stock list and partly a decision-making function in terms of selection of new items and continuing items. Both of these functions must be performed with precision and sound business judgment so that the stores will be stocked with the merchandise customers want.

Customers expect to find the items they want—including new products—in the supermarket. The buyer's job is to supply this demand and, in some cases, anticipate it. The buyer, in selecting items, must disregard personal preferences and attempt to measure *customer* preferences. Buyers must also protect the consumer in terms of quality, value, and economy.

The creation of consumer demand is a highly competitive operation. Through merchandising programs, suppliers create customer interest and, hopefully, demand. The supermarket buyer must evaluate the extent of the demand created. The sales presentation for new items includes a report on research, product, and market; the advertising program, including media used and dates; point-of-purchase materials supplied for in-store promotions; margins; coupons to be used; and the distribution of samples, if used.

The buyer's function is to interpret the information presented by the supplier in terms of the acceptance of the item by the customers in the trading areas serviced by the stores. Buyers tend to evaluate the supplier—that is, the suppliers having a past record of successful product development are likely to have their items stocked.

Buyers interpret the seasonal demands of the consumer. While there is a degree of uniformity, there are local preferences that the buyers must recognize, and he or she must buy accordingly. Customers register their wants with store-level personnel. The store manager should be encouraged to accumulate the suggestions and requests of customers and relay them to the buyers. This enables the buyers to update consumer preferences and measure the demand for new items not stocked. Keeping current on changing buying habits of store clientele is a continual job for buyers.

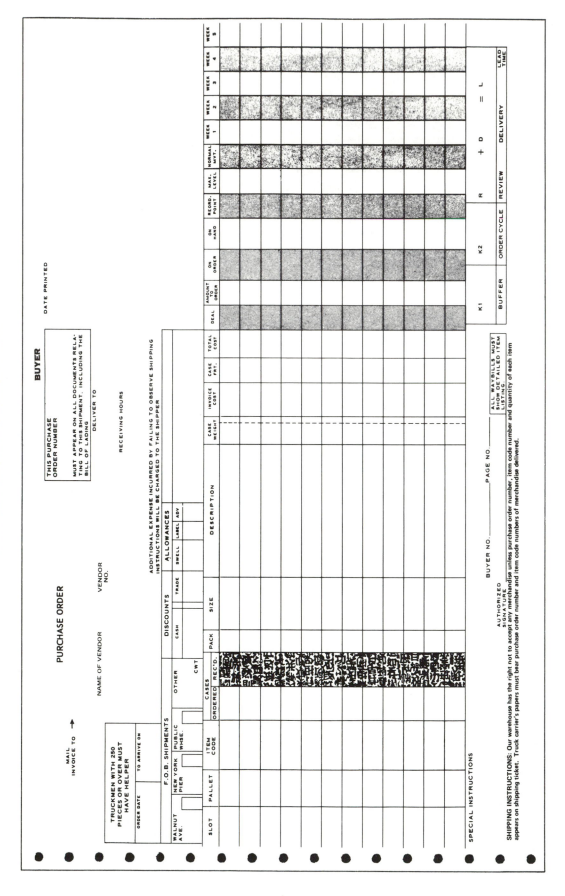

FIGURE 12
SAMPLE PURCHASE ORDER FORM

TECHNIQUES OF BUYING

Merchandise is bought by means of a purchase order or a vendor's order form. Frequently, however, merchandise is ordered orally, either by phone or in person, or through a computer-generated order. Regardless of the means, it is generally accepted that certain information must pass from the buyer to the vendor and vice versa before an order is actually consummated.

The Order Form

The information appearing on buying orders should include:

1. *Merchandise description.* A full description of the merchandise, including a statement of the quantities desired.
2. *Financial arrangements.* The terms of sale, the point to which the vendor pays the freight charges, and the unit price.
3. *Delivery instructions.* Where the goods are to be delivered, or picked up, if backhaul is used, the date and time at which the shipment will be accepted, and the method of shipment.
4. *Special instructions.* Special instructions to the vendor, such as advertising or display allowances.
5. *Facilitating information and other legal requirements.* The buyer's name, the purchase order number, the name and address of the shipper, the date of the order, and the signature of the buyer.

The form of the purchase order will differ from firm to firm; however, the essential elements included will usually be the same.

Legal Aspects of the Order

The legal aspects of buying generally fall within the realm of contract law. This, in itself, is a very broad and general field that requires extensive study to be fully understood. The discussion here will be confined to a few essentials.

An order that is properly filled out, duly signed and accepted by a vendor, constitutes a legal contract. A contract may be defined as an agreement containing a promise enforceable at law. A promise, to be enforceable, must be made by competent parties, must contain an offer and an acceptance, must be based upon a consideration, must be a meeting of minds, and should be in writing. Therefore, the fundamental elements of a contract include:

- Legal offer
- Acceptance
- Consideration
- Meeting of minds
- Importance of a written order.

Legal Offer. The buyer's order is an offer to buy that the vendor must accept before there can be a legally enforceable contract. If the vendor writes the order, he makes the offer, and the buyer may or may not accept. When the buyer receives price lists, catalogs, or other announcements from a vendor, or when prices are quoted on samples and no definite quantity is stated, the vendor is not making an offer, but is rather simply indicating availability. The vendor usually informs the buyer—through literature and sales material, including sales talks—of available merchandise.

To consummate a sale, either the buyer makes an offer by agreeing to take a given quantity at a stated price, or the vendor offers to sell a stated quantity at a stated price and the buyer accepts. To be a legal offer, a proposal must be definite and must apply to a definite amount of merchandise. When the buyer makes out his order, he is generally making an offer to buy that the vendor may accept or reject. Similarly, when the seller writes the order, the buyer may accept or refuse.

Acceptance. An acceptance is an assent to the terms of the offer. If a buyer makes an offer by mail, he may withdraw that offer at any time before acceptance. The time of acceptance is the time the vendor mails his confirmation of the order, not when the buyer receives the confirmation. For example, a buyer mails an order on May 1, the vendor receives the order on May 4, and mails a confirmation on May 5. In the meantime, the buyer sends a cancellation on May 3, which is not received by the vendor until May 6. In this instance, the order would still be binding; the cancellation was not received before the time of acceptance.

When merchandise is bought by phone, the buyer makes his offer, and the contract is binding when the vendor speaks his acceptance.

There is a notable exception to the above concept of acceptance. Should either party make an offer by wire, the other must accept by wire. Otherwise, the contract is not made until the acceptance reaches the party making the offer.

Consideration. Consideration is an act, present or future, bargained for and given in exchange for another act. In a simple contract, consideration is generally simply an exchange of promises. For example, when a vendor agrees to deliver a specific quantity of merchandise under specified terms and the buyer agrees to accept and pay for the merchandise, there is consideration, and a legal contract is consummated.

Meeting of Minds. To be a contract, an agreement must be based on a meeting of minds—that is, both the buyer and vendor must mean the same thing. An example of a meeting of minds occurs when a vendor is quoting the price of powdered milk, and the buyer understands that he is negotiating for powdered milk. If, however, the buyer is thinking of canned milk and the vendor of powdered milk, there can be no meeting of minds. Also, there can be no meeting of minds when one party is forced into a contract against his will or is deliberately deceived by the other party.

Importance of a Written Order. While, from a legal standpoint, a definite, written contract form is not essential, mistakes and misunderstandings are avoided by using regular order blanks; they help assure that all the essentials of the contract are recorded. The written order gives the buyer a permanent record of his negotiations with vendors. The food buyer makes a large number of purchases from a large number of vendors; written orders provide a record of transactions and the terms of each contract. Also, records are basic to inventory control.

Quantity Discounts

Buying a large quantity at one time usually entitles the buyer to a reduction in the billed price and is commonly called a quantity discount. Manufacturers frequently are able to realize certain operating economies from large-volume distribution. The savings that result are passed onto the buyer in the form of quantity discounts. The manufacturer generally provides his customers with a discount schedule that shows the quantities required for certain discounts.

When buying merchandise that carries a quantity discount, the buyer should take into consideration all advantages that may be realized from larger, less frequent purchases, such as reduced prices and lower transportation charges. The buyer should also keep in mind the fact that costs of storing, interest on investment, risk of loss, and price changes may more than offset the quantity discount. Turnover produces more profit than quantity discounts.

A cumulative quantity discount applies to the buyer's total purchases made within a period of time. To offset the disadvantage to the buyer who purchases in small lots but repeats frequently, some manufacturers offer cumulative discounts. For example, a manufacuturer may offer a 5 percent discount if purchases are over $5,000 per year, a 10 percent discount if purchases are over $10,000 per year, and 15 percent for $15,000 and over.

Similar arrangements may be based on the number of units purchased rather than the dollar amounts. The seller may have difficulty proving that a real cost savings exists with cumulative discounts. This may be one reason cumulative discounts are less common than straight quantity discounts.

The legal aspects of quantity discounts are generally encompassed under the sections of the Robinson-Patman Act dealing with price discrimination. Should the vendor be defending his discounts on the basis of cost differentials, he must be able to prove that there are sufficient cost differentials to warrant quantity discounts.

Functional or Trade Discounts

Functional or trade discounts are reductions in price sometimes given to certain classes of customers based on the trading functions they perform.

The courts and the Federal Trade Commission (FTC) regard trade discounts as legal when they are offered equally to all buyers in a particular functional or trade group. Therefore, the buyer should insist on the most advantageous trade classification possible.

Seasonal Discounts

A seasonal discount is granted for ordering and/or taking delivery of goods in advance of the normal buying period. The seasonal discount does not depend upon quantity purchased or trade group, but is an inducement to buy earlier than is really necessary. Seasonal discounts are sometimes referred to as *early-buying allowances.*

Certain discounts are generally offered buyers for buying within certain periods of time. Many times, the discount offered will induce buyers to purchase a large portion of their normal supply for the year at these early dates. In effect, the retailer, in this instance, is performing a storage function for the company; and when payment is made early, some of the financial cost is shifted to the retailer. However, the discount for early payment partially offsets these additional costs to the retailer.

Buyers should use discretion in placing orders and taking delivery of merchandise in excess of current needs. Warehouse space adds to the cost, as does ownership of merchandise. Even when payment is not made ahead of scheduled sale, storage costs add up very rapidly. Thus, the anticipated addition to net profit, in reality, may become a deduction from net profit. Also, inventory taxes may add to the cost, thereby making advance buying unprofitable.

The legality of seasonal discounts is reasonably clear-cut. As long as seasonal discounts are granted to all buyers, they are not discriminatory and are considered legal under the Robinson-Patman Act.

Special Deals

In recent years, many manufacturers, fearing price controls and the problems that such controls created in the early 1970's (when the price-freeze period caught a number of manufacturers with deal prices in effect and forced them to sell these products at a loss for several years or discontinue the sale altogether), have kept some regular prices artificially high. In order to stay competitive, manufacturers have instituted special deal prices on these items for specified periods of time.

This has led to a great deal of confusion, sporadic rather than evenly spaced buying and warehousing, and inventory-financing problems. However, in spite of retailer and wholesaler complaints, it has become a factor that most buyers have had to learn to live with.

Shipping Terms

Shipping terms include the conditions of sale, such as a specified period of time in which a cash discount will apply and the time within which payment is to be made. Most purchases by retailers are made on open account. The vendor has sufficient confidence in the buyer's credit rating to ship the merchandise.

Cash Discounts

To encourage prompt payment, a cash discount is offered to the buyer. Cash discounts are usually expressed as a percentage of the billed price. For example, the expression 2/10-n/30 on the face of an invoice would indicate that the buyer is permitted to take a 2 percent discount if the bill is paid within ten days. If the cash discount requirements are not met—that is, the bill is not paid during the cash discount period—the full invoice price must be paid within the net period, which in this case is thirty days.

Dating

The period of time within which the vendor will grant a cash discount and within which payment is expected, is called *dating*. The most common food suppliers' dating is 2/10-n/30. However, there are many variations, including:

- Regular dating
- Extra dating
- EOM dating
- ROG dating
- EOM ROG dating
- Advance dating.

Regular Dating. The discount period is determined from the date of the invoice. For example, assume the terms of an invoice dated June 15 are 2/10-n/30. This means that if the invoice is paid prior to June 25, a 2 percent cash discount is taken; if paid between June 26 and July 15, the full amount of the invoice is due. After July 15, the account is overdue.

Extra Dating. As with regular dating, the discount period is calculated from the date of the invoice, but a number of extra days are allowed in which to take the discount. For example, 2/10-30 Extra, would indicate that to take the 2 percent discount, the bill must be paid within ten days plus thirty days, or forty days from the date of the invoice. The full amount of the invoice is due after the expiration of the forty days.

EOM Dating. EOM means *end of month;* that is, the discount period is calculated from the end of the month. For example, 2/10-EOM means that a 2 percent discount is taken within ten days after the end of the month in which the invoice is dated. Some vendors permit invoices received within the last few days of the month to be paid at the end of the following month.

ROG Dating. ROG means *receipt of goods;* that is, the discount period is calculated from the date the goods are received by the buyer. For example, 2/10-ROG means that a 2 percent discount may be taken within ten days after the merchandise is received. The full amount is due thereafter. This dating is of particular value when goods are shipped a long distance.

EOM ROG Dating. The discount period in this case is calculated from the end of the month in which the goods are received. For example, 2/10-EOM ROG means a 2 percent discount is allowed within ten days after the end of the month in which the goods are received.

Advance Dating. The discount period in this case is calculated from some future date rather than from the date of the invoice. For example, 2/10 as of December 1, on a bill dated September 1, is payable within ten days of December 1, or December 11, rather than from the date of the invoice.

While regular dating generally is used for grocery deliveries in the food field, in areas where delivery is not normal, or when special problems arise, such as bad weather, etc., many manufacturers will permit the 2/10 to become ROG. However, the delivery problems should be verified with the manufacturer.

Spot and COD Terms

Frequently, the vendor may be unfamiliar with the credit rating of a buyer and may not wish to extend credit. Under this condition, the vendor may require spot or COD terms. The terms are called *spot* when the vendor requires cash at the time the buying contract is completed and prior to delivery. The terms are COD (cash on delivery) when the buyer must make payment to the carrier upon delivery of the goods.

Sight Draft

A vendor may demand cash upon delivery by means of a sight draft instead of selling spot or COD. In this instance, the vendor has the goods consigned to himself in the buyer's city. The vendor then draws an order on the buyer to pay for the goods at the buyer's bank. The sight draft, along with the bill of lading, is sent to the bank. Upon receiving the documents, the bank notifies the buyer that a sight draft is being held. When the buyer pays for the merchandise, the bank relinquishes the bill of lading, and the buyer presents this to the carrier as an order to release the shipment.

Anticipation

When the invoice carries extra, advance, EOM or ROG dating, many vendors will allow an extra deduction—usually the current rate of interest—when payment is made before the expiration of the cash discount period. This *extra* discount is known as anticipation.

Shipping Charges

Transportation charges must be included in the cost of the merchandise. If the vendor pays these charges, they are included in the selling price of the goods. Most accountants treat transportation charges as a part of the cost of the merchandise, not as an expense.

Many wholesalers or chains use a system of backhauls, where the manufacturer allows the freight cost to be deducted, if the goods are picked up at the manufacturer's depot. Often, the wholesaler or retailer is making deliveries in the vicinity of the manufacturer's depot and instead of the truck returning to the warehouse empty (deadheading), it is more efficient to have the truck pick up a load from the manufacturer and bring it back to the warehouse.

This system has been a matter of controversy between the food distribution system and many manufacturers, resulting in many heated battles between the two. Cost-justified backhaul was not legalized by Congress until the middle of 1980. Prior to that date, some manufacturers, by using an FOB (free on board) system based on their depots, were able to legally give cost-justified backhaul before that period. However, firms using zone-delivered prices often felt constrained by a Federal Trade Commission (FTC) advisory opinion not to grant such allowances.

However, Congress, in 1980, in an effort to save fuel (used by trucks returning to their warehouses empty) and cut costs due to the efficiencies gained, endorsed Section 8 of the Truck Deregulation Act to legalize the practice.

Special Buying Arrangements

The various considerations of merchandise selection and the negotiation of terms and discounts are but a part of the intricacies of buying for resale. Vendors frequently offer a variety of services of which the buyer may or may not avail himself. A major part of the buying function involves the evaluation and ultimate selection of the various services offered by vendors. Some of the more important of the special buying arrangements, for which the buyer generally negotiates, are guaranteed sales and guarantee against price decline.

Cooperative Advertising

Cooperative advertising allowances are paid by the vendor to cover part or all of the cost incurred by the retailer for advertising the vendor's merchandise. In the trade, these arrangements are commonly referred to as cooperative advertising contracts or cooperative merchandising agreements. (See pages 112–115 for a more detailed discussion of cooperative advertising.)

Generally, the vendor offers the retailer an advertising contract that requires the latter to run a stipulated amount of advertising in return for an allowance on purchases. Often, the vendor will pay the retailer at the *national* line rate, and the retailer places his advertising at *local* rates. Since, in most instances, the national line rate is higher than the local rate, the retailer is able to offset a portion of his own advertising costs with the difference. However, a number of manufacturers have raised objections to being billed at the national rates while the retailer pays local rates. This currently is a point of contention by some manufacturers.

Since the Robinson-Patman Act requires that advertising contracts must be offered on a proportionately equal basis to competing buyers, some retailers, prior to signing an advertising contract with a vendor, will request that a statement to this effect be included in the contract.

In addition to cooperative newspaper advertisements, some manufacturers contract for cooperative advertising on radio and television. For example, a large chain operator may buy a half hour on television and make arrangements with various vendors to take time on the program. Not only is it possible to offset a major part of the program expense, but it is also possible for the sponsoring company to advertise its own products at a relatively low media cost. The proportionately equal provision of the Robinson-Patman Act applies.

Cooperative advertising may also include: in-store promotional displays, point-of-purchase materials, window displays and/or signs, and handbills. As with other cooperative advertising arrangements, allowances for these advertising materials should be listed in the contract and must be made available to other buyers on a proportionately equal basis.

Buying on Consignment

Probably the most important factor involved in consignment buying is the method by which the title to the merchandise passes. With consignment buying, instead of title passing from the vendor to the retailer and then to the customer, title generally passes directly from the vendor to the customer. Thus, the retailer merely acts as an agent for the vendor. Generally, the retailer has no control over the price of merchandise. He sells at the price established by the vendor, and in return, he receives a stipulated percentage of the profit. Magazines, for example, are frequently handled by supermarkets on this basis.

Guaranteed Sale

Merchandise that is bought on a guaranteed sale basis differs from consigned merchandise in that the title passes from the vendor to the retailer in the normal manner, but the buyer has the privilege of returning the merchandise to the vendor if it does not sell. This can prove to be a very advantageous method of buying, particularly when the selling potential of the product is questionable.

For example, a buyer who is offered a nonfood item, such as plastic tablecloths, the customer reception of which might be questionable, may prefer to buy the tablecloths on a guaranteed sale basis. The price almost invariably will be higher, thereby returning less gross profit, but the risk is reduced, since unsold items can be returned to the vendor. On the other hand, if they do sell, the buyer has lost only the difference between the profit margin on outright sale and guaranteed sale, which generally amounts to 2 or 3 percent. Thus, the buyer can reduce the risk involved in buying merchandise of unknown sales potential and avoid taking a loss through markdowns.

Guarantee Against Price Decline

Buying merchandise that is to be sold over a period of time increases the risk of a price decline. Some vendors offer price protection and will reimburse the buyer if the price decreases within a fixed period after the order is delivered. This practice is referred to as *floor-stock protection.*

In effect, a guarantee against a price decline is an arrangement whereby the vendor agrees to sell his products at a stipulated price and, in the event of a subsequent decline, agrees to credit the buyer with the difference between the new, lower price and the old, higher price.

For example, under one procedure, credit will be issued for the full amount of the decline on all shipments invoiced within a seven-day period prior to the date of the decline. A credit of one-half the amount of the decline will be issued on all shipments invoiced from eight to fifteen days prior to the decline.

Assume that the aforementioned procedure applies to coffee, that the date of the decline was June 20, and the amount of decline was 5¢ per pound. All coffee from this vendor that was invoice-dated between June 14 and June 20 would carry a credit of 5¢ per pound. Any invoices between June 6 and June 13 would be credited at the rate of 2½¢ per pound. There would be no credit due on invoices prior to June 6.

Floor-stock protection contracts take a variety of forms, the period of time varies, and the merchandise covered may be warehouse inventory on the date of the price change instead of invoiced quantities. Regardless of the exact details, the effects are much the same—to give the buyer a degree of protection against the risk of market declines.

PRICING

Philosophy of Pricing

Supermarket operators were the first retailers to deviate from the concept that all merchandise in a store, or at least within a department, had to be priced so as to maintain the same markup percentage. From the standpoint of pricing and confusion to both the customer and retailer, it would be virtually impossible to mark up each individual item in a department by the exact percentage markup that such a department is working on.

It would result in totally unmanageable fractions of 1¢ on individual items. Also, when a manufacturer raised the price of an item by (for example) 50¢ a case for merchandise that came twenty-four to the case, the price rise would be 2.08¢ per item; a 15 percent normal markup for that department would be .312 per item and would result in a theoretical increase of 2.392¢ per item. The retailer, faced with several such price rises in the department, would raise some prices 2¢ and others 3¢ each.

Which items would get the 2¢ increase and which the 3¢ would depend on whether they were raised the higher or lower amount at the last price increase. The department margin also would govern how many of the items got increases of 2¢ or 3¢. Other factors would be the handling of the change by the competition, the total movement in the department of the individual items, and the expected change in such movement that the price increase might produce.

Food retailers pioneered the concept that dollar margins are more important than percentage margins. Dollar margins are earned by low prices that produce high turnover. Space is valuable, and a store is efficient when sales per square foot is satisfactory. Also, capital invested in inventory must earn a return. An item that does not sell in sufficient quantities to pay for the space and capital used should not be stocked.

Pricing for Profit

Profit is the result of pricing merchandise after giving due consideration to the cost of merchandise, direct expenses (expenses directly related to sale of items), indirect expenses (expenses of the store not related to sale of items), the turnover or volume during a given period of time, and the desired net profit.

Most indirect expenses are relatively fixed, which means that increases in sales lower the share of indirect expenses charged to each item sold. As volume changes, the share of fixed costs charged to each sale varies; the lower the sales, the higher the share of fixed costs charged to each item sold.

Price changes tend to vary demand for any given item. In general, as prices increase, the sales decrease, particularly when the price of any item changes in relation to other items of a similar nature.

The supermarket operator must consider all the above mentioned factors in fixing the selling price. There is no mathematical formula to apply, since there is no fixed relationship in the amount of change brought about by changes in any of the variables. Prices must be set, the results observed, and changes made so as to return the best possible profit.

The expense of handling any item of merchandise varies with its speed of movement, its perishability, space required, and handling and bagging costs. In comparing the handling of fresh produce items with canned items, such as tomatoes with canned tomatoes, the fresh item incurs a much greater expense.

Food store operators do not know with any precision the handling and selling costs attached to each item sold in their stores, and accounting procedures do not break down the cost per item sold. These costs are estimated and are reflected in the markup. There is no method of determining the exact cost of handling a specific item; however, the most commonly used method is cost averaging. The cost of doing business varies with each store unit in terms of percentage of sales. A change in the rate of sale of any one item will affect the margin for the entire product mix. Thus, expenses are considered as a package and the total gross profit is compared to the total expense.

Volume is an important factor in the determination of gross profit dollars. The volume for any store is the total of customer purchases of individual items. As the price of an item changes, customer reaction occurs. The extent of the reaction varies with the type of item. If the item is a staple or necessity, price changes will cause little change in demand. However, customers may look for other places to buy, shop competitors, or shop for substitute items. If the item is not considered a necessity, price changes will almost always cause immediate changes in demand—a lower price increases sales, while a higher price decreases sales. Competitors' prices and the possibility of substitute items limit the elasticity of demand.

Items sold in food stores vary greatly as to markup percentage and volume from department to department as well as within commodity groups. Studies of supermarket practices relating to dollar sales, percentage of total store sales, percentage of department sales, dollar margins, and percentage margin on sales for the items sold in the supermarkets studied, revealed a wide range of gross margin percentages on various items—5 to 55 percent.

Psychological Pricing

Merchandisers appear to be in agreement that odd-ending pricing is psychologically attractive. A price of 49¢ on an item seems to indicate a reduction from 50¢, even though it actually may be a psychological price fixed at a level above the 47¢ or 48¢ price indicated by the application of an average markup. Odd pricing permits the retailer to price more closely to the markup percentage desired instead of rounding off all prices or using fixed price increments, such as 1¢, 5¢, 10¢, 25¢, etc. While psychological pricing is not practiced to the exclusion of other methods, it is considered important by many retailers.

A review of the weekly supermarket ads in any newspaper will reveal the extent of odd pricing both within a company and across the industry. Prices ending in the number 9 appear very frequently, either as a unit price, such as 29¢ or 39¢ or as a multi-unit price, such as two for 59¢, three for 79¢, etc. Even numbers are used sparingly, with the exception of $1, which is frequently used for multi-units or so many pounds, such as three pounds for $1.

Multiple Unit Pricing

The use of multiple-unit-price systems, such as two for 57¢ or three for 79¢, has a significant relation to customer psychology. Multiple pricing gives the impression that a quantity discount is being given, i.e., a savings on the unit price. The greatest advantage of this pricing system is that it does stimulate the customer into selecting the multiple units rather than individual units. Multiple unit pricing also allows the item to be priced at a figure that is closer to the desired margin—the ultimate object being that of increasing dollar profit by increasing the volume. Multiple unit pricing makes price comparisons more difficult, especially when stores vary the size of the multiple unit.

Some manufacturers package items in multiple packs. For example, some beverages and canned goods are packed six bottles or cans in a carrier or carton. Obviously only those items with a pattern of regular use in the home should be handled in multiple packs.

Competitive Pricing

Competition is a most important factor in pricing. In many communities, a given operator is looked upon as the price leader. The price leader is checked and sometimes followed. As long as the others follow, a reasonably stable market results, but operators need to be as efficient as the leader to show a profit. The operators that develop efficient methods and reflect their low costs in this pricing structure are managing their stores properly. The others let the price leader make their pricing decisions without considering cost of operation.

In many market areas, *several* operators assume the role of the price leader. This situation leads to severe competition and "price wars." Highly competitive areas force each operator to become more efficient, add high margin lines, and exercise more effective balanced selling. The fact remains, however, that each operator must earn a profit to stay in business. The competitive situation may force low prices on items with a high repeat purchase frequency and high prices on other items.

Chain operators have a multitude of pricing problems. Most chain companies delegate the pricing responsibility to the branch or division with little control from general headquarters. In some companies, there is limited control, in terms of price uniformity, on company-manufactured items and company-label merchandise. However, the local competition often prevents company-wide pricing for any item, even company-manufactured merchandise.

Many branches and divisions operate on a one-price zone basis. This simplifies advertising, order book forms, billing, record keeping, auditing, etc. In some sections, a branch or division is forced to use two or more price zones. The cost of handling these price zones can easily be greater than the gain in dollar margins.

Chain store management is concerned with pricing according to local market requirements, not percentage markup. Typically, top management looks at the profit and loss statement, especially the bottom line, when evaluating each segment of the company. The pressure is on each branch or division for a contribution to the company's net profits. If headquarters management dictated prices, each merchandiser would be handcuffed and perhaps priced out of a given market. Therefore, pricing is the function of the merchandiser for each segment of the company.

Each supermarket must price according to the local market and be sensitive to the effect of price change on volume. Pricing is a continuous function that requires good judgment, knowledge of customer behavior, knowledge of the market area, and a recognition of the pressures exerted by management, customers, suppliers, and the public.

Because of the importance that the consumer places on price, the pricing function is probably the most important function of the retailer. While it is not the only factor that goes into creating a store image, it probably carries the most weight in the consumer's determination of where to shop. While quality of meat and produce, proximity, store cleanliness and courtesy all have some bearing on the choice of a supermarket, price is still the primary consideration for most shoppers.

14

IN-STORE ORDERING, RECEIVING, STORING, STOCKING AND PRICE-MARKING PROCEDURES

THE IMPORTANCE OF EFFICIENT ORDERING PROCEDURES

Efficient ordering procedures can be a key to the success of a store. Overstocks of merchandise tie up capital that could be used to create profits elsewhere, cause waste in perishables departments, make efficient product movement difficult, and impede periodic inventories. Ordering insufficient quantities of merchandise is equally serious. Out-of-stock means loss of sales and loss of customers.

Most stores today use electronic ordering rather than the older, time-consuming and more prone-to-error order book or form. With supermarkets handling as many as 10,000 to 15,000 items, ordering to replenish stock and to anticipate demand for the period between orders becomes one of the most important of the in-store functions.

One system uses an electronic device that records the in-stocks of every item in the store and matches that against what is considered normal inventory plus expected demand beyond the normal which might be occasioned by specials, weather, holidays, etc.

Using this system, an employee takes a physical inventory of those items that are below normal on the shelves, after stocking from the back room. Also taken into account is normal inventory and anticipated demand. All the data is recorded electronically on a hand-held device onto a tape. The tape then is usually played over telephone lines from the store to the central ordering point—either at headquarters or, more often, directly to the warehouse, where the orders are filled.

With a scanner system, this physical ordering process can be sharply reduced, since the computer that governs the scanner keeps track of sales of various items and keeps a running inventory. Such automatic ordering must be corrected periodically to make up for shrink which takes place due to errors, theft, breakage, etc.

The volume of the store governs frequency of delivery from the warehouse, and frequency of de-livery governs how effective another form of ordering—order averaging—can be. Under this system, the history of what a store needs is calculated by computer and an average order is shipped from the warehouse to the store.

If a store's volume is such that daily or every-other-day deliveries are made, regular, frequent inventory taking must be made so that when the average-order supplement or correction is made, stocks can be brought into alignment. Also, under such a system, most warehouses make provisions for telephoned or teletyped instructions from the store to add or delete items from the average order in order to correct store inventory imbalances.

The average-order concept can be extremely efficient and save time and effort at the store and warehouse levels, if used properly. An efficient system will incorporate automatic corrections in the average order to anticipate specials and other conditions that will change buying patterns.

A variation of order averaging is "top-loading." This is used by the warehouse to make efficient use of the space in the truck and entails shipping regular orders, but in addition, lightweight items (generally paper products) are overshipped to fill up the top sections of the truck.

Some stores still use the older, slower and less accurate system of order books or forms. Under this system, a pre-printed form lists all or most of the items carried. After packing-out the store shelves from the back room, a physical check is made of the entire store and orders are entered manually on the printed form, which is then sent to the warehouse.

PREPARATION OF ORDER FORMS

Although nominally the store manager is responsible for all of the functions performed within the store, it is usually the department manager or designee who actually orders items within a class jurisdiction. Some supermarket operators provide each department manager with an order book or form. The order

Photo courtesy of Food Mart stores, owned and operated by Convenient Industries of America Inc.

This department manager is punching data for ordering and inventory control into a portable terminal. The data is transmitted to a central processing center which will store similar information from other units in the supermarket chain. The collection of information will help in future buying and inventory decisions.

ordered marked in the space beside the proper quantity number. At the same time, the order is marked on the order-book sheet. The day or days each item ordered is to be shipped is indicated.

DETERMINING THE QUANTITY TO ORDER (NONPERISHABLES)

A most important facet of ordering is the determination of the quantity to order. Too little means "outs," lost sales, and lost customers, Too much means that unnecessary capital is invested, not only in each store, but in warehouse reorder to compensate for the reduced inventory in the distribution center. A cluttered stockroom results in wasted space and increased cost. If the store is penalized for excess inventory, the store operating profit is reduced.

The most important results of good quantity ordering are good customer service, minimum capital investment in merchandise, and good stock turnover. Additional advantages include: few out-of-stock situations, reduced inventory-taking time, reduced inventory (shelf and stockroom), reduced price-changing (less merchandise price-marked), increased sales, and better store appearance.

Currently, there is a strong move to eliminate the back room as much as possible in the store operation. The theory, as advanced at numerous seminars in recent years is: "No sales are made in the back room."

Many box stores have virtually eliminated all back-room stocking of groceries, and reserves are stored above the selling areas. While this is not always practical in the conventional supermarket, every effort is being made to keep back-room inventory to a minimum.

An exception to this occurs when some independents find they are able to pick up "special deals" directly or through some source other than the regular supplier. In such cases, the back room may become the storage area for such goods. Care must be taken, however, to keep such items from impeding the normal functioning of the store.

book is made up from information contained on punch cards or in the memory unit of a computer which prints the essential information by means of a line printer. The information listed includes: warehouse section, pallet count, line number, profit-margin ranking, name of the item, size, pack and retail price, with space to record the weekly order. As a guide to ordering, the book frequently provides space for recording the preceding orders week by week. The order book provides the store with a record of orders placed in the four-week period during which the book is effective.

The actual order may be placed on a pre-punched, mark-sense card. The order cards are placed beside the order-book sheets and the quantity

DETERMINING THE QUANTITY TO ORDER (PERISHABLES)

Perishable items should be ordered as close to the time of sale as possible. Orders early in the week are generally small, and a larger order is placed for weekend business.

The time element is the most important factor to consider when handling perishable merchandise. Therefore, produce should be ordered on a daily basis. Short orders may be handled by staff representatives or field supervisors.

However, advertising plans have to be made somewhat farther in advance of the actual selling days or even weeks. A section of each ad must be devoted to perishables—meats, produce, and dairy. The dairy items do not vary that much in supply and price, so that there is little problem there.

The produce and meat buying departments of the chain or wholesaler work with their suppliers so that planning can be made far enough in advance to meet ad schedules. The buying departments generally work with the U.S. Department of Agriculture, state agriculture departments, and crop forecasting services as well as get news from trade newspapers about crop conditions so that they can act informatively.

But even the best-informed departments cannot anticipate disasters or freak weather conditions. As an example, the 1980 Bing cherry crop in the Pacific Northwest looked like a bumper crop right up until the week of harvest. A week or more of heavy rains, however, at the beginning of the harvest cut the crop that could be shipped approximately in half. Plans for heavy advertising and price promotions had to be aborted at the last moment for most chains.

ORDERING PROCEDURES

There is a large variety of ordering procedures used by chains and groups. Some of these procedures include:

- Conventional procedure
- Two-order procedure
- Shelf-stock-only procedure
- Modular-ordering procedure
- Direct-ordering procedure.

Conventional Procedure. Many companies simply require that the store list its needs by indicating the quantities desired. The order is assembled at the warehouse, out-of-stock noted, and the load shipped to the supermarket.

Two-Order Procedure. Under the two-order procedure, merchandise ordered is shipped out of the warehouse on two different days to enable efficient receiving and stocking. The first shipment is made up of the fast movers—items that have a large turnover and, therefore, necessitate quantity delivery. The second order consists of normal and slow-moving items.

Shelf-Stock-Only Procedure. Many operators follow the practice of not ordering slow-moving merchandise until it can be placed on the shelf. This reduces grocery inventory, grocery department labor

costs, and makes the back-room operation more efficient.

Modular-Ordering Procedure. Orders are continually scrutinized to determine what is moving and what is not. As a result, it has been estimated that 75 percent of the items stocked move less than a case a week. Studies indicate that sales of fast-moving items do not vary to a great degree. Under modular ordering, fast-moving items (as well as items with a regular movement) are on automatic order. These automatic shipments require determination of the movement of merchandise in each store.

Under this system, an "average" order is sent to the retail outlet; sales are noted, checked and tabulated, and readjustments are made on a predetermined-period basis. The possibility of over-stock is greater than out-of-stocks due to the 75 percent movement factor. The procedure releases the manager from the time-consuming task of ordering certain types of merchandise. Such ordering eliminates routine and minimizes the possibility of out-of-stocks. Computerization of modular ordering further reduces risks. Periodically, actual ordering must be made to adjust for average orders.

Direct-Ordering Procedure. Drop shipments—such as milk, bakery, crackers—are usually ordered from local concerns on a direct-delivery basis. The driver-salesperson keeps the allotted shelf space filled and the stock rotated. A responsible employee is assigned the task of dealing with these drop-shippers. A careful check is necessary to assure accuracy in respect to the number of items needed, removal of outdated merchandise, proper shelf allocation, and billing.

HANDLING DIRECT DELIVERIES

Direct delivery to the store is made by driver/salespeople and rack jobbers of nonfood items. These deliveries must be closely supervised to keep errors, pilferage, and favoritism to a minimum. All delivery people should be supervised to check freshness and/or quality of merchandise received, to control shelf space or rack space, and to schedule deliveries in order to avoid congestion.

GROCERY RECEIVING, STORING, STOCKING, AND PRICE MARKING

Receiving the tons of merchandise sold each week by supermarkets requires well-organized materials handling. Efficiency begins with the receiving of

Sturdy equipment and trained personnel are required to handle the tons of merchandise that arrive each week at supermarkets. Here, a forklift begins unloading from the truck at left in a supermarket receiving area. The men at right are examining the delivery receipts for the shipment.

merchandise at the store. Proper scheduling, maximum loads, fast unloading, efficient checking, and maximum use of mechanical equipment are all needed. Proper scheduling and timing of the arrival of freight at the store keeps the warehouse operating smoothly and at a minimum of expense, lets the store manager efficiently arrange the work and best utilize personnel, prevents overcrowding by trucks at the store, and regulates the amount of merchandise received each day. Materials handling equipment should be used in unloading. Separate unloading doors, if possible, for each class of freight avoid congestion.

Since the delivery schedule is known by the store manager, advance preparations should be made to expedite receiving by preparing space, scheduling personnel, and setting up receiving equipment.

Due to the interrelationship of receiving, storing, stocking, and price marking, it is often difficult to distinguish just where one procedure ends and another begins. Many companies receive, mark, and store their merchandise in one continuous operation. Others separate each function. Still others combine the stocking with price marking on the immediate selling floor. (Also see Chapter 4, "The Grocery Department.")

Receiving and Storing Groceries

Three methods of receiving grocery merchandise at the store level are in common use. They are:

- Central receiving and marking
- Single operation
- The conventional method.

Various companies use variations or combinations of these methods and systems.

The effective use of materials handling equipment has expedited the movement of merchandise. Examples of this type of equipment are forklift trucks, "semi-live" skids, dollies, and "dead" skids.

The successful use of selected equipment at the warehouse level has prompted some companies to extend its use to retail outlets. Factors that limit the use of mechanical materials handling equipment at the retail level are: (1) the high unit cost of the equipment; (2) the absence of loading platforms or truck wells at some stores; and (3) limited aisle and storage space which makes in-store movement of material handling equipment difficult.

The Central Receiving and Marking System. As the name implies, this system of receiving and price marking is performed in one central area. This area may be situated close to the unloading doors and convenient to the conveyors that transport the merchandise to the storage or selling areas.

The central area can be situated on one side of the conveyor or it can be divided into two sections, using the conveyor as the dividing line between the two. The latter arrangement is more efficient. In this manner, employees on each side of the conveyor can unload the merchandise with a minimum of interference with one another.

As the person assigned to unloading the trailer starts the flow of merchandise into the store, it is checked off and examined for obvious signs of disfiguration or breakage, by sight only, and in no way holds up the operation unless a broken case is encountered. Some companies operating their own warehouses have eliminated checking, except for certain troublesome stores, on the premise that the cost of checking exceeds the benefits.

After the unloading is completed and the count verified, employees begin cutting off the case tops and price marking the merchandise. Items having prior demand, such as those needed on the selling floor immediately, are cut, price marked, and conveyed to the selling area.

Some operators have instituted a system of central marking to achieve efficiency and accuracy. With a central system, the ability to obtain accuracy and efficiency increases since the employees specialize, develop skills, and become more efficient at their assigned tasks. Supervision is simplified and responsibility can be delegated to each employee.

Single Operation. Under this system, the entire process of receiving, storing, and price marking is completed in one operation. The order is checked in, price marked, and stored or sent to the selling area for subsequent stocking. (However, in the recent era of rapid price changes, many firms prefer not to price mark until just prior to placing the merchandise onto the shelves. This often eliminates the necessity of changing prices before the merchandise ever leaves the back room.)

This system is highly effective if night crews are used, or the trailer is dropped at the back door of the store and is to be unloaded at the employees' convenience. It can also be used effectively during working hours, if orders are received on "slow" days and sufficient help is available to do the work.

This type of operation demands efficient personnel, well-trained in their duties. One inexperienced or ineffective worker can delay the process considerably, since the work is performed by forming a so-called human-chain which requires a smooth flow of merchandise from employee to employee.

One person unloads the trailer at a steady pace. Another employee, supplied with the invoice containing the retail price listings or a price book as the case may be, marks the unit or multiple-unit price on the case as it passes his station. This is usually done with a grease pencil or a colored crayon. The next man in line cuts the case top or splits it in half according to the price-marking system used. Then the cans or units are price marked by another individual who moves them along the conveyor from where they are stored or sent to the selling area.

The Conventional Method. This system is similar to the previously described methods insofar as receiving and checking the merchandise is concerned. Price marking, however, can be performed either in the back room or at the shelf, depending on the policy of the company.

After using either the item or piece-count method of checking in, the merchandise is sent directly to allocated slots in the storage area. These slots are usually arranged to conform with their counterparts in the selling area. Cases are sometimes price marked with a grease pencil as they are received. Under this system, the merchandise is marked as it is needed on the selling floor. This can be performed at the "up" conveyor, if it is a basement operation, or on the conveyor after the merchandise is "pulled" in the back room. An alternate method is the use of a portable price marking stand. In this manner, price marking can be accomplished at the far ends of the conveyors or adjacent to the gondolas.

Today, most warehouses provide a pricing service that attaches prices on the items (as specified by either chain headquarters or by the retailer to the wholesaler). Affixed to the delivery receipt or attached to each case will be gummed-label price strips which can be inserted into price-marking guns at the store for affixing to individual items, after the cases are opened. This would eliminate the need for marking the cases with grease pencils as noted above, but still does not allow for rapidly changing prices.

Stocking Groceries

The importance of fully stocked shelves and cases cannot be over-emphasized. Adequate stocks of merchandise on the shelves are essential for maintaining maximum sales. Studies indicate that sales increase by as much as 25 percent when full stock conditions prevail. Also, customers are not forced to shop competitors for out-of-stock items.

Stores that are open twenty-four hours a day generally stock shelves during night hours. Some operators who used to keep open in order to stock during the night have discontinued the practice and use day stocking regardless of store size. The two major reasons for this change are: (1) greater flexibility in workforce assignments with better work schedules; and (2) greater efficiency with a lower payroll expense.

The following factors should be taken into consideration when stocking groceries:

● Rotation

There comes a time when manual effort is required. Here, a stock clerk moves dog food onto grocery department shelves. The human factor is still important in maintaining neat merchandise displays.

- Accessibility
- Facing merchandise
- Cleanliness
- Dented merchandise.

Rotation. Rotation is placing old stock in front of new so that a first-in, first-out inventory policy is practiced. All items need to be rotated each time the shelf or case is restocked.

The need for stock rotation is obvious to almost everybody when perishable items are involved. A number of chains and independents, however, are more lax with rotating dry groceries, since the shelf lives of such products are so long.

What such operators overlook is the cleanliness factor and the impression on the customer of a poorly operated, untidy store. Dusty cans or boxes on the shelves tend to create a bad image for most customers. Many customers will note and avoid items with soiled or damaged labels and damaged boxes or cans. If on subsequent shopping trips that soiled or damaged item is still on the shelf, or if there is a layer of dust on the items, the customer may well decide to take his or her next shopping trip elsewhere. This cleanliness factor should be carried further to clean up spills from torn and leaking containers, bags, and boxes.

Accessibility. It is well to remember that "buying power is measured by the length of the arm." Lightweight items should be on the higher shelves and heavier goods on the lower shelves. A customer hesitates to take heavy items from high shelves, and breakage will occur less frequently if lightweight articles are given top-shelf positions.

Facing Merchandise. Facing merchandise is necessary to improve the appearance of the shelf or to give the space allotted for a particular item a full look. Slow-moving merchandise, in particular, is "faced-out" to give a full-shelf appearance. Since stocking and ordering such merchandise is not done as frequently as with fast movers, an out-of-stock impression is avoided. Labels should be faced-out for easy reading by the customer; units should be neatly stacked.

Also, when low stock cannot be replenished, which is bound to happen even in the best-run stores, it is better to face merchandise. This is especially effective on lower shelves, where items are out of sight after the first few rows are sold. Facing merchandise should be a regular day-to-day practice; however, it is not a substitute for well-stocked shelves.

Cleanliness. All shelving should be kept clean. Under pressure of doing business, this important function is often neglected. A damp cloth on the stocking trucks, used to clean each shelf before merchandise is placed on it, can do much to solve this problem.

But cleaning with a duster or damp cloth should be thorough and not just a cursory swipe at the merchandise. If just a pass is made at dusty merchandise with a damp or wet cloth, there is a danger of merely changing the dust to mud and creating an even worse condition.

Some managers insist that *all* stock be dusted daily. At least the slower-moving items, however, should be kept in good selling condition. Nothing repels a customer more than being faced with having to purchase a dirty package of food. Given a choice, that customer probably will start shopping elsewhere.

Dented Merchandise. Dented merchandise should not be stocked; and if it is inadvertently, the dented merchandise should be removed from the shelves as soon as it is discovered. The denting of a can may not affect the contents, unless the can has been pierced, but the appearance is unsightly. A customer who arrives home and finds dented cans will have a poor image of the store. In some areas, the Health Department, as a precautionary measure, prohibits the sale of cans dented at the seam or lip. Swollen cans must never be sold because of the danger of botulism.

Merchandise that is dented or disfigured can be:

- Sold to employees at a reduced rate
- Placed in a bargain display
- Sold to a restaurant, if the quantity is adequate
- Given to charity.

Some manufacturers instruct their salespersons to pick up damaged units and pay the retail price or replace the units. Also "swells" and broken-glass items should be recorded for credit unless the manufacturer grants a flat-rate swell or breakage allowance.

The most commonly used procedures for shelf stocking are:

- Power-phone system
- Complete listing by a responsible employee
- Subdividing responsibility among employees
- Tray-pack method.

Power-Phone System. With this procedure for shelf stocking groceries, an internal telephone is used. The grocery clerk plugs in the headset power phone and communicates with the back-room stockman. Power-phone plugs are spaced throughout the grocery section and the back room. When the power phone on the selling floor is plugged in, the power-phone unit in the back room rings and the stockman answers.

The back room is arranged to conform approximately with the gondola layout. Efficient power-phone operation requires calling items needed from the back room by the grocery clerk on the selling floor.

Price changes are made at the shelf before stocking begins, and the new price is placed on all new and old stock. If the price marked on the shelf stock has not already been changed, a price change ticket placed on the shelf assures accurate pricing. Before using the power-phone system, many operators fill "holes" with a quick visual check and get the urgently needed merchandise stocked first. Then shelf stocking proceeds with the power-phone equipment. Mistakes are held to a minimum since there is no paperwork involved.

Complete Listing by a Responsible Employee. A responsible employee should be held accountable for the complete listing of items needed for the shelves, if this system is used. Under this system, a designated individual makes a systematic tour of the store, listing the items that need replenishing. As he finishes a section, he sends the list to the storage area so that stocking can be started by back-room personnel, and he continues to list the remainder of the store. The merchandise already listed is pulled and sent to the selling area for stocking. In this manner, a continuous operation is attained until the store is fully stocked. Spot checks of shelving may be necessary several times a day on busy days, especially in fast-moving sections. When completed, the lists should be returned to the individual compiling them so that out-of-stocks can be noted.

Subdividing Responsibility Among Employees. With the subdivision system, individual employees are assigned specific sections or gondolas. Their responsibility is to keep the shelves well-stocked and their areas clear and uncluttered. The individual lists, pulls, marks, and stocks his own merchandise.

This arrangement can work well, but a close check should be maintained to ensure that the work load is distributed evenly. In high-volume stores, this procedure is a must.

Tray-Pack Method. The U.S. Department of Agriculture, in cooperation with supermarket operators, has developed a tray-pack method of stocking dry groceries. This method is generally used for high-volume items only. The case is cut to make a tray for the merchandise. After cutting the case in half, the side of the carton is cut, leaving about a two-inch lip on both the top and bottom halves. The trays of merchandise are trucked to the shelf. The hold trays are removed and the new ones added. This method avoids the handling of each item and facilitates stock rotation.

This method can be used with cases packed for tray-pack stocking; that is, the labels are right-end-up on each tray. Also, case size must be suited to shelf space. Since stocking is by half cases, volume must be adequate to justify enough facings to stock a half case.

Also, cases should be designed for tray-pack stocking by having the item identified on the lip.

A number of manufacturers already are shipping in tray packs. These generally are film-overwrapped, and in order to price mark (if the store does price mark) and/or place onto the shelves, all that has to be done is to remove the overwrap from the tray.

Grocery Price Marking

Many price-marking methods are currently in use. Regardless of the method used, the importance of accurate, neat and legible prices cannot be overemphasized. Studies by the U.S. Department of Agriculture indicate that the price-marking operation alone takes up to 22 percent of the grocery department man-hours. This figure can be reduced by improving techniques. Waste of man-hour productivity inevitably finds its way into the store's profit; therefore, established procedures and work methods must be used.

Keeping in mind that there is no hard-and-fast rule applicable to any system of price marking and that variations of any system do occur, some methods of price marking currently being used are:

- Flip-board method
- Bottom-layer method
- Half-case method.

Flip-Board Method. The flip-board table is a simple device used to price mark the bottom layer of merchandise in a case.

Using this method, the case top is removed, and the top layer of merchandise is price marked. The case is then placed on its side and the flip board (a hinged board usually twenty-four inches by twenty inches, attached to a table top or a similar piece of furniture or equipment) is raised flush (45° angle) with the top of the case which is now the side. The employee holds the bottom of the case firmly with his hand, and the flip board is lowered to a horizontal position, thereby "flipping" the case so that the bottom side is up. The carton is then lifted from the merchandise, and the bottom layer is marked. Then, the empty carton is replaced. The flipping process is reversed in order to put the merchandise back in the case.

Using a flip-board table facilitates moving the price-marking function to any area of the back room. Price marking usually is accomplished at the end of the conveyor. If the store manager prefers to price mark on the selling floor, the flip-board tables easily can be moved to the shelf position.

Bottom-Layer Method. Reaching the bottom layer without the use of a flip board can be accomplished by using the following six steps:

1. Cut the top off the case.
2. Stamp the top layer.
3. Remove two rows of the top layer, and stamp the exposed cans on the bottom.
4. Move the remaining merchandise on the top layer over the bottom layer that is already stamped.
5. Continue this process until all bottom units are price marked.
6. Return those two rows originally removed from the case.

It is not difficult to see that this method entails much more handling and moving of the top row of merchandise and, therefore, is not one of the preferred methods of price marking.

Half-Case Method. Another way of reaching the bottom layer is to cut the case in half lengthwise. Cut three slices in one motion, turn the case on its uncut side, and expose both layers by letting the slit halves fall outward. If desired, the last remaining side can be left uncut, the items price marked, and the halves put together again. This is desirable if the merchandise is to be stored. If the merchandise is going to the selling area, the case splitting can be completed by cutting the fourth side. Using this method, as with the flip board, means that half of the items in the case are marked on the top and the other half on the bottom.

Great care should be exercised when cutting cases containing merchandise packed in paper containers. One means of avoiding damage to packages is to cut the packing case diagonally across the top from one corner to the opposite corner in the shape of an "X." In this manner, if the blade of the case cutter pierces the inside of the case, it will cut through only one layer of the box top, which is usually sealed by an overlapping of two layers. The safest method is to "break" the case by hand.

MEAT RECEIVING, STORING, STOCKING, AND PRICE MARKING

Receiving Meat

When a meat order is received at a retail outlet, all merchandise should be inspected carefully to determine if it is in salable condition. When the quality of meat is not acceptable, the meat manager will contact the shipper or warehouse, who in turn will have the merchandise replaced and the inferior product returned. Each piece or box should be weighed and the weights checked against the invoice.

Some preliminary steps to the meat-receiving function are:

1. Arrange the cooler so that the incoming merchandise can be received in an orderly and efficient manner.
2. Mark, date, or place "old" stock so that it can be used first. This stock usually is moved to the front of the cooler.
3. Have the necessary tools readily available.
4. Clean the floor.
5. Check the temperature of the cooler.

Meat must be handled quickly and efficiently. Shrinkage and spoilage can cause lost profits and reduced sales. In order to keep shrinkage and spoilage at a minimum, temperature and humidity should be regulated.

Upon receipt, meat should be:

- Handled carefully to avoid dropping and bruising
- Inspected for spoilage, cleanliness, etc.
- Weighed accurately and necessary adjustments made on the invoices
- Put under refrigeration immediately.

At the receiving dock or door, the meat is weighed and then immediately put into the cooler. Keeping accurate records is as important as the quality of the meat itself. Improperly maintained records of receipts, weights, piece counts, etc., are a constant source of bad inventories and stock shortages and result in a lack of proof in establishing purchases.

Storing Meat

As soon as the meat has been received, it should be prepared for storage. The procedure for placing wholesale cuts in storage varies with different companies. An average storage plan for beef would be as follows:

1. Loins are stored in the cooler on a floor rack, bones down.
2. Top sirloins are hung on a hook with the skin to the wall.
3. Rounds (boned or whole) are stored by hanging by the "heel."
4. Sets of ribs and chunks are laid on a rack in the same manner as loins.
5. Brisket and plates are hung on wall hooks, skin side to the wall.

There is also a proper place in the cooler for the other types of meat products frequently handled:

1. Processed items and smoked meats belong in the warmest part of the cooler, usually near the doors.

2. Lamb, beef, and poultry (usually iced) hold up best in the next coolest spot.
3. Veal, pork, fish, and offal items are best suited for the coldest part of the cooler.

Stocking Self-Service Meat Cases

Self-service meat cases can be stocked either from the front or the rear.

Front Feed. Meat cases located against a solid wall must be stocked from the front. Carts or specially equipped trucks are used to transport the meat from the wrapping area to the front of the case. Stocking is easier since the employee sees the merchandise from the front, the same view as the customer.

Rear Feed. Rear-loading meat cases are used in many supermarkets. An aisle or sliding doors in the wall behind the cases is needed so that the cases can be constantly restocked and kept in good condition throughout the day without interfering with customers.

Mirror-back cases, with the processing rooms directly behind them, are usually fed from the rear by sliding the mirrors out of the way.

Meat Price Marking

The weighing, wrapping, and labeling of meat is time-consuming unless proper equipment is used. The meat package label should show the store name; cut or type of meat; price per pound; weight in pounds, ounces, and fractions; total price; and the date packaged (which may be in code unless local regulations prohibit coding).

Innovations in the field of combination price-weighing, such as the automatic scale, have made the task of price marking much easier and, at the same time, have decreased pricing errors. The use of shrink tunnel wrapping has greatly improved meat packaging. The successful operator incorporates these advances in technology into the operation, and thus takes full advantage of their utility. (Also see Chapter 5, "The Meat Department.")

PRODUCE RECEIVING, STORING, STOCKING, AND PRICE MARKING

Receiving and Storing Produce

The proper receipt of produce deliveries is the first step toward maintaining the quality and freshness that should characterize the produce department. Prior to the time of delivery, the storage coolers should be properly arranged to ensure adequate space for holding the fresh delivery. Merchandise carried over from the previous day should be arranged in such a manner that it is easily accessible for display during the day. Marking the receipt date on the crate is a common practice and helps to assure that merchandise will move out in correct order. The "first in, first out" principle should be strictly enforced unless the merchandise being received is further advanced in the ripening process than that which is presently on hand.

Many produce orders are delivered during the night or as early as possible in the morning. If possible, produce department employees should inspect all merchandise at the time of delivery. If deliveries are made at night, the inspection should be made as soon as possible after the store opens. This inspection is important for the following reasons:

1. The condition of the merchandise is noted; items showing any signs of deterioration or an advanced degree of ripeness can be put on sale immediately. Severely over-ripe items can be reported for adjustment.
2. A count of the containers compared against the invoice precludes misunderstandings concerning overages and shortages.
3. The inspection will aid the produce manager in planning his daily sales programs and display patterns. This is particularly important since items in short supply are often "scratched" from the order sheet.

It is important to have adequate handling equipment available at the time the shipment is received. If deliveries are made at night, the handling equipment should be free of all merchandise and easily accessible at the delivery entrance. If the produce order is palletized, it is important that adequate storage space and a lift truck be available. If a conventional conveyor system is used, the conveyor should be set up and ready to use.

As produce requiring refrigeration is received, it should be placed in the cooler as soon as possible. Tests show that produce loses as much of its "bloom" when left outside the cooler for two or three hours, especially in hot weather, as it does inside the cooler in five or six days.

Due to the bulky and sometimes delicate nature of produce, the following rules should be observed:

1. Merchandise should be stacked to allow circulation of air.
2. Boxes and crates should be stacked so as to prevent bruising and other types of damage to the produce.
3. Merchandise should be stacked according to its position on the produce rack.

4. Wet produce should not be placed on top of dry produce.
5. Bags should never be dragged or stored on a wet floor.

Receiving and storing produce is often performed in one operation. Employees should be instructed as to which items to refrigerate. A classification chart posted at a convenient location near the receiving door is useful as a reminder as well as a check list.

Stocking Produce

Produce stocking begins with the back-room operation of trimming, packaging, and pricing. The produce is then taken by special truck or cart to the produce rack and added to the display. The U.S. Department of Agriculture, in cooperation with several supermarket operators, has developed a tray-stock procedure. Display trays are prepared in the back room and placed on a truck designed to hold stocked trays. The display trays can be held in the cooler or taken to the produce display rack. Trays of

The produce clerk has a double duty in restocking this circular island fixture with bananas. He must lay out the fruit as neatly as possible. And he must check existing stock for unsalable merchandise.

dated merchandise are removed and fresh trays put in their places. The tray-stocking procedure requires special equipment: refrigerated rack, trays, trucks, and racks in the cooler.

Dry racks, in many cases, are "dummied" to give the effect of mass. They should be restocked with small amounts of merchandise to maintain a high degree of quality.

Turnover in the produce department is very important in order to assure freshness; the produce clerks should continually rotate their merchandise.

Customers often "catch on" to the rotation procedures used by the various supermarkets. Such customers select their produce from the rear of a display. If this happens, a leveling effect should be instituted with fresh-looking, desirable merchandise kept throughout the display area. Off-quality merchandise, as mentioned previously, should be pulled to insure customer acceptance of the produce.

As in the meat department, produce racks may be either rear-feed or front feed types. The latter is the more prevalent method. Mirror-back cases should be stocked to the mirror in an orderly fashion to achieve the best results.

Produce Price Marking

Many of the marking procedures used in other departments are also applicable to the produce department, although some fresh vegetables are butt-marked with an indelible pencil. Other items, such as prepacked merchandise, require that the weight or quantity, in addition to the price, be shown. Items that are not marked should carry prices on signs on shelf moldings. Some stores mark citrus fruit with a marker or a price stamp; others use labels. Whatever the system, care should be taken to see that all prices on signs and on items agree. When produce is retrimmed or reconditioned, the old price should be removed before remarking items. (Also see Chapter 6, "The Produce Department.")

RECEIVING, STORING, STOCKING, AND PRICE MARKING OF DAIRY ITEMS, BAKED GOODS, AND FROZEN FOODS

In the dairy department, rotation, cleanliness, and care are important aspects of the receiving and storing process. Price marking is accomplished according to many of the principles applied to grocery items. Cheese and certain other selected items are wrapped, weighed, and coded. Large quantities of merchandise are received in the dairy department. Proper attention and care must be exercised to adhere strictly to the dating and coding procedure.

Commercial bakeries deliver to the retail outlet and, in areas where permitted, stock the shelves. The driver-salesperson price marks items not premarked and keeps them arranged in the allotted space. The major problem confronting the store manager is keeping each driver-salesperson within assigned shelf-space limits. Deliveries are made daily on an assigned schedule designed to avoid delays and congestion. Most driver-salespeople will make fill-in deliveries when needed in order to maintain their merchandise in stock.

Commercial bakery items produced by the supermarket operator are delivered by company trucks—usually in the grocery truck, but at times by the truck delivering perishable items. Stocking and price marking are the function of store personnel.

Direct store deliveries cause problems in terms of congestion in the store and on the receiving docks, inventory control, control of dated items, and so forth. To eliminate some of the inefficiencies and losses incurred through direct deliveries, some supermarket operators are requiring the merchandise to be de-livered to a distribution center for shipment to the stores by company trucks.

Custom or quality baked goods are usually stocked and price marked by store personnel. Leased departments are staffed by their own employees.

Frozen foods are handled in much the same manner as groceries. Frozen foods are packaged; therefore, the receiving procedures used are the same in principle as for dry groceries, except for the urgent need to keep frozen foods under proper refrigeration. A one-hour exposure on a hot day can ruin the quality of an entire shipment of frozen foods. Each shipment of frozen foods should be checked for temperature at the time of delivery to assure quality.

The pricing of frozen merchandise poses difficulties; frost quickly forms on exposed units that are not kept under constant freezing temperature. Therefore, the items should be marked quickly and accurately, either with a stamp that can be inked quickly and requires little physical motion or with pre-printed labels.

Please refer to Chapter 7, "The Dairy Department"; Chapter 9, "Baked Goods and the Bakery Department"; and Chapter 10, "The Frozen Foods Department."

15

MERCHANDISING

A most important factor in food retailing is merchandising. Merchandising is the strategy designed and the action taken to sell the largest quantity of products at a price that will produce maximum gross profit.

Merchandising activities take place both at corporate headquarters and at the individual stores. All merchandising activities engaged in are for the express purpose of increasing sales and profits. Corporate management must, to a high degree of accuracy, estimate future sales in each of its units for each category of merchandise and for each item within each category, since inventory requirements for a store will depend upon the ratio of stock required to the anticipated volume. With the use of a computerized checkout system (described in Chapter 12), management is able to more accurately estimate sales for a particular period and determine quantities of each item required for the period. However, identification of items to be purchased is a far more difficult task.

It is a well-documented truism that there is no "average" customer; there are sharp differences in the kinds of customers that patronize one store as compared with another; and there are sharp differences among customers shopping the same store. Corporate policies that mandate "rubber stamp" operations in all units calling for the same store layout, the same brands and lines, and the same policies, regardless of the store clientele, may gain efficiency and economy of operation, but they may lose customers to competition better geared to serve individual shopper needs.

THE SCOPE OF MERCHANDISING

The modern supermarket scene is characterized by competitive pricing policies, rising operating costs, and sagging net profits. It is complicated by competition from smaller stores with the flexibility that is inherent in smaller operations, from superstores offering "one-stop shopping," and from what had traditionally been nonfood retail operations now offering cut-rate dairy, produce, and groceries for sale. The need for more effective merchandising has never been greater.

To merchandise effectively, the supermarket operator should carefully consider each of the following:

1. The seven "rights" of merchandising affecting profit
   - Buying the *right merchandise*
   - Buying at the *right time*
   - Buying the *right quantity*
   - Buying from the *right sources*
   - Buying at the *right price*
   - Having merchandise in the *right place*
   - Using the *right promotion, advertising, and display*.

2. Factors affecting product movement
   - Customer demographics (distribution, density, and vital statistics of the population)
   - Seasonal buying patterns
   - Promotional influences.

3. Factors affecting in-store merchandising
   - Special displays
   - Store-wide promotion
   - On-shelf stock
   - Stocking procedures.

This chapter is intended as an overview of merchandising. Specific methods and techniques of merchandising are discussed in each of the chapters concerned with specific departments. Advertising and sales promotion and display are discussed in Chapters 16 and 17, respectively.

The Seven "Rights" of Merchandising Affecting Profit

Buying the Right Merchandise. The right merchandise consists of those items that the customer comes to the store to buy, plus the items that can be sold through good merchandising and display techniques. Right merchandise also means stocking a wide variety of items to make the store a more exciting place in which to shop.

Buying at the Right Time. The right time calls for adequate stock at all times, and also involves having special items during certain seasons.

Buying the Right Quantity. Successful merchandising dictates *in-stock*, but not *over-stock*. Out-of-stock conditions nullify all other good merchandising techniques used and send customers to other stores.

Buying from the Right Sources. Many chains, cooperatives, and voluntary groups maintain their own warehouses where goods are stored for distribution to the supermarkets serviced. Store managers expect the warehouse to have merchandise when needed.

Buyers for the chains buy directly from producers and manufacturers whenever possible, use the services of food brokers, and receive food in their warehouses for further distribution to the stores. Independent retailers may buy from cooperative and voluntary wholesalers to obtain competitive price advantages.

Buying at the Right Price. In practice, this means a price not out of line with prices for similar articles in competitive stores. The right price is one that will sell a satisfactory volume of merchandise at a markup that will produce a net profit for the company.

Having Merchandise in the Right Place. An item advertised for sale must be in the store. Care must be taken to anticipate demand on an advertised item. Most chains and wholesalers either frown on or refuse to make special deliveries because of the high cost of such service. Many small chains will interchange merchandise between stores to avoid getting caught without sale items.

The Federal Trade Commission, while it will take into consideration a small percentage of "outs," must be shown that normal, prudent care was taken to order adequate supplies of the item in plenty of time to make sure the items were on hand. Beyond such prudent care, rain checks must be offered.

To keep customers happy, when many stores run out, they will offer to substitute comparable or even higher priced merchandise at the sale price. This procedure often appeases the customer and avoids the time-consuming need to write a rain check.

Within the store, the right place to have merchandise for maximum sales is the place where it will gain favorable attention from the largest number of shoppers. *Traffic items* and *profit items* should be displayed near one another. Preferred eye-level space should be given to profit items on the theory that customers will seek out the traffic items if they are in a logical place. Location itself cannot sell an item for which there is no customer demand.

Using the Right Promotion, Advertising, and Display. In order to buy, customers must know what is being offered and must be able to find it within the store. Promotion and advertising can be directed to building an image for the store and gaining a reputation for fine quality, low prices, and available merchandise of the variety and selection the customer will buy. If you build a "better mouse trap" no one will beat a path to your door—unless they know about it.

Factors Affecting Product Movement

Customer Demographics. In order to merchandise better to the needs of the customer, the supermarket operator should have more knowledge about the people served. Many facts about a community are gathered prior to determining the store location; these facts as well as updated information about the population should keep corporate management in tune with the customers it serves. Demographic profiles for the fifty largest markets, including data on population, housing, and education, can be obtained from the U.S. Department of Commerce; data on employment can be obtained from the Department of Labor. Additional reports and statistics are published periodically by trade papers and magazines and by trade associations. Also, personal observation by management, interviews with customers, and reports by store managers can furnish information needed to better meet customer needs.

Customer information of special interest to merchandisers includes: age, the number of people in each household, ethnic background, income level, education, shopping habits, and average purchases.

Seasonal Buying Patterns. The contemporary supermarket operator must be disabused of the myth that selling in a supermarket is a "steady business." Sales in a supermarket reflect the way its customers work, live, relax, and play. Only a small proportion of

Making it easy for customers to find the "best buys of the week" is one of the ingredients of a successful supermarket merchandising program. These "best buys" cannot be missed, and they are easy to get at, located in a high-traffic area along a side wall.

the products on the shelves sell in the same volume week after week. The other items show changes in rate of sale during different seasons of the year.

Seasonal trends can be estimated for merchandise categories based on figures of warehouse withdrawals during the comparable period for the previous year. From these figures, management can estimate the percentage of change in demand for product groups during warmer weather or cooler weather, can determine which product groups sell relatively steadily during the entire year, as well as which product groups are growing in demand, and when. Common sense may dictate that hot chocolate and hot cereals, for example, will sell better during the winter, but any efficient operator wants to know the percentage of the increase.

Outside of differences caused by weather, there are many variations in weekly selling patterns to which every merchandiser and manager must be sensitive in order to maintain adequate inventories and obtain maximum sales.

The first full week in the month (or the first week with at least three mail delivery days) generally is the heaviest week of the month. This is because social security, welfare, annuity and pension checks generally arrive in the first three mail delivery days of the month.

Many companies and government agencies pay twice a month or every two weeks rather than weekly. If the store is in an area where many of the customers work for an organization with such a pay policy, its shopping-pattern anticipation should take such matters into account. Even the traditional end-of-the-week upswing in the shopping curve may be reversed

A little ingenuity can go a long way, as shown at this urban A&P store. Making the most of unused parking space, the manager features a variety of summer produce at an outdoor sale.

in an area where most of the people are paid on a Monday or Tuesday.

When the supermarket operator has clear evidence of the variation in customer demand for product groups at different seasons of the year, the selection and merchandising of products can be more effective. Greater effectiveness can be achieved by having:

- Merchandise on hand that customers want
- Properly filled shelves with less backing and filling—fewer over-orders, and fewer out-of-stock items
- The right products at the right time, gaining higher sales volume and more profits.

One danger exists in the complete removal of nonseasonal items. Some customers still want hot cereals during the summer, and others still buy charcoal during the winter. While the quantities of non-seasonal items should be reduced out of season, if space exists, sales are encouraged when small quantities are kept on hand. If there is no selling space available on the sales floor, a sign to the effect that such items (as charcoal) are available on request often creates extra sales as well as customer good will. (See pages 101-105 for a more detailed discussion of the merchandising calendar.)

Promotional Influences. Promotion has a direct influence on product movement. Newspaper advertisements have proven pulling power; reaction to advertisements bring customers to the store soon after the paper is off the press. Pulling power is strongest the first day and may continue to be effective for about two to three days. "As advertised" in-store feature displays tied to the newspaper advertisements can produce as much as a 150 percent increase over normal sales for the advertised product, whereas a nonfeatured advertised item can be expected to produce an increase of approximately 30 percent above normal sales.

The supermarket operator should have feedback on the precise pulling power and resultant increase of sales of the various promotional activities of the company. Promotional activities may include: handbills, newspaper, radio and television advertising, point-of-purchase displays and signs, coupons, premiums, manufacturer-provided advertisements and displays, window signs, in-package coupons or refund slips, games and lotteries, continuities, and many more. Although advertising, display, and signs are constant promotional activities for all stores, other promotional activities are utilized in what appears to be cycles; an operator may begin a new promotion or revive one that had been successful in the past.

Factors Affecting In-store Merchandising

Special Displays. Placement of a display can directly affect the movement of merchandise. It is generally accepted that displays sell more goods when placed in a high-traffic area. This is not *always* true, however. Since not all displays can be placed in high-traffic areas, it is important to note that research and experimentation have indicated that the selling characteristics of a product determine the traffic exposure required for increased sales of items in a display. Highly promoted, advertised and specially priced items can move merchandise effectively when placed in lesser traffic areas, whereas, unadvertised and impulse items depend on relatively high-traffic areas if they are to move well.

Special displays do not always result in spectacular increases in sales. Every supermarket merchandiser should be aware of what special displays can be expected to do, as well as what they *cannot* do:

1. Displays cannot sell items toward which customers have a negative attitude, be it toward the brand, the product itself, the packaging, or the selling price.
2. Displays cannot sell damaged merchandise, or items that did not sell through previous advertising or at greatly reduced prices.
3. Display selling performance can be sustained for a limited time only.
4. Display location should be fitted to the product's characteristics. Wrong location can negate the effectiveness of a display.
5. Displays must be maintained properly. They must be kept clean and properly stocked.
6. Displays should have signs attached that are informative, easy to read, and identify the product, the brand, and the price.
7. Display stacking should be arranged so that the customer can easily reach and take the product, and so that the display will not become disarranged or fall as items are removed.
8. Display, to achieve maximum effectiveness, should be backed up by special promotions, retailer-manufacturer tie-ins (limited time offers), introduction of new items, special coupons, and other features.

In summary, displays can be used to: add excitement to shopping and create favorable store image; increase sales of impulse and advertised items; stimulate and increase related-item sales; increase traffic by placing visible-to-shoppers displays in low-traffic store areas; introduce new items; place profit-making related items next to leaders in order to cushion the reduced profit margin of the leaders; and serve as a shopping aid to customers. (See Chapter 17 for more information on displays.)

Store-wide Promotion. Using a thematic approach, decorations, point-of-purchase signs, and promotional devices can add an exciting atmosphere to the store and help build sales, which experience has shown can increase the sales of featured items by more than 150 percent. In-store advertising and promotional activities must be carefully coordinated so that the promotion will result in the movement of the greatest number of items.

On-shelf Stock. Shelf position, level, facings, and the relationship of items on a shelf can affect product movement. Computer programs can provide sufficient information required to achieve maximum efficiency in space allocation for each product and in preventing out-of-stock conditions. Meanwhile, stocking of shelves is done, most frequently, by part-time stock clerks who usually work under the direction of a department manager.

Effective on-shelf merchandising provides flexibility so that out-of-stock conditions are kept to a minimum and slow-moving items are not permitted to monpolize valuable shelf space. Effective on-shelf merchandising includes the following considerations:

1. The size, shape, and weight of a product must be taken into account, since these factors relate to the ease of removing the item from the shelf by the customer. Very heavy or very large packages should be placed on low shelves for ease of reaching and lifting.
2. The rate of sales of the product is an important determinant in allocating the amount of shelf space that the item will occupy.
3. To capitalize on seasonal items, additional facings and space allocation should be provided for products in season.
4. If an item is being specially promoted or displayed in another area of the store, a sufficient quantity of the product should be in its usual shelf space to avoid disappointing customers who expect to find it there.
5. Facing re-evaluations should be made when items are being offered in multiple-unit prices or have "cents-off" labels.
6. New products being introduced should be given a more than normal number of facings during the introductory period; and signs indicating that it is a new product should be placed over the shelf.
7. Within product categories, different brands of a product should be grouped together on shelves adjacent to each other.

Stocking Procedures. The convenience of the customer is of prime importance in stocking merchandise in the store. The shopper, during an average trip, spends less than a half hour in the supermarket and buys between 30 and 40 items out of 10,000 to 15,000 available in the store. Items compete for customer attention.

Out-of-stock is a condition that causes customer irritation and dissatisfaction; if widespread, it might cause the customer to shop at another market—perhaps never to return.

Cases in aisles that leave little room for customer carts to pass or that block access to shelves may defeat any merchandising effort

Where it is possible to avoid stocking shelves during busy shopping periods, it should be avoided. However, when an out-of-stock occurs, it is better for a clerk to hand-carry a case of merchandise to the proper slot and restock quickly.

Stores that are open twenty-four hours a day attempt to stock shelves during the least busy hours. But in those high-volume stores where there is rarely a lull, efforts have been made to stock one section of any given aisle at a time. While that section is being stocked, some stores maintain a portable rack displaying a number of each of the items from the area being stocked. A similar system is used when a section of an aisle is blocked off for cleaning and waxing the floor. Although this requires some extra effort, it is more than made up for in customer goodwill. Regardless of the time the customer comes into the store, it is an annoyance to find a portion of the store or an entire department not available for shopping. (See Chapter 14 for a more detailed discussion of in-store ordering and stocking.)

THE MERCHANDISING PLAN

Effective merchandising requires planning ahead. Some supermarket operators plan as much as six months ahead; that is, a skeleton plan is projected, including the events and themes to be used. Space is allocated in advance for special events and merchandise. Planned supplier promotions also must be included in overall projections. Early planning enables buyers, merchandisers, and advertising personnel to plan, organize, buy and prepare materials to promote the special event. Thus, a promotion package—advertising, store displays, point-of-sale material, etc.—is designed. Effective merchandising is the result.

Each week the promotion plan is reviewed, the plan for the coming week is completed, and the plans for the following weeks are reviewed and updated. The plans are extended either on a weekly or monthly

basis, so planning is at least five months ahead. Buyers need to know the overall merchandising plans to enable them to buy the items to be promoted in the anticipated quantities needed. Media time and space is usually contracted for on a long-term basis with fixed minimum usage plus provisions for additional advertising. The advertising department must plan special events ahead and schedule the added coverage.

THE MERCHANDISING CALENDAR

With the change of seasons comes alterations in living and eating habits requiring adjustments in merchandising. Emphasis should be placed on the appeal that is most appropriate and logical for the particular time of the year. Holidays and the four seasons present a challenge to the initiative, imagination, and ingenuity of a manager, which, in turn, can be presented creatively to his or her customers. Popular consumer motifs or moods can be expressed in original and impressive displays that will tend to stimulate sales, vary the atmosphere of the store, and add appeal so that the supermarket will be a more inviting place to shop.

Spring Merchandising (April, May, June)

Both the calendar indicating that spring has arrived and the holiday of Easter are valid reasons to give the store a new atmosphere. Planning a merchandising program to revolve around the changes in eating or living habits and the general merchandise used is a spring must.

Easter places emphasis on foods typical to the holiday, and special traffic builders should be appropriately displayed and priced. Advertising themes should be subtly related to Easter. Featured and displayed foods for the season should consist of such items as ham, eggs, and Easter candy as well as baking needs, since this is a big family holiday that typically generates a great deal of home baking.

Spring housecleaning affords the merchandiser opportunities for the display and promotion of many high-profit items. Labor-saving cleaning items and devices, through proper display, can result in building customer goodwill by making spring cleaning chores more simple.

Spring, too, is lawn, flower and garden time, lending itself to promotions in suburban areas. Parking lots may be utilized for the display and sale of garden supplies and equipment. A well-merchandised garden center is a profitable addition for spring.

Keeping up with lifestyle trends is important in planning merchandise presentations. Outdoor eating has become part of the suburban residential scene. So this retailer set up a tent with equipment and food to dramatize a patio party theme.

Watermelon time in Alabama. This store receives 800 watermelons daily during the summer months. This dump display shows the merchandise dramatically: The message is clear.

With the arrival of spring, the customer starts looking forward to more outdoor living. Outdoor eating creates heavy demands for soft drinks, beer, steaks, hamburgers, rolls, buns, salads, paper supplies, insect repellents, charcoal, and fire starters. Good promotional items are outdoor cooking devices, such as hibachis or portable grills.

Logically, stores should take advantage of national advertising themes. Among these themes are National Dairy Month, National Baby Week, National Garden Week, and others. There are also special days during the spring season which lend themselves to promotions; among them are Mother's Day, Father's Day, May Day, Arbor Day, etc. In addition, there may be some local or regional events or activities that offer merchandising themes and that help to involve the merchant in community affairs.

Summer Merchandising (July, August, September)

The behavioral pattern of the consuming public calls for changes in the supermarket operator's merchandising and display. The summer slowdown of business, resulting from people taking vacations and trips away from home, schools being closed, and youngsters going off to camp, causes changes, and retailers should strive to maintain their volume.

Summer offers the retailer a different set of prod-

ucts for display and promotion. Produce is available in greater abundance and variety and should be displayed in mass dump and island displays. Watermelons and other melons, as available, should be displayed in bins for customer selection. In conjunction with these fruits, suggestive display material promoting ice cream, cottage cheese, shortcake shells, and the like should be given prominence to achieve balanced selling and provide traffic-building specials.

Of course, outdoor living and picnics continue to be effective merchandising themes. In conjunction wtih these themes, the items to continue to promote are beverages, hamburgers and hotdogs, buns and rolls, and charcoal. These products can be given prominent mass, related or aisle displays. In addition, for balanced selling, the higher than average profit items, such as relishes, pickles, condiments, insect repellents, and picnic supplies should also be given more conspicuous display. It is a good idea to feature suntan lotions and related health and beauty aid items.

Summer, like spring, has its national advertising programs into which the supermarket operator can tie-in, such as National Cherry Week, National Dog Week, and others. Special days include the Fourth of July and Labor Day.

As summer draws on, displays of canning supplies should be placed close to the produce department to remind the consumer of the availability of these items.

To stay competitive, supermarkets must capitalize on holiday events. Publix Supermarkets, Clearwater, Florida, does just that with this prominent aisle display of "Halloween treats."

"Back-to-school" and "normal living" merchandising programs are subtle reminders that summer is ending and that a major change in living and eating is in keeping with the changing seasons. Among the things that should be merchandised are school supplies, clothing, and food items for sandwiches for take-along lunches (e.g., peanut butter and jelly, etc.). After-school snacks add to the product mix.

Fall Merchandising (October, November, December)

The fall season is, by far, the merchandiser's greatest opportunity to convince the consumer to buy. First, the fall season is well-known for beginning the best eating time of the year; second, it includes three big special promotions—Halloween, Thanksgiving, and Christmas. Fall is the merchandiser's delight.

Halloween trick-or-treat merchandise brings extra volume. The annual neighborhood tour by young people in search of candy handouts certainly increases candy sales. Massive displays of trick-or-treat products sell high-margin merchandise.

What was started in late summer, continues into the fall—the freezer-canning season—as long as produce items are plentiful and of good quality. It is essential that inventory of these necessary items be properly controlled because of the seasonal nature and the high perishability of the produce to be canned. Quality control of produce creates a favorable consumer image. Having adequate stocks of these products will invariably help to sell them. Featuring fruits and berries, by the case, bag or bushel, with canning and freezing supplies, helps to sell both.

Thanksgiving Day dinner is traditionally a turkey and trimmings holiday. While the major item is turkey, other poultry and meat products should be merchandised for those not traditionally inclined. While the Thanksgiving menu varies somewhat in various areas, cranberry sauce, sweet potatoes, celery, and pumpkin and apple pie are among the traditional items. These offer a great many varied items to merchandise. Typically, large turkeys are featured items. Smaller turkeys offer a better markup and should be merchandised in the meat case, even though the large size is advertised at the traffic-building price. Related-item displays of a number of different brands or kinds of merchandise increase volume and profits.

December merchandising should include toys, greeting cards, gift fruit baskets, gift food boxes (i.e., cookies, cheese, etc.), decorations, gift wraps, and flowers. Christmas is the best special-promotion season of the year. Most people buy gifts and can use gift suggestions. They decorate their homes and need supplies; and, in addition, they celebrate with a banquet-sized meal. The entire store becomes an arena for Christmas merchandising, and the product mix for promotions is endless. In the supermarket, the special Christmas season begins after Thanksgiving and lasts through December 24. Merchandising a full line of gifts, decorations, and food items adds profit dollars to the year's revenues.

Besides Halloween, Thanksgiving, and Christmas, the other fall holidays that give the merchandiser additional ammunition with which to work are Columbus Day, Veterans Day, and even Election Day. The fall season provides, without a doubt, an ideal situation for the merchandiser; the promotion and display possibilities are rich and varied. There is no question that people spend more money for food and related items during this season than any other—a really challenging opportunity to any merchandiser.

Winter Merchandising (January, February, March)

Continuity with the immediately preceding season is a task that confronts the merchandising team just as soon as Christmas is over. The Christmas holiday brings to an end a big eating season, and for a week after, there is basically a snack, cold cuts and beverage time leading into the New Year holiday. The deli department is the focal point of the Christmas-New Year holiday period for catering. Many firms, both large and small, have Christmas parties; an excellent opportunity exists here for the preparation of cold-cut platters, sandwiches, and other catering services that most deli departments are capable of performing.

In addition to the deli department, stores that have liquor departments find that the holiday season is a heavy-selling season from the standpoint of both gift-giving and parties. A growing number of firms have substituted or added Christmas food-giving to the traditional office and plant parties given at this time of year. This can range from canned hams and turkeys to cheeses, canned cookies, fruit baskets, wines and liquors.

For New Year's Eve, the parties switch from the office or plant to the home. In addition to the deli and liquor departments, snack food and soda-pop sections come in for heavier sales, if the promotion is there.

In recent years, New Year's Day has become more and more a traditional visiting day. Just as

Christmas has come to mean a day to spend with family, so New Year's Day is growing into a day to spend with friends. Here, too, snack foods, cold cuts, wines and liquors are all in demand, and promotional efforts can make the supermarket the place for such purchases. Not to be overlooked are the opportunities for related party-goods sales that this entire period provides for the general merchandise section as well as the paper-goods portion of the grocery aisles.

January requires new and aggressive promotions to combat the post-holiday slowdown and to build sales in an otherwise routine period. In many areas, winter brings cold weather and a consequent change in menu, featuring breakfasts centered around hot cereal, pancakes, waffles, and their trimmings; and dinners mainly consisting of boiled, roasted, broiled and fried meats and poultry, and side dishes, such as potatoes, corn, peas, etc. At this time of year, citrus crops are plentiful and lend themselves to good merchandising at promotional prices. Promoting the sale of hot beverages, such as coffee, tea or cocoa, is appropriate since they are more widely used in cold weather.

In the general merchandise area, the sale of cold remedies, hand lotions, and general health items makes good sense. Because of the possibilities of more cooking and baking, the promotion of cooking and baking utensils are good profit-building tie-ins.

February and March bring the Lenten season and the merchandising of nonmeat meals. These nonmeat substitutes should be featured and used to build traffic. The fact that Lent has arrived should not preclude the use of meats in ads and specials, however. Poultry, beef, pork, veal, and lamb are effective traffic builders. On the usual list of timely promotional items are fresh, frozen and canned fish, eggs and dairy items, macaroni products, spaghetti dinners, and the like. (As with all promotions, the composition of the store's patrons must be kept in mind. Therefore, with a Lenten merchandising program, as well as that for other holidays, the ethnic, racial and religious makeup of a store's clientele must be considered.)

The special days in this period which help to give themes to the merchandising program are New Year's Day, Lincoln's birthday, Washington's birthday, Valentine's Day, and St. Patrick's Day. In some years, Easter may fall in this season.

The supermarket operator should participate in local events and merchandise accordingly. Good consumer and public relations are always important, but winter seems to be a time when local drives and campaigns are particularly prevalent; support of these programs helps the store and industry image.

Ingenuity of promotion must never be under-

The "Party Corner" at Food Giant near Bessemer, Alabama, would like to corner the soft-drink business at parties. It has devoted almost forty feet of wall space for a permanent display of sodas, mixes, and related soft-drink items to capture attention—and business.

The untraditional promotion often pays off for food retailers. Here, this A&P unit is bringing Santa to town in the middle of July. Of course, there will be gifts for all the children, and that should draw a lot of adults to the event.

rated. Normally, most stores find that the January-February period is the slowest time of the year. Wakefern, the co-op flying the ShopRite banner in New Jersey, New York, Pennsylvania, and Connecticut, more than a decade ago, was able to convert this period from its slowest part of the year to its greatest promotional and sales period. While it ranks behind the short, heavy Thanksgiving, Christmas, Easter periods for concerted sales during a week to ten-day selling period, its total sales top any of these periods.

In planning the promotion, which grew beyond the wildest hopes of any of its original planners, the firm decided to make this *the* sale for the grocery department. The promotion is called the "Can-Can Sales." Hundreds of grocery items (most of them in cans, but sometimes jarred or bottled merchandise) are featured. Specials are planned for the period as much as ten months in advance of the promotion.

Brand as well as private-label manufacturers are afforded an opportunity to participate in the event. Television, radio, newspaper and even circular advertising is coordinated—even to using Offenbach's *Gaite Parisienne* musical theme associated with the cancan dance. Promotions are based on multiple items, and the magic number is $1—six cans, three cans, etc., for $1.

The firm moves more than twice the normal amount of canned goods for any given two-month period and probably four times the normal for that particular time period. It is the busiest, instead of the slowest, time of the year for the warehouse and retailers.

16

ADVERTISING AND SALES PROMOTION

The entire consumer appeal of the early supermarkets was low price. Thus, their advertisements used headlines such as "The World's Greatest Price Wrecker," "Champion Price Cutter," "No High Operating Costs," and so forth; and the body of the ad featured low prices.

Today, it is accepted that price is only one of the appeals to be featured in supermarket ads. One of the functions of advertising is to project the store image to customers, both present and potential. Some of the aspects of this image that supermarket advertising must project to the consumer, in addition to price, are quality, variety, new products, leadership, service, convenience, and ultimately, an image.

ADVERTISING OBJECTIVES

The *immediate* objective and purpose of supermarket advertising is to sell merchandise. Sales are increased by increasing the number of shoppers and influencing the shopper to buy more items. The *long-term* objective is to develop continuity in the company's relationship with regular customers.

The food retailer views the creation of demand for specific products or product categories as the responsibility of the manufacturer and processor. This position is generally true; exceptions exist principally in departments that feature perishable items. "Where to buy," therefore, becomes the important issue with which an individual supermarket's advertising is primarily concerned. As a consequence, the retailer advertises that his or her store is the preferred place to shop.

Supermarket advertising is frequently criticized for its lack of variety and creativity. While, to a great extent this is true, a repetitive style in a store's advertising format makes it easily identifiable to the consumers with whom it has developed a following. Supermarket ads are effective when they *generate store traffic* week after week by:

- Emphasizing where to buy
- Projecting a favorable store image
- Taking advantage of demand-creating advertising campaigns by manufacturers and processors

Getting people to talk about you is one way to gain customer acceptance, as Ralphs, Los Angeles, did with this public acknowledgment in the form of a thank-you note. This is an institutional ad with some clout.

- Promoting products through menu suggestions and recipes
- Featuring products that are basic to the trade in the area.

In addition to these direct-action objectives, supermarket advertising can accomplish long-range, indirect-action results, such as promoting goodwill and enhancing community relations.

A single advertisement cannot be designed to combine all of these objectives and purposes. By using a series of advertisements, at least one each week, all desired objectives may be achieved. Advertising must conform to the policies formulated by top management and must be planned, prepared, and evaluated before being inserted in the appropriate media. The advertising must be coordinated with store operations.

Advertising has limitations as well. It cannot sell merchandise that people do not want to buy; it cannot complete the sale, but can only attract people to the store; and, in order to succeed, it must be used *consistently*. In other words, advertising is only part of the merchandising and sales program of any retail outlet.

EFFECTIVE ADVERTISING

To be effective and maintain readership, advertising must be:

- Truthful and accurate
- Clear and specific
- Informative
- Easy to read
- Consumer oriented.

Effective advertising may take different forms and follow various themes:

- Price advertising to build traffic
- Seasonal merchandise advertising, featuring items in big supply
- Advertising based on special occasions or holidays (e.g., Easter—jelly beans; Thanksgiving—turkey; and so on)
- Promotional advertising—store-wide promotions, either sponsored by a supplier or non-sponsored.

Advertising, whether designed to increase store traffic or build community goodwill, should be informative. Participation in community activities, whenever undertaken, should be publicized.

PHILOSOPHY OF ADVERTISING

To whom should supermarkets direct their advertising? This question has its roots deeply imbedded in the basic philosophy of the entire business. No business should attempt to operate without a philosophy; likewise, no business should attempt to *advertise* without a philosophy.

Should advertising be directed to steady customers, to competitors' customers, or to former customers? Sooner or later, good advertising is directed to all of these groups. If there is a story to tell, and it is meaningful and worthwhile, it should reach new, old *and* former customers.

Total merchandising means first segmenting the market—differentiating the kinds or groups of customers who respond to different appeals, be they working people, nonworking people, various nationalities, or gourmets. After segmenting the market, special attention is given to each group, utilizing a sensitive understanding of its special needs and problems. This also means following through in day-to-day operations in order to capitalize on those impressions made during peak efforts. Many supermarket operators have regular programs, handled on a store-by-store basis, of greeting newcomers within the shopping radius of their stores. Some use the local "Welcome Wagon" service. Whatever the method, attracting newcomers is effective.

ADVERTISING TO DIFFERENT TYPES OF CUSTOMERS

Present Customers

Present customers are generally satisfied customers, and no one reads advertising more attentively than the satisfied customer. Each time an ad from a favorite store comes to the attention of a customer, faith in the choice of the store is renewed. These satisfied customers, who purchase regularly, are not only the mainstay of any company's volume, they often bring new customers into the store by their word-of-mouth advertising.

No store should ever become complacent about the customers it already serves. Just as it is seeking to woo customers away from the competition, so the competition is fighting to win the store's customers. Those stores that begin to take their regular clientele for granted often find themselves losing them. Therefore, efforts to keep the goodwill of the old customers must be continued.

Often a store considers changing its image to attract new customers. In arriving at such a decision, the firm must always weigh the fact that some percentage of its current customers may find the new image unattractive and shift its patronage to another store.

Potential Customers

This is the group to which many advertisers direct a great number of their ads. Many in this group have never shopped at the advertiser's store. Generally, it is easier to secure new customers than to win back old customers who have been lost to strong competitors. Traffic-building ads featuring immediate advantages not offered by others are effective in attracting new customers. Whether they *continue* to shop the store will depend upon how satisfied they are with the store's cleanliness, service, and merchandise.

Future Customers

Children, young couples, and persons changing their place of residence all fall into this class. Even though they may not be making any purchases until some time in the future, no advertiser can afford to neglect cultivating these customers. Although they are tomorrow's customers, the presentation to them of a favorable store image is an immediate need.

Competitors

Some advertising is directed to customers of competitors. A number of years ago, one New England firm sent young people into competitors' parking lots to copy the license numbers of cars belonging to shoppers at those stores. During the week following the noting of the license plate numbers, the store took an ad in which it listed the numbers and offered the owners of those cars a gift or free item, if the owner came into the advertiser's store. It was an extremely effective method of wooing customers away from the competitor. Of course, there is a difference between wooing and winning. The store in question had to have enough competitive advantages to hold the customer, once that customer was brought into the store.

Probably no one watches an organization's advertising more closely than competitors, especially if that organization is a leader in its respective field. Since a good offense is always the best defense, the company that commands enough respect from its competitors to have them follow its lead has good evidence of the influence of its advertising.

THE ADVERTISING APPROPRIATION

The appropriation made for advertising provides the cloth from which the advertising campaign is to be cut; therefore, the size of this cloth should be considered carefully before the campaign is planned and started.

Determining the Appropriation

The amount that any particular food store or company should spend for advertising will vary with such factors as the size, location, demographic distribution, trading area, competition, and reputation of that company. The amount of money that a company *needs* to spend for advertising and the amount it can *afford* to spend, are not always the same, however.

Often, it is financially impossible to carry out desired advertising activities. In such a case, management must either reappraise the course of the advertising action to be taken, carrying out the original plan on a more limited basis, or attempt to find suitable alternatives which will be more practical financially.

Before an actual amount of money is appropriated for advertising, some plan or system should be followed which will justify the appropriation. Such a plan should not be set up merely to consume a given amount of money, but rather to establish a relationship between advertising and the target prospective customer to be reached. Such a procedure will tend to keep the appropriation within profitable limits and will provide a satisfactory program.

Unfortunately, there is no cut-and-dried answer to the question: How much should be spent for advertising? Food retailers frequently allocate a percentage of the sales figure as an advertising budget. Consideration must be given to the amount received from cooperative advertising contracts. As an alternative, a retailer may plan the amount of advertising space necessary to create the desired store image and budget accordingly. A few retailers base their advertising on what the competition does; this, however, means turning a portion of the decision-making function over to the competitor.

Once a store or chain is established in a market, it is comparatively simple to determine a budget for advertising. However, when a store is starting or is trying to increase its share of the market, advertising is the primary means of informing the potential customer of the store's merchandising approach. Thus, if a firm is entering a market in which it plans to have five or ten stores within two years, the chain often will budget its expenditures so that the budget per sales dollar is heavier while the chain is gaining a foothold than after it is established.

It is rare that an advertising effort by one store or chain will go unanswered. Therefore, in making plans for a campaign of any sort, follow-up plans must be devised to meet any possible response.

Basically, supermarket operators use two methods to determine the size of the advertising budget:

- The percentage-of-sales method
- The job-to-be-done method.

The Percentage-of-Sales Method. This method is widely used and allows for easy budget determination. A management decision that the advertising budget for the fiscal period will be a specific percentage of sales is made. The sales figure used for computing the dollar appropriation may be that of the past fiscal period, the estimated sales for the current fiscal period, or a combination of both.

This method assumes a definite relationship between sales and the amount of advertising needed to obtain them. If the appropriation is based upon past sales, the assumption is made that advertising follows sales rather than creating them. It also ignores changes in business conditions as a factor affecting the amount of advertising needed. On the other hand, if the appropriation is based on future expected sales, advertising is being considered as a means of creating sales. In this case, the appropriation uses the "building of a store image" approach. Advertising should be considered as a sales builder, not a result of sales.

The Job-to-Be-Done Method. The job-to-be-done method for determining the advertising appropriation recognizes the goals to be achieved and plans an advertising budget adequate to do the job. If the goal is an image of "bigness," being the dominant advertiser, by implication, creates an image as the dominant store or group of stores. To accomplish this dominance requires the use of more space and/or time than any other supermarket operator. Dominance implies: "Everyone shops at our stores. Why don't you?"

The goal may be to increase the size of the sales ticket so as to achieve a higher average sale. This is accomplished by broadening the appeal of the store to include all departments and lines of merchandise.

If the goal is to create a favorable price image, there are many ways of accomplishing this: price advertising of all kinds, including specials, price comparisons, and multi-unit pricing; and the use of price slogans, shelf talkers, and store signs.

Once the advertising appropriation has been determined, the advertising department is responsible for the administration of the program and the achievement of its established goals. In most areas, the major portion of the advertising budget is used for newspaper space. For some stores, however, newspaper advertising is not adequate. For stores with limited trading areas in large cities, selected area newspaper runs are more economical. Some operators use a combination of television, radio, and handbills with or without using newspaper ads. Other operators avail themselves of manufacturer assistance and/or cooperative advertising to defray costs. (See pages 112–115 for a discussion of cooperative advertising.)

The success of advertising is influenced by many factors, independent of the amount of money involved. Choice of the right merchandise and selling appeals, proper timing, judicious pricing, effective presentation, and coordination—all are instrumental in determining the productiveness of the advertising expenditure. Also, the proper balance of outside (newspaper, mail, radio, etc.) and inside (store signs, recipe service, shelf talkers, etc.) advertising is an important factor.

In recent years, a new phenomenon has come onto the supermarket scene—the store that does not have to advertise. The best example is Byerly's in the Minneapolis area. The Byerly stores are so unique that

Don Byerly limits his ads to the following: One ad the day of or preceding an opening, simply announcing it; perhaps one ad just after the opening, thanking the customers for their patronage; and one ad on Easter Sunday and one at Christmas, wishing the patrons a happy holiday. All the ads are institutional, and the only hint of advertising is the small-type listings in a corner of each ad giving the addresses of the store. Just about everything else in the way of advertising and promotion is in-store. Byerly's is thriving; very few stores can create such a powerful image, but they do exist.

WHAT TO ADVERTISE

What can be depended upon to attract the attention of the most people as well as create a desire to visit the store and then to purchase the advertised item? Experience and logic suggest that it is wise to select items that have a popular appeal, are reasonably priced, possess distinct characteristics, and are in demand by the clientele of the store.

TIE-IN ADVERTISING

In an effort to present their merchandise to the consuming public, many manufacturers advertise on a national scale. The channels of communication utilized in conveying this advertising to the public are: magazines, radio, mail, television, and newspapers. These media of communication reach practically every community in the United States. Supermarket operators, realizing that the manufacturer creates demand and pre-sells the advertised items, follow up this national advertising by tying in advertising programs to take advantage of the demand created. Extensive use of "in-ad" coupons sponsored by the manufacturer is a good way in which to cooperate and to promote a product.

CONTINUITY

In order to be effective, supermarket advertising must possess an element of continuity. Infrequent, irregular and inconsistent advertising cannot win new customers or retain the interest of the regular clientele. The customer is constantly being appealed to by a great many advertisers through every conceivable media. Sporadic or unsystematic advertising cannot effectively compete with an advertising program designed to regularly bring the merchandise, services, and company name to the attention of the consumer in a consistent, organized manner.

In many shopping areas, advertising by food retailers appears regularly on specific days of the week, and customers shop the ads for features and specials to plan their shopping trip.

CUSTOMER SHOPPING PATTERNS

Because volume is concentrated on weekends, effective advertising must be scheduled so as to "break" in conjunction with these peak periods. However, in an effort to spread out the business a little more evenly during the week and to eliminate weekend congestion, many food companies are now scheduling early-in-the-week advertising programs.

Customer shopping patterns may include the following factors:

- Local pay periods
- Eating habits
- Income level of community
- National origin
- Average age level.

ADVERTISING MEDIA

Most supermarket operators depend primarily on the local newspaper to advertise to the consuming public. Many operators, however, supplement their newspaper ads with handbills which are distributed in the store's trading area and which are made available

A great deal of behind-the-scenes coordination is required to prepare price promotions in a supermarket chain. Among factors to consider: proper timing, adequate inventories, the right newspapers. This chain advertising director surveys his latest efforts.

in the store for the customer to use as a shopping guide.

As the size of the shopping area increases and the newspaper circulation increases, the cost of buying space increases. In large cities, single-store operators and operators in a limited section of the circulation area cannot afford to use newspaper total circulation space. In cities with more than one newspaper, news ads are generally limited to chains and cooperative groups with stores in all, or nearly all, of the circulation area. For those advertisers able to utilize local newspapers, handbills are a most effective advertising medium.

Many small communities do not have a local newspaper, and using a nearby city newspaper with a wide regional circulation is too expensive for the desired local coverage needed by small supermarket operators. The operators unable to use newspaper advertising use handbills, direct mail, and local radio and/or television. However, newspapers that have special local editions, may offer the advertiser other alternatives. One may be an ad run in special local editions at a considerably lower rate than for complete area coverage. Another alternative that may be offered by the newspaper is an insert distributed in the paper within the local area of the store.

Many wholesalers provide handbill service. Voluntary and cooperative retailer associations advertise in newspapers as a group. The standardized handbill allowing nameplate changes offers inexpensive group advertising to operators unable to use newspapers. Handbills and mail pieces also can be used for special limited area advertising or in addition to newspaper advertising. New store openings and giveaway promotions can be limited to the store's trading area through the use of mail pieces. Handbills or mail pieces have many uses and are usually less expensive on a per thousand coverage basis than other media.

Radio spot announcements are relatively inexpensive and can be used by small stores as well as large, multi-store operators. Radio spots may be the major advertising medium in areas not serviced by newspapers, while in large cities they may be used to supplement newspaper advertising. Radio spots constitute an effective food store advertising medium.

Television, while it is relatively expensive, and while local merchants cannot always buy the best time, is being used more extensively by those who can afford to include the expenditure in their budget.

Which medium is most effective for supermarket advertising? This is a controversial issue. Each operator has formulated an individual advertising plan, and, in general, newspaper advertising gets the largest share of the budget. A recent edition of *Food Marketing Industry Speaks* provides the following composite advertising budget based on answers to a questionnaire submitted by Food Marketing Institute respondents:

Newspapers	63.0%
Radio	4.0%
Television	8.0%
Mailers, flyers	13.0%
In-store coupons	8.0%
Other	4.0%
	Total 100.0%

The small town with a weekly newspaper represents a special problem, since the area is usually serviced by a nearby metropolitan newspaper. If the operator is able to use the metropolitan newspaper coverage, the weekly newspaper may be used for goodwill promotion. If the city paper cannot be used efficiently, the weekly provides the only available newspaper coverage. The ads must be designed for the area residents. In this situation, local operators may augment their weekly newspaper ad with mail and radio.

In the highly competitive price battle among food outlets, the in-store flyer containing coupons plays an increasing role. This customer studies the savings possibilities as he and a curious offspring begin the shopping chore.

For most operators, mail is effective when it is used at indefinite intervals, while for some operators it is effective when used weekly while other media are used sparingly.

Radio spots of one minute—about 125 words—constitute the most widely used radio advertising. Radio has the advantage of being highly flexible since copy can be changed at any time. In fact, the ad should be changed frequently to avoid monotony. Spot ads offer an opportunity to reach a large number of listeners with a concise message at low cost.

Television spot announcements, news and weather reports, and the like can be used most effectively as attention-getters at fairly reasonable prices. Time on radio and television is limited since normal program schedules run for a half or full hour and the number of advertisers per program is limited. It is often a problem to obtain time at desirable hours of the day. Obtaining talent may be a problem, too. Ads should be changed since viewers tire of seeing and listeners tire of hearing the same person and ad over an extended period of time.

THE MERCHANDISING COMMITTEE

A merchandising board or committee is responsible for the merchandising plan (see page 101), including the weekly ad or ads. Typically, the committee membership includes the advertising manager, the departmental merchandisers—meat, produce, grocery—the operations director, controller, and a representative of top management, such as a division vice-president. Nonfoods and dairy, bakery, and frozen foods are represented by the grocery merchandiser in most companies. In a few companies, these departments are represented by merchandisers or buyers from each department.

The merchandising committee usually meets on Mondays. Each department representative comes to the meeting with a departmental sales plan and is prepared to complete the advertising for the following week. Final decisions on the advertising of perishables (meat and produce) must be delayed until the last possible moment because of uncertainty as to availability and current market prices. The purpose of the meeting is to review the advertising for the subsequent week, adding to it any current promotions that may have special impact.

Special-price traffic builders, related item features, cooperatively advertised items as well as balanced selling items are listed by each merchandiser. After all items are considered, space in each ad is allocated, and the items to be used on spot radio and television announcements are selected. It is the responsibility of each merchandiser to get proper representation for his or her department. Perishables usually get a portion of the preferred space and dominant presentation in terms of size of type and pictures. Long-term planning and the equitable, departmental scheduling of feature space is also a function of the committee.

Basically, the procedure as described is the same for voluntaries and cooperatives. The basic differences are:

1. The attendance at the advertising meeting of members, in addition to headquarters personnel (merchandisers, counselors, etc.), who voice their opinions concerning items to appear in an ad.
2. The general discussion of proposed grocery items four weeks in advance in order to allow member survey reports to be submitted indicating the requirements enabling buyers to purchase adequate inventory.

After approval by the committee, the advertising department prepares the ad layout and copy. Copies of the sales plan are reproduced for distribution to the departments and the stores. Changes can be made in the advertising plans for the following week as late as Friday, if only the newspaper ad is involved. However, printing of window posters and handbills or mailers must generally be "put to bed" on the Tuesday or Wednesday before the ad "breaks" because of the need for preparation and distribution to the stores. If a special buy in perishables becomes available at the last moment, it can be advertised at the store level.

MEASURING THE EFFECTIVENESS OF ADVERTISING

The supermarket advertising budget is typically about 1 percent of sales with part of this expenditure recovered by cooperative advertising. To this figure must be added the cost of markdowns on specials or traffic builders. This markdown cost varies and has been increasing because the consumer has become more conscious of sale items, planning a large part of the menu around specials. The net cost of advertising depends upon the extent to which a balanced selling program is successfully executed in the stores.

As previously stated, there are two objectives to advertising: (1) to increase the number of customers; and (2) to increase the average dollar sales per customer. Therefore, return on the advertising expenditure is measured by comparing the number of transactions as recorded by the cash register and the change in the average size of the sales ticket. This should not be a week-to-week comparison, but a long-

term trend. The weekly pattern will vary according to factors such as what the competition does, customer payroll schedules, holidays, seasons, vacations, and the weather.

Knowledge of the effectiveness of a newspaper ad is important in budget planning. In order to measure the effectiveness of the advertising, a survey can be made at store level by using a questionnaire, or a study can be made of the redemption of in-ad coupons that appear in the store ad.

Assuming that a large percentage of the customers are regular customers, effective advertising should be designed to attract new customers to the store. Price advertising will attract the price shopper, whereas advertising to create a favorable store image will attract steady customers. Therefore, nonprice appeals are important in building store clientele.

Any new competition will create new challenges for the advertising director and the merchandisers. Using price alone as the battleground may prove disastrous, whereas an attractive store image plus sound merchandising techniques should prove profitable.

COOPERATIVE ADVERTISING

Earlier in the chapter mention was made of the term "cooperative advertising." Cooperative advertising is manufacturer or processor-dealer supported advertising. The manufacturer agrees to pay the retailer on a predetermined contract basis for advertising specified products of the contracting processor.

Development of Cooperative Advertising

Cooperative advertising originated at the beginning of the twentieth century. The first users were home appliance, women's wear and automobile manufacturers. The Maytag Company and the Warners Brothers Company (soft goods) are credited with being among the first to use cooperative advertising. The early dealers were franchised and had exclusive contracts for fixed trade areas. The manufacturer encouraged exclusive dealers to advertise by sharing the cost. From this beginning, the concept spread to all areas of retailing. Today, about 20 percent of the advertising money spent by national marketers is spent on retail cooperative programs.

Another factor in the development of cooperative advertising was national versus local line rate. During the late 1800's, newspaper advertising space was limited, and newspaper space brokers bought the available space and sold it to manufacturers at a profit. As newspapers became larger and more space became available, the need to sell more advertising to suppliers forced the papers to turn to sales agents. The space broker became the advertising agency, i.e., changed from a space buyer to a space seller. The newspapers offered the agencies a discount. This led to the development of the double-rate system. Since the local advertiser did not use the agency, but received the lower rate, the term *local line rate* was used. The higher rate was termed *national line rate*. The difference in rate may range from 2 percent to 100 percent—the average differential is about 50 percent. Manufacturers turned to cooperative advertising to get space at the local line rate and, at the same time, to encourage the retailer to advertise by offering to pay a substantial portion of the advertising bill.

When cooperative advertising was conceived, and during its early development, its objective—more advertising at lower rates on a shared-cost basis—was achieved. The purpose was clearly to sell more merchandise for both the supplier and the retailer. However, as the concept spread to nonfranchise dealers of mass-produced merchandise, the cooperative advertising contract began to be used to induce retailers to stock items, grant more shelf space, continue the line, and provide special promotions. Co-op payments became just another sales feature of the manufacturer's line. Also, as big retailers came of age, they forced the manufacturer to make concessions or payments for having the line carried in their stores. Today, cooperative advertising contracts require the manufacturer to make partial or full payment for advertising services performed. In some cases, the payment actually exceeds the amount spent by the retailer.

The Robinson-Patman Act

The Robinson-Patman Act of 1936 regulates discounts, allowances, services, and rebates by requiring that any benefit to any retailer must be proportionately available to all competitors. "Available" has been defined as meaning that information covering such concessions must be communicated to all competing customers. The supplier cannot use as a defense the fact that the retailer did not ask for the service or payment. In order to curtail big retailer pressure for special concessions, the Robinson-Patman Act makes both the giver and the receiver guilty of violating the Act.

Under this Act, any cooperative advertising allowance must be available to both large and small retailers in the competitive area. An ad allowance of five cents a case, for example, has value to the retailer with a volume of 1,000 or more cases per quarter (ad allowance payments are generally made on a quarterly basis). The allowance is less meaningful to the retailer whose quarterly volume is less; ultimately, the

allowance becomes so small as to be unimportant. Thus, the greater the volume, the greater the value and importance of the co-op money. Voluntary and cooperative groups collect cooperative ad money through the wholesale unit and share on the basis of volume.

Types of Cooperative Contracts

There are three basic methods of paying retailers under cooperative advertising contracts. There are, of course, variations in the basic contracts. The three basic methods are:

- Cents per case
- Percentage of the invoice cost of merchandise for a specified period
- Cost-of-services method.

Cents per case. This is a simple, easy-to-compute method. The contract specifies the allowance per case which is multiplied by the number of cases delivered during the period. Performance requirements are specified and may be simply two ads of one column inch per quarter. The contract may specify a special display in a given number of stores. There is no relationship between the amount received by the retailer and the cost of the service rendered.

Percentage of the invoice cost of merchandise for a specified period. The specified period is usually a quarter (thirteen weeks). This method is easy to compute and is based entirely on the dollar value of purchases. Performance is specified. There is no relationship between the amount paid and the services received. Contracts may vary from cents per case to percentage of purchases.

Cost-of-services method. This method provides for a reimbursement of all or a specified portion of prescribed advertising and display expenses. Performance can be specified, but supervising and auditing are difficult. Copies of ads must be submitted, but auditing in-store promotions is not practical or economical.

Under the first or second type of contract listed above, high-volume operators collect more money than is spent fulfilling the contract terms. Under the third type of contract, the cost-of-services method, the retailer may make a profit by charging the manufacturer at national line rates and making payments for displays and other services on a contracted rate basis.

In the food business, cooperative contracts have become a discount instead of a payment for services rendered. Auditing the services is difficult, if not impractical. Also, there is a tendency to do as little as possible in return for the payments.

Cooperative Contract Performance Provisions

Early cooperative advertising contracts specified one-column-inch ads to be inserted a specified number of times a quarter. This type of specification resulted in the use of one-inch boxes around the border of the store ad. The ads simply stated the product name and price. The trade referred to these ads as "obituary notices." They fulfilled the performance requirements, but accomplished little, if any, selling.

In recent years, performance provisions have been reviewed, criticized, and discussed in trade association meetings and in trade publications. As a result, most of the suppliers have revised their contracts. The tendency is to require a merchandising package that includes newspaper, radio and television advertising, handbills, displays, and other merchandising support. A concerted effort is being made by manufacturers to get value received for the money spent.

Cooperative Merchandising Agreements

Many companies have changed the contract title to "Cooperative Merchandising Agreement" or some other name that places the emphasis on service rather than the money paid by the supplier. Changing a name or title will not solve all the problems, but the emphasis on merchandising helps retailers think of the real objectives of the agreement.

An example of the innovations possible under the cooperative merchandising service concept is creative merchandising service. This service goes beyond the usual promotional allowances used by suppliers to merchandise their products to retailers. The creative merchandising service places at the disposal of the retailer the services of the staff, the advertising agencies, and the point-of-sale suppliers. The retailer has available what amounts to an individualized merchandising and advertising agency. These services include development of the retail store consumer image, merchandising and advertising ideas, and creative promotional programs.

Food retailers have used these services to develop better approaches to advertising, including the development of an effective format through the various media—newspaper, radio, television, and outdoor billboards. Custom-designed ads that promote the store image to shoppers have been designed for both large and small operators. Display units planned in connection with storewides or for specific merchandising campaigns also have been designed.

These consultation and development services are used by supermarket operators to develop a store decor that will create a favorable shopping image. Also retail-level research (in-store and marketing or customer related) is planned for food retailers and, if requested, the actual research is undertaken.

The retailer pays for the services by merchandising an agreed quantity of products. Each unit or product is assigned point values. Food retailers are encouraged through promotional channels to request services and indicate the type of assistance desired. The servicer's staff submits a proposal and the point cost—quantities of the merchandise required to earn the necessary points. The plan is modified in keeping with the point value quantities of merchandise the operator can handle. After agreement on the program, a contract is signed and production is undertaken.

Trade Practices

In an effort to get cooperative advertising on a sound business base, the Grocery Manufacturers of America drafted a Code of Trade Practices. The Code was approved by all the retail and wholesale trade groups. Suppliers, distributors, and retailers are committed to adhere to the Code.

Co-op Money

Most operators classify co-op money as nonoperating income, since payments are made quarterly—long after the goods have been sold. Therefore, the co-op money is not considered a discount in the sense that it is a reduction in the invoice cost which is reflected in the retail price.

The Future of Cooperative Merchandising

Cooperative merchandising agreements will continue to be used, since the supplier wants the merchandising push and the retailer wants to sell more merchandise. However, the retailer must keep foremost in mind that the primary function of the business is to sell merchandise and that any program that accomplishes this objective is beneficial. The supplier should understand the retailer's emphasis on product mix and merchandising problems. Flexibility is needed and will be successful when the spirit of cooperation to achieve greater sales prevails.

Incorporating cooperative advertising, cooperative merchandising, and creative merchandising service agreements can certainly help to make supermarket advertising more productive and possibly at a lower cost than it might have been without these manufacturers' aids.

CODE OF TRADE PRACTICES FOR THE GROCERY INDUSTRY BY THE GROCERY MANUFACTURERS OF AMERICA

1. Adopt the name Cooperative Merchandising Agreements covering any arrangement for advertising and promotion agreements between manufacturer and distributor.

2. Cooperative Merchandising Agreement will define:
   (a) the payments for specific advertising services,
   (b) payments for specific promotion service, and
   (c) that evidence of performance must be submitted before payment is made.

3. Distributors feel that Cooperative Merchandising Agreements generally limit participation to newspapers, handbills, and window posters and should be broadened to include radio, television, floor displays, and outdoor promotions.

4. Distributors and manufacturers agree that there must be performance of contract and evidence of performance submitted before the manufacturer should be expected to pay.

5. Manufacturers contend that they should not be called upon by distributors to pay extra money for participation in their special events. Such extra payments would legally obligate manufacturers to offer proportionately equal payments to all competing dealers, which is impractical.

6. Manufacturer may participate in distributor's special events which qualify under the terms of the performance of the contract when such cost is applied to the Cooperative Merchandising Agreement available to competing dealers.

7. Contract forms should be short, simple, understandable, and practical; be reviewed periodically and revised to fit changing conditions when necessary.

8. Cooperative Merchandising Agreement should emanate from the manufacturer.

9. Distributors feel that manufacturers can no longer handle Cooperative Merchandising Agreements on a mass basis and that they need to give consideration to what each distributor can do, especially as promotion, and then work out some arrangement within the spirit and the letter of the Robinson-Patman Act.

10. Distributors should receive prompt payment upon submission of their invoice and evidence of performance.

11. Any money received in payment of Cooperative Merchandising Agreement arrangements must not be considered as part of the price of merchandise or as a contribution to profit. Such payments should be made separately by the manufacturer to the distributor for services rendered. No such money should be deducted from the invoice covering the purchase of merchandise.

THE NEED FOR INNOVATION

The supermarket business is a traffic business. People eat every day; consequently, they shop more frequently for food than for any other type of merchandise. One of the functions of supermarket advertising is to generate the traffic needed to make each store profitable. Yet all supermarkets have a sameness —even a monotony. That is, nearly all supermarkets have automatic doors, shopping carts, gondolas, refrigerated cases, display cases, long aisles, nearly the same merchandise, and finally, similar checkout counters complete with checker. This similarity is continued or extended to supermarket advertising— that is, a catalog or listing of items and prices. Very few ads use editorial material, menu suggestions, information of interest, and shopping ideas. All this uniformity exists in a business in which difference generates distinction and projects a powerful image to the consumer desiring to serve attractive meals.

Supermarket advertising is criticized by writers in trade journals, by convention speakers, and by professional advertising people. Criticism is healthy since it forces supermarket operators to appraise, evaluate, and compare the job done by their ad people. As a result, more ads of a greater number of companies are becoming more varied and informative. The fact remains that producing weekly ads for essentially the same merchandise fifty-two weeks a year requires real creativity and originality.

Advertising agencies and mass media companies that consider food advertisers as important clients are interested in providing information, aids, and incentives to improve the food ads as well as public and customer relations.

Through the combined efforts of trade associations, writers, speakers, advertising agencies, and the media, food ads should continue to improve and generate more traffic for the supermarket.

With the advent of the self-service market, the opportunity for selling by display within the store increased. In the service store, the clerk behind the counter has the opportunity to exert personal selling influence on each customer. Self-service has made it necessary for products to sell themselves; therefore, self-service merchandising has made packaging and displays increasingly important. The merchandise package must be an effective selling device. Packages and labels are continually being redesigned to increase their sales appeal. The strategic location and appealing display of these items in the market comprise the store-level contribution to the self-service marketing process. Each time a store manager contemplates a display, he should ask himself the following question: Will it arouse the customer to try it? This is the decisive element of all store display.

SHELF DISPLAYS

While many managers may not think of it as such, the first and foremost form of display is the store's basic shelf area—properly utilized. Most stores consider or assume that displays mean merchandise artistically or massively arranged, forgetting that their shelves are, without a doubt, the most important display form that they have at their disposal.

Considering the fact that only about 5 percent of total store sales are the result of special displays, the obvious importance of shelf displays becomes more apparent. Self-selling of merchandise is aided by:

- Visibility
- Easy-to-reach merchandise
- Neat appearance
- Adequate facings
- Full shelf stocking
- Attractive packaging
- Price marking
- Fixed shelf locations
- Stock rotation.

Visibility. Merchandise being placed on the shelf should be displayed with all labels facing front, toward the customer. The eye-level locations should be

allocated to impulse items with high volume and good profit margins. Shelf space should be allocated on the basis of sales to increase the appeal to customers and to increase shelf stocking efficiency. With declining profit margins, visibility of items on the shelves is extremely important as a means of increasing both sales per square foot and gross margin dollars, while decreasing costs.

Easy-to-Reach Merchandise. Stocking merchandise on the top shelf must be done with the customer's ability to reach it in mind. Every effort must be made to keep the merchandise on the top shelf low enough so that it is within easy reach. This facilitates shopping, improves the appearance of the entire store, and permits better surveillance against pilferage. Although shelving may be high to create maximum sales area and sales per square foot, merchandise on the top shelf must be kept within reasonable limits.

Neat Appearance. Merchandise should be dusted at regular intervals. Unattractive, soiled or dented

Sloppy shelves in self-service markets send a message to many customers—this manager runs a sloppy operation. It becomes important, therefore, for section managers to make sure that shelf displays are neat and inventories maintained, as in this health and beauty aids section.

products should be removed from the shelf and marked down for quick sale (providing it is not in violation of local regulation applicable to the sale of dented merchandise). Loosened labels on salable merchandise should be refixed; while cans without labels should be identified, marked down, and put into a separate display (usually a "dump").

Adequate Facings. The number of facings should be allocated according to volume in order to insure sales appeal and restocking efficiency. Established facings should be maintained for control of shelf stock and to facilitate turnover.

Although it is generally considered best to allocate facings based on the volume done by each item, variations on this have been used effectively. Such variations have only been effective in large, high-volume stores, and they have had to be done extremely subtly because, if manipulation becomes apparent, it totally loses its effect and hurts the store. The variations consist of one- or two-facing shifts from the highest-volume brand in favor of the best-profit brand—generally the house-brand. It must be assured that stocks are never permitted to run out. Testing has shown that under the described circumstances, some changes in sales mix have been affected.

Full Shelf Stocking. Well-stocked shelves give a mass effect and sell merchandise; it takes mass to sell mass. You cannot do business with empty shelves; shelves should be kept filled with merchandise.

When out-of-stocks are unavoidable, a number of chains put fast-moving impulse items temporarily into the space that normally would be occupied by the out-of-stock. To mollify the customer, it is considered good practice to put a hand-printed shelf talker at the substituted facing saying something like: "Sorry, we're temporarily out of 46-ounce Brand X widgets. We hope to have them back in stock on (date)."

Attractive Packaging. In self-service stores, the package is more than a container designed to protect the contents; in a sense, the package is a selling tool also. Customers spend an average of twenty-five minutes shopping. This means that selecting items from the thousands of products available is done at a rapid pace. Therefore, the package with the greatest appeal and visual attraction gets the most consideration and sales. Package design, including label design, is a highly specialized business. Supermarket operators are interested in the sales appeal of the packages as well as the shelf space required to stock them efficiently. It is also important that packages be reasonably pilfer-proof. For example, caps on bottles and jars should not be interchangeable in order to prevent pilferers from exchanging low-priced caps for higher priced units.

Price Marking. Price marking may become a thing of the past when scanning and the Universal Product Code become the universally accepted pricing mechanism. However, while price marking is a "way of life," there are basic procedures that are important. Items must be price-marked correctly at all times, both for consumer confidence and for conformance with government regulations. Shelf price tags (including unit pricing, where used) must be kept up-to-date, and prices must be changed on merchandise when it is on sale.

Fixed Shelf Locations. Customers become accustomed to finding items in certain locations, so changes should be kept within department units and made only for valid reasons. The position of these products should conform with the aisle markers.

Stock Rotation. Movement of product from the rear to the front of the shelf when restocking will comply with the tested and proven merchandising concept of "first in, first out." Rotation whenever the shelves are stocked will minimize accumulation of old stock and spoilage, and will insure fresh inventory. In addition, many product now have "last sale dates," and many others will be added.

Shelf Extenders

Shelf extenders provide a method for improving the effectiveness of shelf displays. They may be constructed of plywood, wire, or metal, extending the display area of conventional shelving. Wire baskets into which merchandise is dumped or shelves on which merchandise is neatly displayed also may be used.

TRAY PACK

The tray-pack method of displaying dry grocery items is another popular way of stocking products, both on shelves (if that many facings fit into shelf plans) and in mass displays. (See page 92 for a description of the tray-pack method.)

A newer and widely used method of outer case wrapping consists of using a film overwrap on the tray pack (actually half cases). Stacking the merchandise in its designated area and removing the film is fairly simple, and the merchandise is held securely until it is displayed.

Among the advantages of the tray pack are:

1. A customer selecting merchandise from a mass display will generally select items from the top layer, front to back, minimizing the "cavity look."
2. Out-of-stock conditions are reduced due to greater ease and efficiency in stocking.

Grab their attention! That is the message of all three of these large-effort displays. Clockwise, from top left: merchandise creates a walk-through display featuring an extensive variety of baskets, pots, and accessories; storefront display of cookout items forms a giant "barbecue pit" and paid off in doubling sales; large plastic tree identifies plant department, spotlights help to accent theme and merchandise.

3. Less time is required in stocking
4. Stock rotation is simplified.
5. Keeping shelves clean is easier.
6. Mass displays are easier to assemble.

A disadvantage can result from allowing the number of facings to be governed by the shelf display packout because it can reduce the variety of products stocked. Another disadvantage occurs when a tray is replaced and a few cans are left from the old tray; sometimes, they are difficult to place.

SPECIAL DISPLAYS

Merchandise properly arranged on the shelves forms the background for good interior display. Special displays, however, provide the basic means for drawing the customer's attention to the merchandise that has been specially selected.

The key to successful displays is the supermarket manager. He or she decides when, where, what, and how to display. The manager knows the value of the various special display locations and the type of display to use in each spot, and decides the product mix that will produce the balanced sales needed to achieve the gross profit goals. In some chain operations, displays are planned by headquarters with limited authority delegated to the manager. This may minimize fullest utilization of the manager's knowledge and experience as it applies to local needs and conditions.

The following are "attention-getters" that tend to attract customers to displays:

- Motion
- Color
- Mass
- Cartoons
- Lighting effects
- Unusual arrangements
- Demonstrations

The mass display of sale-priced cheese in large carts is often used to move fast-turn items. Frequently, these promotions are coordinated with newspaper ads so customers will be pre-sold when they go to market.

- Sampling
- Point-of-purchase signs.

Types of special displays used by supermarket and other mass merchandise operators include:

- Mass displays
- Multiple-item displays
- Jumble displays.

Mass Displays

Mass displays are used basically for staples or well-accepted products with a high turnover. They are based on the principle that it takes mass to attract enough attention to sell a large quantity. Often, feature items at traffic-building prices are displayed in large attention-getting quantities, usually in tray-pack units. Some stores use dummy stands for background with mass displays in the foreground for consumer selection purposes. This is done in the belief that in conjunction with the advertising, the mass display accomplishes the creation of a low-price image. Logically, some part of the mass display area should be devoted to regularly priced merchandise with high-volume potential. The item selected for the mass display should be made with a balanced selling concept and gross margin controls in mind.

Care must be taken that mass displays are not so overpowering or massively created that they inhibit selection from them. Some customers are hesitant about "breaking" a symmetrical display or find it difficult to take product from the top of a high, bulky display.

In order to have a "handle" on sales productivity, records should be kept of sales performance, price, and gross margin of the items used for mass displays. Comparison should be made of the relative success of the item when displayed in various locations in the store; this can be very helpful in planning other sales and displays. Proper input to the data processing center will be a most helpful guide to future display programs.

Multiple-Item Displays

Multiple-item displays are used to display a number of items, related or unrelated, in close proximity. They should be planned in such a way as to sell more merchandise than single-item displays. Analyses and record keeping have shown single-item displays to sell as many as five times normal shelf sales, while multiple-item displays have been known to increase sales ten times or more than the norm for the same item on the shelf.

Although mass displays of single items effectively increase sales, maximum sales are not usually achieved because single-item displays limit their appeal only to shoppers wishing to buy that item. Multiple-item displays are of interest to a greater number of shoppers. The aim is to display more items, get more exposure, thus achieve greater sales.

This desired result is not automatic, however. The display should be planned to include items that have high-volume potential and can be displayed together in such a way as to increase the sales of all items. The items selected for multiple-item display may be related or unrelated, but should be compatible in order to sell large quantities of merchandise.

Jumble Displays
(Shopping Cart or "Dump" Displays)

Jumble displays utilize various types of containers or bases, such as shopping carts, wire baskets, bins, tables, or dump display units supplied by manufacturers. Since the merchandise is "dumped" into the container, the cost of setting up the display is low. Usually each display is stocked with one item. Jumble or dump displays need "talking signs" which convey a message suggesting uses or events for which the item may be used.

Shopping cart displays are popular because:

1. They take little time to arrange; just dump the product into the cart (or basket), and affix a sign.

Grouping related merchandise in multiple-item displays often leads to improved sales figures. You shop for meat and immediately above you find displays of carving knives, seasoning and condiments, utensils, and still higher, roasting pans of varying sizes. It provides a good opportunity for tie-in selling.

So-called dump displays, such as those shown here featuring grocery items in wire baskets, have the virtue, from a store point-of-view, of being inexpensive and easy to set up. Similar displays in actual shopping carts have the added virtue of being mobile. Patrons used to such displays do not seem to mind the jumble.

2. They are mobile; they can be pushed to any desired area.
3. They are effective; customers take note of these displays.

Shopping cart displays have several disadvantages, however:

1. Many customers, without looking closely, will assume that the laden display cart is one being used by another customer who is further up or down the aisle.
2. Some customers will assume that the laden display cart is abandoned, and they might even put some item that they have changed their minds about into the display cart, creating confusion for other customers.
3. Because of its mobility, the cart may be pushed to an area where it was not meant to be and/or where it may block other merchandise. (There are less-mobile wire display racks or bins that are designed for such displays, and managers are probably better off using such display material rather than the carts.)

Another disadvantage is more an operational one and ties into a rule that many retailers make: Use carts only for shopping or placing abandoned merchandise back onto the shelves.

A rule of thumb used by many retailers to determine the number of shopping carts that should be available to the store is to count the number of customers using the store during the highest traffic hour, and then divide this figure by two. If there is a large parking lot in which customers leave carts after loading their cars, this figure may have to be revised, depending on how many carriage retrievers the store uses and how frequently they pick up the carriages. Customers who arrive at a store to shop and find they must wait for carts, may select another store on their next shopping trip.

Jumble displays in baskets can be placed or moved around anywhere in the store. When used in the aisle, a "sore thumb" display for related or tie-in selling is effective, but it must not block traffic or obscure regular merchandise displays. They can be used to suggest tie-in or related items and/or to attract attention. A handmade sign can be prepared at store level to give the impression of a "manager's sale."

Records should be kept of these jumble displays, indicating their effectiveness by item, type of container used, location, price, etc. If the store is a single unit, these records are extremely critical. If the store is a branch of a chain that is governed by headquarters, these records may help the manager to follow instructions or to use initiative if he or she is given latitude.

These records will tell the manager which items to feature.

The store manager, the records, and personal initiative and imagination play an important part in a successful in-store display program. While some displays are contracted for as part of a cooperative advertising program and others are designated by the merchandiser, the store manager has the opportunity to select some of the special displays. Some companies give the store manager very little authority in determining what to display, but there usually are no rules restricting the use of small dump or jumble displays. For example, a basket of topping syrups in front of the ice cream cabinet can prove effective. The manager must be aggressive and imaginative in planning store displays.

Planning for special displays should include not only what to display and when, but expected sales based on figures for previous periods, cost, inventory needed, and man-hours required to set up the display in relation to the labor budget.

WHERE TO DISPLAY

Determining the best display location for each item must be given a great deal of serious thought. The manager or merchandiser should consider the following:

Customer traffic patterns. The store manager knows the heavy traffic areas and traffic flow patterns of the store. This knowledge can be utilized to determine the best locations for displays. Displays must not block customer traffic patterns.

Effective positioning. Displays should be located so that the surroundings add to sales appeal. A good example would be the location of a "sore thumb" display in the regular display area. Related and multi-item displays, as well as an occasional out-of-place display, attract attention. If not used too frequently, the out-of-the-ordinary display can be effective. In order to be totally effective and to maintain the customer image, displays should be located logically and should be a part of an organized shopping pattern.

In planning the regular (permanent) shelf positioning of a product, its effectiveness must be considered. Demand items should pull customers through the store and expose them to impulse merchandise. The layout pattern must make shopping easy, convenient, and logical. Effective positioning will increase impulse sales.

SIGNS

Displays must have signs to attract customers and to add to sales appeal. Signs that are predominantly price markers tend to add to the price image of the store.

"Talking" signs are informational, suggesting menus, preparation, use, source, quality, or special purchase; they are effective sales builders. These talking signs can make shopping interesting and help to build a favorable store image.

Since the purpose of display signs is to sell more merchandise, it must be designed to achieve greater sales appeal. Signs should be compatible with the merchandise, the display, the decor of the store, and the clientele. They must be timely and convey a message of interest. Variety is essential in terms of size, design, message, style, colors, etc.

"Shelf talkers" add sales appeal to regular shelf displays and convey buying messages to shoppers—"as advertised," "new item," "new low price," "new pack," "good value," "new size," etc. These signs, when well-positioned, can help to bring traffic to poorly shopped sections of a gondola. Observations indicate that customers look at end displays and take five to eight short steps before looking closely at merchandise on the shelves. They then take another series of steps and look again. Shelf talkers attract attention and promote more complete shopping.

Simple, homemade signs can prove to be effective. Some merchandisers, however, do not agree with this concept; they feel that the quality of the sign used reflects upon the store image, and therefore, they do not permit the use of handmade signs. Store image is more a reflection of the overall impression, however. A few store-made signs, interspersed throughout the store and attracting attention by being different, will not adversely affect the store image.

Signs attract the shopper's attention to more of the many thousands of items during the typical twenty to twenty-five minute shopping tour of the supermarket, helping to sell more merchandise.

In the past, when a form of food retailing became obsolete, such as the trading post and the general store, another form of food distribution replaced it. The main competitive advantage of early supermarkets over food specialty stores was lower prices and larger varieties. Currently, with intense intra-industry competition and with growing inter-industry rivalries (discount houses, drug chains, department and variety stores, and even service stations), supermarket operators must reassess their position in the food distribution function in the American economy and seek to gain competitive advantage lest they, too, become obsolete.

The main function of the food retailer is to supply goods and services to customers. Since the goods the food retailer supplies are produced, for the most part, by other segments of the food industry, the supermarket offers services to the customer. Customer services include all those functions the food retailer performs that impart value, comfort, pleasure, or satisfaction to the customers.

Providing services other than those directly related to the products sold have long been held by the industry to be an expense which they regard as "frills" to be minimized or avoided. However, the nature and extent of customer services may be one of the ways a supermarket operator can achieve a competitive advantage.

THE NATURE AND OBJECTIVES OF CUSTOMER SERVICES

Customer services are all the activities and facilities within the supermarket premises and surrounding area that will provide customers with value, comfort, pleasure, and satisfaction, as well as with those conveniences that make shopping a pleasure.

The "name of the game" is to increase traffic and, thereby, sales. By providing selected services that will induce customers to choose his or her store and return regularly to make purchases, the supermarket operator can increase sales.

Shopping for food and household necessities is most often regarded as a chore and a bore for the customer, and it is incumbent upon the supermarket operator to make this task a more pleasant one—one that can be accomplished as easily and quickly as possible.

Types of customer services include:

- Ample space and facilities to park the car, and for children, pets, and packages
- Easy entry and egress
- Comfortable, temperature-controlled environment
- Available carts for loading merchandise
- Goods arranged so that they can be easily located
- Full shelves—never out
- Rest-room facilities
- Pleasant, helpful personnel
- Accepting payment by check
- Check cashing privileges for regular, registered customers
- Banking services on premises (bank branch office)
- Advertised specials announced on a public address system
- Soft background music
- Uncluttered aisles
- A wide selection of items, other than food, which the customer buys frequently
- In-store promotions, such as in-store coupons, continuity programs (selling one item from a set of dishes or pots each week), games, and trading stamps.

TYPES OF CUSTOMER SERVICES

A large number of customer services are offered in supermarkets today, but rarely does any single supermarket include in its operations *all* the customer services being offered by the industry. Each supermarket provides the type of customer services that its management feels is justified and necessary to attract customer traffic.

Customer services may be categorized as follows:

- Appearance of store and special facilities
- Courtesy booth services

- Merchandising services
- Checkout services
- Personal services.

Appearance of Store and Special Facilities

This aspect of customer services is concerned mainly with the physical factors involved in the appearance of a modern supermarket, including:

- Cleanliness
- Parking facilities
- Proper store temperature
- Automatic doors
- Rest rooms and lounges
- Store layout
- Shopping carts
- Public address system.

Cleanliness. The old adage, "Cleanliness is next to godliness," holds as true today as ever, especially where food is concerned. People are highly aware of cleanliness. It is not strange, therefore, that shoppers use cleanliness in evaluating the quality of the supermarket they patronize.

Cleanliness begins in the parking lot and the exterior of the building, including the entrance of the store. Often the least attractive area of a supermarket is the entrance, where that vital first impression is formed. Stores that allow this condition to exist are not

making maximum use of the positive impact resulting from the maintenance of clean facilities.

The floor of the supermarket must be kept clean. Debris on the floor is not only dangerous, but also unsightly. Spills from broken merchandise should be cleaned immediately in order to keep carts from going through the spills and spreading them, as well as to help prevent customers from possibly slipping and falling. If a customer bypasses an entire aisle because of a messy condition there, it may cost the store much more than the extra effort spent between a quick cleanup and a more leisurely one.

Odors also are a major source of customer annoyance. Spoiled foods should never be permitted to remain in the store, let alone the selling areas. The odors of rotting produce, fish, or meats in the back room carries into the store proper and is as much of a customer deterrent as the same odors emanating from the selling floor. Ventilation systems should be used to carry away the odors of strong cheese and those that accompany fresh fish and deli departments.

The cleanliness and personal hygiene of a store's employees is just as vital to the success of the supermarket as the cleanliness of the selling area.

Even if the foods purchased by the consumer are all sealed in containers, the image of a dirty or smelly store carries over in the minds of most shoppers to the packaged goods as well. When customers are questioned about the factors which influence their shopping habits, cleanliness appears near the top of the list.

Photo courtesy of Giant Food Inc.

The suburban supermarket, generally part of a shopping center, must be able to tell its patrons: We have adequate, convenient parking facilities. That means roomy parking stalls, adequate exits and entrances, wide lanes, good signage, cleanliness, good lighting and security.

Parking Facilities. Supermarket operators were the first retailers to recognize the importance of adequate parking facilities.

Early stores were built in crowded downtown areas or in the center of neighborhood districts. Most customers patronizing these stores lived nearby and, therefore, parking facilities were not considered an essential customer service. Today, people living in cities still shop in neighborhood stores. Frequently, they may be carrying packages from previous shopping stops along the way. These city stores would do well to consider facilities for storing packages.

Suburban customers have different shopping habits. They may shop once or twice a week for their major purchases and stop for fill-ins on other days. The parking lot is an important factor in suburban shopping in particular. Such customers are usually unable to carry all their purchases and live far enough away so that it is necessary to use an automobile in order to shop. Thus, adequate parking facilities are a basic and needed service a suburban supermarket must offer its customers. If a supermarket does not have a parking lot, or only an inadequate one in which the parking stalls are so narrow that it is necessary to squeeze out of the car, the customer will simply drive to a competitor.

Proper Store Temperature. Air-conditioning and heating equipment (in climates where it is required) is standard in supermarkets. It is important to keep the store temperature at a level where customers are not too hot or too cold. Personal comfort is important to the customer and may affect the length of time spent and the number of purchases made in the store.

Particular attention must be paid to the frozen foods area, particularly in the summer. Often a great deal of cold "leaks" out of the coffin cases. Shoppers in the summer are generally clad very lightly. A frigid zone often is created in this area, which drives the shopper out a lot faster than their shopping needs would dictate. They will often choose another store where they "won't catch cold" for this reason alone.

Automatic Doors. Automatic doors are a customer service as well as a goodwill builder. Opening the door for each customer is an invitation to enter; both a courtesy and a service. Automatic doors are especially appreciated by the shopper with an armload of groceries or a cart filled with groceries.

The use of "in" and "out" doors helps direct traffic without creating an impression of being directed. Definite traffic patterns are established for the store, and at the same time a favorable store image is created.

Rest Rooms and Lounges. Two relatively new customer services are the installation in supermarkets of rest rooms and lounges for the customers' convenience. These are new services in the sense that they are slowly gaining prominence in the industry as a whole.

Many companies maintain that customers do not need this service. Some claim that pilferers use the privacy of these rooms to hide items in their clothing. On the other hand, others feel that rest rooms are a valuable service which is highly appreciated by customers, especially those bringing children with them when they shop.

Rest-room facilities are essential to superstore operations where customers spend more time shopping for nonfood items and remain in the store for longer periods of time. The lounges furnished in some of the supermarkets consist of an air-conditioned room; magazines, newspapers, and in some cases, television sets, are provided.

To be an attractive customer service, rest rooms and lounges must be maintained. Customers judge the entire store by the condition of any part or section. It is better not to have any lounge or rest room than to have one that is poorly maintained.

Shoppers in markets without customer rest rooms are often directed to employee facilities. This type of facility is usually located near a back room or in a downstairs storeroom and may create an unfavorable impression of the store.

Store Layout. Many customer services are first formulated on the drawing boards of the designers, architects, and layout specialists who plan the supermarket. These people know that management must be conscious of the cost involved in building a supermarket. Within this framework, however, everything should be done to provide the customer with the most modern and comfortable structure possible.

Shopping Carts. Shopping carts are essential in operating a modern supermarket since most customers buy far more merchandise than they are able to carry in their arms or in hand baskets. Also, shopping carts are used by customers to transport purchases to their cars, thereby reducing the amount of carry-out services required.

Shopping carts should be removed from parking lots promptly so that they do not obstruct parking stalls and so that a sufficient number of carts are available for use by other customers. Shopping carts should be kept clean and in good working order; it is frustrating for a customer to try to move a cart with wheels that will not turn. A damaged cart may result in damaged merchandise. Also, keeping carts in good order reduces the expense of replacement; with the cost of carts constantly increasing, this is an economy measure.

Public Address System. Many shoppers do not have an opportunity to read the advertisements placed in newspapers, and they may purchase items image. Also, the use of the public address system can help the store move products that require quick disposal because of perishability.

Excitement and extra sales can be built to a store's advantage by the proper use of the public address system. "Unadvertised specials" announced over the system, particularly when the store is crowded, accomplish this effectively. On the East Coast, Waldbaum's is a primary example of a chain that uses this technique to advantage. In the late hours, announcements over the public address system often are used to clear out perishables that the manager does not want to carry over until the following morning, when they must be marked down more sharply than in the evening special or even discarded.

Courtesy Booth Services

Many supermarket operators have found it advantageous to install courtesy booths. These booths are generally located in the vicinity of the checkout counters near the front of the store and are designed to provide a central location for the handling of a number of customer services.

Courtesy booths may be used to perform one or more of the following services:

- Cashing checks
- Redeeming coupons
- Handling bottle returns
- Handling returned merchandise and customer complaints
- Issuing rainchecks
- Selling big-ticket, small items
- Providing miscellaneous services
- Selling tobacco items.

These same services are generally provided in all supermarkets, whether or not courtesy booths are used. Each of these services is discussed below.

Cashing Checks. Check cashing has become an integral part of supermarket operation. Personal checks made out by customers for the amount of merchandise purchased, as well as other personal checks, traveler's checks, government checks, and payroll checks are cashed by supermarket operators. In many ways, the supermarket resembles a medium-size bank. One New England chain handles an average of 100,000 checks a year, amounting to over $5 million. Some stores cash checks totalling two to three times store volume each week.

On the basis of average pre-tax earnings of 1 percent net profit, a store would have to sell $3,000 worth of merchandise to make up for the loss on a $30 bad check. To keep bad check losses at a minimum, a few companies use protective identification devices,

Photo courtesy of Harris-Teeter Super Markets, Inc., Charlotte, North Carolina.

Customer convenience in carrying purchases to the checkstand, and then getting purchases to cars, is essential to the supermarket that hopes to gain success. In the photograph at top, the shopping cart eliminates the need for the customer to lift purchases from the cart onto the checkstand conveyor. And when the customer is really stocking up, as in bottom photograph, help from a store clerk becomes crucial.

suggested to them on a public address system. This system may be connected to the music system, or it may be an independent unit. The suggestions made on the public address system should truly be considered a public service to the customer, and the message should not be "blasted," but kept within the store

Keep them smiling is the message here, with a variety of services offered to keep customers happy. Among other things, the courtesy booth of this store cashes payroll checks, sells registered checks as well as lottery tickets, offers cigarettes for immediate purchase, offers film processing, and runs a stamp machine.

such as photoelectric machines which take pictures on film to identify the individual tendering the check, the date, the hour, and the check; or identification cards provided to regular customers upon request.

Although there are costs involved in cashing checks, most supermarket operators feel that the return in customer satisfaction more than overcomes the expense. They point out that customers spend more money in a store that cashes their paychecks than in stores that do not. The customer may be prompted to buy something in a store offering this service even when the purpose for entering was to cash a check. Finally, by using proper equipment and an efficient check-cashing system, the supermarket will keep the losses from check cashing to a reasonable minimum.

Regardless of which of these attitudes are held by supermarket operators, check cashing must be looked upon as a highly desirable customer service used by a great many customers.

Redeeming Coupons. Another customer service is the redemption of manufacturer coupons. These coupons are premium offers made to increase sales. Accepting coupons slows the checkout procedure, creates additional clerical work in claiming redemption, and ties up capital until payment is received from the manufacturer.

Despite these disadvantages, coupons are an effective promotional device. They induce customers to buy the couponed item and tend to force retailers to stock the merchandise. The attitude of food suppliers is that as long as the customer redemption rate remains high, coupons will continue to be a prime promotional

tool, and retailers will have to stock the merchandise and redeem the coupons.

Most stores have the cashier handle coupon redemption as part of the checkout procedure; cashiers are instructed not to accept the coupon unless accompanied by a purchase of the item.

In recent years, one promotional tool that has come into ever greater use is the device of double or even triple couponing—that is giving the customer twice or three times the face value of the manufacturer's coupon.

This is a costly promotion, but once one store or chain in an area starts the practice, it is almost mandatory for the competition to match the promotion or risk losing customers. The initiator of the promotion generally hopes to get the jump on his competitors so that he can attract new customers to his store before the competition can react. Once started, this promotional device is difficult to end, since each factor in the market is afraid to end the practice, lest the competition continues it and gains a competitive advantage.

Handling Bottle Returns. Receiving empty bottles and refunding deposit money to customers may once again become an important service. Many supermarkets handle bottle returns at the checkstand. In keeping with the trend of removing as many extraneous tasks from the checkstands as possible, efforts are being made by some companies to perform this service in other parts of the store.

Some supermarkets have a bottle return area adjacent to a back-room work area. Customers ring a bell when requesting service, and an employee assists them. Other companies have located conveyors inside their courtesy booths to handle bottle returns. The empty bottles are lowered into a basement area for temporary storage.

The use of nonreturnable bottles and cartons has greatly reduced the bottle return volume. However, in order to discourage littering, a number of states and municipalities have instituted mandatory deposits on "nonreturnable" bottles and cans.

Strong efforts have been made over the past few years to get a federal law to ban no-returns or at least place mandatory deposits on all no-return, soft-drink containers. There is some question as to how effective such laws are in reducing or eliminating litter. Quite effective to date have been recycling efforts tied in with supermarkets.

A difficulty faced by all supermarkets is the extra costs and sanitation problems involved in handling the additional returned containers brought about by such laws. The store must hire additional personnel to handle and sort the containers. Few, if any, customers clean the containers before returning them, and thus a serious sanitation problem arises. Also, a great deal of extra space is required at the store for sorting, handling, and storing the containers.

Handling Returned Merchandise and Customer Complaints. If it is properly staffed, the courtesy booth provides the supermarket with an excellent means of receiving returned merchandise and handling customer complaints. Although people performing this customer service will be confronted by habitual "gripers" and "complainers," for the most part, customers complain because they have a legitimate reason, or at least they feel their complaint is justified. The person handling complaints should avoid any further irritation of the customer.

The method used to handle a complaint is vital to maintaining customer goodwill. If customers are antagonized, they will no longer shop in the store. Courteous, efficient handling of complaints improves the store image and helps build goodwill.

Issuing Rainchecks. The Federal Trade Commission frowns on out-of-stocks on advertised specials. One way to ease its displeasure (after convincing the FTC that all possible effort was made to have an adequate amount of such merchandise on hand) and appease the customer is the issuance of a raincheck for the out-of-stock item.

Before issuing the raincheck, the courtesy booth attendant should offer the customer a substitute, such as a similar reduction on a different size of the same item or on a competitive brand. If this does not satisfy the customer, a raincheck should be issued with the utmost courtesy and an apology for not having the item.

Selling Big-Ticket, Small Items. As supermarkets have added general merchandise items, one of the problems has been how to eliminate pilferage of small items that have high prices. One solution was the creation of the blister pack on a fairly large backing, which discourages insertion into a pocket.

However, some items, such as wristwatches, traditionally are offered for close inspection by the consumer. Here the manning of a courtesy booth makes it a natural place for the sale of such goods. Such sales generally are rung up right at the courtesy booth.

Once one such item is handled at the courtesy booth, it could lead to a host of similar items being sold there, and in many stores, it creates a profit center in what otherwise would be only a service area.

Providing Miscellaneous Services. Several other customer services—such as collecting utility bills and selling traveler's checks and money orders—may be handled at courtesy booths. Some supermarkets offer film developing services to their customers.

Selling Tobacco Items. Since cigarettes have become so expensive and are so easy to pilfer, many stores have placed them behind the courtesy counter so that they are paid for as soon as selected.

Merchandising Services

A merchandising service is any planned activity on the part of a retailer that is designed to implement the presentation of goods to consumers. Among the many factors involved in merchandising services are:

- Price
- Price identification techniques
- Labeling and packaging
- Displays
- Quality
- Variety
- Special promotions
- Aids for locating merchandise
- Service departments.

Price. Perhaps one of the most sought-after merchandising services is low price. Supermarket operators perform a valuable service by offering merchandise at prices that are a real value. People do not expect their supermarket to have the lowest prices in town on every item, but they do expect the store to be competitive. Fair prices commensurate with competitive conditions are characteristic of the food industry.

Price Identification Techniques. Merchandise must be legibly price marked. This not only aids customer shopping, but is also an aid to people who like to check their order when they get home. Also, there is a reduction in the amount of congestion at checkout lanes (where no scanning is available) when effective price-marking techniques are used.

There are a variety of price-marking techniques. The sale price of a unit of merchandise may be attached by stamping the price or by using a label gun to attach the price. Prices should also be placed on the moldings of the shelves where food is displayed. In many countries, cities and states, retailers are required by law to place unit prices on the shelf moldings. Since many items of canned and prepackaged merchandise are packed in less than full ounces, pints, quarts, or one hundred count, the prices for these items must appear in comparable full measure or weight on the unit price shelf marker. Maintaining unit pricing on shelf labels has been a problem; some stores use individual unit price labels on all products, either placed on the item or on the shelf marker.

Labeling and Packaging. Food manufacturers are responsible for convenient labeling and packaging of food products. Federal and state laws specify the type of information required on all packaged food items. These requirements include: net weight, ingredients, packer or distributor, grade (on some items), and other information.

The placement of the Universal Product Code (UPC) on the label of canned and prepackaged merchandise is revolutionizing the supermarket industry;

it is anticipated that during the 1980's, most major food chains will have installed the computer hardware needed to utilize the standardized Universal Product Code. (See pages 66-69 for a more detailed description of the UPC and technological changes in front-end operations.)

The purpose of the UPC is to increase speed and accuracy at the checkout counter, to eliminate pricing errors, and to improve inventory efficiency. The UPC is made up of bars called the *symbol*. The numbers printed under the symbol identify the manufacturer and the item. The thickness of the bars of the symbols are "read" as the cashier passes the item over an electronic scanner built into the checkstand. The scanner translates, through the use of a preprogrammed computer, the UPC symbol into an item description and price which appears on the cash register view screen and is printed on the cash register tape. The checker, after moving items over the scanner, is only required to make change and bag the items purchased.

Consumer advocates object to not having each item price marked. These advocates would like to see laws preventing a change of price once articles are placed on shelves and have had some such laws passed. Proponents of the system have expressed fear that states might adopt laws that are overly restrictive.

Since the late 1960's, federal, state and local governments have been considering legislation to require "open dates"—legible to the consumer—on packaged, perishable foods, and many local governments have passed such legislation. (New York City has had such a law since 1971.)

More than 55 percent of the food processors surveyed by the U.S. Department of Agriculture (USDA) have reported using some form of open dating. Fluid dairy products, other refrigerated foods, and baked goods are the items usually open-dated.

Open dating is called a consumer right by its advocates, and is often perceived by consumers as an assurance of product freshness and quality; there is little doubt that the use of legible dates at least encourages wholesalers and retail stores to improve inventory control.

There are four distinct types of open dates in general use:

- Pack date
- Pull date
- Quality assurance date
- Expiration date.

The *pack date* is the date of final processing or packaging. The *pull date* is the last recommended day of retail sale which allows enough time to store and use the product at home. The *quality assurance date* is the date after which the product is not likely to be at peak quality. It may be expressed as "Best when used before..." and often appears on cereal products. The *expiration date* is the last day the product should be used to assure quality. A processor who voluntarily uses an open date is not obliged under federal regulations to explain it.

Recognizing the need for the consumer information required to prepare balanced, nutritional meals, the Food and Drug Administration (FDA) and Federal Trade Commission (FTC) are working on rules to guide producers, packers, and supermarkets on adding nutritional information to their label and/or packages of selected items.

Displays. Displays are an effective way to stock merchandise and can increase sales by taking advantage of in-store traffic. There are many different types of displays, including: shelf displays, end-of-aisle displays, aisle displays, dump displays, and checkstand displays.

Since supermarket operators seek to obtain the greatest return for their advertising dollar, displays are frequently tied to store and national brand advertising.

Displaying related items next to each other (in addition to having them available in their usual shelf positions) can increase sales. Customers appreciate the convenience of being able to locate more easily that for which they are looking. Grouping all cake mixes together, for example, or grouping related items, such as cake mixes and frosting items, in the same display or on the same shelf, is an aid to customer shopping. (See Chapter 17 for a more detailed discussion about store display.)

Quality. To be effective, the merchandiser must offer the consumer "value," i.e., the quality of the products should be in line with the price—a good value for the money.

Variety. In addition to self-service merchandise methods, the modern supermarket offers its customers a large variety of items. This helps balance store image. One-stop shopping is an appreciated convenience which helps promote a greater sales volume.

Special Promotions. The supermarket operator must entice large numbers of customers to come into the store and buy merchandise. Promotions are vital factors in developing sales volume for the store and provide an element of interest for the consumer.

The kinds of promotions used by supermarket operators include: holiday and seasonal promotions; special events; "specials"; leaders; multiple-unit pricing; games; coupons (cents off on a particular item); continuities (a series of related sales spread over a period of time; e.g., a set of dishes or encyclopedias);

trading stamps; and promotional games (bingo, lottery, and the like).

The supermarket operator can be sure that a successful promotion will soon be imitated by competitors. Promotions run in cycles. As customer interest fades, new promotions are devised; frequently, old promotions are recycled. (Also refer to Chaper 16, "Advertising and Sales Promotion.")

Aids for Locating Merchandise. Greater sales result from the use of aids for locating merchandise, such as aisle markers and store directories. They also have a positive psychological effect on customers. Frustration and irritation are greatly reduced when customers are able to quickly and easily locate specific items on the shopping list. Aisle markers and store directories should be easy to read; therefore, location, color, and size of type are important considerations.

Service Departments. All the service departments added to the supermarket are an effort to win extra sales or traffic by providing a service that the customer desires. This is true for the service deli, bakery, etc. Additional service departments or boutiques vary from shoe repair shops, such as Schwegmann stores have in the New Orleans area, to film service booths, found in many stores in many areas.

These service departments must provide something that the customer desires in order to be effective for the store as a traffic and/or profit builder. Supermarkets that have service departments find that they make their stores distinctive and are effective in bringing customers into the store. Once there, the tendency is for the customer to shop the entire store.

Such service departments generally are profit centers, but in some cases, do no selling directly. A case in point is home economist personnel instituted by a number of retailers to help shoppers in meal planning, preparation, and budget meeting. In this same category are cooking classes, etc., which many retailers sponsor.

Byerly's was one of the first retailers to experiment with such nonselling services, and in addition to the personal help that the home economist department personnel supply individually, the department turns out weekly booklets offering recipes, meal suggestions, nutritional information, and numerous other household suggestions.

Little touches, such as a bulletin board placed somewhere in the store, accessible to all shoppers who can place or find notices of neighborhood activities and services (e.g., baby sitters, handyman services, etc.) also are nonselling services. Another example is a postal service which may include selling stamps, weighing mail to tell customers how much postage is required, etc. Such postal services bring no direct profit to the store, but help generate traffic. Another

This store makes it easier to locate merchandise. Each section has its own directory which lists merchandise categories in alphabetical order. This cuts down sharply on patron frustration.

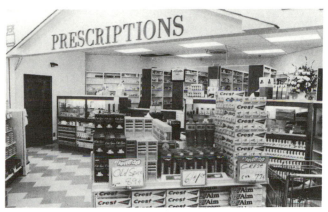

Since it sells toiletries and over-the-counter medicines, this supermarket also adds a prescriptions department. This is another aspect of the one-stop shopping trend as supermarkets add to their food market base.

nonselling service is a laundromat, which is both a traffic builder and profitable.

Among the many sales-oriented departments that are part of the service area are a host of varied departments that may be unique to individual stores or areas. The most common are the bakery and the service deli.

Either a scratch bakery (makes the entire product from "scratch") or a bake-off operation (the final baking step to finish generally frozen items prepared elsewhere and then baked on the store premises as required) are strong customer builders. (See Chapter 9, "Baked Goods and the Bakery Department.")

One small, Midwestern regional chain even has just a doughnut machine, which has been extremely helpful in building customer traffic; it provides hot doughnuts throughout the store's shopping hours. One East Coast store has an automated oven which makes only loaves of either Jewish rye or Italian bread as well as rolls. The baked items are used as leader items and help create traffic.

The snack bar or restaurant can contribute to traffic as well as sales in the supermarket. Some patrons, in fact, will stop off at the snack bar during their shopping experience, as indicated by the partially filled cart near the table.

Although some supermarkets run buses to bring customers to and from the store, this bus, sponsored by the Buttonwood IGA, near Reading, Pennsylvania, is extra-special; it provides transportation for senior citizens who live in a downtown high-rise apartment complex.

A number of chains have cakes in their display cases which can be iced and printed at short notice so that a festive cake can be ready for even a last-minute remembrance of a birthday or anniversary.

Service deli items, such as salads, hot dishes, and fast foods—all are features that attract customers. Also, many customers still like the personal service of having deli items prepared or cut just to order. (See Chapter 8, "The Delicatessen/Appetizing Department.")

The average sale per deli transaction is much higher in the service rather than self-service deli department. For customers who do not want to wait, most large stores also have self-service adjuncts to the deli department.

One debate has raged for years between the advocates of greater productivity and the merchandisers. Without question, the service department, be it deli or bakery, is much less efficient than the self-service counterpart, and it cuts productivity considerably. However, many of the more successful merchants—particularly independents who thrive on the customer who wants personal service—find that although their productivity may be down with the more service-oriented store, their sales and profits are up. And in the total picture, that is what they are in business for.

This even carries into the produce and meat departments. In many small-town stores, it is not unusual to see a produce department clerk helping to pick out product based on ripeness or other factors that the customer feels unqualified to do. Special cutting of meat to order may be the rarity in some large supermarkets; it is the rule in others.

Checkout Services/Personal Services

Customer services at the checkout counter are of prime importance; a mistake at the checkstand can nullify all the earlier efforts made throughout the store to satisfy the customer. Customers may spend many minutes deciding upon the smallest purchase, but they do not want to wait after they have completed their selections and reached the checkstand. Surveys have shown that waiting at the checkstand is the customer's greatest source of dissatisfaction in a supermarket. Abandoned carts, either partly or completely filled, are a sign of such customer dissatisfaction. Frequently, customers will choose to shop at stores that have a poorer selection of merchandise, and perhaps higher prices, rather than wait at the checkstand.

Employee training, the use of sophisticated and automated equipment to pare checker activities, offering express checkout lanes, and bagging should be constantly evaluated by the supermarket operator in an attempt to solve wasteful activities. This topic is discussed in detail in Chapter 12, "The Front End—Checkout Management and Control."

Another important customer aid is a well-trained and courteous staff willing to help customers in a friendly and intelligent manner. No matter how much customers enjoy the convenience of self-service in the supermarket, they still value the personal touch of employee-shopper contacts. Through these contacts, a store can develop a personality that will materially improve the store image.

Every personal contact at departments that offer services and at the checkout counter should be made as meaningful as possible. Courtesy is needed to make customers feel their patronage is appreciated.

The store manager must assume the responsibility for making certain that employees uniformly offer pleasant personal services to customers. This is one of the manager's most important functions. How well he or she makes store personnel aware of this fact affects the entire supermarket operation.

19

THE SUPERMARKET MANAGER

During the early period in the development of chain supermarket operations, clerks frequently served as store managers. Actual management came from the central office. Many chain operators used manuals outlining all activities, techniques, and procedures. These manuals were loose-leaf, and as changes were made, new pages replaced the old ones. Under this procedure, a store manager simply read the manual and the daily directives and followed central office orders. Some of the largest food chains developed and grew under this type of store manager. There can be no doubt that central office store management was successful.

As stores increased in size (in terms of total area, sales, number of employees, number of items, stock, number of customers, and size of financial investment), management by the central office became more difficult. The changing competitive situation, including the emergence of the owner-manager of the voluntary or cooperative group store, forced chain operators to reappraise the role of the store manager. As a result, the position of store manager is now *management* in the true sense of the word.

Increasingly, top management of supermarket firms realize that the store manager is probably the most important link in the chain. In some high-volume stores, he or she is reponsible for managing a business that does as much as $40 million a year or more. Pathmark, for example, has a chain of stores that averages nearly $12 million a year for each one of its stores—more than $225,000 a week as an average and a number of stores that do between $500,000 and $750,000 a week.

Many stores find the manager's function so important they have specialist managers who are put in charge of new stores for the first three to six months of the store's opening. These are specialists who can fine-tune the store and make adjustments quickly, when required, in the initial days of the store's operation.

A great many chains feel the store manager is so important that he or she is given a part of the profit and an even larger share of the improved profits for his or her store.

QUALITIES OF THE STORE MANAGER

The key component in the human equation involved in the operation of a supermarket is the store manager. Certainly no one person may claim the credit for the success of such an enormous operation. Lower-level attitudes are often a reflection of upper-level competence. The skill and capability of the store manager is reflected throughout the entire organization of the store and can help to achieve the desired profitable results.

The qualities usually considered important for successful store management are:

- Organizational ability
- Leadership ability
- Management skills.

Organizational Ability

A small store with a limited number of employees needs a *working* manager; the payroll budget is small and the manager or owner must do whatever work is required. The greater the number of employees, the greater the need for organization. Operators of large stores, therefore, are concerned first with a manager's ability to organize and get the job done by others, leaving him available to meet customers and supervise the store operation.

An organization-oriented manager recognizes that each job should be performed by an employee who is rated and paid for that level and type of work. Therefore, a store manager earning a relatively high salary is a very expensive checker, stocker, or bagger. Full-time and part-time employees can be hired to perform these jobs at the prevailing hourly rate of pay. The organization-oriented manager uses his payroll money effectively, devoting most of his time to management functions.

Leadership Ability

Leadership may be defined as the art of influencing and directing people in such a way as to obtain their *willing* obedience, confidence, respect, and loyal cooperation to accomplish the goals of the organization.

The store manager can use the leadership approach by orienting each employee to company policies, store layout and operation, the other employees, the types of customers, and the specific job. Effective leadership helps produce high employee morale, high-level job performance, good customer relations, and a satisfactory operating profit.

Management Skills

Management is the process whereby the resources of man, money, material, time, and facilities are utilized to accomplish the goals and tasks of the organization. The manager needs to have both technical and conceptual skills.

The operation of a supermarket requires a vast amount of "know-how." Each type of merchandise stocked requires specific knowledge as to methods of handling, merchandising, pricing, margin, and other factors. For example, meat must be cut, packaged, and priced; temperature must be controlled, freshness maintained, and displays kept full and fresh. The store manager needs to know how meat is cut, but he does not need to be proficient at it; neither does he need to be a meat expert. The same is true for the other operating areas.

The store manager must know company policies and procedures. This includes handling money and records, supervising people, maintaining property and equipment, and controlling expenses.

In addition to technical skills, a store manager must possess conceptual skills. This involves the ability to visualize the supermarket as an operating unit and to see how the various store segments and activities interrelate to maintain good operations. The manager should be able to see the company as a whole and each unit as part of the whole. The greater the conceptual skill, the greater will be the understanding of the total job.

Large supermarkets must be managed at store level by a competent executive. The annual volume, the number of employees, the variety of functions, the responsibility, and the public relations operations justify the need for an executive to be in the position of supermarket manager. To fill this position, the manager must possess the necessary technical skills plus the ability to organize and lead.

THE DUTIES OF THE MANAGER

The actual work of developing store-level plans, promotions, and policies can be delegated to others, but the manager is responsible for the final results. Some of the activities involving manager responsibility may be peculiar to a particular situation or company, but in general the items listed apply to most store managers. The duties of the manager fall into five main categories:

- Merchandise-related activities
- Personnel-related activities
- Clerical functions
- Communications-related activities
- General management functions.

Merchandise-Related Activities

The merchandise-related duties of the supermarket manager include the following:

1. Ordering merchandise and supplies from the company warehouse and authorized vendors.
2. Receiving merchandise and supplies. Storing and/or stocking all items received.
3. Pricing merchandise offered for sale according to company price lists and policies. Changing prices according to established procedure.
4. Displaying merchandise for maximum sales results.
5. Conducting "balanced selling" so as to produce a satisfactory gross profit.
6. Controlling merchandise so as to minimize shrinkage of all kinds.
7. Controlling checkstand operation for greatest efficiency and customer satisfaction.

Personnel-Related Activities

The personnel-related duties of the supermarket manager include the following:

1. Supervising the activities of store employees. This includes scheduling work hours, assigning jobs, and checking employees on the use of approved work methods and procedures. Approved union contract procedures must be followed.
2. Checking employees on compliance with company policies.
3. Maintaining the necessary staff of employees. In some stores, this may mean also recruiting and hiring.
4. Rating employees according to approved company procedures.
5. Following up personnel ratings with corrective and promotional aids, advice, and instruction.
6. Maintaining personnel records.
7. Developing employee morale.

Clerical Functions

The clerical duties of the supermarket manager may include the following:

1. Checking and approving all vendor invoices before submitting them to headquarters for payment.
2. Maintaining payroll records and approving payment.
3. Maintaining a vacation schedule and assigning or approving vacation requests.
4. Handling cash and banking.
5. Reviewing the daily checker reports.

Communications-Related Activities

The communications-related activities of the supermarket manager include the following:

1. Setting up and advising employees on work and vacation schedules.
2. Providing payroll information to the accounting office.
3. Disseminating sales and promotional programs to employees.
4. Advising staff on changes in merchandise items stocked.
5. Advising staff on price changes.
6. Supervising orders to warehouse and suppliers.

7. Directing reports to accounting, personnel and merchandising offices.
8. Advising on policies and policy changes to all concerned.
9. Advising employees on approved standards and procedures.

General Management Functions

General management functions of the supermarket manager include the following:

1. Seeing that customers receive courteous and intelligent attention.
2. Directing all merchandising, operational and administrative activities in accordance with the authority assigned by the company and according to company policy.
3. Controlling store operating expenses, including regulating the use of lights; controlling the use of telephones; controlling the distribution and use of supplies, forms, tools, price cards, price markers, etc.; requesting necessary repairs, maintenance, and equipment; seeing that controlled temperature areas are properly maintained; and controlling labor costs and adhering to the labor budget.
4. Participating in community activities, arranging for donations to the extent of the manager's authority, and forwarding other requests to headquarters.

20

SUPERMARKET MANAGEMENT, CONTROL, AND SECURITY

The supermarket manager controls the store operations within the limits of the policies and procedures established by top management. Basically, management involves getting the work done through other people. The management process includes:

- Planning
- Organizing
- Directing
- Leading
- Communicating
- Controlling.

PLANNING

The actual objectives, goals, standards, procedures, budgets, and rules for the store are usually established by top management. At the store level, the manager's prime objective in planning is to meet the established goals and objectives. (In some high-volume stores or super stores—often where the store is the only one of that chain in an area—the manager does the actual policy setting, but this is the exception rather than the rule. What policy making is unique with the manager is generally spelled out beforehand and entails some leeway in reacting to a local competitive situation.)

The manager plans work schedules for the employees, display installations, security procedures, work procedures, receiving and marking procedures, and how all functions are to be performed.

ORGANIZING

In order to carry out the plans, it is necessary to organize and structure the various tasks and activities involved in performing functions necessary to operate the supermarket.

Related activities are grouped together and assigned to specific people who are given the responsibility and authority needed to accomplish the assigned work. In the supermarket, activities are grouped by related products into departments: the grocery department, meat department, produce de-

partment, and so forth. Depending on the store (structure, size, volume, special handling, philosophy, etc.), some product lines may be combined with dairy and/or grocery departments.

The most efficient approach to a formal structuring of organization is to put everything in writing, preferably in chart or manual form with the duties, functions, and responsibilities for each job. Each employee then knows which tasks are to be performed on the job. This should ensure more efficient store operation. However, the manager must be aware that the organizational chart is subject to change and should be altered when new conditions internally or externally present themselves. An astute manager will be aware of each employee's qualifications and change the organization chart as needed, utilizing strengths of employees to best meet the work-flow demands of the store.

Organizing into departments (product related) or work-related activities provides some distinct advantages, including:

1. Responsibility for the work may be assigned to specific employees.
2. Employees may specialize in product or work.
3. Productive and nonproductive personnel are more easily identified.
4. Losses are more easily detected.
5. Managing becomes easier.

Staffing involves the recruitment, interviewing, and selection of prospective employees as well as training, orientation, and evaluation. This is discussed in greater detail in Chapter 21, "Personnel Management."

Underlying the organizational process is managerial authority. Fundamental to its proper exercise is the transmission of authority from superior to subordinate, commonly referred to as delegation of authority. Various experts consider delegation as:

1. Entrustment of work (entrustment of work responsibility) to an employee.
2. Granting of authority to carry out this work (powers and rights).

3. Holding that employee accountable to perform the work according to set standards.

However, the person in management who delegates a job to an employee is still responsible for its completion. A store manager may delegate the responsibility of the produce department to a produce manager. The produce manager may be given the authority to operate the department and may be held accountable for predetermined goals. In the final analysis, however, it is the store manager who is responsible for the results of that department and for every department of the store.

Some useful suggestions for effective delegation are:

1. Establish goals expected for whatever tasks are assigned.
2. Decide on all the specific tasks that must be performed and duties that must be assumed.
3. Place specific employees in charge of each job with full responsibility for accomplishing the desired goals.
4. Institute proper controls and standards so that corrective action can be taken when necessary.

DIRECTING

Directing the work is a process that will determine the effectiveness of the operation. Directing involves motivating, training, leading, and communicating. Properly motivating employees can result in obtaining appropriate behavioral responses from them. The manager must get the "team" to behave in a particular manner. There are many theories as to why people act in the ways they do, and it has been established that individuals behave in a manner for which they feel they will be rewarded.

Strong motivation should:

1. Last for a long period of time.
2. Be directed toward the completion of a specific objective.
3. Have behavior produced from a felt need.

A good store manager is aware that:

1. Employees generally have many needs that may be different.
2. More than one need may be operating at any particular moment.
3. Once a need is satisfied, it is no longer a motivator.
4. Money can satisfy many different needs, but it is not necessarily the strongest need.

LEADING

Leading is motivating others to get the job done, while at the same time sustaining their morale and providing the proper psychological environment. Research studies on effective leadership have concluded that there is a definite pattern of leadership traits.

Successful managers are generally brighter; more aggressive, self-reliant, persuasive and capable supervisors; better decision makers; and better educated than those managers who are not considered to be as successful. They usually accomplish the jobs they are given and at the same time appear to satisfy the needs of their employees.

The manager maintains the authority of his or her position by communicating to the employees that it is the manager's right to make decisions about matters in the store. Top management should continually support this concept so that the position is solidified with subordinates. However, informal approaches, such as leadership ability, style, attitude, soliciting management by participation, etc., will impress subordinates more effectively. It is important to keep employees informed, but there must be consistent interpretation and enforcement of policy, procedures, rules, etc.

The following are suggestions that can help a manager develop into an effective leader:

1. Develop positive, personal traits.
2. Know each subordinate and attempt to get complete support from him or her.
3. Appear and act like a leader.
4. Delegate as many duties as possible to competently trained subordinates.
5. Develop a team approach so that all members feel that they are part of the team.

COMMUNICATING

Successful leadership and control in supermarketing depends upon proper communication with employees. This communication must be bilateral—downward to the last employee and upward to top management. The employee's response and reaction must be considered. Complete understanding of orders, rules, and instructions is essential to effective communication.

In a supermarket organization, the general manager, whether division, branch, or total company, channels communications to the store manager. The store manager interprets the instructions and channels them to the various employees affected. This phase of communication is best carried out orally with explanations, reasons, and procedures. Oral instructions permit an interchange of ideas and information, creating better morale and cooperation. Understanding of instructions and a willingness to comply is, therefore, better assured.

Lines of communication are the lifelines of a business; however, management too often takes them for granted. Communication ranges from the most simple method of speaking with a person to a very complex system of written reports and directions. Regardless of the method used, communications must be two-way. If management is to communicate to the employee, then employees must have a way to communicate with management.

Oral Methods of Communication

There are a number of ways the store manager and employees communicate orally:

- Direct
- Public address system
- Intercommunication system
- Meetings

Direct. Probably the easiest and most common oral communication is personal conversation which permits modifications to meet the situation.

Public Address System. The public address system broadcasts the message throughout the store for customer entertainment or information. Therefore, the use of the public address system for employee communication during store hours should be limited.

Intercommunication System. The intercom is distinguished from the public address system in that the audience is selected, and it provides two-way communication.

Meetings. The store manager should take advantage of every reasonable opportunity to have meetings with the employees. Meetings should not be used merely for the purpose of solving a problem, but also should be held as a means of preventing problems from arising.

Meetings may be held with any particular group with which the manager wishes to communicate. For instance, if the manager wants to discuss the importance of the produce department in creating a favorable customer image, a meeting of the produce employees would be called. If something needs to be discussed concerning the entire store, such as pilferage control, a meeting would be called of the entire staff, either in one session or several sessions.

Store meetings are also an effective leadership and control device. Once responsibility is defined and authority delegated, it is important to maintain a high degree of coordination and control in order to insure the accomplishment of predetermined goals. Regular checks should be made to ascertain whether each person is performing assigned tasks in the most efficient way. Store meetings constitute an effective way of informing employees of company policies and directives.

Store meetings should accomplish three things: inform, build teamwork, and instruct. They should be held on a regular basis with a definite time. The meetings should be well-organized so that the objectives can be accomplished in the shortest possible time. Meetings should be conducive to group participation. It should be the responsibility of the store manager to conduct and monitor the meeting to prevent discussions from drifting away from the subject. The meetings should be scheduled during working hours (on company time) when customer traffic is light. Meetings should be scheduled for employees in groups, so a crew is always on hand to operate the store. The major purposes for store meetings are:

- To inform employees
- To build teamwork
- To provide instruction.

One of the primary purposes of store meetings is to give employees information on company directives, company policies, general announcements, sales plans and promotions, work schedules, and other pertinent items.

The manager can review current sales plans and assign duties. The meeting provides the store manager with an opportunity to familiarize each employee with information on the products to be featured and their respective sales prices. It is a good time to enlist employee suggestions on the merchandising plan for the week. Store meetings enable the manager to review past operations and isolate areas that need improvement. A manager should remember that, when dealing with employees, praise should be given publicly and criticism privately; always find something to praise before criticizing.

A manager who knows the employees, is in a better position to develop team spirit by recognizing that each individual is an entity with individual likes and dislikes, personality, and faults. Each person needs to feel important, assigning responsibilities and being requested to make suggestions will help promote the individual's self-esteem. Recognizing satisfactory performance and using employee suggestions whenever possible develop team spirit which is reflected in greater job efficiency, increased sales, and better customer reactions.

Store meetings provide an opportunity to compare store averages with those of other stores of similar volume. This is extremely useful during company-wide contests. Each person can be asked for plans to improve a particular section. If, for example, any ideas on displays, simplifying operations, or reducing costs are suggested by employees, the manager can give credit to this person in front of the group.

Intrastore contests establish team spirit and, at the same time, accomplish operating objectives. One West Coast grocer wanted to insure accurate pricing without calling attention to errors. A program was initiated in which each employee was encouraged to check for price-marking errors. Whenever an error was found, the person who made the error would contribute a small fine to a central "kitty." If an employee discovered his/her own pricing error prior to detection by others, no fine was paid. After the fund reached a set amount, the manager contributed to it, and a party was held for all of the employees. So much enthusiasm resulted that pricing errors became negligible. The employees enjoyed policing each other in this friendly way.

Store meetings also serve as a release valve to settle disputes and frustrations. Frequently, friction between employees and/or personal problems outside the store adversely affect job performance. These grievance sessions enable them to voice their complaints. Most often, these problems are simple and can be alleviated by sound reasoning. Personal or more serious problems should be dealt with in private; problems that are encountered frequently in many areas may be dealt with in group sessions.

Grievance sessions are particularly good in situations in which the entire group is misinformed about certain issues. The manager should determine what is bothering employees and help settle their differences. Once harmony is established, a strong foundation is laid upon which to build teamwork.

Store meetings can be planned so that individuals take turns in presenting topics to the group. Suggested topics include: group benefits, working conditions, a career in the food industry, a better understanding of company operations, new improvements in materials handling within a supermarket, company history, company policies, new methods and procedures, pilferage, safety, fire prevention, and customer relations.

Some store meetings should be organized at headquarters so that procedures and material to be presented can be efficiently and effectively distributed to the managers. By mastering the technique of handling store meetings, the manager is able to exercise more effective control.

Written Methods of Communication

Generally, written communications are not as effective as oral ones because indiviuals have to exert more effort reading than that required for listening. However, written communications can be very effective in controlling the store if they are carefully written and properly used. The wording of written communications is a universal problem. The writer understands the meaning of his message, but the reader may not properly comprehend the content as intended by the writer. Methods of effective written communications include:

- Bulletin boards
- Store publications
- Pamphlets and booklets
- Oral-written combinations.

Bulletin Board. The bulletin board should be placed in a prominent, employee-traffic location in a nonselling area. It should be divided into the following sections:

- Permanent material—safety signs, etc.
- Communications from headquarters
- Communications from the manager
- Personal notices concerning employees—weddings, births, etc.

Oral-written Combinations. Often, it is a good idea to make sure the written communications are read and understood by devoting a portion of each meeting to underlining key points in them. Important points (perhaps clearing up something that appears ambiguous or indistinct) that may have come up in individual questions about the notices also should be aired.

Communications Upward

Communications upward are encouraged by an "open-door" policy and a suggestion system. The former is a policy under which the manager is available to store personnel for consultation on any problem. An open-door policy often exists more in theory than practice; the manager encourages employees to communicate, then is too busy to see them. If this policy is to be successful, the manager must take time to listen to employees when they want to talk.

Store Publications. House organs, if used by the company, provide an opportunity to publicize both store events and interesting personnel activities. In addition, a store bulletin, posted on the bulletin board and published regularly, could keep employees informed of happenings and coming events.

Pamphlets and Booklets. A manager should see to it that each employee receives bulletins and booklets which the company distributes from time to time. These booklets may cover such topics as company history, company benefits, etc. Also, the company may distribute current literature on new products, methods, and procedures.

Some companies use a suggestion system. If it is used, employees should be encouraged to make suggestions. A reply to each suggestion should be made by letter. Each employee should be informed as to what was done about the suggestion and the reasons for the action. Often, a system of awards is used to encourage employees to be creative.

Fast Area Coverage

Frequently, rapid communications to all stores in a trading area are desirable. The "fan-out" phone system is used successfully by many operators.

This system is used on last-minute price changes or other matters requiring immediate action and is accomplished by making store managers part of a telephone communications team. Headquarters calls the designated store managers in an area. Each of these managers has a list of two others to call; and these, in turn, call others. This fan-out method is practical for companies having a substantial concentration of stores in an area.

The fan-out phone system was adopted by a supermarket operator after a study showed the company was sending out four and one-half pounds of mail per week to stores. The mail volume was reduced to one pound, and the phone system costs were paid with the money saved on mail. Also, this system spreads information much faster.

The most efficient method of getting communications from the wholesaler to the retailer or from headquarters to the store is used almost universally these days—on the truck with merchandise deliveries. Today, almost all deliveries to the store contain a pouch of information as well as delivery-ticket information. With the slow and expensive mail system that exists today, this saves time and money.

CONTROLLING

Managerial control attempts to maintain conformity between actual and desired performance of its personnel and resources so that the established objectives of the firm are accomplished. The steps in the control process are:

1. Standards are established from objectives, policies, plans, procedures, budgets, etc., for the various activities involved in the operation of the store.
2. Actual performance is checked against the

established standard within the appropriate time period.
3. Differences between actual and desired performance are isolated so that the type or size of the difference can be established.
4. A decision is made on what type of corrective action should be taken.
   (a) Should the standard be corrected?
   (b) Should the performance be corrected?

The control function is interrelated with the various functions of management so that a desired standard is derived from a plan that is dependent on organizational design. Personnel and other resources are essential in effecting the plan, which in itself must be controlled.

There are many reasons for establishing controls, including:

1. Protecting the store's property and merchandise from theft, misuse, and waste.
2. Establishing bounds that delegated authority can use, i.e., auditing systems, job descriptions, etc.
3. Setting the measurement for performance of activities designed to increase efficiency.
4. Standardizing quality that is geared to accommodate customer specifications.
5. Aiding the manager in meeting the desired results of the firm.

When the appropriate measurement of results cannot be accomplished and corrective action is not taken, the end result is ineffectiveness, leading to loss of profits.

Types of Controls

There are three basic types of controls:

- Precontrols
- Concurrent controls
- Postcontrols.

Precontrols. Designed to prevent an undesirable occurrence, e.g., control sheets insure merchandise is in stock before specials are advertised.

Concurrent Controls. A control device instituted while an activity is taking place, e.g., checking an employee's performance during the execution of a task in order to correct or adjust work for greater efficiency.

Postcontrols. The appraisal is performed after the completion of the activity, e.g., a register tally at the end of the day.

Different types of controls that are important to the store manager are: quality standards for personnel, equipment, and merchandise; various types of budgets dealing with personnel, equipment, and supplies; and quotas and other centrally imposed criteria.

Many managers find it difficult to measure performance. The difficulty lies in the fact that some information or data is not quantifiable. Today, there are complex reporting systems that help simplify this process; however, simple, personal observation in many cases is just as useful. Regardless of the system or method, it is important to achieve a rapid compilation and transmittal of information.

An actual comparison of performance to the established standard is sometimes overlooked or avoided for various reasons. Obviously, the control process will not operate unless this is done. However, this step has an even greater significance. For instance, a clerk who is being rated will probably be more motivated and do a better job. Corrective action should be taken immediately by the person who has the responsibility and authority for such action.

A factor that must also be considered when deciding on controls is the cost of implementing them. A budget for each department or major activity (e.g., snow clearing in the parking area) is established. When considering the costs for a control, it is important to consider the objectives that have been set, the courses of action, and the attitudes of the management staff and the subordinates towards that control. Employees must be made aware that the controls are interdependent and interrelated to other controls. The control in sales is directly related to the amount of inventory controls that are established as a standard.

The store manager must also be aware of some of the pitfalls in implementing the control process. These include:

1. Do not emphasize postcontrols, but attempt to institute precontrols and concurrent controls.
2. Do not spend too much time in seeking and criticizing the personnel who are responsible for the deviation at the expense of taking the corrective action immediately.
3. Avoid friction with staff specialists who establish the implement controls that appear to be bothersome and useless.
4. Examine the cost of the control to make sure the benefit is greater than the cost.

INVENTORY CONTROL

Inventory control includes the maintenance of a proper relation of stock-on-hand to sales as well as efficiency in handling stock. The store manager is concerned primarily with the phases of inventory control necessary to obtain and maintain an adequate inventory with a minimum amount of loss. An important part of inventory control is "breaking a good inventory," that is, keeping shrinkage within established tolerance limits.

Shrinkage is an important control factor. Most food chains bill the store for merchandise at retail, especially groceries. Billing at retail enables the accounting department to hold the store manager responsible for the total value of the merchandise received. For any period, the retail value of the beginning inventory, plus the retail value of the merchandise sold, minus sales, should equal the final inventory at retail. The difference between the book inventory and the physical inventory is the shrinkage.

To achieve complete accuracy, adjustments should be made for all changes in selling price, all losses due to breakage, etc. Instead of incurring the expense of recording all losses and changes in value, multiple store operators use *average* shortage or shrinkage allowances. Frequently, pilot stores are used; all known changes in merchandise value are recorded for adjustment and average shrinkage figures are set on the experience of these pilot stores. Other operators use the average shortage of the entire number of stores, and deviations from the average, whether high or low, are investigated.

Since each store is charged for the retail value of the merchandise, it is important for the store manager to establish a system of price marking that will assure a high degree of accuracy. Also, the accounting department should make frequent checks to assure accuracy. Price marking is audited whenever a store inventory is taken.

Accurate pricing is important from a management point of view. As the price of merchandise fluctuates and the replacement cost changes, the selling price should be changed to provide the operator with the funds to replace store and warehouse stocks. Store managers are often quicker to increase prices than to decrease them, since their thinking is primarily in terms of "breaking a good inventory" by using price increases to cover losses. If price increases are absorbed by inventory losses, the capital required to maintain inventories will not be available and additional financing becomes necessary. The store manager must price to maintain working capital instead of "breaking a good inventory."

Price changes on a declining market are important competitively. Alert and aggressive operators are the first to decrease prices and, thereby, gain an advantage over the operators who lag on price reductions. Customers attracted to other stores by the lure of lower prices are difficult to win back. The long-run benefits derived from immediate and complete price adjustments to the market are satisfied customers, continued high volume, and increased sales.

Shrinkage allowances will cover changes in value due to price changes. Any effort to cover inefficient operations by lagging on the execution of price changes is a short-sighted policy. Store supervisors need to understand price change problems and should check store managers to insure prompt compliance.

Accurate pricing is important from the customer's point of view also. If a price is too high, customers will become dissatisfied with the store and shop elsewhere. If the price is too low, an inventory shortage is incurred and the store loses on the transaction. Illegible prices are costly in terms of time at the checkstand and customer dissatisfaction.

A number of years ago, a major chain was publicly accused of instructing its meat department managers to cheat on weight and fat content in ground meat. The chain denied the charges vehemently and depite all denials, had a difficult time recovering an acceptable image in the community. Although the chain was technically correct, in that it did not instruct its department managers to cheat, closer checks of top management policies did prove that the fault lay with top management.

It seems that some overzealous upper-level executives were dissatisfied with the profit margins, and in attempting to reduce shrink too far, were telling their store department managers that the profit margins were much too low. The store personnel, fearing for their jobs, began cheating the customers in order to protect their jobs. They short-weighted. After hours, when they felt no inspectors would be working, they added to the fat levels in ground meats, etc.

Officially, the management did not order cheating, but in effect, they "forced" the employees to do it. Fortunately, top management discovered the problem and rectified it, but not until heavy and considerable damage was done to the chain's image in that area.

Balanced Stock

Inventory control also refers to the activities carried on for the purpose of keeping merchandise offerings balanced with respect to expected sales and customer demand—that is, quantity control and turnover, both of which are a result of proper ordering.

Insufficient quantities on hand result in out-of-stock conditions. Too much merchandise in the store—including the backroom—results in decreased stock turnover. Out-of-stock decreases sales and causes customers to shop at other stores for the items wanted. A low rate of turnover decreases the controllable operating profit for the store.

Some operators limit the quantity of stock a store should have in the backroom to a percentage of weekly sales. A limitation of this type requires the manager to exercise control over the items in the backroom.

An oversupply of a case or two of many slow-moving items could lead to insufficient quantities of fast-moving items. Out-of-stock in the slow-mover category is less serious than out-of-stock on volume items. Whether a backroom limit is imposed on the manager or not, the quantity *and* types of items in stock should be controlled in order to assure a satisfactory turnover. Out-of-stocks must be held to reasonable limits, primarily on slow movers.

Damage Control

Improper handling and stocking of merchandise causes damage and resultant losses. Cartons should be opened without damaging their contents. Items with loose labels should be made salable by affixing the labels with glue. (If the repair is noticeable, however, the items should be discounted.) All employees should be trained to prevent loss and to salvage as much as possible when there is damage.

Merchandise should be stocked so as to avoid situations that cause customers to knock items off the shelf or to drop breakable units.

Control of stock rotation reduces the quantity of merchandise that is unsalable. Customers patronize the stores supplying fresh-looking merchandise that is neatly arranged on clean shelves. Old-looking merchandise must be reduced in price and sold on special displays or to employees and volume buyers.

PILFERAGE CONTROL

Losses incurred through pilferage have been estimated to be anywhere from 0.5 percent to 5 percent of sales. No one really knows the exact figure. Pilferage accounts for a sizable loss in net profit, and anything that can be done to control it will help increase profits.

The prevention of pilferage is a continuous problem. Each day, shoppers in the United States walk away with more than $200,000 in merchandise for which they have not paid.

Dishonest vendors, clerks, and cashiers are also responsible for pilferage losses. It is very difficult to measure the amount of pilferage accounted for by each of these groups. However, it can be assumed to be a substantial amount. It has been estimated that one dishonest checker will take an average of $10 a day, or about $2,500 yearly. Thus, cash and shortage control is essential. The success of the supermarket manager in controlling pilferage will be directly reflected in the controllable operating profit of the store. (Using 1 percent of sales as net, a store would have to sell $250,000 a year just to cover that loss.)

Control of Customer Pilferage

In a recent study of apprehended shoplifters, it was found that the average value of merchandise stolen by a shoplifter was $1.55. In most cases, the shoplifter stole only one item. The study also revealed that the sex of the offender is not a factor; the number of shoplifters was almost equally divided between men and women. Ninety percent of them did not need to steal; most had good jobs and a sufficient amount of money to pay for what they wanted.

The items stolen are usually small packages of high-unit value, such as meat, cigarettes, health and beauty aids, butter, cheese, canned salmon, etc. A great portion of the shoplifters are everyday working people, not professional shoplifters. Some of them may be very good customers of the store.

One method of controlling shoplifting is the use of "spotters," who observe the sales area from behind one-way mirrors or on a balcony lookout. An additional method is the placement of large mirrors at strategic points in the store enabling a person in the office to view the entire sales area.

Still another method is the use of store detectives, who appear to be ordinary customers doing their shopping, but are continually on the alert for shoplifters. In some inner-city stores, uniformed guards are used to detect pilferers. Operators not wishing to establish a store security department use an outside security service. Some operators feel that this is an expensive way to combat shoplifting. Other operators feel that the amount saved through the use of store detectives is considerably higher than the salary expense of the detectives.

A number of stores (first tested in Pathmark stores in New Jersey) are using a system similar to that used by many libraries or department stores. A magnetized sales tag is used on the merchandise, and unless it is demagnetized or passed over the checkout counter, when passed through an electronically monitored area, the tape signals a detector and a loud alarm is sounded. This system is too expensive to use on all items in the store, but has been used with high-ticket items, such as expensive packages of fresh meat, canned hams, etc.

Another method of controlling shoplifting is the use of television cameras placed strategically throughout the store, monitored by a person situated in an inconspicuous location. The monitor generally has a switching device so that observations can be made of various points in the store. It may also have a zoom lens so that it can zero-in more closely. In order to bring down the cost, dummy cameras are interspersed among the live ones, serving as a psychological deterrent to shoplifting.

A closed circuit television monitoring system is being widely used as a device for preventing and apprehending shoplifters. Monitoring screens are placed in strategic areas of the stores and monitored by remote control in a back-room area.

The "friendly method" prevents pilferage before it happens. Shoplifters do not want to be acknowledged, recognized, or noticed by store personnel. They avoid clerks in the store and want as little attention as possible drawn to them. By training store personnel to be alert to recognize customers, acknowledge their presence, and show an interest in them, they are doing a good customer relations job and at the same time are discouraging the would-be shoplifter. Training store employees to greet customers and call them by name, whenever possible, is a good technique.

Control of Vendor Pilferage

Vendor pilferage is more easily controlled than customer pilferage. It will usually be found that the manager who trusts the vendors and is lax in checking their deliveries and returns will have more vendor pilferage than the manager who strictly controls them. The complacent manager soon gets a reputation of being a "pushover" among vendors and loses money through padded bills or stolen merchandise.

A full-time employee should be assigned to handle all receiving and returning of merchandise. It is also a good policy to assign an alternate to take over when the regular receiving clerk is not on duty. These clerks should be trained to check all deliveries and returns and not take the word of the vendor. They should also be trained to stay with and check the work of the vendor until the vendor has left the store. Once an invoice has been checked and signed, the store copy should remain in the possession of store personnel.

The back door should be locked at all times, except when receiving or returning merchandise. A clerk should watch the door as long as it is open. All merchandise being delivered should be checked at the receiving point.

The manager should occasionally check the deliveries to prevent collusion between vendors and the receiving clerk. This will help remove temptation and prevent pilferage.

Vendor deliveries should be scheduled so as to avoid confusion and mistakes which may occur when too many vendors arrive at the same time. Vendors should not be permitted in the store unless an employee is available to check their actions.

Approximately 80 percent of the merchandise received by a supermarket is from the food distribution center—chain or wholesaler. This percentage will vary with store location and the completeness of warehouse stocks and departments. The amount of checking of distribution center deliveries varies from no check, to a piece count, to an item count.

The cost of checking is a factor, but the store manager must be assured that the merchandise billed is delivered. Errors will occur, but an efficient warehouse operation is cheaper than costly checking. When one company owns both the distribution center and the stores, the money spent checking is considered a loss. The use of a piece count assures the store that the number of items on the invoice has been received. This assurance may justify the cost of counting merchandise received. Separate ownership of warehouse and store facilities may justify using an item count.

The store manager should be alert to the schemes and devices of delivery personnel who profit by making short deliveries. A few items to be alert for include: hollow pallets; short count or weight; not removing returns and counting them as deliveries; additions to the invoice, such as adding in the date; bringing in empty containers and charging for full units, etc.

In general, people are as honest as the system allows. Therefore, the best safeguard is complete supervision, checking, and auditing. When accomplished as a matter of routine procedure, there is no need to question the honesty of anyone—just how company policy and procedure have been followed.

Control of Pilferage by Clerks and Cashiers

Controlling pilferage by clerks and cashiers is not too difficult. Clerks and cashiers should know that pilferage of any degree will not be tolerated and will result in immediate discharge and possible prosecution.

By keeping all back doors locked and requiring all purchases by employees to be checked out by the head cashier or other designated checkers, much of the opportunity to pilfer is removed.

Controlling cashiers requires that they be observed as continually as possible while "ringing" and that they have their own cash drawers for which they are responsible.

The cashiers should also be required to observe specific rules and regulations in the performance of their work. A deviation from the required pattern

should be easily detected. If such a deviation has occurred, the cashier should be kept under more strict surveillance to determine whether the deviation was a mistake or the result of a dishonest act. (See Chapter 12, "The Front End—Checkout Management and Control," for a more detailed discussion of checkstand staffing and control.)

SECURITY

Supermarkets handle large sums of money daily, making them attractive targets for robberies. Every supermarket manager and owner should be alert to the danger and follow safe money-handling procedures.

The first step is to limit the amount of money in each cash register by making cash pickups regularly. The money should be counted, credited to the register operator, and deposited in an armored service safe. This safe should be marked: "Cannot be opened by store personnel—only by armored service personnel." Checks should be endorsed "for deposit only." This prevents the checks, if stolen, from being cashed. Careless handling of money invites trouble, since the registers are visible and procedures are subject to the scrutiny of the public, including interested robbers.

Large amounts of money attract robbers. Store personnel should be instructed not to resist attempts to rob the store at gun point. The employees should protect themselves from injury and not attempt to be heroes.

Night robberies or burglaries are attempted by breaking into the store and the safe. Adequate safeguards, such as built-in safes, alarm systems, keeping the store illuminated, having the safe visible from the street, etc., should be used.

Some robbers have been known to kidnap the store manager and force him or her to open the safe. The store manager should be protected by being unable to open the armored service safe and being able to open only the store safe which has limited funds at any given time.

At no time should a store manager or anyone having a key go to the store at night without the police being notified. A night "emergency" telephone call to the manager to open the store may be too old a technique to be effective, nevertheless store managers should be reminded of this subterfuge used by robbers.

The best safeguard is to keep available funds limited and follow safe procedures. Other safeguards include: signals and silent alarms to employees in other parts of the store to call law enforcement officials, checking the "get-away" car for a description and license plate number, etc. Some operators use a camera or cameras mounted so as to take photographs of the checkout area during a holdup in order to help identify the robbers. An independent, whose store was often robbed at night, installed a concealed microphone near the safe and a speaker in his bedroom. This device proved very effective.

Daytime or store-hour holdups present another type of hazard—being locked in the freezer or cooler to prevent store employees from calling the police. Being locked in a freezer is not only potentially dangerous, but the insulation makes the box soundproof, so that shouting for help is useless. Also, freezer-door catches can be jammed so that opening the door from the inside is impossible. Having some sort of alarm device inside the freezer connected to police headquarters is one type of safety precaution. All employees should be told the steps to take if locked in a walk-in freezer or cooler.

Strict control of keys is a vital security measure. Locks should be changed periodically. Tumbler-type locks can be changed easily and at nominal cost. Whenever there is any doubt as to the number of keys in circulation for a particular unit or changes in key-carrying personnel occur, the tumblers should be changed and new keys issued.

Avoiding publicity as to the amount of money stolen, and giving the impression the amount was nominal, whether it actually was or not, eliminates the appeal of holdups. Also, publicity on holdups and robberies shold be kept to a minimum so customers will consider the supermarket a safe place in which to shop.

Close cooperation with law enforcement agencies has proven very effective. Fast police action, combined with the arrest and conviction of thieves, is the most effective method of discouraging holdups.

In the past several years, a new method for theft has been tried, which involves the manager of a store and his or her family. The manager's home is phoned by an impostor claiming to be a telephone repairman. He tells the family that in order to test the circuits, the phone company is requesting that the phone not be answered, regardless of how many times it rings in the ensuing two hours.

The store manager is phoned and told that the family is being held hostage and that unless a certain amount of cash is delivered to a specific spot in an hour, without notifying police or anyone else, the family will be harmed. When calls home are unanswered, the threat seems to be authentic. Police advise that all families of supermarket personnel immediately inform police if such an alleged phone company request is made to the family.

Managers of stores and other officials who have access to and control of store funds should have certain code phrases or words which, if injected into otherwise normal-appearing conversations, will either alert or verify a kidnapping or holdup situation. Such a system might well have saved the life of Julie Kravitz, head of a large Ohio chain, who was murdered by a kidnapper several years ago when headquarters personnel were not alerted quickly enough to respond to real kidnap demands. Kidnap and hostage reaction programs should be adopted by companies before they occur so that firms can possibly save lives should such an event take place.

21

The supermarket manager must help establish and implement objectives through planning, organizing, directing, and controlling resources and people. Probably no other member of management is directly involved with so many staff employees as is the store manager. Since management gets the various functions of supermarketing done through people, it is essential that we examine the one management function that is directly responsible for dealing with people—the personnel function.

The main purpose of a personnel program is the effective utilization of human resources, a working relationship among all members of the organization, and a maximum development of each individual. These objectives are accomplished through:

- Procurement of capable personnel
- The development and effective utilization of their efforts, skills, and abilities
- The development of their willingness to work in a motivating atmosphere.

Operators generally agree that the personnel administrator is a staff official. Staff officials provide specialized services to the line officials (the store manager) and advise and counsel them. Personnel administrators, as staff officials, are primarily advisors and service agents, not only to top management, but also to all segments of line management. Personnel administrators do not issue orders to the line organization or to employees even when personnel matters are involved, except within their own department. They advise management on sound personnel policies and their application, but do not establish these policies. Policies are established by the top echelon of management as guides to active management; thus, policies establish the framework within which each department functions. Within the limits of company policies, the personnel department recommends, cooperates, and counsels. Line management applies the techniques and procedures to the work situation.

FUNCTIONS OF THE PERSONNEL DEPARTMENT

The role of the personnel administrator, in terms of the broad functions and relationships to the line organization, must be understood by all levels of management. The principal responsibility of the personnel administrator is to develop and maintain an effective human organization. These responsibilities typically include:

1. Procuring new personnel, including recruitment selection, and placement.
2. Developing and administering training programs.
3. Developing and administering employee evaluation programs.
4. Conducting management development programs.
5. Developing, aiding, and consulting in promotion, administering, demotion, transfer, separation, layoff and leave of absence policies.
6. Developing and administering the fringe benefit program; e.g., insurance, retirement, health benefits, incentive plans, credit union, and unemployment insurance.
7. Developing and administering wage and salary plans.
8. Supervising the implementation of company personnel policies.
9. Maintaining satisfactory employee relations and communications.
10. Acting in a staff capacity to the labor relations department in union negotiations.
11. Administering the safety program.
12. Maintaining personnel records.
13. Maintaining check on compliance with federal, state and local labor laws.
14. Maintaining a stable work force.
15. Forecasting and projecting manpower needs.
16. Establishing and maintaining a relationship with community, religious and educational groups as a resource for personnel.
17. Complying with Title VII of the Equal Employment Opportunity Act.

Some companies separate labor relations and personnel. Labor relations advisors negotiate the union contract with staff assistance from the personnel department. The assumption is that the personnel director cannot be the "friend" of the employees as well as the "enemy" of the union at contract negotiation time.

PERSONNEL POLICIES

Seventy years ago, personnel policies and personnel departments were little known in almost any field. The hiring and firing of employees was left to the supervisor or executive who had immediate responsibility for workers; problems of training, compensation, and discipline were handled by numerous supervisors throughout the company, largely as they saw fit. Proper treatment of employees, or lack of it, depended primarily upon the humanitarian interests of the boss.

The "personnel movement," as it is known today, received its greatest impetus during World War I. During this period, because of the demands of the War, the labor force was smaller and wages rose, causing management to demand increased production. Business executives turned to the pioneers in personnel work for assistance in handling this problem. Also, labor legislation, fixing the responsibility of management for workers as well as the protection of the rights of workers, helped employee relations to improve.

As the employer became more responsible to his or her workers, morale-building activities and company-sponsored training programs developed. Consequently, employees gained in stature and dignity, a process that was fostered and encouraged by the early union movement. All of these activities changed personnel practices, and the modern concept of personnel management—the direction of human effort—emerged.

Once formulated, personnel policies should be subjected to continual appraisal and scrutiny by members of the management team. Policies should be reviewed in the light of experience, current trends, changes in labor laws, etc.

Since personnel policies should be clear and definite, they must be in writing. It is the responsibility of the personnel department, in cooperation with managers, to publicize and communicate these policies to all employees so as to avoid any problems.

The principal means of communicating information on personnel policies, practices, and procedures is through a personnel manual which, in a sense, is also a training manual. However, merely having this manual is not enough. Employees must know what is in it, especially the sections affecting the employees themselves.

Probably the most effective and popular method of presenting policies to the employees is the use of an employee handbook. It has become an established means of communication between management and employees, designed to inform new employees regarding policies and procedures, while at the same time providing a reference for all the employees. In addition, the employee handbook provides a means of conveying information about the company, its history, executives, products, customers, etc. Of particular importance to all employees is the information on wage payments, training, promotion, and fringe benefits.

Changes in personnel policies can be announced in many ways, including employee magazines, bulletins, letters, oral communications, and a combination of written and oral methods.

Communication with all employees is vital to a successful operation. The practice of "send a memo" establishes the fact that a message was sent, but does not provide effective communication because there is no real effort to gain cooperation or achieve mutual understanding.

As communications pass through the chain of command, the wording and method of communicating should be revised to fit the situation. A statement of changed personnel policy may be satisfactory to the top echelon, for example; but the second level needs an interpretation of the change in terms of its specific area or department, and the work-performing level needs instruction and training as well as an understanding of how the change is an improvement. Originating communications at the top level is a relatively simple task. Getting the change made at the work level, however, requires time, patience, training, and follow-up.

PERSONNEL PROCUREMENT

An important aspect of developing an efficient organization is a program of personnel procurement satisfactory to both employer and employee. Procurement is concerned with recruitment, selection, and placement of suitable employees within an organization. Recruitment can be defined as the function of seeking applicants for jobs, while selection is the function of choosing employees for job openings after considering the available candidates.

Expansion and labor turnover create a continuing need for new employees and, in turn, requires a continuing flow of job applicants. The total number of job-seekers must be large enough to permit the selection of well-qualified applicants. Therefore, a satisfactory selection ratio can be achieved only if adequate sources of labor supply are developed and maintained.

The retail food industry has had a poor history of retaining employees, especially part-timers. The store manager and the personnel department must be conscious that employee turnover is very expensive. It costs a great deal of money, time, and energy to train personnel to adapt to an organization's way of doing business. Therefore, steps should be taken to avoid turnover of employees, not only by proper procurement methods, but by good employee policies, and strong superordinate-subordinate relationships.

A number of supermarket firms prefer such turnover, however, particularly those firms with union contracts, where a three-month period is permitted for testing an employee before he becomes a union member. Even part-timers are subject to these restrictions and do not become eligible for union pay scales or benefits (or have to start paying dues) for the first three months. Since the salary levels and fringe benefits rise considerably after the first three months, these firms encourage turnover in those first three months where the supply of part-time help is plentifully available. Such short-sighted policies make for poor help and, in the long run, are more costly than the increases would be if the help were retained into the union-status phase.

More young people work their way through college in the supermarket field than in any other industry. The same is true for young people who have to work during their high school years. Yet, in survey after survey, when these same people who have worked in the supermarket to help defray school costs are asked if they would consider careers in the food field, most of them refuse to consider it. For some reason the initial image that these young people get of the supermarket industry is a negative one. Perhaps some study should be made to see why this is and what can be done about it.

RECRUITMENT

Recruiting varies with the conditions of the current labor market and with the qualifications required. The employment manager should know the most productive sources of qualified applicants as well as the most effective means of reaching them and encouraging them to apply.

Recruitment involves four major steps:

1. Preparing job analyses with job descriptions and specifications.
2. Developing satisfactory sources of supply.
3. Instituting application forms, comprehensive interviews, physical examinations, and general and specific tests for potential applicants.
4. Complete orientation to the company and the job for each prospective candidate.

An analysis of each job must be undertaken jointly by the sotre manager and the employment supervisor. In this way, there is no question of what the job requirements are and the necessary characteristics of the candidate. The duties required for the job are referred to as a *job description,* while the requirements for the individual are called *job specifications.* This analysis can be accomplished by questionnaires, interviews, and observations. It includes:

- Title and description of the job
- Exact duties
- Working conditions
- Training
- Compensation
- Advancement opportunities
- Physical requirements
- Mental ability
- Experience and education requirements
- Personal characteristics.

The personnel department should maintain a file of promising candidates to take care of anticipated turnover, planned expansion needs, and future management replacements. Periodic surveys should be taken among department heads, store managers, and district supervisors to determine the anticipated personnel needs. Promotable employees should be trained in depth at all levels to assure adequate selection when positions are to be filled.

Perhaps, if something could be done to change the image of the supermarket prevalent among the in-and-out students who work part-time in the stores while attending school, a new pool of highly trained and already experienced workers might become available to the industry. Most of these short-time employees see only the least desirable jobs in the field. Perhaps some effort should be made to let them know of the better jobs that become available a little higher up the ladder.

Internal Sources of Labor Supply

Basically, there are three important *internal* sources for filling vacancies. The first of these is a policy of transfer and promotion from within the organization. This policy assures workers an opportunity to advance and encourages individual development. Management positions are filled with experienced personnel familiar with the organization. Promotion from within increases morale and enthusiasm.

Another source of applicants is the friends and/or relatives of present employees. A very effective aid to recruiting is the recommendation of an applicant by an employee. Some administrators discourage this source of applicants on the grounds that it may lead to nepotism and the formation of cliques within the organization. This method, nevertheless, is a valuable source for employees below the executive level. Many companies use a "friend-card system," whereby employees recommend their friends and relatives for jobs on specially prepared cards. For each new employee hired, the worker providing the recommendation may receive a monetary reward.

The third internal source for filling vacancies is to recall former employees who have been released, provided, of course, that their service records were satisfactory. Many permanent positions are filled by persons who formerly worked on a temporary or part-time basis.

External Sources of Labor Supply

Most companies must look to outside sources for new employees. Time, effort, and effective publicity must be utilized to uncover suitable job applicants.

Many supermarket operators use state employment agencies, which are a part of a state-federal organization unified by the United States Employment Service of the Department of Labor, to locate available job applicants. Government employment agencies maintain a list of jobs available and send qualified, interested applicants to apply for the jobs.

Community resources, fraternal organizations, such as religious groups, schools, adult education centers, local clubs, fraternal organizations, and senior citizen centers are valuable outside sources for applicants. As with government employment agencies, careful screening is important.

Many large organizations conduct annual recruiting programs for executive-type personnel by visiting placement bureaus for graduates of colleges, universities, and professional schools. Arrangements are made with the placement officer to interview potential applicants. College recruitment is a highly regarded source of executive personnel. In carrying out a college recruitment program, care must be taken not to oversell the job; it can have a dampening effect on future relationships with the colleges as well as creating dissatisfaction on the part of the new employee.

Often, recruiters develop a sort of friendly rivalry as each tries to attract the more desirable students. One such recruiter for a nationally known chain, perhaps carried away by this spirit of rivalry, described a training program for new college graduates which was extremely attractive. The only problem was that it existed only in the imagination of that recruiter.

When some of the recruits from a number of colleges appeared at the headquarters of the company the following June to claim the jobs offered them earlier, the company was quite embarrassed. An effort was made to appease some of the angry applicants who were top students and had turned down other offers that had seemed less attractive. The firm even tried to go part way toward creating what the recruiter had described, but the damage and ill will engendered resulted in not one single new graduate joining the chain that year. A warning was issued to the firm by the colleges involved that their recruiters either be more truthful or not participate in the recruiting programs of the colleges.

If a store is fortunate enough to be close to schools that offer food marketing or supermarket management as a career interest, management should arrange for these students to be recruited while they are sophomores or juniors. Studies have indicated that after graduation, they will usually stay with the company with which they have trained.

In addition to placement offices, most colleges, high schools, and professional schools have employment services for students who are seeking part-time employment while pursuing their educations. This offers students a "pay-as-you-learn" plan. A number of firms select students who have expressed an interest in the supermarket field, helping them through college with tuition scholarships and permitting them to work part-time in the stores. Very often, part-time help acquired from these sources become valuable full-time employees.

Most colleges and universities operate organized recruiting services, while high schools arrange to coordinate recruiting through designated teachers. Ordinarily, applicants hired through these channels are carefully selected and screened; therefore, they are more desirable than the average applicant applying directly to the employment office. For specialized jobs, qualified applicants can often be contacted through business schools. It would be wise for store managers or personnel directors to contact schools with distributive education programs, since their students are more highly motivated and must answer to both the school coordinator and the store manager as to job progress. Here again, studies have shown that turnover rates are greatly reduced.

Just about every state in the nation has at least one college or junior college in which distributive education programs include some course on food distribution and supermarkets. Several hundred such colleges have two-year courses that deal heavily with the food distribution field.

The following colleges have full four-year degree programs that specialize in food distribution: Food Marketing Academy, St. Joseph's University (Philadelphia); Cornell University, University of Massachusetts; Michigan State University, and Western Michigan University. Michigan State, Cornell, and the University of Southern California also have graduate programs that offer masters degrees in the field.

Just about every graduate of each of these schools has at least one job offer in the field long before his last year at school is completed. Many of the students are helped through the various programs by firms in the field. All of these schools welcome recruiters.

Newspaper advertising is another method used to recruit prospective employees. Open or signed advertisements are often used to attract large numbers of people for store openings. "Blind" advertisements (i.e., the company name is not given) are commonly used when recruiting for higher level positions. This form of advertising avoids incurring the resentment of present employees who may consider themselves qualified for the position.

Additional methods used to recruit prospective employees include: in-store posters, radio advertising, leaflets, handbills, and special brochures. Radio advertising is not generally used for announcing job openings, but it is effective when emphasizing that a company is a "good place to work." Brochures are useful in presenting employment possibilities to students and specialized groups. Leaflets, handbills, and posters generally emphasize good starting pay, interesting work, extra benefits, rapid promotions, secure future, and stable employment.

Each step in the recruitment process involves a contact between the public and the company through the company representatives. Persons who are not applicants are also exposed to the recruitment program; they often form their opinions of the company because of the recruitment program. For this reason, a positive public relations attitude must be taken. A company should protect its own reputation and relationship with the community in determining the methods and techniques used.

Retailing is looked upon by young people as a clerk-type operation with advancement only for those financially able to own the store. In reality, the food industry offers a vast selection of careers with good possibilities for rapid promotion and frequent pay increases. In fact, very few businesses offer career opportunities equal to those in the food industry.

The food industry is the largest single employer in the United States. The range of different types of jobs available in the field run the gamut of engineering, computer processing, accounting, law, advertising, transportation, finance, production, selling, manufacturing, chemistry, and agriculture. It is difficult to find any other field that requires such a diversity of skills. Yet the average person thinks of supermarkets in terms of checkers, stockers, and bag boys.

The need is for more career information, especially for the guidance and placement people in high schools, colleges, and universities. Better career publicity will provide retailing with an improved occupational image, attracting more capable people. A good starting place to achieve this is building morale and pride in the job for both full and part-time employees by providing information on career opportunities as well as company growth and development. Much progress in this area has been made, but much more still needs to be done if food retailing is to achieve sufficient stature to attract capable people, especially among the young.

For many years, the supermarket industry has done a poor job of public relations when it comes to attracting personnel. Many of the better executives in the field "backed into" the food industry. Few have come into the field because of the same desire that attracts young people into fields considered to be more glamorous. However, bringing food to the consumer conveniently and at low prices affords an exciting and challenging opportunity.

More recently, a few of the more progressive firms in the field have become active participants in sponsoring and recruiting actively the more capable and desirable personnel available. These recruits to the food industry find more and more that the field they represent can be as attractive as the engineering, aerospace and other "glamour" fields.

THE SELECTION PROCESS

In the selection process, the personnel department determines which applicants are to be hired. Thus, the process is one of obtaining and interpreting information through which to predict the probable success or failure of an applicant. The high cost of replacing an unsatisfactory employee makes effective selection of vital importance.

Obtaining information on the relevant factors concerning each applicant is important and involves a series of steps and techniques. To be of value, each technique must contribute to the interpretation of information about the applicant. These steps include:

- Filing of the application blank
- The employment interview
- Testing
- Physical examination
- Checking references
- Making the decision.

These techniques are not necessarily used in the specific order shown and vary with the level of the job and the procedure followed in obtaining the application.

An important initial step, often overlooked by employment offices, is the proper reception of applicants. The employment or personnel office is capable of making a strong, first impression on the candidate. Therefore, it is important that good physical surroundings be provided in order to give applicants a favorable image of the company. Furthermore, all applicants should be treated courteously and in such a manner that they feel the organization is a good place to work. It must be remembered that applicants and their families, relatives, and friends are food store customers. Their good image of the store must be maintained or enhanced.

Studies conducted by the Food Marketing Institute have indicated that full- and part-time cashiers and clerks were most often hired at store level. About 70 percent of the part-time jobs were filled at store level, while 50 percent of the full-time cashiers and clerks were hired from central headquarters. Large-volume stores usually hire more employees at the central office than do smaller volume stores. Therefore, it is essential that the store manager become familiar with employment practices and each step in the hiring process.

The Employment Application. If properly designed, the application form can serve many purposes. The basic reason for its use is to determine whether an applicant meets the company's general standards of employment. Many organizations use a preliminary blank for higher level positions, which does not go into as much detail as the regular application blank. This preliminary application, however, does provide information that can aid the interviewer in screening applicants and determining which qualified people should be requested to fill out a more comprehensive form.

Although forms used will vary greatly in detail and layout from company to company, they provide the employment office with:

1. A means by which the candidate's handwriting, spelling, and ability to follow written instructions can be observed.
2. Detailed information that relates to the applicant's capacities, interests, and experiences. Although this information must be analyzed and verified by additional investigation, it provides the basis for the employment decision.
3. A guide to the direction of the employment interview. Information obtained by subsequent questioning aids in developing an understanding of the applicant's abilities and ambitions.
4. A basic record of a potential candidate, who may be called upon at a future date if there are no openings at the time of the application.

In addition to the applicant's name, address and social security number, the application blank serves as a permanent record of education, past work experience, and interests. While a broad picture of the applicant's background is helpful, care must be taken so that the application blank is not excessively detailed. Many employers are discovering that their application blanks contain questions that are either irrelevant or misleading to the candidates. Forms should be as brief and simple as possible, requiring only essential and useful information.

Federal and state laws and regulations prohibit discrimination based on race, religion, national origin, age, and sex; therefore, requests for information in these areas should not be included either on employment applications or in job interviews.

The Employment Interview. The employment interview is by far the oldest and most commonly used technique for selecting new employees. In some stores, the interview is the only tool used in the selection process. This initial meeting with the candidate is management's opportunity to make preliminary decisions concerning the applicant's suitability. Speech, dress and other obvious characteristics should be noted.

Although the circumstances under which they are conducted vary considerably, employment interviews cannot be held in a hurried manner. A well-placed interview will put the applicant at ease, which, in turn, should elicit honest responses. The interviewer must remember that performing the function of the interview is of prime importance to the public relations of the organization. To the applicant, the interviewer represents the management of the organization.

Even though interviewing techniques vary, there are two basic methods in common use today: the directed or patterned interview and the nondirected method. In using the patterned technique of interviewing, the employment manager seeks answers to directed questions, such as: "What did you especially like about your former job?" or "What are your reasons for leaving your last job?" In this manner, the interview is limited to desired information and the interview is kept brief. Questions should be posed to elicit as much information as possible, and those that provide yes or no responses should be kept to a minimum.

The second basic interviewing technique is the nondirected method. In this method, the applicant is asked a general question and is encouraged to talk freely and openly on whatever subject or area to which the question might lead. A typical question might be: "Tell me what appeals to you about this company?" By using this technique, authorities feel that the underlying motives, opinions, and attitudes of the interviewee can be brought to the surface more readily than in the directed technique. The nondirected interview takes more time and requires the elicitation of a greater amount of information from the applicant; therefore, it is used primarily for executive-level employment applicants.

The exit interview takes place when an employee terminates employment with the company. This type of interview is used either when the supervisor takes action to discharge a worker or when the worker resigns. In either case, the exit interview is usually held as soon as possible after it becomes known that the worker is about to leave the organization. The value of the exit interview is that it:

1. Establishes for the record the reason for termination.
2. Promotes good relationships with workers who are to be separated involuntarily.
3. Attempts to keep the worker and his or her family, relatives, and friends as customers.
4. Helps identify problems in the store that may require correction.

Generally, personnel administrators consider it a poor practice to use the interview as a sole selection technique. Two equally competent interviewers often do not give the same rating to the same applicant. For this reason, many companies usually supplement the interview with reference checks, testing, and other available methods in personnel selection.

Tests. Many organizations are finding that tests, both of the psychological and skill types, can supplement other employment procedures and provide a considerable aid in appraising objectively the capacities and interests of applicants. Test scores must be interpreted and used as guides in conjunction with other information—not as absolutes. Tests should be given and interpreted by experts. Many large companies have employment counselors qualified to give and interpret tests. Among the types of tests used by food distributors are the following:

- Mental ability tests
- Temperament and personality tests
- Interest and preference tests
- Aptitude tests
- Skill tests.

In the food industry, tests are used to:

- Select new workers

- Assign specific jobs
- Select workers for training assignments
- Select workers for transfer to other positions
- Determine promotion levels
- Locate potential executive talent.

Physical Examinations. Physical examinations are sometimes required by law for people handling food. Furthermore, the physical examination protects both the applicant and the employer. Waste and costs mount when a person, although mentally qualified to do a job, lacks the physical characteristics of health and strength essential to job performance. Also, it is equally costly to employees to be assigned to work for which they are not physically qualified, both in terms of health and job satisfaction.

Physical examinations are not designed merely for purposes of rejection or to discriminate against handicapped applicants. Instead, these examinations permit new employees to be accepted with a minimum amount of risk to themselves, their fellow employees, and their employer. The object is safe, productive employment.

Reference Checking. The purpose of reference checking is to verify the information given by the applicant and to collect additional information. Basically, there are four methods of checking on an applicant: by telephone, personal visits, written inquiries, and outside investigating agencies. There are several sources that can be used to obtain the information. These include: former employers, schools and colleges, personal references, social security numbers, police records, and military discharges.

Of the four methods of checking references, probably the best is that of telephone checking. This method is generally preferred because unfavorable, but honest and accurate information is more likely to be revealed when it does not have to be placed in writing. In addition, the time and cost factors necessary to obtain the information by telephone are more favorable. Some operators use the Retail Credit Bureau for checking applicants.

Some companies place employees under fidelity bonds. The bonding company checks the applicant's past record. People with questionable or clouded records most often will not seek employment with companies that bond employees, thus these firms are eliminating undesirable applicants without the expense of checking them.

Making the Decision. The final step in the selection process is to interpret the findings and make decisions. Of course, this is a phase of selection that takes place at all stages of the process, as some candidates may fail to qualify at any step along the way.

The overall recommendation by the personnel officer concerning the probable success or failure of the applicant is based on a number of factors that should be considered in relation to the job being filled. These include informational, motivational, emotional, behavioral and physical factors. The best of the available applicants constitutes the labor supply from which selection must be made.

After the applicant for employment has been selected, agreement must be made as to wages, hours, and so forth. All matters relating to the employment should be carefully explained. This includes the general job description, union contract provisions, pay scale, fringe benefits, evaluation procedures, and the like. It is imperative for the prospective employee to understand all of the above before a final commitment is made.

EMPLOYEE ORIENTATION

The purpose, methods, and feedback of the orientation must be clearly developed, since most employee turnover occurs within the first few days. If properly handled, the employee orientation can reduce this number, but more important, it will lay the foundation for a productive and happy employee.

The new employee should be introduced to the store manager or person-in-charge. Next, the specific job should be explained, including work methods and standards. Fellow employees are introduced and a general orientation to the company and the job is achieved.

EMPLOYEE AND MANAGEMENT OBJECTIVES

To build an efficient work force, management must know what employees want and expect of the employer. When they are asked what they want (many of them have been asked in various opinion surveys, interviewing programs, etc.), they are likely to answer with such phrases as: "fair pay," "good working conditions," "a chance for promotion," "security," "to be treated as a human being," and so forth. In reading between the lines of such responses, it can be concluded that there is one general, basic objective: the desire to feel useful and important.

A survey of store employees will reveal that the opportunity to advance, to be creative, to use initiative, and to learn will often rate higher than good pay. The job factors considered important by store employees, not necessarily in order of priority, include:

- Opportunity for advancement
- Steady work
- Opportunity to be creative
- Opportunity to use initiative
- Training programs
- Recognition of achievements
- Competent supervisors
- Good pay
- Good working companions
- Comfortable working conditions
- Security.

The desire to feel important, creative, and useful is an important factor in producing good employee morale. Workers are willing and anxious to be productive, efficient, and loyal if it is felt that the employer is interested in them, is watching their efforts to improve, and is willing to reward their efforts.

The loyalty and devotion of employees cannot be bought. It must be earned by management through intelligent and honest efforts to treat all members of the organization with understanding and consideration. Management's recognition of the self-respect, the needs, and the responsibilities of the individual as well as his or her desire to succeed, makes a group of widely different individuals into an efficient working team. Management should recognize that the aims and goals of labor are not inconsistent with its own.

Simply stated, the objectives of supermarket management are to achieve efficient production and a good consumer image, to meet consumer needs at the lowest possible cost, and to earn a profit. Basically, the reduction of waste and increased efficiency on the part of all workers and executives are required to operate a supermarket successfully.

EMPLOYEE COMPENSATION

While "good pay" is relatively low on lists of employees' stated wants, this rating assumes a satisfactory pay scale in terms of the labor market. Therefore, wages and salaries are still important criteria in the creation of a satisfactory work force.

A compensation plan must satisfy both the company and the employee. Such a plan should attempt to do the following:

1. Reduce discontent, which in turn will keep labor turnover at a minimum.
2. Act as an incentive so that better performance is recognized.
3. Control wage costs.
4. Be recognized as a fair plan by employees.
5. Provide a feeling of security.
6. Be competitive within the industry.
7. Be easily administered.

Wages and Salaries

Fundamentally, wages and salaries must be fair and equitable. They must be related to the importance and difficulty of the work performed, and they must compare favorably with what other companies are paying for similar jobs. In all categories, people expect fair pay for the kind and amount of work done. Moreover, internal inequities are generally considered more serious than differences between one company and another.

Incentive or supplementary compensation will not make up for a salary structure that is inadequate in the first place. The whole salary program should be an incentive in itself. A salary program must enable employees to increase their earnings as they improve their job performance.

Incentive Plans

The old compensation concept considered adequate salaries, based on the responsibility and importance of the position, comparable with salaries paid for similar responsibilities by other employers, and fairly and equitably administered, as sufficient incentive and reward for maximum effort and accomplishment. The more modern concept, however, recognizes that a good incentive plan will produce improved performance far beyond the cost of the additional compensation and will be an important factor in attracting and retaining efficient employees.

One of the practical considerations in the adoption of an incentive plan is competition. Companies adopt incentive plans in order to keep their compensation policies in line with competition in the labor market. Incentive plans are either discretionary in nature or based on a fixed formula established and known by all concerned at the beginning of the period covered by the formula.

A discretionary incentive plan is a pure bonus, since both the funds and their distribution are discretionary. At the end of each year, management allocates an amount for bonus payment, selects those who will receive payments, and decides the amount each employee receives. This plan provides incentive if the payments are substantial and if the employees have confidence in management.

A variation is the semi-discretionary plan. This plan has the additional incentive of a predetermined formula for establishing the total amount of the bonus fund. A typical formula is: "Up to 10 percent of profits before taxes, after a 6 percent stockholders' equity has been set aside as a return on investment." The participants and the amount each is to receive is determined by management. This plan has added incentive because the participants know in advance that the bonus

fund will increase as profits increase and that each participant's share is likely to increase accordingly.

The next step toward increasing the incentive in bonus plans is to provide some basis for determining in advance each participant's share prorated on a salary basis. This eliminates the possibility of bias and personal favoritism and distributes bonuses according to the employee's contribution insofar as his or her salary reflects the individual's contributions.

Salaries alone, however, even though they are geared to the relative importance and difficulty of jobs, do not adequately compensate for outstanding performance. A formalized performance-appraisal plan distributes 40 to 60 percent of the bonus fund according to salaries. The remainder is distributed by management on an appraisal-of-performance basis.

A fixed-formula incentive plan has the advantage of notifying employees in advance of their participation and giving them some basis for calculating their potential bonus earnings throughout the year. Each employee is assigned shares or partial shares based on his or her responsibilities. The bonus fund is a fixed portion of earnings and frequently increases as profits increase to a fixed maximum percentage of the profits. Usually, the bonus payment to an employee may not exceed a set percentage of his or her annual salary.

The purpose of an incentive plan is to increase employee morale and productivity. To accomplish these purposes, incentive plans are tailored to fit the company. Thus, each plan is unique, but is basically either discretionary or a fixed formula. A discretionary plan is better suited to top-level personnel, but is used by a few companies for store-level employees. As long as payments are continual, and employees feel that the distribution is just, morale remains high. A fixed formula is frequently used for store-level employees. They know the conditions in advance and work for greater profits.

Important to establishing a good compensation plan is the continual process of job evaluation so that an appraisal of the value of the job and an equitable relationship with other jobs are attained. It should establish:

- Equal pay for equal work
- Salary scales for different quality and quantity of work
- Competitive wages within the community
- An explanation to employees of salary scales
- Salary commensurate with responsibilities and difficulty of work.

Supplementary Compensation

Supplementary forms of compensation are commonly referred to as "fringe benefits." Among the more common forms of supplementary compensation are:

- Retirement plans
- Stock options
- Life and health insurance.

Retirement Plans. The general function of retirement plans is to provide a sense of security, to reduce turnover, and to provide generally for better morale. Retirement plans have become so widespread that they are almost a necessity from a competitive standpoint.

Retirement plans are of two main types: fixed pension plans and profit-sharing retirement plans. The latter are again subdivided into plans that are adopted because the company wants to provide a retirement plan without the obligations of a pension plan; and plans that are used to supplement a pension plan to provide more liberal benefits.

Employee contributions can be used to increase the benefits. The favorable tax treatment granted these plans makes them an attractive employee saving program subscribed to, on the average, by 85 percent of those eligible. Employer contributions, either directly, as in contributory profit-sharing retirement plans, or indirectly, in the form of vested interests in pension plans, make the plans very attractive.

Stock Options. Stock option plans provide company employees with an opportunity to buy stock at favorable prices. Stock options are more practical for high-level employees—those more likely to understand stock values and prices and having large enough salaries to benefit from increased stock ownership. Favorable treatment by the income tax laws increases the attractiveness of stock options plans to higher salaried employees, since they are classed as capital gains rather than income.

A number of small and medium-sized regional chains have adopted employee stock option plans (ESOP) in which a portion of the company's stock is turned over to employees each year. The amount is based on profits of the firm, and the stock becomes the property of the employees on a prorata basis. (Eberhard's was one of the first chains in the country to adopt such a program, although many have since adopted similar programs.) It is a good incentive program for the employees and provides the company with tax-free investment capital. In the case of the Eberhard program, the employees eventually will own the firm. All employees who work more than twenty hours a week are in the plan, and in the case of separation, the employee is paid his or her share of the plan.

Life and Health Insurance. Many companies provide executives with supplementary compensation in the form of company-paid life and health insurance

policies. These plans provide additional security for employees and are important primarily in retaining employees.

Nonfinancial Incentives

In thinking about compensation, it should be recognized that virtually all employees are motivated by nonfinancial considerations as well as cash payment for their services. In fact, once a person's salary enables him or her to live comfortably, the nonfinancial factors become increasingly important. For example, some people respond to the urge for power, others desire social prestige, and some will sacrifice additional income for greater security. These factors and the techniques that have been developed to provide for their interplay form an integral part of any effective incentive program.

No purely formal system of financial rewards is sufficient in itself to encourage an individual to give his or her best. For example, a number of chains encourage their employees to further their educations, and after an employee has been with the firm for a fixed short period, the firm will pay the tuition for courses successfully completed. Some firms will limit the courses they will pay for to those approved by the firm as being beneficial or helpful to the work of the employee and the company. Others will pay for any successfully completed courses on the theory that any education is beneficial to both the employee and company.

A number of employees of Supermarkets General Corporation have received college degrees under such a program, one receiving his B.S. some years after the last of his three children received his. Some firms will take young people who say they will stay with the firm and loan them money to complete college, and after the employee has received the degree and worked a number of years, the loan is cancelled. This and other programs that look to the fulfillment of the employee outside of the workplace create more contented and loyal employees.

At all levels, there must be a consciousness of, and a pride in, being part of a well-run organization; some opportunity for the exercise of individual judgment within the limits of assigned responsibilities; a fair chance at promotion and advancement; and an awareness of the human need for recognition of individual accomplishment. Supermarket operators must bear in mind, therefore, that financial incentives in themselves are not likely to be effective unless the work environment stimulates each employee to put forth his or her best efforts.

A recent survey conducted by the National Opinion Research Center reported that 51 percent of those surveyed thought that important work and a sense of accomplishment were the most important things to look for in a job. Only 19 percent stated that income was the most important aspect of a job, while 18 percent looked at the chance for promotion as most important. A relatively small 7 percent considered job security, and only 5 percent considered hours.

EMPLOYEE RELATIONS

Employees are human beings with individual temperaments, needs, problems, hopes, fears, skills, abilities, and idiosyncracies. As such, they have desires and motives of which they are only vaguely aware. Unless management recognizes and satisfies these, the workers will either turn to other areas of endeavor that can satisfy them, or they will become frustrated and unproductive.

One of the reasons that employees in many cases demand higher wages is that the worker knows he or she is not satisfied, but cannot really pinpoint the source of the dissatisfaction. Thus, the worker demands higher wages, thinking that this will bring satisfaction. Actually, even though wages are important, the employee is really more interested in wage differentials than in the absolute amount of his or her wages. Wage differences express the relative social status of different jobs. Thus, when wages are sufficient to satisfy the employee's basic physical needs, a greater interest in his or her wages in relation to those of co-workers becomes more evident.

Management should display a concern for the welfare of the employees and a recognition of their needs and feelings. These attitudes will be reflected in regular consultation with subordinates before actions affecting them are taken, a clear recognition on the part of management that workers are people, and that labor is not a commodity which can be purchased and manipulated as can the other elements of the production process.

Unions

Workers increase their bargaining power by acting collectively through a union. Most employees of large companies, especially chain operators, are organized. A few companies have internal unions; however, most supermarket employees are members of industry-wide unions, such as the United Food Workers Union. Management has learned to live with unions, and many firms deal with a large number of them.

A study conducted by the Food Marketing Institute found that 53 percent of the companies reported at least some of their store-level employees were unionized. Within this group, meat department employees and cashiers were those that most frequently belonged to a union. Unionization of supermarket employees was found to increase as the company volume increased, so that 75 percent of the companies that do over $100 million annually had unions.

The Store Manager

The store manager is probably the most important single factor in building a happy, efficient work force. He or she is management's contact with the workers. Nevertheless, the manager's concern should be not only with meeting production needs, but also with meeting the needs of subordinates. Studies have shown that the most successful supervisors, in terms of high team spirit and productivity, achieve this success by the indirect route of knowing their workers as people and allowing room for individual differences and self-expression—not by using the force of authority.

Some important qualities that the store manager must possess are: the ability to build teamwork through a continual display of team spirit; the ability to integrate human needs and technical demands; the ability to give clear, precise and timely orders so that the work can be done through people; handling complaints quickly and fairly; and identifying and resolving problems efficiently and rapidly.

The store manager should develop a communications system that will maintain understanding and a sense of working toward a common goal. Communications should be used to give the worker a chance to identify with the work group and with the organization. Training and knowledge of the personnel function will help enable the store manager to achieve the overall goals of the store and the company.

TRAINING

A major responsibility of personnel management is training. This is usually done in conjunction with the store manager. Many food industry authorities see a direct correlation of store success with the calibre of the training program implemented. It must not only be a permanent part of store policy, but a continual part of every supervisor's job.

Some firms differentiate between training and development. Training is usually a formalized method of developing specific kinds of skills and knowledge, while development is a long-range plan usually associated with management development.

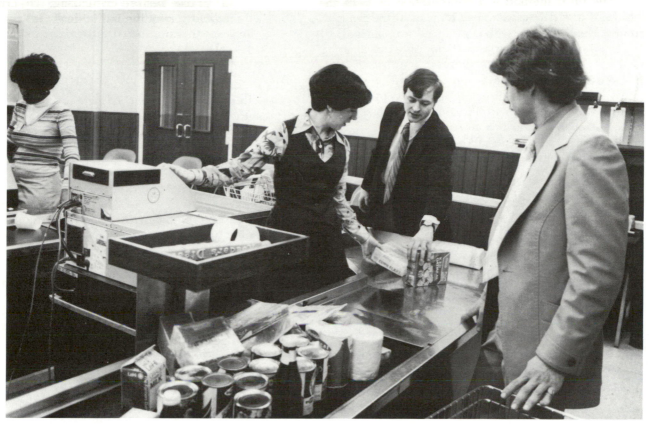

Learning about checkout operations is what this scene is all about, at Acme Markets' corporate training center in Philadelphia. Giving instructions is Acme's corporate training manager. The realistic setting here makes it easier to adjust to actual store conditions.

There are very clear advantages and benefits to an effective training program, including:

1. More effective job performance and greater productivity.
2. Adhering to objectives, procedures, rules, and regulations, which in turn increase customer satisfaction and reduce errors.
3. Improving and helping reduce employee turnover.
4. Increasing the opportunity for greater earnings of all employees.
5. Helping to simplify management problems and responsibilities.
6. Developing skills and better attitudes.
7. Standardizing procedures.

Guidelines to Training

Although employees learn in many different ways, there are some basic concepts that can help a supervisor in training an employee. Employees will learn when they are ready and motivated to learn.

They must be made aware of a need to learn which will be satisfied during the learning process. Actual involvement facilitates the training; employees should actually participate in the activity they are learning. This is why on-the-job training can be such a successful part of a good training program. If possible, an attempt should be made to associate the learning activity with something in which the employee is interested or familiar.

There are three major methods of training: the centralized, the decentralized, and the combination approach. The centralized method places the training function within a special department under a supervisor responsible for establishing various types of training programs. Classrooms, audio-visual materials, programmed instruction, training manuals, and other instructive devices are used. Training may be on-site or at a training center.

The decentralized training approach provides the store manager with the responsibility of training people within the store. This responsibility is usually delegated to specific subordinates, such as department managers, to provide on-the-job training.

The third method is a combination of both the centralized and decentralized systems of instruction. Training usually begins with centralized training and is then completed at the store with the store manager and the management staff. A successful approach is the sponsor system, whereby an experienced staff employee is assigned the direct responsibility of training the new employee. In addition to the prestige, the sponsor is rewarded for this activity.

There are some basic guidelines to training an employee, no matter which method is used. These include:

1. Define objectives to be learned clearly.
2. Know and outline the information to be taught.
3. Emphasize the reasons for learning the material being taught.
4. Arrange material in sequential order, breaking down the information into small steps.
5. Give complete instructions without leaving out any details.
6. Demonstrate how the job is done.
7. Allow the employee to participate and practice by doing what was taught.
8. Check performance and give assistance, where necessary, using the following approach:

(a) praise before criticizing; (b) criticize the activity, not the individual; (c) criticize employees in private; and (d) provide a positive atmosphere.

9. Review progress.
10. Retrain if necessary.
11. Allow the employee to see the learned activity in a whole sequence as part of the entire function.

Who Should Be Trained?

Training is a continual process and should not be restricted only to new employees. The following are some of the groups in need of training:

1. New and inexperienced, full-time employees, providing them with full orientation and basic skills.
2. Experienced personnel, providing them with new, updated information.
3. Employees designated for promotions or job changes.
4. Part-time, inexperienced employees.
5. Management training—for the development of the employee and the store.

22

HOUSEKEEPING: SANITATION, MAINTENANCE, AND SAFETY

The store manager must satisfy the customer by providing a clean, safe environment in which to shop, must abide by government health and safety regulations, and must also apply preventive maintenance to avoid costs that may be incurred through neglect.

There are three basic objectives of a supermarket housekeeping program: the protection of health, the safety of employees and customers, and the maintenance of equipment. Many thousands of dollars a year in lost profits may be attributed to poor housekeeping procedures. Stores that do not maintain proper housekeeping programs may sustain a reduction in gross profit as high as 10 percent. At least half this amount could be saved through store housekeeping management.

An effective program of housekeeping is essential in order to maintain a favorable store image. The following elements contribute to the total store appearance.

- Spotless fixtures
- Clean and fresh-looking merchandise
- Pleasant surroundings
- Noncongested aisles
- Nonlittered floors
- Clean and well-groomed employees
- Safe walking surfaces
- Odor-free atmosphere
- Clean and sanitary environment.

SUPERMARKET SANITATION

Good sanitation management can control the microbial growth that causes meat discoloration and spoilage as well as the loss of other products. Effective sanitation procedures can result in longer shelf life, which in turn can result in savings in labor costs, materials, and products.

The following factors are an absolute necessity for a successful sanitation program:

1. Complete commitment by top management.

2. Proper training and indoctrination of store personnel.
3. Establish cleaning procedures and schedules.
4. Allow sufficient time and money to expedite this program.
5. Follow up on cleaning procedures and schedules.
6. Inspection by designated person who has been properly trained.
7. Establish high sanitation standards.
8. No smoking where food is being processed.
9. All wooden surfaces must be cleaned and sanitized every four hours. (Lag phase: it takes bacteria four hours for accelerated growth.)
10. Food handlers must wash their hands using hand detergent with sanitizers after every absence from their stations.
11. Trash receptacles must be thoroughly cleaned after each dumping; eliminate decomposed food particles and breeding places for roaches, flies, maggots, and other vermin.
12. Meat packaging procedures must comply with state and local regulations, such as the preparation of chicken and pork away from beef. (Chickens may become infected with salmonella bacteria; pork with a parasite causing trichinosis.)

Refrigeration is an important tool in bacteria control. The lower the temperature, the longer the case-life of the product; 32° F. for meat is proper. Dairy—milk and cheese—should be kept below 40° F. Salami, ham, and other delicatessen meats should be maintained below 39° F.

Bacteria are divided into four general categories:

1. *Benign.* They just sit there; neither harmful nor beneficial.
2. *Useful.* Needed to make various foods, such as cheese, yogurt, sour cream, beer, and wine.
3. *Spoilage.* Will spoil food, but will not cause illness.

4. *Pathogenic.* Capable of causing disease. Among the most widely known of this type of bacteria are:

- Staphylococcus—affects the respiratory tract.
- Salmonella—affects the intestinal tract, causing nausea, regurgitation, and diarrhea.
- Botulinus—usually found in infected canned or jarred foods. This type of bacteria is especially virulent; attacking the nervous system, it causes paralysis and death.

To avoid contamination of food and to assure cleanliness in the store, clean floors, shelves, fixtures, and refrigerated and freezer cases; and in the back rooms, implement regularly scheduled cleaning procedures. Selection of the most effective cleansers for each area should be based on the characteristics of the cleanser.

To be most effective, detergents should be noncorrosive, nontoxic, able to dissolve easily and rapidly in water, and stable when stored for long periods of time.

The most common detergents are:

1. *Alkaline.* The most widely used, normal cleaner for equipment.
2. *Germicidal.* These detergents contain sanitizing (germ killing) agents and are usually referred to as one-step cleaners.

Good sanitizers include:

1. *Chlorine.* Kills most types of bacteria; inexpensive to use; does not require rinsing; may irritate the skin.
2. *Quaternary (Quats).* Highly stable; nonirritating; noncorrosive; effective in destroying vegetative organisms; must be rinsed.

Rodent and Insect Control

Pests are the scourge of the food industry. They cause hundreds of thousands of dollars in damage annually. Food inspection officers are very concerned about this area of food store sanitation. Probably more retail food stores are fined and/or closed because of rodent and/or insect infestation than for any other sanitation violation. And yet, many operators consider the presence of insects and/or rodents as normal and routine. These operators feel that the main objective is to keep these pests from being seen by the customer.

Naturally, no operator wants pests in the store,

but most feel the only thing they can do is keep the store as clean as possible and employ a good pest control company. This is a good start, but an adequate pest control program must go further than that; it is also necessary to know something about the characteristics and habits of the pests.

Rodents and insects can affect at least two vital areas of retail food store operations: economics (spoilage, waste, customer rejection) and health (foodborne illnesses).

Rats and mice carry disease-producing organisms in their fur, intestinal tracts, and on their bodies. They often feed in garbage dumps and sewers; sewage is largely made up of human waste, which very often contains disease-producing (pathogenic) organisms. The same is true of insects, such as flies and roaches, found in places where food is stored. Basically and simply stated, there are four very important steps that must be taken to control pests:

1. Do not let them in.
2. Do not give them a home.
3. Starve them.
4. Kill them with a professional, ongoing extermination program.

Eliminate all possible sources of entry by making certain that there are no openings around doors (especially at the bottom). This is a common problem with receiving doors. Seal all cracks in walls, doors, or openings which may provide an entrance for pests.

Make sure that windows and screens are in good repair and that air curtains are working properly. Openings around pipes should be covered with an adequate protective material, such as sheet metal or concrete. Rodents also can gain entry by climbing pipes or wires; therefore, metal shields or guards should be placed over them. In addition, vents or exhaust fans, common sources of entry, should have suitable coverings to keep out both rodents and insects.

It is inevitable that a few pests will get into any food store, in spite of the best control efforts. Once they do get in, however, their ability to survive depends entirely on the store operator's skill as a housekeeper. A cluttered store is an invitation for pests to make a permanent home. If boxes, for example, are allowed to sit directly on floors or against walls, this provides a perfect hiding place. Old boxes, lumber, rags, trash, or any other rubbish lying about make perfect nesting places either inside or outside the store.

Without food, rodents and insects will starve and die. If they cannot find a meal at the store, they will go elsewhere to satisfy their hunger. Therefore, control of these pests is possible by limiting their access to food and water. It does not take much to feed a hungry rodent or insect; just a few leftover scraps will satiate them for quite some time. This is why a *thorough*, store-wide cleaning job is necessary every day. Meals for pests may result from:

- Poor storage practices
- Improperly cleaned equipment
- Improperly cleaned facilities
- Improper containers for garbage
- Garbage receptacles not covered tightly
- Trash and garbage left outside, but near, the store.

Most retailers have regular visits by an exterminator to provide preventive maintenance in keeping pests out of the store and to eliminate them quickly, should they gain possession of the premises. In city stores, shopping centers, and strips, however, the supermarket may share premises with another enterprise that may not have to be as concerned with vermin as the supermarket. Also, with many areas now requiring mandatory container return, vermin often may enter the store in cases or large containers of such bottles and cans.

One New Jersey regional chain had a disturbing incident occur during the price-freeze era of the 1970's, when stores were lucky to earn ¼ to ½ of 1 percent of sales and the total industry earnings figure was almost zero percent. As an economy move, the chain discontinued its preventive maintenance visits by an exterminator firm.

One of the chain's stores was in a shopping center that had open and wooded areas on one side. About a mile from the store, the state highway department was cutting a depressed highway and in several cases had to cut and move existing sewer lines. Infestations began to occur within five miles of the highway by rat colonies that had been uprooted by the highway activity. Homes in the $250,000 value category suddenly started to have rat problems.

The store was no exception, but by the time it was discovered, the problem in that store had become a major one. The local health department shut the store for more than a week before it was ready to let the store reopen. The chain has been on regular preventive maintenance with an exterminator firm ever since.

It is advisable for every store operator to have an ongoing pest control program administered by a reputable, professional company. In the long run, however, the success of the program remains in the hands of the retailer. If the manager does not take corrective action, as given in the first three steps listed on page 158, no professional program will be able to guarantee the control of pests.

Sanitation Program Planning

A good sanitation program can only be achieved with properly trained personnel. Top management as well as store personnel must be convinced that sanitation is one of the most important factors in the proper management of food stores. Therefore, it is important that all concerned be properly trained in the management of the sanitation program.

Many store operators object to becoming involved in a sanitation program because of its cost. However, the initial outlay of money will result in a greater financial return, as well as creating better relations with consumers and government agencies. The results in the financial area will be marked reduction in shrinkage, such as rewraps in the meat department, and reduction of spoilage because of rodent and vermin infestation.

A well-designed housekeeping program, as with any management objective, must follow a prepared plan. This includes:

- Assigning areas of authority and responsibility for each function
- Selling the program to all employees
- Training employees
- Establishing work and performance standards
- Providing needed equipment and supplies.

Photo courtesy of Food Mart stores, owned and operated by Convenient Industries of America Inc.

Sanitation must get high priority with supermarket managers. You can see the floor shine in this grocery department. Health standards are making supermarket management more concerned about this aspect of store upkeep.

Areas of responsibility for the sanitation program should be assigned by departments. The meat managers and meat specialists should be responsible for the meat department, the produce manager for the produce department, and so on throughout the store. Department heads should assign the necessary duties to subordinate employees and arrange for just and equitable distribution of such duties. Above all, the wholehearted cooperation of everyone concerned is needed.

A project to sell work-level employees on proper maintenance procedures can be accomplished through established channels. Such techniques as suggestion boxes, posters, and regular employee meetings can be used to "sell" the housekeeping program to employees, who must be reminded to be continually alert to maintaining the program.

Federal agencies are just about ready to promulgate a nationwide store sanitation code on which they have been working nearly a decade. After being adopted, the program will be enforced at state and local levels, if the respective agencies adopt the code as their own. Enforcement will be partially funded from the Federal level. Federal agencies have stated at hearings that they do not have the personnel to enforce the store guideline codes.

SUPERMARKET MAINTENANCE

Preventive maintenance can be scheduled on a simple check-off chart. Such charts are usually supplied by the home-office maintenance departments. Duties would include oiling motors, checking wiring and electrical outlets, listening for unusual motor noises, checking temperature gauges, and so forth.

The maintenance program must be adaptable to each department. Basically, this necessitates establishing a set of general principles which are, in turn, applied specifically to each department and each person in it. Such a program serves the dual role of encouraging the employee to feel proud of the work area while encouraging cooperation with others whenever necessary for the good of the whole store.

Complicated repairs and preventive maintenance procedures are the responsibility of the maintenance department. Large companies operate and staff their own departments as an integral part of the organization. Others contract with outside firms for heavy repairs and preventive maintenance service. Often, a combination of these two policies is practiced; for example, store managers may be authorized to contact local repairmen whenever necessary.

Regular maintenance crews usually handle the necessary repairs on refrigeration units, electrical equipment such as air conditioning, heating systems, and plumbing. In addition, it is often their responsibility to transfer equipment from one store to another.

Excluding major repairs, a preventive maintenance checklist with time schedules and directions should include:

1. Oiling motors in refrigeration units, fans, heaters, air conditioners, compressors, and door opening systems.
2. Cleaning condensers in refrigeration units.
3. Inspecting machines incorporating belt systems to see that the belts are in satisfactory condition.
4. Checking refrigeration equipment for operating condition and proper temperature level. (A daily record of temperatures should be kept.)
5. Checking air-conditioning systems in summer and heating systems in winter.
6. Cleaning or replacing air filters in air conditioners and heaters.
7. Replacing any burned-out indoor and outdoor lighting; also checking for defective wiring and maintaining a ready supply of fuses where they can be easily located.
8. Inspecting faucets, piping, traps, and toilet bowls for leaks and congestion.
9. Checking for signs of rodents and pests.

The following points should act as a guide for all store managers:

1. Establish a systematic program of maintenance.
2. Arrange daily inspection of equipment, plumbing, etc.
3. Post information giving instructions for emergency action. Keep employees alerted to emergency procedures.
4. Inform employees of company policy relating to maintenance and emergency procedures.
5. Secure prompt action on all maintenance and repair work.
6. Keep employees alerted to safety and accident prevention.
7. Train employees on fire prevention action and procedures, including what to do in various emergencies.
8. Train employees to use authorized procedures, supplies, and equipment.
9. Inform employees on the relationship between maintenance and consumer image.

Store managers should assign specific employees the responsibility for the daily preventive maintenance work. It is not enough that supermarket personnel have a knowledge of how to prevent accidents and properly police the retail unit—the knowledge must be translated into action. This can be accomplished by setting forth sound personnel policies and efficient operating procedures. Contests, bulletins, training courses, and the frequent briefing of store employees are especially helpful for this purpose.

SAFETY AND ACCIDENT PREVENTION

Since the supermarket customer most often self-selects items in the store and moves quickly through the aisles of displayed merchandise, he or she may be oblivious to the hazards that may exist. A prepared supermarket manager, with the aid of employees, can decrease the chances for most types of accidents.

Large supermarkets with a large variety of merchandise lines, heavy customer traffic during peak hours, and a large work force have a high accident potential. The safety problem is sufficiently great to cause large supermarket operators to establish safety departments with safety directors in charge. Reduction of accidents is a customer relations problem as well as a cost reduction consideration. Small operators can assign the safety program to an existing department or area, such as personnel.

Store image is an important consideration in terms of accidents to shoppers. The average customer is not safety conscious, but expects the operator to provide safe shopping facilities. Reports of injuries, either in the local news media or by word of mouth, are detrimental to the consumer image of the store.

Also, employee accidents are costly in terms of lost work hours and compensation. One large operator estimates that it takes the profit of one out of each twelve stores operated to pay accident costs. When an accident happens, the cost is not just limited to medical costs, but to compensation, legal fees, and other costs that may surface at a later date. There are estimates that accident costs are actually four to five times as great as insurance claim dollars. These include: the loss of the injured party as a future customer, the employee time lost in attending the injured party, the purchasing power of those customers observing or involved in the accident, and any broken merchandise itself.

Customer accidents usually fall into the following three categories:

1. Personal injury which represents 69 percent of the accidents and has a 95 percent settlement cost.
2. Property damage which represents 22 percent

of the accidents and has a 31.5 percent settlement cost.
3. Other claims which represent 9 percent of the accidents and have an 11.5 percent settlement cost.

Within the personal injury area, falling has the highest incident rate, with more than 40 percent of all accidents in this category. Almost 80 percent of the falls occur within the store. Most of these would be controllable and preventable if store personnel were made more aware of accident prevention—of the causes and the preventive action that should be taken. Some of the causes include damp, wet and icy floors; spilled merchandise on the selling floor, including food matter from the meat, deli or produce departments; poor floor maintenance; cases left in aisles; poor illumination; and broken floor surfaces.

Another preventable cause of accidents is falling cans, especially from displays more than six feet in height. Some precautions that can prevent this from happening include: placing heavy items in lower bins, using dividers between beverage displays, and not placing more than three units on top of one another on the top shelves.

Other accidents can be traced to poor housekeeping in the store. The following checklist can be used as a guide to instruct employees in accident prevention:

1. Keep floors clean and uncluttered. Police the store floors regularly for broken glass, wet leaves, and other items of a similar nature.
2. Keep aisles clear for customer traffic. Remove unused shopping carts and empty cartons.
3. Build safe displays. Massive displays are impressive, but can cause injury unless protected and constructed to withstand customer shopping and bumping.
4. Keep sidewalks and parking lot areas clean and policed. Common causes of accidents occurring outside the store include cracked sidewalks and improperly parked cars.
5. Dispose of waste materials according to company policy.

With ever bigger stores, warehouse stores, and similar types of retailing that keep reserve stocks above regular selling areas in the stores, new potential hazards are created. Extra care must be taken that such reserve stocks are secure in the overhead racks with no danger of cases falling. Particular care must be taken to insure the in-stock position of all product, not only from the standpoint of losing sales, but for customer safety. On occasion, some customer, finding the regular shelves out of product, may attempt to climb the racks to bring down a case of the desired item himself.

Safety Programs

A preventive approach to accidents must be practiced. This can be accomplished by establishing safety programs tailored to fit each individual company.

Getting a safety program "off on the right foot" can be accomplished by incorporating it into the regular orientation and training program used for new employees. New employees are impressionable, and the importance of safe work habits, the elimination of hazards, and proper housekeeping procedures should be impressed upon them as soon as possible. Also, refresher training should be undertaken at frequent intervals to keep employees alert to safety procedures.

A common, easy-to-operate type of program is the use of safety volunteers on a rotating basis. The duties assigned to the safety volunteer include daily safety checks throughout the store for careless work habits, potential hazards, and any carelessness which might lead to or cause accidents. Daily reports are given to the store manager, summarizing the findings as well as remedial action taken and recommendations for action to be taken by management.

The store manager submits a monthly report to the safety committee at headquarters summarizing the monthly findings and the work of the volunteer safety officers. The company or division accident prevention program is the responsibility of a safety committee which usually includes the divisional vice president, the controller, the construction engineer, and the transportation, warehousing and training directors.

Another type of program is the use of a continual safety education program under the direction and supervision of a safety engineer. Safety is communicated to employees by various media. A very successful medium for personnel information is large, colorful, cartoon-type posters supplied to all stores for posting. These spotlight the causes of accidents and emphasize careful work habits, clean floors, careful stocking, and efficient use of operating equipment, display fixtures, and work tools.

In addition, each store has a safety promoter or inspector. Some variation exists in the selection and length of service; usually, each employee is assigned to serve as the safety inspector for a period of one or two months. This provides each employee with a detailed look at the causes of and remedies for accidents. The duties of the safety inspector include a daily inspection of sales, processing and stockroom floors for removal of any hazards; check operating equipment and displays; and search for evidence of careless work habits. A monthly report of safety activities is then made to the store manager. Stores are rated according to their safety record.

Another approach to improving the safety record is the use of a safety manual. Each new employee is given a manual which includes safety practices. Safe work procedures and practices should be an important part of the training program. Specific instructions on the proper use of knives, tools, and equipment, as well as the proper methods for lifting objects, are important and should be reviewed periodically. The manual should emphasize the "how" and "why" of accident prevention.

New employees are also told how workmen's compensation and public liability insurance operates. Also, many employees are trained in first aid procedures and how to handle more serious injury cases.

A somewhat novel method of communicating to employees involves the use of hourly safety reminders in the form of musical jingles over the store loudspeaker system.

Other devices to help keep accidents at a minimum are: posters, safety buttons, articles on safety in company publications, and contests calling for safety slogans with cash prizes. The winning slogans from such contests could be used as a "Safety Slogan of the Week" for each store.

Safety Follow-Up

The safety record of each unit of the company should be reviewed at fixed intervals—monthly or quarterly. This review uncovers problem areas. For example, if half the accidents that occurred are falls caused by floor conditions, and most falls are in the produce department, the remedy would be better housekeeping with emphasis on the produce area. If employee accidents are largely cuts and strains, instruction on work methods and procedures are called for.

Accident reports coupled with periodic summaries provide the information needed for remedial action. The responsibility for remedial action must be fixed and checked by management. Aggressive and alert follow-up, plus effective communication regarding safety procedures, will make each unit safe for both employees and the public.

Procedure for Handling Accidents

When accidents do occur, the store manager and the staff should be aware of procedures to aid the injured parties as well as to demonstrate the store's concern for them.

All accidents must be reported promptly. This is necessary to assure prompt, effective care of all people injured and to supply information needed by the company. Attention should be given to even the slightest injuries. Each store should be equipped with first aid supplies, and employees should be trained in first-aid care.

Following the proper procedure for handling accidents will not only help reduce the settlement claims, but can create a more positive store image. In case of accident:

1. Act calm, confident, friendly, and interested in the injured party. Indicate that his or her welfare is the most important consideration.
2. Attempt to determine if the injury is serious enough so that qualified medical care should be administered.
3. Do not discuss insurance or the cause of the accident; do not argue with the injured party.
4. If the party can be moved, transport him or her to a private, comfortable area away from the selling floor.
5. Determine the facts, by discussing the incident with the injured party. Do not cross-examine him or her.
6. File an accident report, including all the pertinent information.
7. If possible, obtain a signature on a release form. This will aid in forestalling future legal actions in cases of minor accidents.

FIGURE 13
STORE SAFETY INSPECTION REPORT

	Yes	No
1. Is PARKING LOT free of (1) holes, (2) dangerous irregularities?	□	□
2. Is SIDEWALK (1) free of dangerous holes, (2) slippery, (3) amply lighted?	□	□
3. Are STEPS at store entrance painted with (1) yellow bands, (2) entrance and exit signs?	□	□
4. Are AISLES free of (1) stocking trucks, (2) cartons, (3) incoming merchandise, (4) merchandise residue, (5) blind corners, (6) shopping carts?	□	□
5. Is GLASS in all display cases free of cracks and breaks?	□	□
6. Are FLOORS in produce department free of (1) water, (2) produce particles?	□	□
7. Are FLOOR DISPLAYS safely stacked?	□	□
8. Are FLOORS free of (1) loose boards, (2) holes, (3) uneven surfaces?	□	□
9. Are protruding NAILS removed from (1) baskets, (2) crates, (3) fixtures?	□	□
10. Are MEAT KNIVES kept in rack when not in use?	□	□
11. Are GUARDS used on meat (1) saws, (2) slicers, (3) grinders? POWER shut off?	□	□
12. Do ALL DOORS work properly—including cooler and freezer doors?	□	□
13. Are STEPLADDERS in safe condition?	□	□
14. Are BASEMENT STAIRWAYS (1) in good condition, (2) lighted, (3) clear, (4) provided with railing?	□	□
15. Does store have properly stocked FIRST AID KIT?	□	□
16. Are recent SAFETY POSTERS displayed?	□	□
17. Do employees LIFT merchandise in a safe manner?	□	□
18. Do employees wear safe CLOTHING?	□	□
19. Is merchandise in BACK ROOM stacked in a safe manner?	□	□
20. Are AUTOMATIC DOORS as accident proof as possible?	□	□
21. Are DISPLAY FIXTURES and CHECKSTANDS accident proof? (No protruding edges, etc.)	□	□
22. Are NO SMOKING signs obeyed?	□	□
23. Are REPORT FORMS for all types of store accidents readily available?	□	□
24. Have all PREVIOUSLY REPORTED HAZARDS been corrected?	□	□

FIGURE 14
ACCIDENT INVESTIGATION REPORT

Store No. _____ Department _____ Date of Report _____

Employee _____

Person Involved _____ Customer _____

Date of Accident _____

Description of Accident _____

_____

_____

Where in the store did accident happen? _____

_____

Was employee off the job? _____ How long? _____

In your opinion, what caused the accident? _____

_____

_____

_____

What could have prevented the accident? _____

_____

_____

What has been done to prevent similar accidents in the future? _____

_____

_____

_____

Signed _____

_____

(Position)

23

There will be an estimated 245 million consumers in the United States by 1990, compared with fewer than 225 million in 1980. More than 75 percent of this population will be concentrated in metropolitan areas and their suburbs; and it is anticipated that there will continue to be a shift in population to the South and to the West.

A market area is not static; it is constantly changing. Food retailers must be alert to trends and anticipate changes in the market areas. Soaring building, renting and operating costs increase the risk involved in opening new units. Selection of a site demands careful consideration, be it for independent operations, cooperatives, small chains, convenience stores, or large supermarkets.

No one formula can be used for selecting the best location, but there are several generally accepted factors which should be investigated. The data from the investigation of these factors, combined with good judgment, offers a good basis on which to select a new supermarket location.

TRADING AREA APPRAISAL

Research is the tool most frequently used in selecting a store location. The researchers must consider many characteristics of the trading area, including:

- Types of trading area
- Size and nature of the population
- Traffic volume
- Sales potential
- Competition
- Progressiveness of the community
- Availability of services, including advertising, banking, and utilities
- Availability of suitable employees
- Proximity to sources of supply.

Types of Trading Areas

A study of any trading area reveals that retail trade is conducted in a number of locations of varying types and sizes within the area. It may be desirable to locate a supermarket in any of these areas or in none of them. Each area must be analyzed to determine its potential as a supermarket site.

A knowledge of the various types of business location areas already in existence is an ideal starting point for a study of possible supermarket sites. These include the following:

- Downtown area
- Secondary shopping area
- Strip location
- Neighborhood area
- Shopping center.

Downtown Area. Downtown is an area where department stores are usually concentrated and where public transportation facilities converge. Typically, food retailers do not consider downtown areas desirable places to locate because of parking costs, high rentals, and the distance from residential areas.

Secondary Shopping Areas. A large metropolitan area, in addition to the central downtown area, has numerous secondary shopping areas in which stores were established without an overall plan.

Strip Location. Specialty stores, such as fashion specialty shops, thrive on competition from other stores of the same type. These stores are often found clustered along a single street or "strip" along with food, drug, variety and service stores.

Neighborhood Area. This type of location is characterized by a number of convenience stores and service establishments in a residential area.

Shopping Center. A shopping center is an integrated group of retail stores, under one management, designed and built as a unit, with complete shopping facilities and adequate free parking space.

Each type of trading area has its own particular characteristics. Any one of these trading areas is a possible location for a supermarket.

Densely populated residential areas make excellent locations for supermarkets. Any part or section of a city, town or community having a concentrated, highly populated area is a potential location for a new market. The number of people who are potential cus-

Ingenuity sometimes plays a role in selecting a store site. This is a former warehouse in the Charleston, South Carolina, historic district. Notice the rafters and skylight. It serves as a downtown location for Harris-Teeter Super Markets.

tomers should be the greatest single factor in determining whether or not to locate a supermarket.

Most new supermarkets located in large cities are found in residential areas, out of the downtown district. Concentration of the population in apartment houses in residential neighborhoods of a large city, necessitate the location of food retailers in these areas.

In large city stores, studies have shown that the predominant reason for the patronage of one supermarket over another is proximity. Trading areas in large cities may be limited by factors such as the necessity to cross busy intersections, expressways, railroad tracks, industrial areas, and so forth.

The accessibility of the trading area is another important factor to be considered. Can shoppers from outlying regions get into the area? Can those in the area get out easily to shop away from the area?

For convenience stores and small local supermarkets, the customary flow of traffic may be a limiting factor. People tend to move with the flow of traffic, and a location in a different direction will not attract shoppers. However, traffic patterns can be changed over a period of time with aggressive promoting. In general, it is easier to locate in the traffic pattern than to effect a change.

Many locations draw customers from a trading area larger than the community or city in which they are located. In small cities and towns, especially in sparsely populated regions, a store may benefit from a trading area that is several times the population of the city or town itself.

Unfortunately, population data is not published by trading areas. Such areas cannot be represented by distinct boundaries. Neutral zones are usually found between competing city market areas. In these areas, the attraction of each supermarket or each city is closely related to its population, size, and accessibility. There are a number of qualitative and quantitative factors that must be taken into account; each site is considered on its own merits, weighing the specific variables involved in that site location.

Probably one of the best methods of determining the trading area of a proposed site is to examine a map of the area surrounding the site. Maps showing streets, rivers, parks, schools, public buildings, and the like, are usually available. Also, the number of houses in a given area can be obtained from the city or county recorder's office.

Many site selection specialists plot a series of isochrones on a map to delineate the trading area. To do this, points spaced in terms of fixed intervals of driving time are plotted along each street leading from the proposed site. The lines of the isochrones are formed by connecting the points of equal driving time. Along residential streets, the dots, plotted in accordance with minutes of driving time, are close together; in the case of highways where higher average driving speeds are normal and safe, the dots (each representing five minutes of driving time, for example) are farther apart. On winding, narrow roads and through densely populated areas, the points are closer together.

By plotting time-distance isochrones on a map, distance factors become more evident. Some locations appear geographically remote from the site, but in terms of time-distance, are very accessible. Major highway construction has greatly enhanced the ability of cars to reach areas in which stores are located.

By using the proposed site as the center point and drawing isochrones for five, ten, fifteen and twenty minute driving-time intervals, operators can determine the number of potential household buying units within shopping distance of the proposed site. Experienced operators, however, recognize that driving time varies. Also, the amount of business that can be expected from each five minute driving-time interval will depend on the traffic flow pattern for each section.

Some site selection specialists prefer to use the actual distance in miles to determine the extent of the trading area. The proposed site is then used as the center point, and concentric circles are drawn on the map representing radii of one-fourth, one-half,

Where to build? In each city, supermarket specialists check out many factors, including population, size of the area, and accessibility to proposed site. First things first: Take a good look at the map to determine trading area potential.

one, two, four, and five miles. Estimates as to the percentage of business expected from each circle vary. The neighborhood market in a congested urban area will obtain a very large percentage of its customers from within a short radius of the store. Suburban sites will draw on a larger area.

Size and Nature of the Population

The size of the population, its density, dispersion, growth trend, and characteristics are all major factors in site selection. All people are consumers and, accordingly, are potential customers of a supermarket. The size of an area's population will, therefore, help supply a *rough* estimate of the sales potential of the trading area.

Population data for the trading area can be obtained in numerous ways. Some sources of population data are:

- Census tract data
- Public utilities
- Post office data
- School enrollment

- Churches
- Banks
- Newspaper circulation data
- Surveys of the trading area
- City, county and state records.

Many food chains have established rule-of-thumb requirements for population in the trading area. The requirements vary considerably according to the income level, the proximity, the quality and quantity of competition, and the size of a proposed supermarket. Since there cannot be hard-and-fast rules concerning site selection, the operator must consider the anticipated volume as a guide to the site of the store being built—thus, the size of the trading area must be larger in order to support a larger store. The area of greatest population offers the greatest number of potential customers, provided people can get to the site easily.

While present population is of major importance, the future population possibilities also need analyzing. Many questions must be answered. Is the area considered stable, growing, or contracting? Has the population of the area increased substantially in recent years? Is there room for new homes? Has substantial new home construction been carried on in the area? Answers to these questions are needed to evaluate the past, present and future growth of the area.

Locating in an area with an expanding population and with room for future construction of new homes is usually desirable. At times, the present trading area may not fulfill the required needs for establishing a new supermarket; but when the future of the area is considered, the potential may warrant the risk of constructing a new supermarket.

The potential of the trading area will have some influence on the size of the market constructed. There has been a steady increase in the size of the average store from about 20,000 square feet to over 33,000 square feet. The reason for the increase has been the addition of more general merchandise and nonfood items to the store offerings in an attempt to attract more customers from greater distances, thereby increasing the size of the trading area.

Additional information concerning the population can be obtained by checking the birthrate and school construction in the area. High birthrate indicates a growing town, and school construction usually indicates a growth in the number of families with children. It is important to note, however, that the high costs of building and mortgage loans have curtailed new construction.

When analyzing the population of the trading area, a study of the composition of the population is essential. The predominance of a foreign nationality or a religious faith should have a bearing upon the type of merchandise stocked. Any and all characteristics or predominant factors concerning the population of the trading area should be analyzed carefully for possible relation to the proposed supermarket.

The average size of households and the average ages of household members are useful data. The number of schools, the enrollment, and the school age distribution give a fair indication of the age ranges in the area.

Fundamental to a sound analysis of the trading area is a study of the disposable income, the distribution of that income among the population, and the sources that provide the income. (A means of estimating sales potential of a trading area is discussed on the next page under "Sales Potential.")

There are other considerations. An area in which a large portion of the population is dependent upon a particular industry or manufacturing concern may be less desirable than an area in which the income originates from widely diversified sources. A single industry or concern may be influenced by seasonal or cyclical variations. Income paid to the employees is less secure because of the possibility of industrial relocations or work stoppages due to strikes or other causes.

Estimates of the income of the area can be taken from census tracts, local tax records, local property records, rentals in the area, as well as many published reports on local and national income averages. Determining the current general income level of the area and making predictions for the future are important.

Traffic Volume

The amount of traffic passing the proposed site will help determine the potential of the location. A close check of streets and highways near the site is useful in estimating the sales potential for transient customers.

In a study of the type of traffic, it would be helpful to know:

- Traffic count passing the site daily
- The percentage of local cars
- The percentage of county cars
- The percentage of out-of-county cars
- The percentage of cars driven by women (since women do most of the shopping)
- The heaviest traffic periods.

The idea of counting the number of persons passing a given point in the course of a day and classifying them according to desired characteristics has been basic to sound site selection practice for many years. Inspection should be made on a scale sufficient to obtain a reliable sample of the trading area.

The opinion was once held that the total volume of traffic passing a site was the most significant factor determining its value for merchandising purposes. Experience indicates, however, there is no dependable general relationship between quantity of traffic and the potential sales of a site; factors not apparent from casual observation are often discovered.

Sales Potential

The annual food expenditure for the actual or potential number of families in a trading area can be estimated. Subtracting the sales of the competition from the estimated annual sales of the trading area will give the estimated sales available to a new store. However, the strength or drawing power of the new supermarket still must be evaluated.

A new supermarket may be able to draw some percentage of the total food sales of an area. An aggressive operator may obtain a higher volume. How much depends on many factors, many of them predictable, but not all. If site selection were an exact science there would be no poor or marginal stores, no "overstoring" or "understoring," and all stores would be successful.

In any estimate of potential volume for a new supermarket, an appraisal of existing stores must be made to determine their effectiveness in competition with a new supermarket in a given location with a given store image.

Supermarket chain organizations can estimate potential sales by comparing the proposed site and trading area with similar areas in which they are operating. The estimated total food business of the area is calculated, and the competition is evaluated. Usually, three stores of a similar size in a trading area that has approximately the same population and income level as the area of the new store to be opened are selected for comparison. The sales of these stores are combined, and an average of the sales per thousand people in the trading area's population is computed. When this figure is multiplied by the population of the trading area under consideration, the expected volume of the new unit can be determined.

Many chain operators rely on similar trading area comparisons for accurate sales forecasts of new stores. The methods used to estimate the sales of a new supermarket will vary from one organization to another, depending on the size of the stores, competition, and other characteristics of the different trading areas. Again, no one method can be considered the best. The results of the analysis, combined with good judgment based upon past experience, will be much more valuable and accurate than either the analysis or judgment alone.

Competition

Both the extent and the nature of the competition in and near the trading area must be thoroughly investigated. The amount of sales of the competition in the trading area can be estimated, and this amount, subtracted from the total potential supermarket volume, will give the approximate potential sales for a new supermarket. There is less risk in locating in an area where the existing stores are not able to meet the needs of the customers and where they are forced to shop outside the trading area.

Many times, a new supermarket will be able to attract a portion of the customers from other food stores in a highly competitive area, thereby still making it profitable to open a new outlet in such an area. Chain stores rarely stay out of an area because of excessive competition, if they can do a better merchandising job than the existing stores, and if they are able to obtain a specific, desirable location at a reasonable cost. Emphasis is more on the nature of the competition than on the extent of it.

Progressiveness of the Community

Retail food store organizations, when evaluating a trading area, place a great deal of emphasis upon the progressiveness of the community. This quality is evidenced by population trends, industrial character, income level, competitive circumstances, and the general improvement made by retailing.

Progressiveness may be judged by questionnaires used to get a "feel" for the potential of the area. Among the most commonly used questions are the following:

1. Is new construction being undertaken regularly?
2. Is the school system modern and adequate?
3. Is the Chamber of Commerce active?
4. Is the local transportation system adequate?
5. Is the park and recreational area program effective?
6. Are the churches and social organizations strong and active?

Affirmative answers to these questions are indicative of the ability of the area to continue to develop and grow.

Availability of Services:
Advertising, Banking, and Utilities

Advertising is an integral part of a supermarket's merchandising success. The absence or presence of suitable advertising media and its cost, relative to coverage, should be fully investigated. All media, including radio, television, newspapers, and handbills, should be evaluated in terms of their potential effectiveness for supermarket promotions.

Adequate banking facilities are needed to facilitate the handling of supermarket funds and to avoid delays in transferring funds. Funds on deposit and in transit are unproductive and increase the capital requirements.

Availability of adequate utility services should be assured before time and money are spent investigating any site for a new supermarket. Also, the cost of providing water, electricity, and other services, if not already available, is an important factor.

Availability of Suitable Employees

A lack of adequate transportation facilities may be a handicap in terms of employee accessibility to the store, and, therefore, may limit the availability of workers. If a limited number of people can get to a place of employment, the wage rate will be higher and the pool for selection will be more limited. These factors may limit the profitability of the store.

Proximity to Sources of Supply

Transportation costs, speed of delivery, and investment in inventory are all influenced by proximity to the company warehouse and/or other sources of supply. Consideration must be given to the distance of the proposed supermarket from the various supply points and the route that must be used to complete deliveries.

SELECTING THE SITE

After the trading area has been selected, the next step is the selection of the site. Many of the previously mentioned factors dealing with the trading area have a direct effect upon the selection of a particular site. Once the sales potential of the trading area has been estimated and the sales potential of a new supermarket in the area has been predicted, the size of the building and parking area can be projected.

The *sales per square foot of total store space* or the *sales per square foot of sales area* of a store in operation in a similar location and with characteristics similar to the proposed site, may be used as a guide to determine the size of the building needed. Assuming that the proposed supermarket is to be similar to a store with an average weekly sales per square foot of selling area of $4.80, and assuming further that the

proposed store has a potential volume of $100,000 per week, 20,833 square feet of selling area would be required. Assuming also that the selling space is 75 percent of the total supermarket, 27,777 square feet would be required to handle weekly sales of $100,000.

But other factors have to be taken into consideration. Some high-volume stores may have a sales mix that as much as doubles or triples the sales-per-square-foot averages of its competitors. The firm's merchandising abilities, its ability to find the right product mix which can obtain maximum results in different areas, and its ability to be a promotion leader rather than follower are just a few of the factors that must be taken into consideration. Here, modesty is no virtue, but a strongly critical self-appraisal also can keep the less dynamic firm from stumbling.

However, even more is involved. In planning the site, the store operator is required to consider zoning variances, zoned commercial conforming ordinances, Board of Adjustment approval, and Planning Board site approval. Local and regional ordinances and codes may restrict the use of signs, lighting, store hours, promotional activity, etc.

A site plan should be prepared, which includes:

- Parking
- Store position on site
- Topography
- Drainage
- Utilities
- Curb cuts—county, state approval
- Lighting and signs
- Borings—foundations
- Entrance location.

Parking

Adequate free parking is a major consideration in the selection of a supermarket site. If the store is located in a local shopping area, the amount of space required varies according to the type of location—that is, the percentage of customers that use an automobile when shopping for food. Only city locations in apartment house areas have walk-in traffic; they need little or no parking space. Suburban-type locations have 100 percent drive-in traffic and need five times or more parking area as store area. A five-to-one ratio of parking to store area is more or less standard.

In addition to being large enough to offer sufficient parking, the parking area must be located so as to afford easy entrance and exit. Parking must be provided for store employees, but the more convenient spaces, must be reserved for customer use.

The size of the parking area needed is not difficult to determine. The estimated peak-hour traffic for which the store is planned should be part of the estimates. Multiply that figure by the square number of footage needed to park a car (including access space), and add an allowance for entrance and exit lanes, the parking spaces that will be occupied by employees, and cart storage and deposit areas. That is the minimum parking area that should be paved and available for use before the store opens.

If there is the possibility of future expansion, it is the wise operator who can have a reserve area available for expanding the store and the parking lot. Periodic surveys should be made to evaluate the adequacy of the parking facilities.

Accessibility

Vital to the success of any supermarket is the accessibility of the site to the customers. The entire road system in the trading area is important because roads influence the traffic a site can readily attract. Difficult stretches of winding roads, very low-speed sections, detours, steep hills, narrow and/or unpaved roads, and crowded areas through which drivers must pass, all discourage regular shopping trips. Traffic congestion during peak sales hours can destroy an apparently good site. A high-speed highway can also be detrimental if potential customers are not able to reach the store easily.

Emphasis must be placed on the ease of ingress and egress from the street or streets bordering the site. Location on one side of the street or the other may have a negative effect if cross-overs or left-turn lanes are not provided.

The accessibility of the site to delivery trucks must be considered. Rear entrances from an alley or side street are preferable to the use of front entrances where deliveries may conflict with customer traffic. Since most major deliveries are frequently transported by eighteen-wheel tractor trailers, adequate approach areas to unloading docks must be provided.

Making a site viable depends on the sophistication and imagination of the particular chain or store operator. Roof-top or indoor parking, irregularly shaped stores, and multi-deck parking are just a few of the means that have been used to solve problems. One chain uses air rights over a major turnpike in Massachusetts, while another uses a subway station location with indoor parking.

Site location is a complex affair that is based on many factors, problems, and restrictions. Today's road patterns, retail partners in shopping centers, ethnic considerations, and socio-economic levels must also be considered in the decision-making process, in addition to population density and competition.

Imagination and ingenuity in this entire area certainly are additional factors to be considered especially by chains that anticipate continued successful expansion in a competitive market. The relatively recent decision of some larger chains to close some of their stores may at first appear to create an inconvenience for shoppers and to heighten the vacancy problem of the nation's retail space. However, in urban areas, local and independent operators have been leasing these stores. In low-income areas, however, the number of closings is greater, and some stores never reopen. Sixty-five percent of the stores closed were free-standing supermarkets with 8,000 to 12,000 square feet. The large chains cannot operate these stores profitably with absentee management, but small independent operators who demonstrate merchandising ability can create successful, independent operations.

Often, an independent operator may be able to outperform a chain because of flexibility and the potential of almost instantaneous maneuverability. A regional, aggressive small chain can often be a "David" to a major, large chain's "Goliath." However, larger chains often have considerably more capital reserves and, in the case of a price war, can outlast the smaller, more limited independent.

Because of the many factors involved and the weight that must be given to each, site selection teams for chains or wholesalers must be highly skilled. When one considers that between $1 million and $3 million in investment is risked every time a supermarket or superstore is opened, one can understand the importance of the site-selection function.

A number of regional chains have grown because of the astuteness of its site-selection team. On the other hand, a number of small chains have suffered badly because of poor judgments. In West Orange, New Jersey, one store site, originally built for a major national chain, changed ownership three times (because it was a marginal store) until it became a ShopRite, and then did so well that the owner (Village Supermarkets) had to build a larger store at a nearby site to accommodate the heavy traffic. On the same street, about a mile away, another store changed hands three times in five years before a Pathmark opened on the site. Within a week after opening, the Pathmark was doing more than four times the volume of the previous tenant of the site and the store has never fallen under that mark.

Hundreds of similar instances could be cited. None of them is that unusual. With the right merchandising strategy and store image, a firm attracts the consumer. Without the proper formula, a certain number of customers may shop the store because of proximity, but the magnetism that will make it a success is missing.

The shopping center boom began in the 1950's. Neighborhood centers were mostly anchored by supermarkets, as was the case here. An A&P unit is the key store at Colonial Village Center, built in 1963 in Sarasota, Florida.

SHOPPING CENTERS

Shopping centers first appeared in significant numbers in the suburbs of United States cities after World War II, producing one-stop shopping for enormous numbers of consumers. Basically, they consist of stores and service shops centered around a common parking lot.

When the shopping center boom started in 1949, there were only 75 centers in the United States. Today, it is estimated that there are about 20,000. Some of the country's largest retailers claim to do more than 50 percent of their volume in branches located in shopping centers.

Several factors contributed significantly to the growth of shopping centers: population movement out of inner cities and into suburbs, the increased mobility of the shopper, the expansion and building of highways, and the lack of parking facilities in the downtown areas of cities. As they have grown and developed, shopping centers have become increasingly important to the food industry.

Background History

The early American general store can probably be considered the forerunner of the shopping center; at least, the convenience of one-stop shopping evolved from the general store concept.

The first major retailer to move to outlying locations was Sears, in the late 1920's. It built large stores on what were then the outskirts of large cities to obtain "better" locations with sufficient parking facilities. For years, the locations were unsuccessful and the buildings became mail-order stations. However, as the cities expanded, other stores were added; informal and unplanned shopping centers evolved.

During the late 1920's, a few planned shopping centers were built. Kansas City, Kansas, and Houston, Texas, were among the first cities to have planned centers. These centers featured architectural uniformity, protective covenants, parking, and operating restrictions.

While shopping centers were built in the late 1920's, the concept was slow to develop due to capital restrictions during the Depression. World War II curtailed construction of all kinds. Thus, very few shopping centers were in operation prior to 1950. The decade 1950–60 witnessed the construction of approximately 4,000 centers—large and small. These groups of stores were developed, designed, and built as a unit.

Importance of Shopping Centers

Presently, there are about 20,000 shopping centers in the United States. These centers account for over 40 percent of the total U.S. retail dollar volume. It has been estimated that the shopping center share of retail sales will increase slightly each year. In recent years, about one-half of the new supermarkets opened have been in shopping center locations.

The question may well be asked: How long can this rate of shopping center development continue? Another question asked in supermarket circles is: When is the saturation point reached in any trading area for shopping centers and/or supermarkets? The only answer that can be given is that as long as new stores and centers are profitable, they will continue to be built.

The expansion and development executives in food distribution believe that desirable locations exist in every trading area—thus the urge for expansion continues. In some areas, shopping centers are in competition with each other—that is, several centers compete for the same customers in the same trading area. The retailer considering a shopping center location should analyze the situations using all the criteria discussed earlier in this chapter along with special factors related to a center.

Types and Sizes of Shopping Centers

If the trading area analysis indicates a potential for the establishment of a shopping center, the next step in any evaluation is the plan for the shopping center. What kind of center should it be? What types of stores are to be included, and how much does each type contribute to a successful shopping center?

The most common types of shopping centers are:

- Neighborhood shopping centers
- Community shopping centers
- Regional shopping centers.

Neighborhood Shopping Centers. These centers are located in the immediate neighborhood within six minutes driving time of the customer. Establishments here are generally classified as convenience stores and include foods, laundry, dry cleaning, drugs, barber shop, etc. The main tenant is the supermarket, and the trading area population extends to 40,000.

In small or neighborhood centers, those having less than 100,000 square feet of store area, the supermarket is usually the main drawing power. The developer, therefore, looks for a highly rated or regarded supermarket operator to sign the first lease (before other tenants). In these centers, the variety store and the drug store are also important in attracting shoppers. The other miscellaneous shops and stores add relatively small amounts of traffic. The important consideration regarding the small stores is that they be compatible with the center operation.

Community Shopping Centers. Because the trading area includes up to 150,000 people, the merchandise includes convenience and shopping goods. This, of course, means that shoppers will comparison shop. A branch department store, a large variety chain outlet, and a supermarket are the leading tenants in this type of center.

In large community or semi-regional centers having 100,000 to 400,000 square feet of store area, a department store branch is generally the most important drawing power. The supermarket and the variety and drug stores—whether exclusive or multiple—are next in importance. The other stores are important as a group and must maintain the customer image set for the center.

Regional Shopping Centers. An in-depth assortment and variety of home furnishings and general merchandise, in addition to the merchandise listed under the smaller shopping centers described above, characterize the regional center. The trading area could be between fifteen to twenty miles, or more. Regional centers have over 400,000 square feet of store area.

The large department store or stores constitute the major traffic builders. The specialty stores add to department store drawing power, while the supermarket or supermarkets add little, if any, additional traffic, unless, of course, the chains are strong enough to do their own drawing. The regional center is a complete one-stop shopping area, competing favorably with the major downtown area.

Many of these centers are totally enclosed with climate-controlled malls that allow for greater family shopping comfort and convenience. An attractive and unique decor makes shopping especially attractive as does the large variety of merchandise and stores. Today, there are super-regional shopping centers with multiple levels which include bowling alleys, motels, offices as well as luxury restaurants.

Shopping Center Layout

The layout of shopping centers has taken various shapes and forms; the most common are the:

- Strip shopping center
- Court shopping center
- Mall
- Enclosed mall
- Cluster arrangement.

Strip Shopping Center. The strip shopping center derives its name from the location of the stores in a line along the street. The buildings face the main thoroughfare, usually with parking space in front. Most neighborhood shopping centers are of this type.

Court Shopping Center. In a court shopping center, as the name indicates, the buildings are usually placed in a square or rectangle to form an inner court, with parking on all sides around the buildings as well as inside, if the enclosed area is large enough to accommodate parking. This type of center is best used with a square building plot that cannot accommodate a string of stores.

Mall. The mall concept is that of a self-contained shopping street. The stores are arranged somewhat as they are on any shopping street, the chief difference being the absence of vehicular traffic and street noise. The usual practice is to place a department store at one end, with another large store at the other end.

Enclosed Mall. The enclosed mall is very popular for large centers—those over 100,000 square feet. In this type of mall, the area between stores is enclosed and is usually climate controlled. The enclosed-mall concept encourages shopping the entire center, not just the store closest to the available parking space.

Cluster Arrangement. The cluster arrangement of stores derives its name from the fact that the stores are clustered around a large central store, usually a department store.

In this shopping center mall, the supermarket's checkstand area opens directly onto an enclosed "shopping street," which is climate controlled and free of vehicular traffic noise. The Acme Market, here, is at the Granite Run Mall, Philadelphia.

Location of Supermarket in Shopping Center

Every tenant wants to be in the path of maximum traffic. The supermarket operator is no exception. The great amount of customer traffic and the necessity for frequent deliveries usually relegates the supermarket to a position near the end or the perimeter of the center. Ease of entry and exit with a great amount of parking space to handle peak traffic periods are important factors in the supermarket's location.

A great deal of consideration must also be given to the parcel pick-up area. It should be located so as to be entered easily by the customer; also, the area must provide easy exit to avoid traffic congestion. Supermarkets located on the end of a shopping center strip have an advantage in that the parcel pick-up station can be located at the side of the building, thereby offering greater accessibility to customers.

In large shopping centers where there is a large department store, it is generally agreed that the supermarket should not be located near the department store. The average shopper spends between twenty and forty minutes shopping in a supermarket as compared to two or three hours in a department store. When the department store and the supermarket are close to one another, department store customers may occupy parking space for a longer period of time, reducing available parking facilities for supermarket customers.

Number of Supermarkets in Shopping Center

Supermarket operators seek centers where competition, both actual and potential, is minimized. The vulnerability of a center to competition after the center is established is a vital point in measuring the value of its location. The chances that a competitor or a competitive shopping center may open in the same trading area, with popular name stores tending to outdraw the first center, should be considered.

The question of exclusive supermarket leases or multiple supermarkets in shopping centers is far from settled. Some operators will pay a premium rental for an exclusive lease, while others prefer to see two, or sometimes more, supermarkets in exceptionally large centers. This indicates a real difference of opinion as to drawing power.

Exclusive-lease operators believe that most shoppers make separate food-buying trips and other shopping trips, seldom mixing the two. Food shopping is more frequent and regarded as "comfortable clothes" shopping, while shopping for garments and other nonfood items is less frequent and looked upon as "dress-up" shopping. Nonexclusive-lease operators believe they can draw shoppers who visit the center and that two supermarkets increase the drawing power. However, many store operators and chains still feel that a fashion center is not a good supermarket location.

The shopping center developer and operator is interested in total drawing power and maximum total sales. Here again, there is a difference of opinion. The center operators favoring exclusive supermarket leasing believe that a single unit is most efficient. They agree that a second unit will increase supermarket sales, but not enough to justify the capital required to provide the facility. Therefore, these operators feel that the return on investment is greater with exclusive leases. The multi-lease proponents view total drawing power as being greater with two supermarkets and as resulting in greater total center sales, thus producing greater returns than the exclusive-lease situation. This may be helpful to the shopping center, but not necessarily helpful to the supermarket.

Supermarket operators and shopping center operators are as successful in exclusive-leased centers as those in multi-leased centers, depending upon the specific situation. Who is right? Obviously, both are.

Size of Supermarkets in Shopping Centers

The size of supermarkets in shopping centers varies considerably. In regional centers, the gross area runs from 30,000 to 60,000 square feet. In medium-sized centers, a supermarket customarily occupies 22,000 to 30,000 square feet. In small centers, the gross area of a supermarket is from 12,000 to 22,000 square feet. However, the general trend has been for national chains to open only large stores. This gives independents the opportunity to occupy the smaller stores.

Shopping Center Leases

The lease and its provisions and restrictions must be analyzed with major attention being given to:

- Rental rates
- Length of lease and renewal clauses
- Provisions of merchants' association
- Center opening
- Promotional clauses
- Parking facilities
- Restrictive clauses
- Other vital clauses.

Rent. The rental rates usually vary according to the type of retail business of each leasee and are figured on a square-foot-of-area basis. A minimum rental figure is usually established for each occupant. The minimum rental is paid until sales reach an established figure. A percentage of gross sales is charged, in addition to the minimum, on all sales over the established minimum figure. The rent for supermarkets should not exceed 2 percent of sales. Some leases are written with a base amount plus a percentage based on sales over a base amount.

Leases may be written with exterior maintenance being the landlord's responsibility or with the tenant responsible for the care of both the interior and exterior. Others charge actual maintenance costs on a pro rata basis. Many chains feel that the rental of shopping center locations should be all-inclusive with respect to miscellaneous expenses such as maintenance, increases in taxes, etc. However, the trend is unmistakably in favor of additional charges for maintenance, merchants' association fees, increased taxes, and other items. Generally speaking, the larger the store, the lower the rate of the percentage-of-sales paid for rent. Bargaining position is usually affected by the ability to pull traffic to the shopping center.

Length of Lease and Renewal Clauses. Lease lengths vary, but the trend is to longer leases. The principal reason for the increase in length is that lending agencies are demanding better guarantees on length of occupancy. Many shopping center developers are asking for leases that run the length of the mortgages on the center. Most shopping center leases are for fifteen to twenty years with some for twenty-five to thirty years.

Many leases provide one to four renewal options of five years each. Individual variations in renewal options exist, varying from no option, to longer options, to a varying number of renewals. Desired leasees are able to force renewal option concessions.

Merchants' Associations. Membership in a merchants' association or shopping center association, along with promotional agreements, which include the shopping center developer and tenants, should be checked closely. In some leases, membership in the merchants' association is required of all tenants. Most association contracts require each tenant to contribute as dues a specified percentage of sales or an assessment based on gross land area. The center developer may or may not contribute to this fund. Shopping center activities are coordinated by the merchants' association.

The association acts as a governing body within the framework of the lease covenants and the center constitution and by-laws. The shopping center merchants' association is the key to center-wide cooperation and requires participation by all tenants as well as effective leadership by the developer. Required membership is the only way to obtain the cooperation of all tenants; however, some will be more active than others.

The association develops uniform store hours to keep all of the center's stores open when the largest number of shoppers are present. They also have the responsibilities of maintenance and housekeeping (in parking lots, common areas, etc.). A variety of center-wide special events and promotions are usually planned and executed by the association to attract potential shoppers to the center. These may include concerts, fashion shows, celebrity appearances, and the like.

Center Opening. Clauses covering the grand opening may also be included in the lease. The opening of any store may be restricted until a certain percentage of the stores in the center are prepared to open together. Naturally, the more stores that participate in the grand opening, the greater the chances for a successful event. Shopping centers that have allowed stores to open at will have frequently failed to become successful as quickly as those which have required simultaneous openings. Anniversary sales or promotions may be included in the lease along with possible periodic assessments to be applied to the promotional activities of the center.

Promotional Clauses. Many chain operators will participate in special promotions. The developers of shopping centers are usually anxious to promote the center until such time as all rental space is occupied and the center is a success.

To help in this promotion, the developers may match the tenants' expenditures for advertising center-wide promotions. Other developers, who feel that the first three years are the most important in the successful development of the shopping center, agree in the lease contract to match (dollar-for-dollar the first year, 50 percent the second year, and 25 percent the third year) any monies spent by the tenants for center-wide promotions. By doing so, an advertising program can be planned for three years. The details of this promotional program are usually worked out through the merchants' association.

A few center developers hire and pay for the services of an advertising and promotion specialist to aid and assist all the tenants. The promotion specialist works with the merchants' association in the planning of center-wide promotions. Much of the success of any shopping center depends upon the sound planning, enthusiasm, and support afforded the tenants by the developer.

Parking Facilities. The problem created by lack of parking facilities in downtown business districts has been one of the primary reasons for the success of the shopping center. Supermarket operators should investigate carefully the proposed parking facilities available at the center. The amount of parking space available and the total number of cars that can be parked at one time are very important.

An acceptable parking area to sales area ratio is about four square feet to one; however, a ratio of five, six or even seven-to-one is more desirable. The supermarket operator should estimate the parking available for his customers. The actual ratio for supermarket customers can be calculated by dividing the total parking area accessible to supermarket customers by the total space occupied by the supermarket.

If the center is located in an area where foot traffic is anticipated, a lower parking ratio may be satisfactory. Most operators want a five-to-one ratio, or better, for that portion of the parking lot that is accessible to the supermarket.

Many operators feel that the number of car spaces offers a more accurate measure than the parking ratio. The space needed to park one car, plus allowance for lanes, is at least 300 square feet. However, if access drives, pedestrian walks, bumpers, and landscape areas are planned, the allotment must be increased accordingly.

The following points should be considered when planning or analyzing the parking facilities in a shopping center:

1. L, U, square and strip-shaped shopping centers work best when parking facilities are provided in front of the buildings.
2. Reserved parking areas, employee parking, and delivery areas should be in the rear of the buildings.
3. Customers do not like to park in back of a building, particularly at night.
4. Double-deck and underground parking can be made economically feasible and easy to use.
5. Well-lighted and clearly lined parking areas are advantageous.
6. Walkways from the parking lot to the shopping area enable safe and easy movement of customers to and from the store.
7. Straight-forward parking (as opposed to parking on a slant) makes it easier to get in and out, but requires more space for lanes.
8. The best size for each parking stall is nine feet wide and twenty feet long.

Restrictive Clauses. Some companies require restrictions in their shopping center leases that provide exclusive rights to sell specified merchandise. For example, a druggist may force the developer to insert a clause in the shopping center lease giving exclusive rights to the drugstore to sell drugs and proprietary items; or the hardware merchant may require an exclusive on hardware, paint, etc.

These restrictive clauses create two problems: (1) desirable tenants may find that the restrictions cause them to eliminate one or more departments; and (2) the definition of exclusive rights may be difficult to interpret. For example, if a drugstore has an exclusive on drugs and proprietary items, can the supermarket, variety store, and department store sell health and beauty aids? Or, if the hardware store has the exclusive right to sell hardware, can the other stores sell housewares? Restrictive clauses have resulted in numerous court cases, reinforcing the importance of specific definitions.

Other types of restrictions cover the type, height, and location of store signs. This clause may apply only to the original group of stores and not to added units. Exclusive store covenants may also apply to the original construction and not to later additions.

One restrictive clause, which should be looked at closely, concerns hours of operation. While few supermarkets will be concerned with having to open early in the morning, some restrictive clauses may prevent their opening before other stores open at 9 or 10 a.m. Generally, such clauses prohibit twenty-four-hour openings or Sunday openings, even when the supermarket in a large center may be a free-standing building.

If such restrictive clauses are a problem, there should either be a guaranteed exception (one that competent legal experts consider valid and binding) to the clause included in the lease or the site should be rejected.

All restrictive clauses should be evaluated in terms of their effect on the leasee and the possibility of involvement in a law suit with the center operator and/or other tenants.

Other Clauses. Zoning restrictions that pertain to the shopping center may or may not be included in the lease. A thorough investigation of zoning restrictions that are in effect at the time the lease is signed or that possibly may be established in the future, need attention before entering into a shopping center agreement.

In checking over the lease, close attention should be given to options, subleasing, and exclusive clauses. Tenants whose business has not become successful after a fair period of time should be given some consideration. Subleasing with the approval of the developer and/or the merchants' association serves this purpose. Exclusive clauses are included in almost all shopping center leases and should be investigated for their present and future effect on each tenant.

Some arrangements should be included to allow for possible expansion should the shopping center prove to be successful. Provisions should be made for future expansion of stores and parking facilities, maintenance and repair of the buildings, and parking lot upkeep. Also, some allowance should be made in the lease concerning physical improvements and the liability of both tenant and developer.

A number of large supermarket operators have formed subsidiary corporations to develop shopping centers. By this method, the supermarket operator is in a position to control lease clauses, operating conditions, etc. To date, some of these subsidiaries have been very successful and have provided desirable locations for the supermarket operator.

24

Store layout is considered by many to be one of the basic ingredients in the success of a supermarket. Despite this recognition, many supermarkets have developed a uniformity in appearance which makes it difficult, if not impossible, for shoppers to make distinctions among stores. There is so little difference in design, fixtures, layout, decor, etc., that customers can hardly tell which store they are shopping.

Supermarkets offer the same items, at the same or nearly the same prices, with similar if not identical services. Merchandise is displayed on similar gondolas, temperature-controlled cases, and display fixtures and tables, adding to the sameness. To shoppers, the checkstands are the same; the differences in the design and model used are unnoticeable. Also, the various makes of shopping carts are basically the same in appearance.

Although developing a distinctive consumer image of a store is difficult, supermarket operators must realize the importance of being original and of making their stores look different from other stores in the trading area.

A survey of 4,500 shoppers conducted by the A.C. Nielsen Company found that consumers wanted: (1) bigger stores, (2) faster checkouts, (3) more personal attention, (4) fewer stockouts, (5) prepared take-home foods, (6) more variety, (7) more and better parking, (8) elimination of cart clutter, (9) improved transference of groceries to car, (10) easy-to-read store signs and directory, (11) rest or snack area, (12) readable cash registers, (13) clearly visible meat and produce, and (14) uncluttered aisles. These factors must be considered when planning store layout and design.

CREATING CUSTOMER IMAGE

Image building should be considered when designing supermarket layouts; the store should entice customers with pleasing surroundings which invite sales. Colorful store interiors, adequate modern lighting, modern fixtures, easy-to-read signs, comfort (temperature control), and cleanliness are factors of importance in the creation of proper store atmosphere. Store layout must keynote convenience and atmosphere to the customer in order to be appealing and build a favorable image.

The emphasis on modernity forces at least 50 percent of the supermarket operators to remodel their stores every three to eight years, based, of course, on financial ability. Since these interiors are changed with such frequency, a static image should not be perpetuated.

LAYOUT PLANNING

Most supermarkets are planned by specialists. Large operators have a store planning department; group members use the services of the store engineering department of their wholesale unit on a fee basis; others use the engineering and planning services offered by leading store equipment manufacturers.

The services of specialized consultants and engineering firms are also available. These consultants plan, design, and supervise the building and layout of new stores. Of course, the nature and amount of service as well as the fee depends on the individual contract.

Some operators plan new stores by visiting and copying markets recently opened by successful competitors. They take those features they like from the stores visited and consult with an architect on the planning and construction of the building. These operators then plan their own interior layout by copying specific pictures as well as varying the layout of the store or stores visited. Getting ideas from other proven operations *and adapting them* to the specific operation has proven successful. Copying entirely the physical structure and layout seldom succeeds; in fact, one highly successful Eastern operator claims many operators have failed because they copied his stores exactly, but were unable to duplicate the operation, management, and quality of the employees.

Planning a modern supermarket is an intricate operation, requiring a combination of architectural and engineering skills, a knowledge of supermarket operations, and an understanding of human behavior. This is essential in order to make the store layout effective under local conditions.

Planning must reflect the local trading area's peculiarities. However, there are certain basic factors to be adhered to regardless of trading area. These include:

- Convenient access to the parking area and the store
- Effective and efficient utilization of plot and instore area
- Low-cost operation.

OBJECTIVES OF STORE LAYOUT

Layout refers to the arrangement of the fixtures, merchandise, selling and nonselling departments and areas, displays, and aisles in relation to each other.

The overall objective is to make the store as attractive, inviting, and convenient as possible for the shoppers, and at the same time provide effective utilization of space so as to achieve satisfactory sales and profit for the owner. Therefore, layout is primarily a vehicle for facilitating sales; that is, providing maximum merchandise exposure by planning the layout to achieve:

- Customer circulation throughout the entire store
- Balanced selling by the sale of high-margin impulse merchandise
- Logical shopping patterns
- Attractive surroundings which create a favorable image and invite the customers back
- Efficient space utilization.

To accomplish the desired objectives, the layout should integrate impulse, convenience and demand items. When this is done, fast-moving items serve as magnets to draw customers through the entire store, thereby exposing them to a wide range of goods for sale, including the high-margin merchandise. Good layout helps achieve balanced sales and a satisfactory net profit.

SPACE REQUIREMENTS

Before deciding upon the building and the supermarket layout, the operator should determine the amount of space required for the type of store being planned. The merchandise to be included—departments, sections, variety, quantity—should be determined, and the total space required should be calcu-

lated. Next, the area necessary for service functions—back-room area, receiving area, checkstands, office, aisles—should be calculated. The total is the area that is required for the planned operation.

A visit to similar stores is helpful in determining the space requirements. Remember, however, that copying is not successful; but getting ideas and advice from others can be beneficial.

LAYOUT AND SPACE ALLOCATION SERVICES

Consultants may be hired or equipment manufacturers may be contacted for information on space requirements. The operator should obtain such information—whether paid for on a fee basis or provided by equipment manufacturers—and base any decisions on facts. The planner is cautioned, however, to beware of outside sources that may benefit themselves by stressing certain aspects of the layout—as do equipment manufacturers or consultants whose fee is based on store area. Their suggestions may not be compatible with the operator's best interests.

As a part of their selling program, most equipment manufacturers offer supermarket operators complete store planning services. Their store planning departments will plan the remodeling of a supermarket or the layout for a new unit.

For supermarket operators desiring ideas, equipment suppliers offer recommended layouts for various sizes of stores. These plans should be used as guides. Supermarket operators are not expected to design and equip a store to conform to these general plans. However, plans tailor-made for a specific situation can often be used with minor modification. The important factor is that the equipment manufacturers are promoting the concept of a "balanced store"—that is, each department is allocated space according to its sales and space requirements. Of course, the objective is to sell equipment that will successfully accomplish the plan.

Many supermarket suppliers provide layout and space allocation materials and services to retailers. Their services are usually restricted to the space allocated for their products or the section in which their products are displayed. Supplier space allocation services originated as a means of obtaining more shelf space for company products or to obtain a better position on the shelf. However, in recent years, suppliers have based their recommendations on research and are providing basically sound information relative to sales figures and proven procedures for achieving greater sales and operating efficiency.

BASIC FLOOR LAYOUT

Storage and Processing Areas

A major cost consideration in all supermarkets is that of labor. Labor costs fluctuate drastically as the result of such minor considerations as walking, reaching, and stooping. To eliminate unnecessary walking, merchandising departments should be located as closely as possibly to their prospective storage and processing areas. Another major consideration is real estate costs and limitations.

These are a number of different types of merchandise and storage processing layouts, each with its own advantages and drawbacks:

- U-shaped storage and processing area
- Back-room storage
- Basement or subfloor storage
- L-shaped or end loading and storage.

U-Shaped Storage and Processing Area. (See Figure 15.) This type of layout offers a versatile work and storage area; it can be varied in size as necessitated by the number of merchandise deliveries that will be received by the supermarket in any given time period, by merchandise turnover, and by the amount of reserve stock to be carried, without drastically varying the interior of the store. However, many authorities on layout find this approach to be too wasteful of costly real estate. Too many doors are needed, creating a security problem. An estimated fifty car spaces are lost because the building cannot be moved back to the property line, since space is required for the trucks to back into the loading areas.

Back-room Storage. (See Figure 16.) This method is not as wasteful as the U-shaped storage area, since the space on the side of the building is still available for parking cars. However, the building is still away from the property line, eliminating parking spaces, and there are many doors, creating security problems. It is desirable if land is available and cost is not a major factor.

Basement or Subfloor Storage. (See Figure 17.) This is rarely used in planning new stores, except where space is at a premium.

L-Shaped or End Loading and Storage. (See (Figure 18.) This provides the greatest number of parking spaces for the same land area as used in U-shaped and

---

EXAMPLES OF BASIC STORE LAYOUT

FIGURE 15
U-SHAPED STORAGE AND PROCESSING AREA

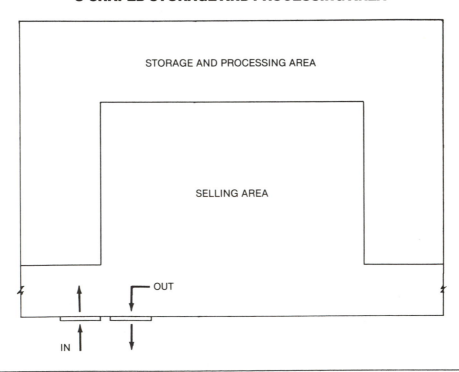

FIGURE 16
BACK-ROOM STORAGE AND PROCESSING AREA

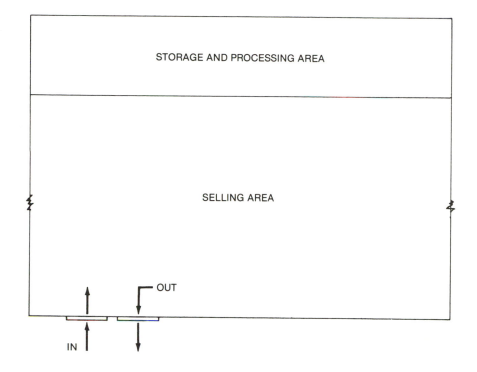

FIGURE 17
BASEMENT OR SUBFLOOR STORAGE

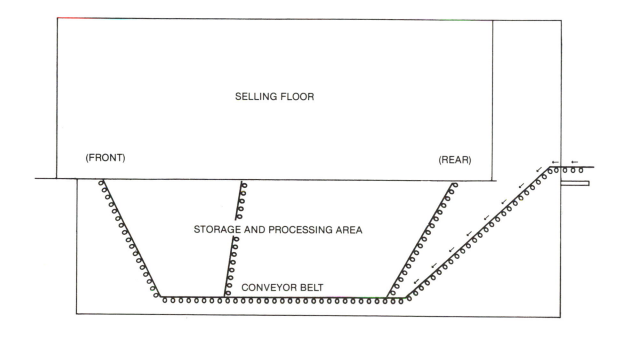

FIGURE 18
L-SHAPED OR END LOADING AND STORAGE

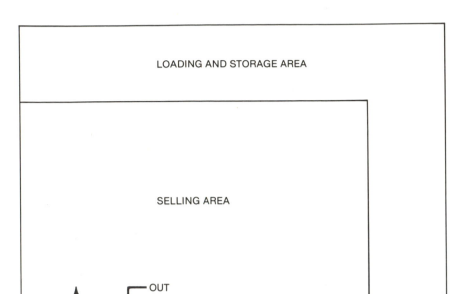

back-room storage and processing areas, since, with this layout, the building is placed close to the property line. This produces more potential dollar sales; greater parking capacity allows for the handling of more customers. Security problems are minimized since there are fewer entrances. The disadvantage of this layout is the distance that merchandise has to be conveyed to the designated department storage area. However, this may not be too high a price to pay for the potential of additional customers.

Selling Area Layout

Since supermarket operators are convinced that labor expenses have risen faster than labor productivity, which is pushing the need for higher gross margins, they are adding new departments as well as new items. These departments usually are selected because of volume and also because of increased margins. They include plants and flowers, mini-drug departments, garden centers, bakeries, cafeterias, take-out foods, and service deli departments. These departments are easier to install for larger stores

which draw from wider trading areas. It should be noted that a supermarket does not necessarily accommodate all these departments. Efficiency and profit will determine which products and departments will be promoted.

A greater emphasis is being placed on the increase of selling area from total store space. This can be accomplished through the use of new computer-based store ordering, full case shelf-stocking, more exacting space allocations, and better case packages. Central processing for meats and produce also cuts space requirements for processing and packaging at store level.

New items constantly put pressure on available space which, in turn, means the layout must be flexible, since store managers should be promoting proven winners. This is not easy with over 10,000 items in a store vying for space. Contenders for increased floor space appear to be frozen foods, general merchandise, health and beauty aids, and grocery and deli items. However, each store will promote the department or merchandise that it feels can cater to its clientele. This, of course, means greater space allocation to that merchandise or department.

EXAMPLES OF SELLING AREA LAYOUT

FIGURE 19
INTERIOR PERIMETER

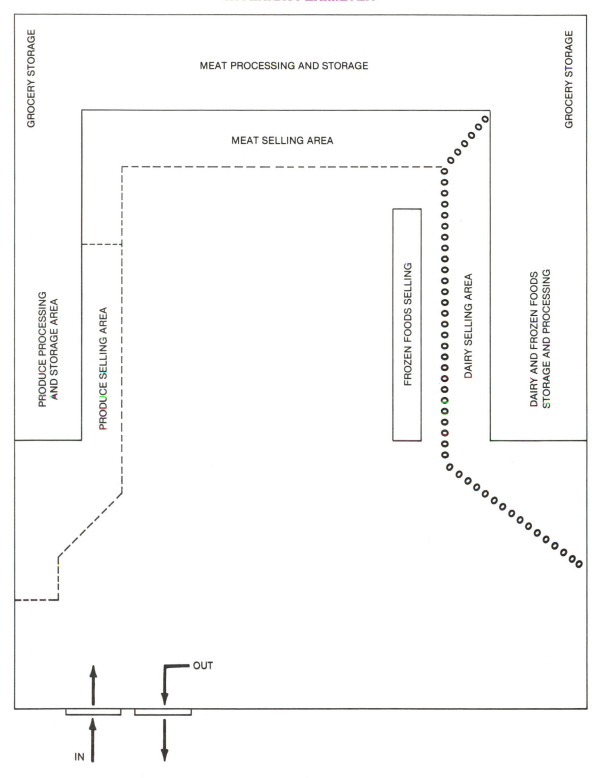

FIGURE 20
LOCATION OF PERISHABLES

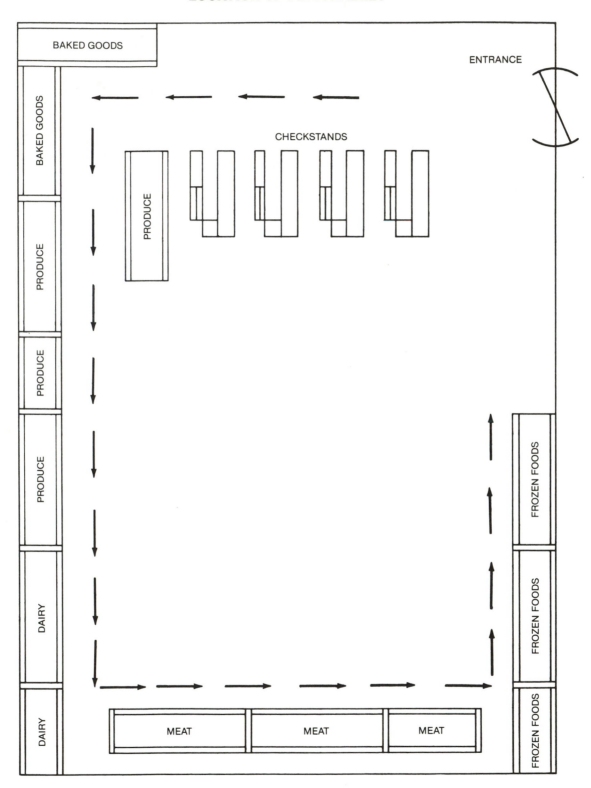

FIGURE 21
LOCATION OF GONDOLAS AND AISLES

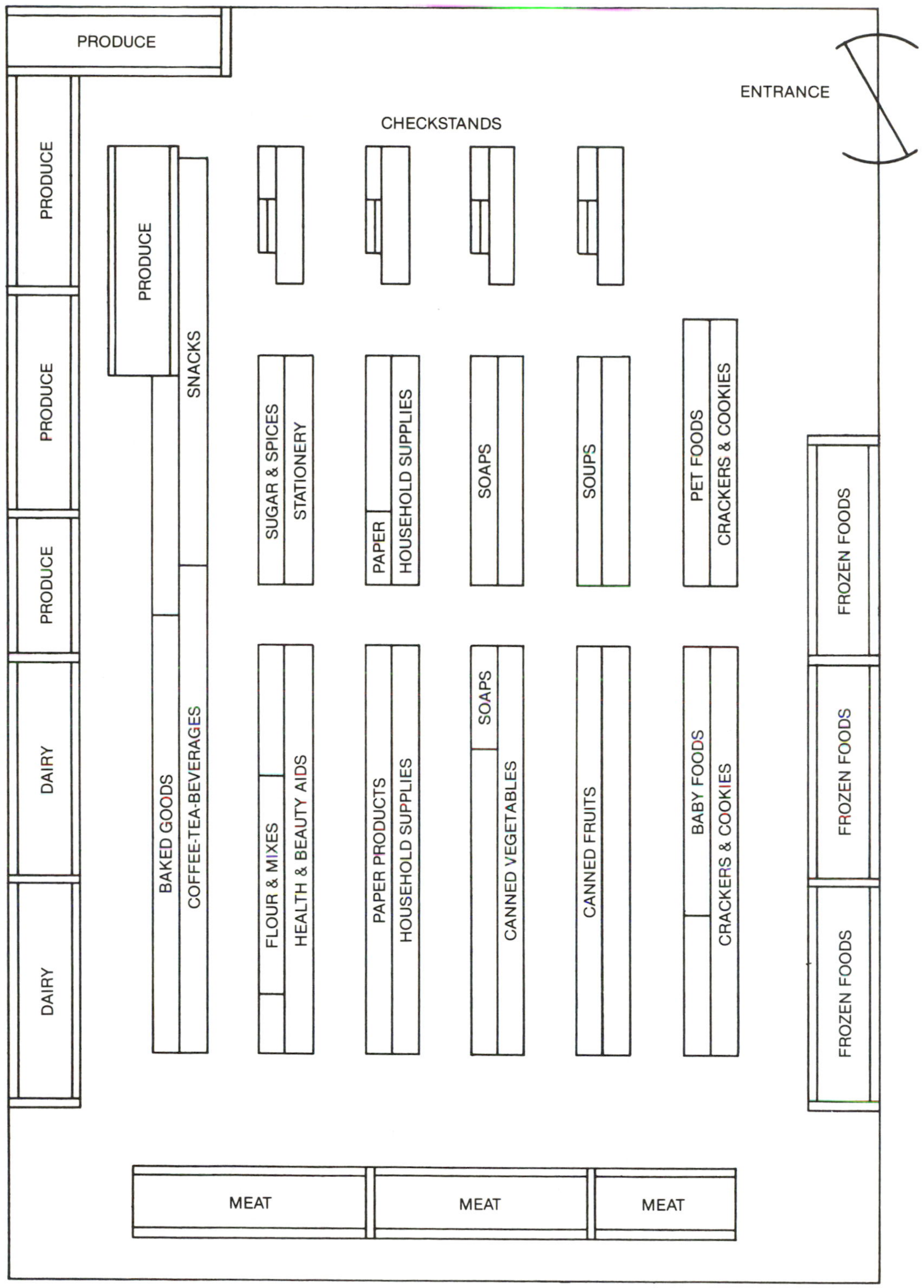

The first step in planning the selling area layout is to locate the perishables around the perimeter of the supermarket in order to draw customers from the entrance around and through the store. (See Figures 19 and 20.) Merchandise is usually grouped into the following departments:

- Meats
- Produce
- Baked goods
- Frozen foods
- Dairy
- Grocery
- Appetizing and delicatessen
- General merchandise (nonfoods).

Meats. Self-service meat departments usually are located along the rear wall or a side wall of supermarkets. Meats will draw the customers through the store and increase full store shopping. Also, the self-service meat case should be located near the work-room area, where it can be restocked easily and efficiently. (See Figure 19.)

Produce. After shopping for meat, the customer usually shops in the produce department to purchase vegetables to be served with the meats. Many supermarket operators prefer to situate the produce department in an area that is conveniently located in relation to the meat department.

In some stores, the produce is displayed at the beginning of the shopping tour because it is a high-profit department, and it is good to expose the customers to it before they spend too heavily in other departments. It is possible to arrive at a compromise between the two schools of thought by placing the produce department along one of the side walls of the store, thus meeting both requirements. (See Figure 19.)

Baked Goods. Many supermarket operators place the bakery section near the entrance. (See Figure 20.) Since nearly all shoppers buy bread, the bakery section starts the buying and prevents shoppers from walking a long distance without picking up some items.

Baked goods that are packaged are generally placed near the dairy department, and if space permits, near cookies. However, if the baked goods are baked in the store, the department is generally placed in the rear of the store or near the deli department. The aroma of baked goods serves to sell them and other products in the store. The high-impulse value of many bakery items makes a location early in the shopping tour desirable. An objection to this is that it is more likely for baked goods to become crushed by piling on top subsequently purchased heavy merchandise.

Frozen Foods. There are two prevailing ideas concerning the placement of the frozen foods department. On the one hand, many operators feel that frozen foods should be at the end of the shopping tour (see Figure 20), since the growing demand for frozen foods will draw traffic without the aid of the meat or produce department, and the length of time the item is without refrigeration will be reduced. On the other hand, they are now being placed in other areas strategic to the store, e.g., the center of the store running parallel to the gondolas.

Dairy. The dairy section is frequently the last perishable-shopping stop for most customers. Therefore, many operators place the dairy department along the wall opposite the produce department. (See Figure 19.) Note that the dairy section is often conveniently located in relation to the frozen foods case. This is desirable since the two departments will tend to mutually support each other.

This completes the inside perimeter of the supermarket. The customers are drawn around this perimeter by the perishable merchandise. At this time, the customers are deep in the store and are consequently ready to shop the grocery section.

Grocery. Supermarket operators have experimented with many different arrangements of gondolas. The most poular arrangement places the gondolas parallel to the checkstands, thereby permitting the checkers to look down the aisles. (See Figure 21.) Diagonal or herringbone arrangements are not generally accepted by customers or operators. The arrangement of the gondolas is designed to encourage, if not force, the shopper to shop the entire store. Other methods used to facilitate traffic circulation are:

- Identification of departments by use of signs and banners
- Maintaining point-to-point visibility throughout the store
- Locating heavy demand displays where they will facilitate circulation
- Eliminating excessive floor fixtures
- Merchandising stock by department.

(A more detailed discussion of gondola and aisle layout is given later in this chapter.)

Appetizing and Delicatessen. Although the contribution of the appetizing and deli department to sales and profit of the store is not great, it is considered important in drawing customers to the store. Since labor is an important consideration in the operation of this department, many stores have experimented with a self-service department. Pathmark, a successful Northeast chain, has been extremely successful with this approach. This, in turn, has influenced the layout of this department in their stores. The appetizing department may also provide prepared take-out and ethnic foods which also create store traffic and yield high margins.

General Merchandise (Nonfoods). With the changing patterns in food spending (eating out has become increasingly popular), the supermarket operator has been seeking items and departments to increase the dollar volume. General merchandise has been selected by many large stores to meet this need. Managers anticipate that most of their profit will come from nonfood items. The in-store location for these items is usually near impulse areas.

Alpha Beta's San Diego store, for example, gives more than one-third of its floor space to nonfood items, including clothing racks that are placed next to the bakery department. On Long Island, a supermarket offers auto supplies, linens, hardware, and a pharmacy. Another typical example is the A&P Family Mart which has a 50-50 split of food and nonfood items in 56,000 square feet. The frozen food area separates food from nonfoods.

Gondolas and Aisles

After locating the perishables around the perimeter of the supermarket, the next step in planning the selling area layout is to locate the gondolas and establish aisles. A typical layout consists of having the checkout lanes and gondolas placed parallel to the side walls. The gondolas are parallel to the produce, dairy and frozen foods departments, and perpendicular to the meat department. The long rows of gondolas often have no breakthrough. By not allowing a breakthrough, the customer is forced to move to the back or front of the store before being able to shop the next aisle.

Minimum aisle width should be six feet for convenience. However, in city stores, where space is both extremely expensive and difficult to get, the aisles may be as narrow as 4.5 feet wide. Smaller shopping carts, as much as twenty-four inches wide, should permit shoppers to pass each other easily. There are many different size shopping carts manufactured which differ in length, width, and depth based on the needs of each store.

Shoppers unable to get around other shoppers get irritated and may not return. Eight-foot aisles are about the maximum, since customers tend to shop only one side when the aisles are too wide; that is, customers will either shop only 50 percent of the merchandise, or they will have to take time to travel up and down the same aisle, which is not likely. Many operators believe that six- to seven-foot aisles are best for high-volume stores, and encourage shopping of both sides of the aisle.

Frequently, in planning new stores, small, independent operators plan for wider aisles, hoping for a

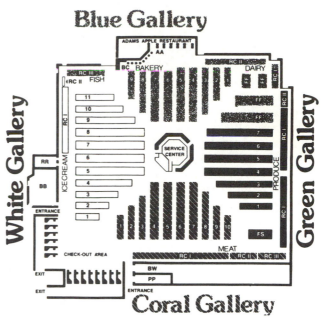

Adams Superama, Pittsfield, Massachusetts, takes a rather distinctive approach at store layout with its almost-symmetrical design, a service center at the hub. It is believed that the design encourages more leisurely shopping. Departments and sections are color coded to make it easier for customers to locate merchandise and departments.

Aisle width is a vital element in planning store layout. Aisles should be wide enough to allow shoppers to pass another customer easily, while being able to shop both sides of the aisle at the same time.

clean, open look which will be pleasing to the customer and will enhance travel down the aisles.

When one such store was complete and the gondolas in place, one owner recently was suddenly assailed by the fact that the space between the gondolas was too wide. The first impulse was to set up a line of wire-basket dump displays to end the barren look of the store. In reality, what that would do is double the number of aisles, and to shop both sides of the original aisle would mean two trips. When this retailer noted this after the gondolas were in place, he had them moved closer together and had an additional aisle created with a cheese boutique, barbeque foods area near the deli department, etc., to fill out the space and eliminate a potential problem area.

More space is needed in front of the meat cases in order to permit shopping for various cuts. Typically, customers leave the shopping cart and walk along the meat case to check prices on the various items. Nine- or ten-foot aisles are used by many operators here in order to avoid confusion and congestion.

The aisle in front of the checkstands should be wide enough to permit customers to shop the end displays and turn down the next aisle. An eight-foot aisle is considered to be the minimum width, with some operators allowing as much as sixteen feet. The operation of the checkstands determines the amount of space needed; *efficient* operations without long lines at peak periods require less aisle space.

Attempts have been made to direct traffic through the store by using one-way aisles. This has not proven very satisfactory, and in some cases, customer dissatisfaction was voiced against being forced to follow prescribed patterns of traffic.

Location of Demand and High-Markup Merchandise

After the aisles and gondolas have been located on the plan, the next step is to locate the merchandise on each gondola. Consideration should be given to locating the fast-moving demand items so as to draw shoppers to impulse items. Geographic differences will affect the location of merchandise items in different stores, since the degree of demand and impulse vary with differences in living habits and standards. The overall plan is to draw traffic to each aisle of the store by disbursing staple commodities in different areas of the store.

The next step is to position the high-markup impulse merchandise. Generally, it is desirable to group related high-markup items together near the faster moving items. Items such as party foods, mixes, snacks, beverages, and glasses sell successfully when displayed together. The fact that the customer is "exposed" to the high-markup merchandise has a great effect on increasing their sale. By strategically placing the fast-moving demand items, complete store shopping is almost assured.

The customer must be able to see, examine, and purchase the merchandise without the assistance of a salesperson. The preferred shelf position is at eye level. Customers do look at merchandise at higher and lower levels, but their attention is usually on eye-level items first, and then on items at other levels. It is for this reason that high-profit impulse items should be at eye level, when possible.

With eye-level impulse stocking, staple items are usually placed on lower shelves and stocked horizontally rather than vertically. Shelving is adjusted so that high-profit impulse merchandise is stocked over the staple items. The customer's eyes automatically come in contact with the high-profit impulse merchandise when he reaches down to pick up the staple items.

Eye-level impulse stocking or "layered merchandising," as some operators refer to this arrangement, has been successful in increasing sales and margins. Also, customers registered no complaints when stores were rearranged. Store managers should determine the type of layered merchandising that is best for their store.

Of course, underlying these considerations concerning the location of demand and high-markup items, it must be borne in mind that merchandise should be within easy reach of shoppers. Most shopping is done by people of average height, with limited reach. Stock clerks frequently stock top shelves out of reach for most shoppers who hesitate to reach for items stocked high on top shelves.

Space Allocation

Space allocation is a major problem, since some items sell in volume, while others sell slowly. The first consideration is allocation of space by sections or merchandise groups. Section space allocation is usually based on share of sales; e.g., a section selling 5 percent of the grocery sales is allocated 5 percent of the grocery shelf space. Allowance is made for variations in size of packages and other display factors. Within sections, the space allocated to each item is important. Consideration must be given to weekly sales movement, importance of the item, size of package, and margin.

Efficient use of selling space is a major problem for all food store operators, whether large or small, since margins are meaningless without volume. Volume means turnover; and effective utilization of shelf space creates turnover, which reduces the share of the expenses charged to each item.

Efficient use of shelf space cannot be reduced to a simple mathematical formula. However, computerized data processing information provides detailed movement reports by item, and shelf space allocation can be assigned based on specific facts and figures. Adding variables for size and shape of the package is helpful, but from an operational point of view, nonmathematical consideration must be added.

Stocking considerations are important. From the standpoint of cost, stocking would be done in case lots or, for some items, half-case lots. Costs are increased by taking cases to the selling floor and back to the storeroom. Half-case packout prevails primarily in smaller, urban stores. Merchandise may be damaged, overlooked, or pilfered when handled in less than case lots in the storeroom. Efficiency in stocking includes frequency of restocking.

Operators agree that proper allocation of space is essential in maintaining full shelves with a minimum of effort and cost. However, unless information is computerized, the task of analyzing and interpreting product movement, varieties handled, unit sizes, and gross profit on sales is not easy. As a result, space is not generally allocated in terms of these factors.

Frequently, space is allocated on a "hit-and-miss" basis. Many operators use warehouse movement as the basis for store space allocation. Warehouse movement does not conform to the movement of any one store, but is the total for all stores. If the stores are similar, this procedure is satisfactory. Usually, customer demands will differ; therefore, the store manager should have authority to make adjustments or request changes in space assignments. (Stores using scanning and the Universal Price Code have exact count and tracking data for that store at all times.)

Adding new items creates space allocation problems since the shelves are already full. Therefore, an item or items must be discontinued and/or facings of some item or items must be reduced to make room for the new item. Usually, fewer items are discontinued than are added; therefore, a reduction in facings as well as the elimination of some items takes place. Company policy frequently gives the responsibility for new-item decisions, as well as which items to discontinue, to a committee. The new-item committee evaluates warehouse movement in making its decisions, and no special consideration is given to the requirements of any particular store and its customers.

Store managers are allocated new items as they appear, and a memo as to the space allocation for each item is prepared. Discontinued items are listed. Some companies send store managers complete space allocation instructions periodically as well as changes whenever new items are added. Many operators permit store managers to vary the overall space allocation plan to fit the particular store and its clientele.

The amount of shelf space that should be allotted to any particular grocery commodity cannot be precisely determined and applied in one sweeping realignment of all stores. Each supermarket, depending upon its location and character, is an individual unit and should operate as such. However, by using commodity turnover and profitableness, the store manager can allocate shelf space for more efficient operation.

Progressive Grocer magazine, *Chain Store Age*, and *Supermarket News* continually publish research on sales by commodity groups, margins, and store profit. The purpose of the various studies is to determine how consumers spend their money and thereby to reveal important facts regarding item sales and profitability. These facts are applied to store design, layout, and space allocation with the view that sales, profitability, and productivity can be increased. As a result of these studies, *Progressive Grocer* has suggested the following procedure for determining space allocation:

1. Determine the total linear feet of shelf space in the grocery section.
2. Determine the space allocation for each commodity group. The share of grocery shelf space is the same as the share of grocery sales accounted for by the commodity group. For example, if canned vegetables account for 10 percent of the unit sales, 10 percent of the shelf space is allocated.
3. Adjust space allocation to allow for size of unit. Average cubic displacement for all grocery items is figured. Allocated space is decreased for small package items and increased for above-average-size units. *Progressive Grocer* figures canned vegetable cubic displacement is below average; according to their calculations, only 71 percent of the average size. Therefore, 10 percent of the grocery linear space × 71 percent is the adjustment for size (1,000 feet × .10 = 100 × .71 = 71 feet).
4. Adjust for shelf width. The average shelf width is used as the base for adjusting space. Accordingly, if the average shelf width is nineteen inches and the canned vegetable shelves are seventeen inches, the allocated space is increased 11.8 percent.
5. Adjust shelves for height suitable to needs so as to obtain maximum visibility of product and not to waste space.
6. Finally, to make allowances for special factors, such as slow-moving items that must have a minimum number of facings to be seen by shoppers and for efficient stocking. Also, direct-store delivery items require space enough to avoid an out-of-stock condition between deliveries, etc. Commodity groups must be a complete unit so as to enable shoppers to recognize the unit. For example, with good space allocation, several facings of another com-

modity are not placed in the canned vegetable sections so as to conform to the mathematical figures.

The *Progressive Grocer* studies showed an increase in sales, turnover, and store profit as a result of allocating space according to the above six-step formula.

Progressive Grocer experimented with the use of colored price channel strips as a shoppers' aid in locating product categories by color-stripping peas, green; corn, yellow; tomatoes, red; etc. Their experiments indicated that color stripping is effective when products are arranged in a block so as to present a noticeable group. Operators, however, have not accepted color stripping as an aid to product location. Operators are using unit-pricing stickers or stickers prepared by their warehouses indicating product and number of facings to be maintained; these stickers are affixed to the shelf molding in order to assure the proper positioning of product on an ongoing basis.

Supermarket operators use a space allocation system of their own design, which uses the store layout as a base, auditing sales by units for a period of time as a base for making adjustments. This can be a formal procedure involving the following steps:

1. Record the facings and the full stock count.
2. Audit sales by units to determine weekly movement. Weekly sales will vary. The audit is over a sufficient period of time to provide a usable average.
3. Determine the number of weeks the shelf supply will last before restocking is required.
4. Check unit pack to determine whether the allocation of more or less space to the item will increase efficiency. Buyers should use this information to make recommendations to manufacturers and to request more efficient case sizes.
5. A few operators add a final step: average inventory investment in shelf stock (average shelf stock in units × unit cost).

Store managers can use this procedure to reallocate space and as a means of providing space for new items. It can be undertaken by sections and should be continuous. The number of items is not static; consumer demand is not static; therefore, space allocation cannot be static.

Many store managers use an informal procedure to measure stock movement. They note the frequency of reorder and/or restocking and reallocate space accordingly. All too often, the store manager recognizes the fast movers, but fails to recognize the lack of movement by the slow movers.

This situation was proven to a store manager by the simple procedure of placing an inconspicuous code mark on the shelf stock of several items which the manager estimated move from one-half to one case a week. A month later, only one to four of the coded units were sold. The manager was shocked to learn that his informal method gave him such inaccurate results.

Equipment manufacturers furnish guides for determining the amount of space needed for various volumes. To use these guides, a total sales budget must be prepared, and the percentage of sales each department is expected to contribute is determined. Area, location, type of operation, degree of efficiency, class of customers, etc., are all influential factors for each store. Operators must adjust to their own territories and types of stores.

The method used to determine the unit movement of items stocked is not important. In fact, 100 percent accuracy is not vital, since adjustments must be made so as to present the merchandise by commodity groups and in sufficient quantity to achieve efficient stocking. The important consideration is that weekly unit sales be determined with reasonable accuracy, allowing for weekly and seasonal variations, and that space is allocated in relation to movement. This is not to say slow movers should not be stocked. However, good management requires that the slow movers be identified and controlled. (Again, this is an advantage of UPC data.)

Grocery Storage and Work Area

The storage area for the grocery items should be convenient to the sales area and accessible for incoming merchandise. Stocking the sales area shelves represents one of the highest expense items in the store. Therefore, anything that will increase productivity will increase store profit.

The purpose of a storage area is to serve as a place where merchandise is stored and prepared for display. The storage area should be laid out so that the operations can be performed with a minimum of handling, walking, carrying, or searching for merchandise. Excess handling and searching can be eliminated by commodity group segregation and by proper arrangement of the stocks within the storage area. (See Figure 22 for an example of a grocery storage and work area.)

Many years ago, Grand Union devised a system of stocking perimeter shelves from the back room. The system, called Slant-o-Matic, consisted of shelves that were slanted downward toward the front of the gondola. At the gondola facing, a fixed metal rod, several inches up from the bottom of each shelf, held the merchandise in place. The merchandise had to be lifted so that it could be removed from the shelf. Stocking the items was done from the back room by feeding product from the rear of the gravity-fed shelves. The problem with the system was that only perimeters could be so used and it eliminated the conventional placement of meat, dairy and produce departments. It was a complicated and expensive system and never really caught on. The last system of this sort in place was removed from a Grand Union store in Elmwood Park, New Jersey, in the mid-1970's.

Factors that control the size of grocery storage areas are sales, number of deliveries of merchandise per week, merchandise turnover, and amount of reserve stock carried.

Studies by the U.S. Department of Agriculture indicate that a long, narrow, rectangular area provides

Well-stocked at all times: That was the aim of this special ninety-eight-foot canned goods unit installed at Sid's Supermarket, Berkeley, California, in 1958, which operated like Grand Union's Slant-o-Matic shelving. Shelves, located along the perimeter of the store, slanted downward and were filled from the back room. This stocking system never really caught on.

the best type of storage area. The area should be separate from the meat and produce receiving areas, if possible. In all new stores, palletization is the choice method of delivery and storing merchandise in this area; palletization increases the productivity of those working there. Some stores still use a conveyor to reduce the time and effort expended in the storage and movement of merchandise.

In the narrow storage area, the bays or stacks of merchandise should be in double rows, perpendicular to the wall, with an aisle wide enough to permit easy removal of merchandise. A conveyor may be set up parallel to the wall and perpendicular to the bays or stacks. The distance from the bays or stacks should be no more than twelve feet, a reasonable distance to carry merchandise for anyone unloading or loading the conveyor.

The merchandise should be stacked in the storage area to coincide roughly with its location on the selling floor, if possible. It is much easier to locate any desired item when this arrangement is followed. Signs designating the commodity group or aisle number corresponding to the selling area location are helpful. If the merchandise is to be centrally marked, the stamping table should be located at the end of the conveyor near the door leading to the sales area in order to save stock clerks unnecessary steps.

By setting up bays with racks so that merchandise can be double-decked, much time is saved in removing needed merchandise because of the shorter height of the stacks. Also top-deck space for items that are crushable—cookies, crackers, cereals, etc.—is multiplied.

Adequate frozen foods storage space is a major problem, unless the supermarket is equipped with walk-in freezer storage. The number of frozen items stocked continues to increase, and backup stocks are necessary to maintain full selling displays.

While it is desirable to plan the size of the building to fit the needs of storage, work and sales areas, this is not always feasible. Usually, the storage and work areas are the ones that must be adjusted. However, the trend is to establish the minimum needs of each department of the store, along with storage and work area, and then construct a building to fill these requirements.

Meat Storage and Work Area

Years ago, when carcass beef was cut in almost every supermarket, much greater areas had to be maintained in order to prepare meat for sale. Today, however, with primal cuts coming into the store either in the form of boxed beef or other systems, smaller areas are needed for storage and preparation.

EXAMPLES OF LAYOUT FOR STORAGE AND WORK AREAS

FIGURE 22
GROCERY STORAGE AND WORK AREA

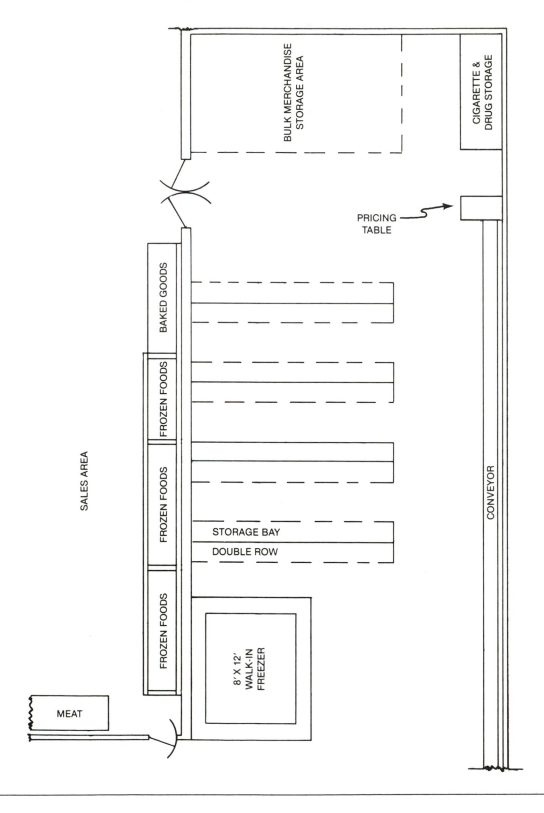

FIGURE 23
MEAT STORAGE AND WORK AREA

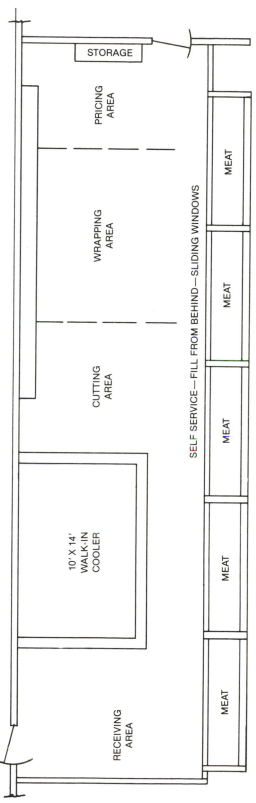

FIGURE 24
PRODUCE STORAGE AND WORK AREA

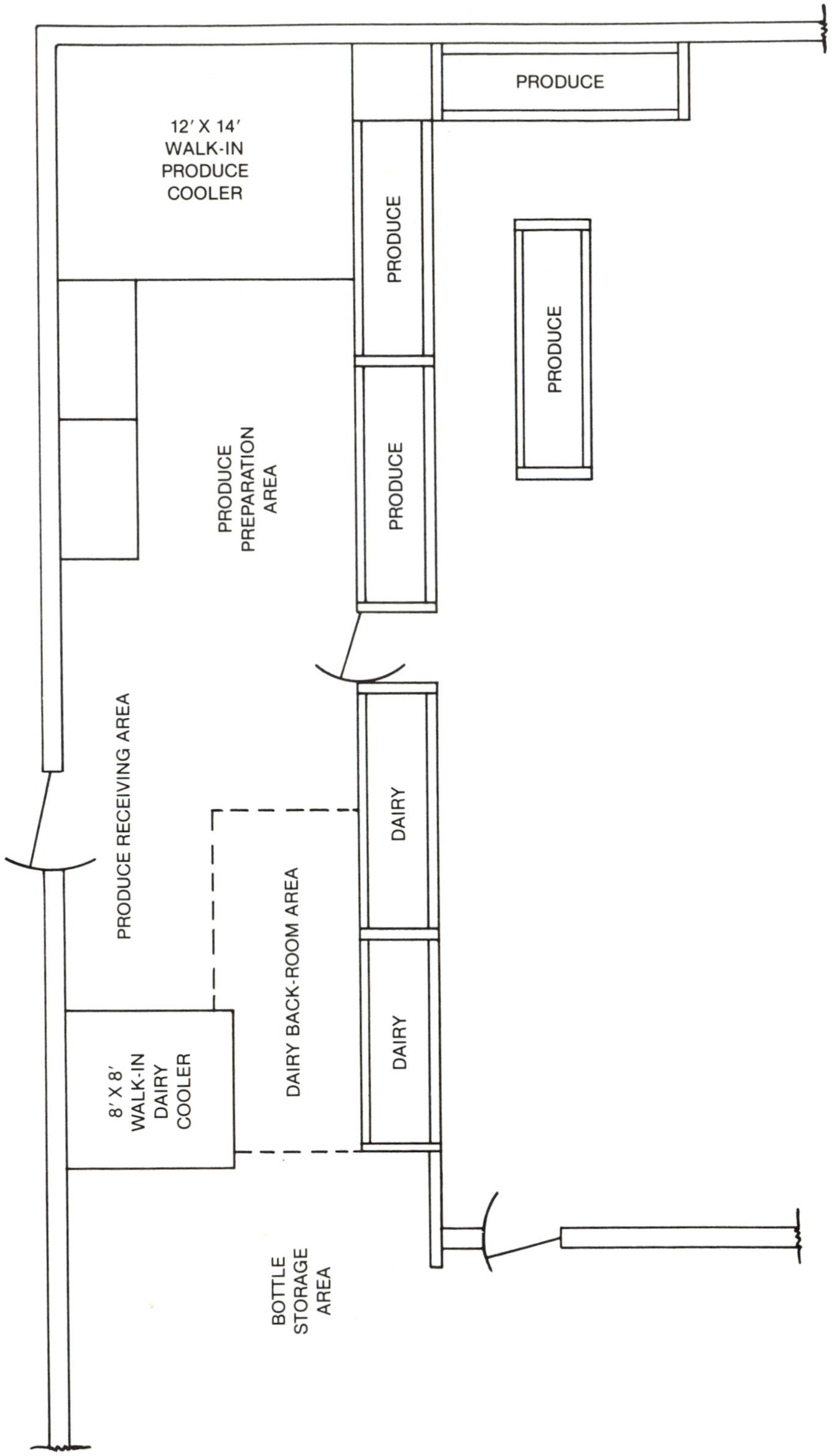

12' X 14'
WALK-IN
PRODUCE
COOLER

PRODUCE

PRODUCE

PRODUCE

PRODUCE

PRODUCE

PRODUCE PREPARATION AREA

PRODUCE RECEIVING AREA

DAIRY

DAIRY

DAIRY BACK-ROOM AREA

8' X 8'
WALK-IN
DAIRY
COOLER

BOTTLE
STORAGE
AREA

In older stores, much of this space has been converted so that walk-in freezers can be accommodated. However, sufficient space must be maintained so that primal cuts can be trimmed and cut into store or retail cuts and the resultant items can be wrapped and priced.

Such areas generally are directly behind the meat display cases, and a bell or buzzer signal system permits the customer to call someone from the department up to the case so that special cuts or items not on display can be ordered.

Glass walls generally are used here so that customers can see how sanitary the department is. Some customers still prefer to see their chopped meat ground up in their presence. The glass walls permit this visual inspection without the grinder being in the sales area or necessitating the customer's entry into the meat preparation room.

Figure 23 shows the typical layout of a meat department work area.

Produce Storage and Work Area

The produce storage and work area varies with sales, the number of deliveries each week, merchandise turnover, amount of reserve stock needed, and seasonal demands.

Figure 24 shows a typical layout for a self-service produce work and storage area. In those markets where produce is packaged in-store, there is an increase in the amount of space and machinery used in the preparation area. As larger supermarkets are constructed and produce sales increase, a product flow plan coordinating layout and equipment must be developed for each store.

The size of the dairy storage area will vary from supermarket to supermarket, depending upon the number of dairy items handled. This area should be close to a door leading to the selling area and as near to the dairy department as possible.

Many stores now prefer an open wall with removable partitions between the dairy storage area and the milk and egg cases so that product can be put into selling areas from the back room merely by removing an empty section of the case and putting in a filled section, thus saving time and effort and creating improved productivity.

SINGLE-FLOOR VERSUS BASEMENT OPERATION

The single-floor storage and work area overwhelmingly has preference over the basement storage and work-area operation. It provides easier move-

ment of product from work and storage area to the selling area. Currently, new supermarkets are being constructed with a one-floor plan. In urban stores, however, where space is at a premium, stores must utilize basement space (or in the conversion of a building with a high ceiling and/or a second floor, there are possibilities of a balcony type operation).

The principal reasons given for the use of basements are:

1. The size of the lot on which the supermarket is to be built is not large enough to accommodate large storage areas.
2. Construction costs for basement space is sufficiently lower than for ground level space.
3. In renting shopping center locations, a full basement is usually rated at half the price of

There is generally a message for customers in so-called store "looks." For example, in the photograph at top, the interior roof simulating a warehouse translates to "no frills" and means low pricing. However, the massive product graphics and "high hat" lights may convey modernity as well. The Early American theme says stability, nostalgia, and simplicity, in the store at bottom. Also a bit of humor—note the "jail" and "saloon."

the main floor, and a partial basement may add no additional rent, dependent on the lease terms.

Improved conveyor equipment makes basement space economical. Apparently, no hard-and-fast rule exists for resolving this question, and many large food organizations have both single-floor and basement-type operations. The deciding factors seem to be the size of the plot of land that is available, the cost of the land, and construction costs.

Steadily increasing construction costs have obliged some operators to reverse their attitudes on the use of basements. It pays to install basements where ground costs are extremely high and use of a basement would cut the overall cost of building a market. Most operators prefer single-floor stores whenever adequate space at a reasonable cost can be obtained.

Some operators use trailer trucks as additional back-room space; that is, the trailer remains at the store until the next delivery, and the merchandise is unloaded as needed for stocking. This is practical and recommended for high-volume outlets, both from the point of view of the store as well as the distribution center.

Another approach to reducing costs of handling and stocking is the containerized stocking of merchandise. Items such as milk are received in special containers and moved directly to the display coolers on carts. When refills are necessary, another container is rolled into place for easy access and self-service. The movement of bulk items, such as sugar, flour, large bags of pet foods, paper goods, and bulk produce, have been handled successfully using this method.

STORE "LOOK"

Endless rows of cans, bottles, and boxes can create a monotonous appearance and mood. To avoid this and add interest at the same time, many stores have reorganized departments, such as grocery, into subdepartments, so that each is a shop in itself. The proper use of color and lighting with a modern decor, and even carpeting, provide a fresh and interesting appearance which encourages shoppers to stay in the store longer and shop. New, automated and computerized systems facilitate the checkout process, so that checkout, pricing, and bagging are done in one operation, conveying a feeling or look of modernity, efficiency, etc.

There are many layouts and designs that can be used to project the desired store image. Some store groups have selected an early American decor. A store-within-a-store arrangement has been used effectively. A warehouse look projects a low-price image. Others have even moved to a high-fashion look. Any theme can be used to identify with a store, chain, or locale. Whichever theme or "look" is used, the basic concept should possess the following characteristics; it should be inexpensive, neat, bright, utilitarian, and easy to maintain.

25

With the expansion and growth of supermarkets, extensive changes have been made in the types of equipment and lighting used. A number of factors have contributed to these changes: new merchandising techniques, labor-saving devices aimed at efficiency and productivity, updated knowledge of consumer buying behavior, traffic patterns and, most recently, an emphasis on energy saving. No doubt, supermarket operators, in conjunction with equipment manufacturers, have attempted to develop equipment that would meet the required needs of the stores, giving thought to increasing self-service efficiencies.

As a part of their selling program, most equipment manufacturers offer supermarket operators complete store-planning services. As indicated in the previous chapter, their store-planning departments will plan the remodelling of a supermarket or the layout for a new unit. Of course, the objective is to sell equipment that will successfully accomplish the plan.

Changes in equipment are being made continually. Supermarket operators complain that the equipment changes occurring between the time a store is planned, including contracting for the equipment, and the completion date, render some equipment obsolete. It is truly an industry of change!

Experts in the field, identify six types of equipment: refrigeration, lighting, heating and air conditioning, nonrefrigerated display cases, cleaning and control equipment. Studies recently conducted by *Supermarket News* indicated that there was an increase in expenditures in five of the six categories. Cleaning equipment was the only category that experienced a decline. However, even in the other five categories, the equipment buyers, representing 22,126 stores, suggested a cautious rather than an all-out, "no-matter-what-the-cost" search for energy-saving equipment.

The three energy-demanding categories of which most equipment buyers were conscious, in order of priority, were: refrigeration, lighting, and heating/air conditioning.

When purchasing expensive equipment, approximately 50 percent of the firms rely on purchasing committees to make the decision or review the equipment buyer's decision. There is no doubt, however, that the accent is on dealing with energy problems, since this expenditure has now exceeded rent in many stores. Many equipment manufacturers have addressed themselves to this problem and have designed their equipment specifically to attempt to alleviate the retailers' concern.

Despite these energy concerns, the store building, its lighting, and the appearance of its equipment remain among the most noticeable factors and major influences in the creation of store image.

LIGHTING

Modern advances in supermarket lighting have kept pace with changing patterns in merchandising. Whether in new store construction or old store remodelling, lighting is a major factor in influencing visual impression and creating an attractive atmosphere.

Well-planned lighting helps develop the visibility needed to influence impulse buying in supermarkets. Lighting should be designed to reveal the inherent quality of the merchandise—color, texture, form, pattern, workmanship—by means of an overall pattern of illumination that provides light of appropriate quality, color, direction, and diffusion to create a buying impulse.

Lighting helps develop a distinctive store appearance which is an asset to a modern supermarket. Self-service merchandising requires a higher-than-average illumination level to help speed customer traffic and merchandise selection.

Circulation areas require an illumination level of 30 to 50 foot-candles; general illumination, 100 foot-candles; display spotlights, an additional 200 foot-candles; thereby establishing a bright, clear appearance throughout the entire store as well as highlighting displays. The use of spotlighting helps to attract attention to featured items and high-impulse merchandise. A level of 200 foot-candles for the checkout areas aids in making change, tends to speed up checkout operations, and reduces errors.

Lighting is a competitive merchandising tool; that is, overall store appearance and customer impression is, to a considerable extent, a result of light. Also, sales

Well-run supermarkets recognize the importance of modern lighting in an essentially self-service setting. The merchandise must be seen by the customer. Good lighting helps in another way; it creates a comfortable atmosphere. Notice the combination of fluorescent and incandescent lights in the general ceiling lighting of this store. An additional light source is found on the top shelf of the perimeter shelving fixture on the left.

are increased by good overall lighting; if the customer can see better, he or she will make buying decisions faster. Thus, lighting is a sales tool.

Modern store lighting must contribute to the sales appeal of the merchandise, attract attention, permit fast shopping, and create a pleasing atmosphere. A good lighting system accomplishes these objectives by using three components: general, display and perimeter lighting.

General Lighting

General lighting is used for traffic areas, including the aisles in a supermarket. Much of the light for appraising merchandise is supplied as general lighting: fluorescent, incandescent and high-intensity discharge lighting system lamps with inconspicuous fixtures. The recommended illumination level is 100 foot-candles of combined light to balance the ceiling appearance, store atmosphere, and effect on merchandise.

Since the increased costs of energy, many stores are re-evaluating their lighting programs and are making changes in order to lower costs and improve efficiency. These include:

- Buying more expensive bulbs that use less electricity and that in the long run are cheaper
- Replacing lighting systems with more efficient layout
- Increasing the number of switch locations to improve lighting flexibility
- Reducing the level of lighting
- Reducing the number of bulbs or using lower wattage lamps
- Using mercury lamps instead of fluorescents.

However, in spite of all these cost-saving measures, the stores have continued to register an increase in the cost of lighting.

Display Lighting

Display lighting is a point-of-purchase sales tool which attracts attention by contrast, emphasizes color, provides sparkle, adds a change-of-pace in brightness, and adds to store atmosphere. The most commonly used light source is the spotlight, which adds 200 foot-candles to the general lighting.

A newer display of display light is the luminous panel which is used to transilluminate transparent or translucent merchandise. Merchandise suited to this kind of lighting includes bottled liquids, jams, jellies, honey, etc.

Perimeter Lighting

Perimeter lighting is used to emphasize merchandise near the walls and to add a pleasing decorative element. It creates a favorable overall store image and highlights signs, including the store directory, when one is used.

Uniform lighting is accomplished with fluorescent lamps or high-intensity discharge systems. Valances can be used to reflect light upward on walls, creating an illusion of greater size. Incandescent light is added to highlight special displays along the perimeter.

Fluorescent lighting fixtures are now installed at right angles to gondolas, aisles, etc., contrary to the former practice whereby the lights ran in the same direction as the equipment.

Lighting should create a store atmosphere that invites shoppers to enter. Inside the store, the overall atmosphere determines the degree of continued acceptance and is an important factor in the customer's decision to continue to shop the store or to look for another place to buy merchandise.

Parking Area Lighting

Parking area lighting should be adequate to assure the safety of shoppers. People will not park in dimly lighted parking lots and will drive miles to shop in a supermarket with a "safer" parking lot. The two to five foot-candles needed can be supplied by street lighting-type fixtures using incandescent, fluorescent or color-improved mercury-vapor lamps. High-mounted flood-lighting equipment, using filament lamps or color-improved mercury-vapor lamps, will adequately light the parking lot.

Store Identification and Building-Front Lighting

Adequate store identification and building-front lighting may be accomplished with luminous plastic signs or panels, or flood lighting. Store identification can also utilize exposed-lamp signs with either neon tubes or filament lamps.

Storefront lighting should be designed to harmonize with the interior view customers get of the store while driving or walking nearby. A well-balanced lighting system is a direct invitation to the public to enter the store and shop.

The offbeat use of lighting can be an effective promotional tool. Here, panels of lit bulbs meeting at right angles form frames for merchandise sections. The focus: Get the customer's attention.

Lighting Maintenance

Lighting maintenance should be built into the design of the lighting. Dirt and deterioration decrease the effective illumination of all types of lighting. Therefore, a regular cleaning and replacement program is needed to maintain lighting at the installed efficiency.

Group relamping and cleaning at regular intervals is usually the lowest cost procedure. The labor cost of replacing all bulbs or tubes in a fixture is not much greater than replacing one. Also, as bulbs and tubes age, they become less efficient; the amount of electricity consumed remains the same, but the foot-candle output is reduced.

Decreased light intensity affects sales and alters store image. Scheduled maintenance reduces costs, maintains the level of lighting, and contributes to greater sales and more favorable customer image.

Lighting and Color

Color appearance often enters into the making of buying decisions. Lighting should render colors in a familiar and realistic manner. Also, the color characteristics of light affects the appearance of people, the impression made by packages, the impression made by perishables, and the character of the store.

Unless lighting is carefully selected, the color of many items may be far from their familiar or "natural" look. This is particularly true of meats and vegetables; however, it applies almost equally to packages, since color is a major element in their design. When incandescent light bulbs are used in supermarket lighting, colors have a familiar, though often imperfect, appearance. Incandescent light creates a "warm" atmosphere; the yellow side of the color spectrum is dominant, and the cool side—the blues and greens—is subordinate. Many lighting experts recommend mixing fluorescent and incandescent light.

Fluorescent lighting has largely replaced incandescent lighting in supermarkets, providing a higher level of illumination which helps make shopping quicker and easier. Also, fluorescent lights burn "cooler" and use less energy; therefore, they last longer and are more cost efficient.

With all its virtues, fluorescent lighting had been unable to produce familiar or "natural" color effects. After much research and experimentation, fluorescent lamp colors were developed which retained the advantage of fluorescent lighting and, in addition, provided familiar color rendition. The "natural" effect is accomplished by the use of a new fluorescent powder combination which adds more red and green to the light, while keeping the correct amount of yellow and blue.

Fluorescent tubes are available in four basic types. "Deluxe Cool White" tubes create a cool atmosphere which simulates daylight and emphasizes all colors equally or nearly so. "Deluxe Warm White" creates a warm atmosphere and simulates incandescent lights, emphasizing warm colors and dulling blues and greens. "Cool White" creates a cool atmosphere which simulates daylight on neutral surfaces; cool colors are emphasized as are yellow and orange; reds are dulled. "Warm White" creates a warm atmosphere and simulates incandescent light on neutral surfaces. The yellows are emphasized, and the cool colors and harsh reds are dulled. More and more general lighting is being furnished with either fluorescent or high-intensity discharge systems.

Tubes of this type, both cool and warm, are recommended for selling areas. Also, interspersing incandescent light will add the reds lacking in fluorescent light.

Warm white lights should be used on meats and vegetables, emphasizing the natural reds of the meats and the bright varying colors of fruits and vegetables, and creating a brighter and more vivid appearance. Packages and canned goods also have greater sales appeal under this lighting. The cool whites are less expensive, but create a "bluish" look.

In other departments, the "Deluxe Warm White" lamps are also the best lighting choice. Poultry and dairy products take on an added rich yellowness. The rich tans and browns of baked goods are also emphasized for better appearance.

Placement of Lighting

Because the eyes are attracted first to areas that are unusually bright, a market area lighted to a high level by a system of bare fluorescent lamp fixtures makes the eyes overly conscious of the bright light sources overhead. This situation is most noticeable when a customer first enters the store because there is a contrast with the natural outside light and the bright lights are more in the shopper's field of vision, creating a ceiling glare and distracting the customer's attention from merchandise displays.

Similarly, upper wall surfaces finished in pure, glossy white produce annoying reflections of high brilliance as well as distractions for the eye. Overhead glare, combined with unlighted display cases, contribute to changing the showcases from desirable pieces of display equipment to mere storage bins.

Besides the direct glare problems, exposed fluorescent lamp systems develop a further distracting atmosphere when the bare tubes accumulate a visible coating of dust and dirt. This condition, together with symptoms of lamp aging or early burnouts, present what customers usually regard as an unsanitary, neglected appearance. In many cases, the situation is aggravated further when more than one shade of fluorescent white lamp is used. (There are several different whites.) Many times, as replacements are made, the wrong color or shade is used, contributing to a confusing, undesirable atmosphere.

Many of these objectionable situations, which distract from the customer's buying impulse, can be minimized by using some form of shield to deflect the direct glare from the lamps and to conceal dust and dirt accumulations on the bulbs as well as early burnouts and mismatched lamp types. Valances may be used over the lighting on the shelves and upper walls, producing a softer, luminous background against which merchandise and department signs may be displayed. Perimeter lighting using valances can also make a contribution to overall store appearance by increasing the apparent size of the store. The use of valances, however, can reduce lighting efficiency as well as result in some dust accumulation.

Lighting Special Displays

Standard shelving and merchandise in the stores of today are combined with numerous displays. Either direct or internal lighting may be successfully utilized to accent these displays. For this purpose, miniature spotlights can be utilized for highlighting the merchandise or the area. Internal lighting of displays, such as jellies packed in clear glass containers, creates an interesting and impulse-buying situation; an internal source of illumination can produce a uniquely effective display.

AIR CONDITIONING

Most supermarket operators are aware of the need to have air-conditioned stores, regardless of the section of the United States in which they are located. Three principle reasons for air conditioning are:

1. To bring additional customers to the supermarket while retaining the present customers.
2. To maintain a competitive position in the trading area.
3. To keep employees comfortable, promoting greater productivity.

An air-conditioning system, in order to create a favorable customer image, must control both temperature and humidity. Controls that maintain a comfortable inside temperature, in relation to the climate outside, are very important. Too great a change, especially on very hot days, is unpleasant and will keep customers away.

A written agreement outlining the conditions that will be maintained in the store by the equipment should be obtained from the manufacturer, dealer, or contractor. Maintenance service may be contracted and should be investigated to assure that qualified and dependable repair service is available on short notice.

Two principal types of air-conditioning units are in general use. One type is a self-contained unit, usually available in sizes from 24,000 to 36,000 BTU-per-hour (12,000 BTU units equal one ton of cooling capacity). These small units are especially adapted to older structures and buildings having limited space available for a central plant. By spacing two or three of these packaged units throughout a store, even temperatures can be maintained.

The condensing unit may be either air or water-cooled. Very few units being made today, however,

Supermarkets are aware that lighting can be distracting, and therefore counter-productive, if brightness is not controlled. Here are two ways to reduce glare. In photograph at top, plastic shields are used to deflect light rays; at bottom, lighting is encased in no-glare paneling. Merchandise is the beneficiary.

are water-cooled, since a tank and circulating equipment must be provided. Very often local ordinances require the use of water-saving equipment in order to control the use of limited water supplies. If possible, a separate well to supply water for the refrigeration equipment is advantageous. Therefore, operators favor the air-cooled condenser units which eliminate the water supply problem. These packaged units vary in cost for each 12,000 BTU of capacity. If heating units are combined, the cost of the equipment and of installation will be increased.

The second general type of air conditioning being used is the central unit. The large, centrally located unit supplies temperature-controlled air (cooled or heated) for the entire store area. Air is blown through ductwork located in the ceiling or near the ceiling along opposite sides of the building. The air conditioning or heating is thermostatically controlled; this type of system provides temperature regulation and humidity control. The air is filtered and dehumidified before being cooled and redistributed.

A central air-conditioning plant is especially advantageous where the requirements necessitated by climate and square footage are greatest. Air-cooled units for large installations have been improved and the efficiency increased; as a result, they are widely used.

Centrally located air-conditioning costs vary for each 12,000 BTU of capacity (per ton), including ductwork, piping, and wiring. Local conditions and locations of dealers who can supply maintenance service are usually determining factors in the selection of the refrigeration equipment.

Nearly all new supermarket buildings are air conditioned, using centrally located systems that provide both heated and cooled air. Air conditioning is a customer service that is expected by shoppers.

Since the energy crisis, store operators have been conscious of reducing energy costs and have sought heating/air-conditioning equipment that can reclaim heat in the winter and cold air in the summer from other existing equipment being used, such as refrigeration units. The equipment manufacturers claim success for a 10 percent reduction in heating and air-conditioning costs, while at the same time providing comfortable aisle temperatures throughout a store.

In new installations, and even some older ones where they lend themselves, efficient reclamation systems for recapturing heat have eliminated all heating costs for the stores in winter.

The high costs of energy have also caused retailers to look to other efficiencies to save energy. Winn-Dixie, for example, has installed solar heating systems in virtually all of its stores, and depending on the store and location, some of the stores have been able to generate all of their hot water needs from just the solar system.

Other efficiencies and energy planning programs have been among the prime considerations in planning new stores—locations, store layout, heat reclamation systems, etc.

AIR-CURTAIN DOOR

The air-curtain door was developed in Switzerland. In principle, a current of air is used as a curtain to keep outside air from entering the building. The air curtain keeps insects out, and small animals hesitate to cross it. Directional nozzles installed above the entrance produce an air wall, with the air being exhausted from the entrance through a floor grating, where it is cleaned, heated or cooled, and recirculated. Dirt is accumulated in a pit which must be cleaned regularly.

Controls automatically change the velocity of the air so that outside air does not enter. The depth of the air curtain permits the use of a velocity so gentle that it will not disturb hairdos. Since the installation and operating costs of the air curtain are high, and it is of limited use, the air curtain has not become very popular.

AUTOMATIC DOORS

The electric-eye door opener was standard for supermarkets until the invention of the electric-mat door opener. Nearly all supermarkets use automatic doors, at least on exits, to enable customers with packages to leave with ease. As an added convenience, supermarket operators have also installed automatic doors at entrances. The electric-mat door opener is more dependable and not as subject to interference as the electric eye.

Availability of service is an important factor in the selection of equipment. Therefore, another device has become extremely popular—the sensor sliding-door installation which operates without mats, but is controlled by an overhead beam. An outstanding advantage is a reduction in the possibility of accidents.

CONTROLLED-TEMPERATURE DISPLAY EQUIPMENT

Typically, between 45 and 55 percent of supermarket sales are perishable and must be displayed in temperature-controlled equipment. In addition to new equipment, major remodelling ($50,000 or more) is done each year on about 6 percent of all food stores. The most frequently remodelled and expanded department is frozen foods. Meat comes next, with dairy following closely. Dry groceries, produce, and nonfoods account for the remainder. Estimates are that supermarkets spend over $250 million annually for refrigeration equipment.

A major consideration in store planning is the kind of equipment to use and the location of each unit.

Photo courtesy of Hill Refrigeration Division, Emhart Corporation.

Frozen foods have to be kept colder than meat, dairy products, and produce. That is where these sophisticated parallel compressor condensing units come into play. In effect, by customizing refrigeration needs, the store saves on overall energy costs.

Each unit must be connected to condenser and compressor units. The heat removed in the cooling process will tend to heat the store and make air conditioning more expensive. To avoid heating the store area, the refrigerating units are located in the back room in order to permit venting to the outside or the use of water to carry off the heat. Remote units—either air- or water-cooled—are used. Having all the mechanical units together, daily inspection and checking is easily performed, and no units are overlooked. Maintenance is also easier, since the units are open (not enclosed in a cabinet) and easily accessible.

The danger of costly losses in merchandise, which would result if compressors were to fail and such freezer and cooler cases did not function properly, has caused a number of firms to install alarm systems that alert the manager or even a central headquarters person to the fact that a danger temperature has been reached on a given piece of equipment. A repairman is quickly dispatched to the store to repair or replace the faulty piece of equipment before excessive damage results.

The layout plan of a new supermarket must provide the necessary ductwork to permit piping the refrigerant to each display unit. An important cost factor in building construction is the number of feet of ductwork, tunnels, or troughs needed to operate the controlled-temperature units. However, engineering, construction and installation costs are secondary to sales considerations, since it is only through sales income that costs are paid and profits earned.

The display cases, from the customer point of view, are all about the same, the major differences being the merchandise on display. All cases have a heated front-trim-sill for greater customer comfort. The color of the case or some of its panels adds to the decor and contributes to the total store image. It is interesting to note that merchandising appeal is still probably the number one consideration in the selection of refrigerated display equipment, with energy a close second. In a recent survey, for example, meat departments with upright cases or multidecks and compressors were most frequently mentioned, while door cases were cited least.

Control equipment includes thermostats, environment control panels, and computerized energy control systems, with an eye toward balancing "peak and valley" use of energy. There appears to be an increased consciousness of this type of equipment on the part of management.

Many large firms use energy management systems as a means of lowering energy expenses, while smaller stores seek remodeling of equipment as an alternative to total replacement.

Planning considerations include the various case types, such as the low back-front shopping case, frequently used as the typical meat case; the high back-front shopping case with display shelves for nonrefrigerated items, used as a wall or back-to-back frozen food case; the mirror-backed case, used primarily for produce; the island-type case which can be shopped from both sides (with or without a superstructure for nonrefrigerated items) and used primarily for frozen foods; and the various service display cases used for meats, delicatessen items, fish, poultry, and so on. There are many variations, such as high-back cases with refrigerated shelves, and door-type upright cases.

Location of the case and operating considerations dictate the type of case that is best suited. The amount of display space needed must be translated into the unit capacity. Most cases are either eight or twelve feet long or are a combination of units joined together to make larger single units (e.g., four sections of twelve feet each to create a forty-eight-foot case). There are exceptions or variations, such as the end cases for "jumbo island" freezer units, built to fit across the end of these large units. Thus, factors relevant to planning include the basic layout pattern, the equipment best suited to each location, engineering considerations, service factors, etc.

The circulation of air removes heat from merchandise in the various display cases. Over-filling a case, and cutting off or breaking the flow of air, reduces the removal of heat. Therefore, the load limit line on all cases should never be exceeded, since the entire display is no longer being cooled when circulation is discontinued. Gaps also strain the equipment, use excess energy, and are as inefficient as loading over limit lines. Many retailers use dummy or filler boxes to eliminate gaps. Quality control rests upon temperature control, which, in turn, depends upon proper circulation of cooled air.

All temperature-controlled cases should be checked frequently so that any malfunctioning of the equipment can be discovered and corrected before the merchandise deteriorates. A prime consideration in the selection of mechanical units is the availability of service. For temperature-control equipment this means day and night service, complete with parts and competent technicians.

Meat Display Equipment

The fresh meat case is a low-type case about thirty-seven inches high in front and about two inches higher in back to provide visibility for the price molding and to avoid a totally flat appearance. The cases may be filled from the rear. The merchandise shelf or rack is adjustable to create the appearance of a full case with a minimum quantity of merchandise on display as well as to hold larger quantities when needed to maintain a well-stocked condition.

Many operators use the same type of case for all meat items. Display footage can be increased by using a multi-shelf unit for prepared meats. Canned hams, frankfurters, bacon, and other high-volume items are placed on the deep, bottom shelf, and cold cuts are placed on the two upper shelves. The top of the case is used for nonrefrigerated items.

Small island cases are used for dislocated or aisle displays of specials or for continuous displays of canned hams, bacon, various sausage items, etc.

In this long produce display case, mirrors along the top of the unit are used to duplicate the visual experience. Fruits and vegetables look twice as luscious. This produce wall unit is refrigerated.

A service case is used by some operators for service fish, delicatessen, poultry, specialty meats, etc. Service cases are in standard lengths of eight, ten and twelve feet with a single shelf or rack. Pans and trays can be used in all or part of the case for bulk salads and cooked items.

Generally, markets have a freezer in the meat department from which frozen meats, such as turkeys, ducks, and lamb, may be sold.

Produce Display Equipment

Many operators use refrigerated produce cases for highly perishable items. The high, mirror-backed unit is a popular case. The spacing of items for color contrast is highlighted and the size of the display made to appear much larger by means of the mirror. A well-arranged display looks bigger and better, but the disarray of a display that has been shopped and sorted is accentuated by the mirror. A mirrored case must be maintained in good display condition at all times.

Some operators use iced display cases or ice channels on refrigerated cases, since some produce needs moisture as well as temperature control. The ice creates an eye-appealing quality and enhances the impression of freshness. Sprinkling produce with water increases the fresh appearance of the display.

Manufacturers are producing triple-deck produce cases in eight- and twelve-foot sections. The bottom or main shelf is used for demand bulk or packaged items, the second shelf for small unit or packaged items, and the top shelf for packaged specialties. By alternating colors on each shelf, an attractive, eye-appealing display is possible. These cases increase the display capacity for each linear foot of floor space and have received industry approval.

Dairy Display Equipment

Three types of dairy cases are in common use: the five-deck shelf, the door case, and the air-curtain case.

The five-deck shelf dairy case is very popular. The bottom shelf is used for milk, butter, oleomargarine, eggs, and other high-volume items. The upper shelves are used for cream, various cheese items, roll and cookie doughs, cottage cheese, etc. The top of the case is used for nonrefrigerated dairy items, such as processed cheeses.

The door-type case uses the diary cooler as part of the display by placing shelves and doors on the traffic side. Usually the milk, butter, oleomargarine, and eggs are stored in the cooler and added to the shelf stock from the rear; that is, the shelves are stocked from inside the cooler. Some operators feel that the doors are a sales deterrent. A case for cheeses also must be maintained.

The air-curtain dairy case uses an air curtain in place of doors and is front-loading. The large lower shelves are used for milk and eggs, and the upper shelves for small items, such as cheeses and refrigerated doughs.

Most dairy cases are against the wall and are front-loading, except for the door-type case which has had limited acceptance. Separate refrigerated cases to display milk, juice, or eggs are also used.

Frozen Foods Display Equipment

One type of frozen foods case is a front-loading case, with one or two back shelves for displaying related items or impulse items, or it is open for shopping on both sides. The freezer is a deep unit, with about twelve to seventeen inches from the load limit line to the bottom. Most items are stocked in one row for the entire width of twenty-five to thirty-five inches. The number of facings per foot of floor space is very limited, since the total case is thirty-five to forty-five inches wide and in eight- or twelve-foot lengths. These are nicknamed "coffin cases" and are not now as widely used as formerly; they still can be seen in combination with multi-deck and door cases.

An improvement on the double-faced cases is the island freezer unit. It is a wider unit; the smaller units of this type are forty-four inches wide inside and fifty-

six inches on the outside. Larger cases are about sixty inches inside and seventy-eight inches outside. Some of these island units have a double-T-shelf in the center. Usually, the top shelf is wider than the lower shelf. These units require more floor space, but offer two facings—one on each side—as well as an impulse display area in the center.

The next development in terms of space utilization was the multi-tier freezer cabinet. The first step was the two-shelf unit, using the same base, but with a freezer shelf for specialty frozen items. Next, came the triple-shelf unit. These units also provide space for impulse items on top of the cabinet. Production of tiered, frozen-foods cases has increased rapidly, indicating an enthusiastic reception by retailers. Today, the multi-tiered freezer is also available in a five-deck model, and is in wide use because of the expansion of the entire frozen foods department. Door cases, in existence for quite some time, have risen greatly in popularity as a result of rising energy costs.

Another case that is used in small stores is the self-contained, portable display case used primarily for juices and sale items.

Manufacturers of freezer cabinets have been developing cases that will permit greater display area per linear foot of floor space. With the increase in the size and importance of the frozen foods section, we can anticipate innovative ideas for cases that will not only merchandise the product better, but will use less energy.

GROCERY AND NONFOOD DISPLAY EQUIPMENT

Since the perimeter of the supermarket is frequently used for perishables, most of the grocery and nonfood items are displayed on gondolas and island stands or racks.

The most widely used supermarket equipment for grocery and nonfood display is the gondola, usually made of metal, with adjustable, narrow shelves, and a narrow base. Deep shelves hide merchandise, especially on the lower levels, and require large quantities of merchandise in order to create a full-stock image. Items that appear to be out-of-stock or in low supply discourage shopping. On the other hand, too much shelf stock may cause merchandise to appear aged. Also, heavy shelf stock reduces turnover and increases capital invested in inventory. Therefore, gondolas with narrow adjustable shelves are of greater service to the customer, providing them with more shopping space and reduced congestion.

Spreading merchandise out must be kept within reasonable limits so as to avoid a difficult-to-shop store image. The shopping time required to shop a

Gondola and pegboard fixtures are combined in this permanent cookout display at Western Supermarket in suburban Birmingham, Alabama. A movable-shelf gondola contains food items, including sauces and pickles, as well as bowls; pegboard at back of top gondola shelf holds barbecue tools. Results were excellent.

This forklift moves into the store during slow periods, and takes backup stock from the top shelves. The wire baskets or bins at top contain refill merchandise to replace items sold from fast-moving floor-level bins.

particular store is a design and layout problem which must be given increased consideration as store size increases.

The adjustable-shelf gondolas, permitting varying shelf height for each section, are well-suited to eye-level impulse or layered stocking. By increasing the sale of high markup merchandise, adjustable shelves add to store profit.

Equipment manufacturers are providing end-display fixtures to match the gondola shelving units. A number of variations are available; the bin for dump displays, with a backing of merchandise arranged for mass eye appeal, is very popular. Some table-type units are equipped with casters to permit stocking in the workroom area.

Pegboards are used to display nonfood items, such as housewares, cleaning equipment, utensils, etc. Small sections of pegboard are frequently used to display packaged nuts and candy.

Special racks are used for magazines, records, books, greeting cards, and cigarettes. Some of these racks are provided by the supplier.

There are many manufacturers who have modified the methods of displaying merchandise by the use of their equipment. For example, the Vendex system has advanced their continuous baskets which are mounted on the slotted uprights of store fixtures. The chief benefits are that it displays the merchandise with a see-through design and does not require shelves for support. It also is designed to cut stocking time, thereby reducing labor costs. It can be cleaned easily and can be used to separate various types of merchandise. This basket-type equipment can be tiered in a mobile rack which can be moved from one location to another as desired.

Various types of box stores (limited-assortment stores and warehouse stores) use their own types of display cases. High-volume items in such stores generally are brought right onto the selling floor on their shipping pallets and sold from the pallets in cut cartons. Slower-moving items are displayed (also in cut cartons) on gondolas or platforms with shelves wide enough to take one or two cartons in height.

Some warehouse stores use huge heavy-wire metal baskets into which product is dumped. Such baskets have hinged front sides so that the sides can be lowered for easier access when the baskets are about half full.

Such stores generally have little or no back-room storage, and space above the selling area is used for reserve stocks. Thus, special overhead racks are usually loaded and unloaded by forklift trucks. Some stores have these forklifts move into the stores during selling hours, but others limit their use to either very slow periods or nonselling hours.

CHECKSTAND EQUIPMENT

After shopping the store, the customer proceeds to the checkstand to check out and pay for purchases. Many companies manufacture checkstands with the same basic principles of operation. Tests have shown that the advantages of one type of checkstand over another are few. Actually, if the latest model checkstand of each manufacturer was tested under the same operating conditions, very little difference in efficiency would be noted. Thus, the choice of one feature over another is mainly a matter of personal preference and service consideration.

Claims as to the amount of dollar sales per checkout per day or week for various units must be considered in the light of such variables as the speed of the cashier, number and speed of the baggers, and whether the cashier cashes checks, handles bottle returns and/or trading stamps, processes coupons, or weighs produce. All of these functions take time and affect the dollar sales per checkstand.

In planning a store, the number of checkstands that will be needed to handle the estimated sales must be determined. The expected sales per checkstand differ greatly, since the functions performed vary. Equipment manufacturers provide standards that may be used as guides and that must be adjusted to suit the particular situation.

A relatively new development in cash registers is the electronic cash register (ECR), which, if equipped with a scanner, is called a terminal. They have helped to speed the checkout operation. Older, motorized equipment was dependent on the speed and accuracy of the operator. New scanners allow the merchandise to pass over it with ease and accuracy, immediately registering the price and product on a cash register tape while other information is fed into the control device at store level. After an item passes over the scanner, it can be bagged immediately, saving on labor and time. Since the entire system is computerized, it performs other important functions (e.g., inventory stock control, etc.), which make its installation valuable to many stores. (See Chapter 12, "The Front End—Checkout Management and Control," for a more detailed discussion of this subject.)

While these checkout devices are expensive, their manufacturers present information that assures stores that the benefits will more than offset the initial cost. It should also be noted that the scanner system fully utilizes the Universal Product Code (UPC).

Before stores select a particular system, most experts agree that they should investigate the various systems and then set up a plan for testing types of equipment, choosing the one that best suits the needs

Photo courtesy of NCR Corporation.

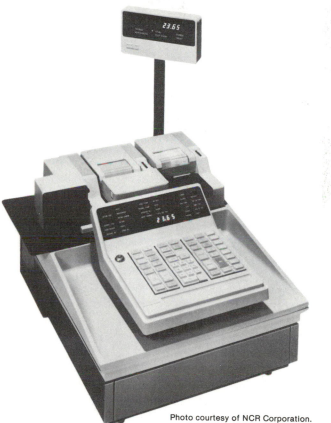

Photo courtesy of NCR Corporation.

Cash registers have come a long way, to say the least. Much more, in fact, than the eighty-year span between the old pre-World War I decorative brass register and today's NCR on-line retail terminal which provides all sorts of marketing and merchandising data, including best-sellers, volume patterns, and stock requirements.

of the company. Store operators should look for a system that can:

- Do more than simply replace the slower cash register
- Increase productivity
- Reduce store operating costs
- Improve grocery and other department merchandising
- Possibly link central headquarters with the various stores
- Provide data input
- Display a description of the item and its price
- Perform all calculations for tax and change
- Print a customer receipt containing descriptions and prices of all items, totals, and a customized promotional statement for each store
- Handle items that are not symbol marked (UPC)
- Have minimal, but immediate, repair service.

Needless to say, there are many manufacturers who are producing this equipment. All of the companies have spent a great deal of money for the research and development of equipment specifically suited to the supermarket industry. Some of the advantages claimed for these systems are that they:

- Help to lower back-room inventory through point-of-sale data
- Make available data about item movement to assist in:
  Advertising and promotion analysis
  New item tracking
  Better vendor analysis of store door deliveries
  Placement management
  Demographic merchandising
  Extended departmental control
  Immediate implementation of price changes
- Facilitate warehouse and transportation procedures
- Simplify price changes
- Provide a complete store inventory at any moment
- Aid in personnel scheduling.

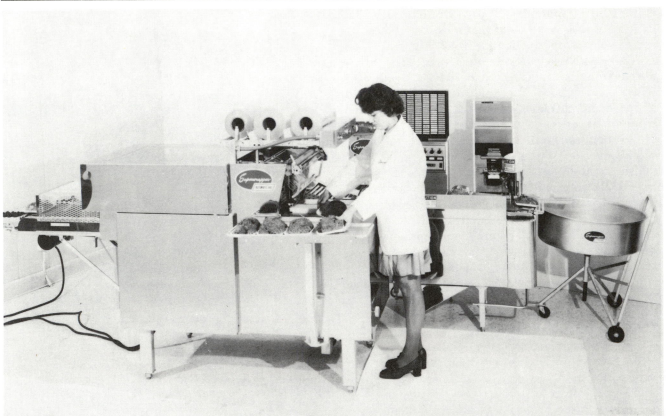

Photo courtesy of Toledo Scale, Division of Reliance Electric Company.

This backroom equipment provides big support for the meat department. This machine gives controlled-weight portions. A wrapping machine is also included in this unit.

There is no doubt that this equipment has already revolutionized supermarketing. The store manager will find it necessary to become familiar with all aspects of this electronic innovation.

OPERATING EQUIPMENT

Grocery Department Operating Equipment

The operating segment of the grocery department is primarily devoted to handling the tons of merchandise delivered each week. Depending on the nature of the physical facility at the receiving end (size, location, and other factors), the incoming merchandise is handled differently.

In city stores with no unloading platform, the likelihood is that roller conveyors are placed into the delivery truck to be unloaded, running out toward either a back door or chute leading into the basement, where the merchandise is then rolled away into its storage position.

On the other hand, when the store has an unloading platform, the truck can back up to it and be unloaded by using a pallet jack or forklift truck on those loads that come in palletized. In many instances, where the facilities are available, the trailer can be left at the store, unloaded by store personnel, and picked up by a tractor after it has been emptied. Some operators take the pallets of merchandise directly onto the selling floor, where the products are packed out.

Usually, however, merchandise is handled in the back room—cases cut and price marked—and hauled to the selling floor on four-wheel trucks. Greater efficiency is possible if the pallets are loaded according to store layout and the shelves can hold case units.

New procedures and equipment are slowly being introduced to improve materials handling. Warehouse racking with the fork lifting and binning done at the store is now available. Every store manager should be innovative in improving procedures for materials handling at his or her supermarket.

Meat Department Operating Equipment

The current tendency is the delivery of boxed meat rather than hanging meat. Various types of hand trucks are used to move boxed meats to storage, and packaged items, such as smoked hams, directly from the receiving dock to display cases in order to reduce unnecessary handling.

Separate storage equipment for frozen meats and fish is available in most new supermarkets. Air-conditioned cutting and packaging rooms, roller-type conveyors—some of them refrigerated—and refrigerated holding cabinets, in which counter-ready trays of meat are stored as a part of the meat flow plan, are used in self-service meat operations.

One of the greatest time-saving devices in the meat department is the electric band saw that proved to be a major factor in developing the production line which increased the efficiency of the meat operation.

Practically all supermarkets today have computer scales, package sealers of the hot-plate and hand-iron type, convenient label cabinets, and various wrapping supplies and dispensers to aid the packaging operation. Other devices now being used include: automatic and semi-automatic packaging machines, label-making devices, automatic seals, activators for use with pressure sensitive labels, and vacuum sealing equipment for use on luncheon meats and variety items.

Another real time-saver for the meat-packaging production line is the automatic scale. This scale eliminates error by weighing in units of one hundredth of a pound, computes the selling price at the set price per pound, and prints the selling price, price per pound and type of cut on the heatseal label.

The temperature in the meat-cutting area should be maintained at approximately 50° F. or less. Some operators cut meat in the meat cooler. This separates the workers from the display area. By using a refrigerated roller conveyor, the scaling and wrapping can be performed behind the display cases. In this way, the workers are available to customers and at the same time are productive—cutting, sealing, and wrapping. Most operators prefer a glass partition between the cutting room and the display area. Customers can see the workers and ring for assistance. This system is more efficient, but less personal.

In some supermarkets, rotisserie cookers for barbecuing chickens, ribs, and roasts are now being used as a special customer attraction in the deli department. Most meat departments prepare ground beef patties by using a patty-making attachment on the meat grinder. A special machine, called the "Hollymatic" and used solely for patties, forms and packages each patty. The patties can be made to weigh from two to four ounces and can be prepared at a rate of forty to eighty patties per minute.

Produce Department Operating Equipment

Supermarket operators use the same product-flow production methods in the produce department as those developed in self-service meat preparation. The computing scales and labeling machines are identical in most cases to those used in the meat departments. The same procedures and equipment are available for the bakery, deli and appetizing departments.

Some operators prepare produce during the early evening hours and use the meat department equipment during the night to weigh and package. When this is done, extra care must be taken to ensure that the equipment is clean. A few workers can accomplish more by utilizing the wrapping machine, automatic sealer, and other apparatus in the meat department during the hours this equpment is not being used than by using the limited equipment available in the produce department. This also increases the productivity of the equipment.

Probably one of the most useful inventions adapted to supermarket use has been the garbage disposal. The problem of garbage removal has always plagued the supermarket operator. The garbage disposal has helped reduce the cost and worry of removing many tons of waste resulting from trimming. The compactor, too, has saved time and space and removed many sanitary problems from the store. Careful supervision is required to prevent salable merchandise from being run through the disposal or the compactor.

Bagging machines are available which permit easy bagging of hard produce, such as apples, oranges, grapefruit, potatoes, and onions. Automatic machines have been developed to wrap lettuce and many other produce items.

MISCELLANEOUS EQUIPMENT

Music may be available through store-owned facilities, such as tape players, or through a central service, such as Muzak. Tapes with several hours of programmed music are available at nominal cost. Music service costs are reasonable and may be paid for by supplier advertising; however, customers are likely to object to being subjected to commercials while shopping. A microphone unit can be added to the music player to announce specials and items of current interest to shoppers. Music can be helpful in creating a shopping mood and in reducing the irritation of waiting in line.

As operational costs rise, more pressure will be exerted on equipment manufacturers to develop and market more efficient, cost-cutting equipment.

26

A food distribution center is basically a warehousing operation whose function it is to assemble large quantities of merchandise and distribute it in relatively small amounts to its store outlets or to chain, voluntary, cooperative or independent customers.

DISTRIBUTION CENTER LOCATION

For a particular site to be considered a suitable location, special attention must be given to a number of factors, the most important of which are:

- Highways—easy access to existing and planned highways
- Availability of railroad track service
- Finding the "ton-mile" center
- Traffic conditions
- Expansion space
- Labor supply
- Cost of available land
- Local considerations.

Often other factors enter into the site selection picture, such as: Will employees consider it a good place to work? Is adequate fire protection available or possible? Will the cost of bringing in power and other utilities, including sewage lines, be reasonable?

Comparison of these factors usually proceeds through three stages. The first stage is selection of the region. Once the general area has been determined, the search for a warehouse site narrows to the second step, the selection of the particular community. And, third is the selection of a specific site.

Food distribution center location is generally a matter of costs tempered by circumstances. Theoretically, the most favorable location of a warehouse is that area where, in consideration of the business as a whole, the total cost of delivering merchandise to all retail units is the lowest. Actually, however, the location decision is tempered by financial, local and other judgments.

Three trends in food distribution center location are discernible. The first is the trend to locate warehouses away from the cities, in the suburbs or smaller towns.

Suburban areas offer practically all the advantages, facilities, and services supplied by cities and usually do so with a lower assessment value and tax rate. Also, more land can be obtained at much lower cost in more sparsely settled areas. There is room to spread out the warehouse, allow for expansion, provide off-street loading and unloading facilities, and furnish adequate parking areas for employees. While travel distance sometimes is greater, travel time is usually less since city traffic congestion is avoided. The public- and customer-relations value of a modern, functional warehouse, well-landscaped in pleasant, roomy surroundings, should not be underestimated in terms of building a favorable consumer image.

Secondly, there is a trend toward planned industrial centers or industrial parks. Planned industrial parks, composed of a group of manufacturing and distributing firms, are considered to be the industrial equivalent of the planned shopping center.

Developers of industrial centers maintain close control over the use of the land. They provide for orderly and attractive growth, minimize congestion, and aim to increase the value of the property. Sometimes, the industrial districts supply architectural, engineering and construction services for concerns locating in the park and supervise all the details involved in building a plant. The developer may help to arrange the financing of new plants.

The third trend in warehouse location is to large one-story distribution centers. These mammoth one-story centers are set up to increase the market area serviced, increase productivity, improve service, and increase efficiency.

FUNCTIONS PERFORMED IN THE DISTRIBUTION CENTER

There are certain basic functions that must be performed in all distribution centers, including: ordering, receiving, storing, order assembly, shipping, inventory control, data accumulation, reporting, guidance, store bookkeeping (available in some centers), and the processing and packaging of perishables

This merchandise will be moving out to truck loading facilities, at right, for distribution to stores located primarily in the Dallas area. This is the Kimbell Distribution Center, typical of the new trend of one-story warehousing operations which service growing marketing areas.

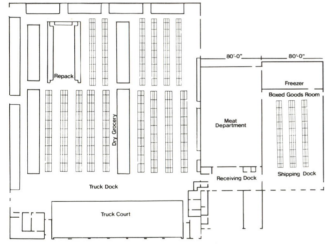

Maximum efficiency and the ability to handle growing amounts of merchandise frame the purpose of the modern distribution center, such as this one planned by King Kullen. The careful plant structuring here is to eliminate product, time and labor wastage.

(in centers that handle produce and meat). While the nature of these tasks are fundamentally the same for each comparable center, the methods, techniques, and procedures of performing them vary, since the management, personnel, facilities, and handling equipment differ among the centers. Each distribution center operator endeavors to achieve the highest level of efficiency possible by handling the greatest volume of merchandise at the lowest cost, while at the same time, providing the most effective service.

Labor represents the greatest variable as a percentage of the cost of operations of the center; therefore, it is vital that the best labor-saving equipment and techniques be used.

There are functions performed from behind a desk, there are those that take place on the distribution center floor, and others on the road behind the wheel of a truck. While each job may be performed in a different locale, one job is dependent upon the other.

The supermarket relies heavily on the smooth functioning of the warehouse for its performance. Scratches, tardy deliveries, mistakes of various sorts in order selection, all have a direct bearing on the smooth functioning of the store.

Virtually all warehouses today are computer oriented. From the smallest and most labor intensive to the largest and most automated, the computer plays a larger and larger role in the warehouse operation.

A&P scrapped a $6 million automated warehouse in Edison, New Jersey, because it could not be made to function properly, and a highly automated warehouse was turned back into a manual operation. One of the reasons for the backward step was that it did not, at the time, have a software package for its computers which could make proper use of the equipment, and so the warehouse was a liability rather than an asset to the firm.

TYPES OF DISTRIBUTION CENTERS

Basically, warehouses are grouped by their order-selection system:

- Manual
- Semiautomated or batch pick
- Fully automated.

The oldest and most traditional is the manual system. Yet, even with the "manual" warehouse, the computer plays a major role. While orders are selected manually, most such warehouses slot their warehouses (store merchandise) for receiving and order-picking as well as replenishment by computer.

In most such warehouses, the computer tells the selector the sequence and slots from which to select the order and even prints out the time, in seconds, that it should take the selector to assemble the order. Inventory control, ordering, billing, and even price-label stickers to be attached to each case are prepared by the computer and arrive at the shipping dock in time to affix to bills of lading or to each individual case directly.

The manual warehouse has a number of types of mechanized equipment that assists the order selector, from forklift trucks and tuggers to cherry pickers and

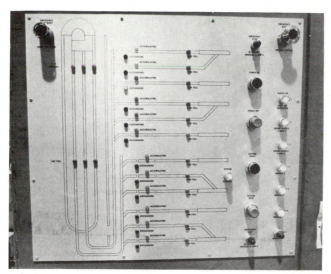

"Future is now" at the center featuring this automated flow control which moves merchandise on belts from every point in the warehouse to appropriate assembly points. Goods move onto pallets, into trucks, and are on their way to supermarkets.

a host of other equipment. But the order itself is manually selected.

The next type of warehouse up the automation ladder is the batch-pick system. In such a warehouse, receiving and storing goods is still a manual operation, even though slotting is computer-governed. Order selection, however, is not for an individual store, but cumulative selection for a group of stores is done simultaneously. Thus, each selector works one aisle in the warehouse and selects multiples of each item for the group of stores, placing them on a moving belt which carries items from each of the selector aisles to an assembly point. Here, the orders are divided into the actual, individual store orders. If the warehouse has sufficient volume to afford the cost of this system, it is faster and more efficient than the manual warehouse for order selection.

The ultimate in rapid order selection is the fully automated warehouse. In this system, a computer runs a machine that has thousands of lanes loaded with various of the items that are normally in the warehouse. On a signal from the computer, various lanes disgorge the number of cases ordered from that particular lane, and on moving belts the items selected for the particular order are carried to an assembly point where the merchandise is palletized for delivery to the store.

Depending on the warehouse and the products it carries, only some 50 to 70 percent of the items in the warehouse can be selected through this system; the

balance must be selected manually and integrated at the assembly point.

The reasons for the inability of all items to go into the system are numerous. Very slow movers should not go into the system because they tie up lanes for little use, and it is simpler to manually select those few items when needed. Fast movers would either tie up too many lanes or cause the machine to be stopped too often for replenishment. Therefore, fast movers are stored near the assembly point and added to complete the order. Often, fast movers can be shipped to the store as a complete pallet load, thus saving considerable handling. As a matter of fact, some wholesalers and manufacturers are making special allowances for firms that take a full pallet of a single product because it saves handling.

Since the system has a gravity-feed, some glass items cannot go through the machine because of breakage. (Weight is concentrated on the sides of cartons during the feeding process.) Also, bagged goods, because of the tearing and spilling of product, cannot go into the system. Some cases and overwrapped items, where the coefficient of friction impedes or is too fast for gravity feeding, also cannot go through the machine. Another serious drawback to the system is that the machine is limited by the rapidity of replenishment of the various lanes.

Springfield Sugar, at its New England Grocery Supply Division, Northborough, Massachusetts, experimented successfully with combining a stacker crane (for storing product and making replenishment readily available) with this automated system. It took several painful years before the software package joining these two dissimilar pieces of complex equipment could be perfected, but once the programming was successfully completed, the firm had the most efficient automated warehouse in the world—automated receiving, storage, and order selection.

ORDERING

Ordering is a function of the buying office, which maintains constant vigilance over product movement. The data processing unit provides the buying office with information about weekly movement, year-to-date movement, product on hand, merchandise en route, and other pertinent data that may not apply specifically to ordering, but which may influence buying decisions. (Buying strategies and procedures are discussed fully in Chapter 13.)

RECEIVING

In order to properly receive merchandise most expeditiously, it is necessary to schedule arrivals based on need as well as the ability to receive quickly and efficiently. The function of receiving begins with the arrival of product at the platform, either by rail or motor carrier, which may be either an outside carrier or the distributor's own vehicle making backhauls. Approximately 15 to 20 percent of the grocery merchandise is received by rail, with the remainder arriving by truck. This, however, will vary with geographic location, size of order, and variation of shipping rates.

Receiving must be integrated with the flow of activity in the center; its efficiency is dependent upon avoiding conditions that cause congestion. As receiving documents arrive at the distribution center, the buying and the accounting offices are advised of the arrival of the shipments. Based on the logistics of the particular operation, either the accounting department or the buying office will arrange for the addition of the incoming merchandise to the inventory records as soon as possible so that items will be listed as being in stock.

Every morning, the receiving foreman and the buying office receive an updated list of out-of-stock items, as indicated by the data processing files. This information helps to determine the speed and need for putting these items in the selection lines as quickly as possible. In some operations, the out-of-stock items are placed on the outgoing dock as soon as they are received so that they can be added to the store orders awaiting shipment. Filling in "scratches" can cut the "out" list by as much as 50 percent, keep store managers happy, and help satisfy the consumer.

There are numerous procedures used for planning the arrival of merchandise. For truck arrivals, the most widely used procedure is to advise the shipper of the date and time delivery is wanted so that it will fit into the receiving area (door and warehouse space). For backhaul using the facility's own truck, receiving must coincide with available door time, need, and proximity to outgoing delivery planned for that truck. With rail delivery, there is not as much flexibility as with truck delivery, and delivery planning is based mainly on previous experience. If these procedures are followed, the distribution center should have very few out-of-stock situations, especially on high-volume items.

Proper inventory control is designed to keep scratches at a minimum, thereby providing better service to stores. Depending on the procedure used by the distribution center, scratches may or may not be back-ordered. (In most cases, unless otherwise advised, they are back-ordered.)

In order to maintain a more even workload at the warehouse and expedite faster and better shipments to the store, many chains and wholesalers have worked out systems of average orders. Such orders are shipped to the stores on a regular basis. The order is selected using historical patterns (and when teamed with a computer, can take into effect such factors as what items are "specialed" and expected weather. A number of such orders can be supplied to the store before a new inventory position and actual order is needed to correct for actual rather than theoretical store needs.

Many chains and wholesalers will provide the store manager with a copy of what the average order will be in order for him or her to add or subtract specific items in time to make that shipment. Naturally, such a system is much easier to institute in a chain than with wholesale customers. However, many wholesalers provide incentives to their customers to induce them to accept average orders. Without the average-order system, many warehouses would operate only about three days a week and would require about double the space, equipment, and employees to fulfill its function.

Methods of Receiving

Loads arriving at the center by *truck* are usually palletized on forty-eight-inch by forty-inch pallets. If the center uses smaller pallets, the merchandise must be restacked by hand on the small pallet at the dock before being put into inventory. In order to unload the trucks quickly, if the incoming pallets are the same as those used at the center, the merchandise is unloaded using a forklift, pallet and all, and the truck driver takes other pallets in place of those on which the products arrived. This is known as the pallet exchange program.

A number of years ago, a Pallet Exchange Council was formed in order to facilitate the exchange of pallets. However, as with the adage about currency, bad pallets drove good ones out of the exchange system. Thus, receivers of merchandise would accept good pallets, but return only the worst. All firms that were part of the exchange program were supposed to repair damaged pallets before putting them back into circulation, but many did not do so.

The Pallet Exchange Council went out of business in the late 1970's, and the entire pallet system was endangered. Many firms did not adhere to the forty-eight-inch by forty-inch standard. Railroads and truckers, which at one time returned empty pallets without charge, began to charge for their handling, arguing that they were heavy and occupied space.

A substitute was available that was much lighter in weight, took almost no space, and was disposable— the slip sheet. (The slip sheet is a cardboard base for load of product which replaces pallets and acts as a base for a unitized load.) Although it had many advantages, it also had a number of disadvantages, the chief one being that many warehouses and practically no stores had equipment for handling slip sheets.

To date, there is still a strong debate between the shippers and receivers about the use of slip sheets. The shippers point to the shipping economies, while the receivers point out that the burden of the cost of such equipment falls upon the warehouse. (It is estimated that it would cost nearly $100,000 per warehouse for push-pull or tugger equipment to handle slip sheets.)

One suggestion made at intergroup meetings on shipping problems has been a trade-off—warehouses accepting slip-sheet loads, if manufacturers would institute modular packaging. According to the suggested compromise, the extra cost to the receiver would be offset by the benefits of modular packaging, which would be an added cost to the manufacturer. (Modular packaging consists of having secondary packages—the outer cartons—all in predetermined modules of a constant that would fit exactly on a standard pallet. Thus, if the module were determined, all secondary packages would have to be 1 module; ½, ¼ or ⅛ of a module; or 2, 4 or 8, etc., modules in each of the three dimensions.)

Rail receiving may have several variations:

- Dead-loading or floor-loading
- Palletized on wood panels
- Slip sheet.

Dead-loading or floor-loading. Each case must be removed from the car by hand and palletized, then moved by forklift, and either placed in the slot from which it will be selected or put in reserve.

Palletized on wood pallets. Forklifts remove the complete pallet and then move items to the reserve area or the picking slot.

Slip sheet. Merchandise arrives on a cardboard sheet, is removed by equipment known as a push-pull, which picks up and moves both the paper pallet and products, and is then placed into inventory. If it takes about eight to eleven man-hours to unload a freight car that is dead-loaded, it takes only one to two hours to unload the same car that is on slip sheets or palletized, with considerably less damage, according to a study by the U.S. Department of Agriculture.

Mechanization for continual flow as well as separation of the unloading and moving tasks into two separate operations are keys to the efficient handling of merchandise. One of the methods used is the tractor-trailer gang units for long warehouse hauls. Forklifts place the loaded pallets on trailers and, when the gang unit is loaded, tractors move the unit to the storage area where the pallets are then moved by another forklift.

Another method used is to double-tier pallets utilizing low-lift fork trucks or hand jacks on the receiving dock. The larger, more mobile forklifts are then used to move the merchandise to the storage area.

A similar procedure is followed in using the "towveyor" system. In this procedure, the trailer is coupled into an in-floor chain conveyor that acts as the prime mover.

Another efficiency in receiving procedures implemented by industrial engineers is to physically lay out the facility in such a way that merchandise is received as close to the storage area as possible in order to avoid long hauls.

An important consideration for the receiving function is the dock itself. If there are individual dock doors, they must be wide enough to accommodate the railroad car or truck. The floor or the dock should be level with the floor of the railroad car or truck bed for

The railroad comes right up to the loading platform in this distribution center in the Dallas area. The track area between train cars and platform edge has been literally bridged—with a steel bridge in order to unload the cartons and crates at left.

greater ease in loading and unloading. In order to make the dock level with the truck, there are load-levelers mounted into the platform and a lip set into the truck which goes up or down depending on whether the truck is higher or lower than the dock. This type of leveler also can be used for railroad cars.

However, centers most frequently use dock-boards to bridge the space between the railroad car and the siding platform. If two spurs are parallel to the platform, a steel bridge can be placed between the cars in each track so that the merchandise can be moved through the car immediately alongside the platform and into the building.

The job of receiving clerk is one of responsibility, since he checks the incoming goods for item and quantity against the shipper's invoice and the purchase order. In addition, the clerk usually puts a sticker on each pallet load indicating the item code number, the tie and the high (called "ti-hi"), and date received. (The tie equals the number of cases on each tier; the high is the number of tiers; therefore, the tie by the high equals the number of cases to the pallet load.) Many warehouses use differently colored stickers to represent different months, making it easier to identify the length of time the product is in the warehouse for the purpose of inventory rotation.

The receiving clerk also has the responsibility of seeing that incoming merchandise is in good physical condition as well as for the standardization of pallet loads. Keeping the pallets uniform is essential for good stocking and inventory control.

Finally, the receiving record and accompanying documents must be forwarded to the data processing department as soon as possible in order to avoid unnecessary out-of-stock in the inventory files. In the few warehouses that still do not use computerized slotting (where the computer keeps track of which slots are empty and where to store and retrieve merchandise), the receiving clerk will also determine where to store the merchandise and record this for retrieval purposes later.

STORING

Keeping storage to a minimum is an important objective of an efficient distribution center operation. At the same time, merchandise must be accessible and in good order.

In a warehouse that does not use computerized slotting, storing can be divided into two basic types: long-term and short-term. Items intended for short-term storage should be placed in areas that are easily accessible. They are usually placed in a designated floor slot and/or racks placed directly over this floor area. If the merchandise is slotted on the floor, a number of pallets of the item are stored one on top of the other. Products should be kept in the front of the pallets to allow for easy selection. Merchandise on the upper tiers of the steel racks should be used for short-term reserve or storage. Selection is done from the bottom two, or possibly three, decks (floor and one or two steel shelves); this is ordinarily the height that can be reached by a selector without climbing. The upper sections of the rack accommodate pallets of merchandise placed there by a forklift to be brought down and put into the lower selection slot as needed.

Long-term storage, or remote storage as it is sometimes called, is for products that have been purchased for various reasons in quantities larger than needed within a seven to ten-day period. Reasons for this may include: a planned advertising promotion, deal price, future prices increasing, shortage of product looming, and quantity buying price. This merchandise, as the word "remote" would indicate, is stored in an area especially designated for this type of storage, away from the short-term selection area.

There are two basic systems for positioning merchandise: commodity grouping and the slot system.

Commodity Grouping

In this system, merchandise is stored by family groupings (e.g., all types of pickles together, all soups in another location, etc.). Each item in the center has a fixed location, which creates handling and distribution problems. For example, incoming merchandise must often be placed in reserve storage space until the stock on hand in the designated bay is depleted. Then the merchandise in the reserve area is moved to the assigned location necessitating a second moving of the merchandise. Furthermore, commodity grouping does not fully utilize distribution center space, since space must be held open if the new merchandise has not arrived.

A variation of the commodity grouping system is the use of random positioning within the commodity group. This allows for some flexibility because the item is not always in the same position, but is placed in an open bay within the commodity grouping.

Slot System

This system is more complex to set up than commodity grouping, but is more versatile and utilizes space more advantageously. Using the slot system, merchandise, as it comes into the distribution center, is placed in a free area large enough to accommodate it. These areas are formed by a combination of steel racks and floor space. It is not located in a specific area, as in the commodity group system, but rather is placed where the merchandise will best utilize space. This space is termed a slot and, as such, is given a slot number.

Slot numbers remain constant; for example, five-pound sugar bales may be in number 1251 for a period of time, and the next time sugar is received, it may be located in another slot, numbered 1034. In other words, goods may occupy one or more slots in the warehouse at the same time, and each with a different slot number. With the use of automatic tabulating equipment, the oldest stock's location is indicated on the order sheet, and it is selected first.

The slot system utilizes space more efficiently than commodity grouping, since, in the former system, it is not necessary to hold space open until merchandise arrives. It is possible to use two slots for an item if merchandise is received before the first slot is open. Then, the advantage of the slot system is that when the first slot is emptied, the second slot can be used, and moving the shipment from reserve stock is eliminated. Under commodity grouping, the old stock must be moved out before new merchandise can be stored, which may mean using reserve stock space until the assigned space is available.

With the arrival of computerization in the warehouse, the storage of product became a function of the computer. Using the memory function to locate merchandise, it became easy to store product wherever there was an empty slot and retrieve it based on a first-in, first-out basis, except for specially marked items, such as cents-off merchandise, which must be handled specially.

Using computer slotting, there is no wasted space. Every single slot can be occupied. This system also creates greater efficiency in inventory replenishment for order selection. The warehouseman charged with replenishing merchandise in the selection lanes is told by the computer where to find the oldest of the item desired, and he can then go to it directly.

ORDER FILLING

Order filling includes obtaining the invoice or selection sheet, selecting the listed merchandise, and transporting it to the loading dock.

An accurate, fast, low-cost, order-filling system is essential for efficient, smooth distribution center operation. Since nearly 40 percent of distribution center man-hours are used in the selection of orders, increasing efficiency through mechanization and time-and-motion study is indicated.

The system used in order selection varies, based on physical layout, equipment used, frequency and size of orders, and so forth. The prime function of

service to the stores must be incorporated into the center's operation. Center costs must be kept to a minimum, and store cooperation is vital to an efficient operation.

The number of deliveries per week and the time that orders are received at the distribution center must be planned so that operations can be scheduled efficiently. Store management must be discouraged from requesting extra deliveries, which are expensive and disrupt planned schedules. Schedules should be followed. Very few chains or wholesalers will make special deliveries except in cases of extreme emergency; the expense is almost incalculable.

The first step in the order-assembly process is the obtaining of store orders by the warehouse dispatch office from the data processing office. From that point, the selection sheets are distributed to selectors who proceed to pick out the items that appear on the order form.

At this point, it would be advantageous to trace the order as it travels from the store to the distribution center so that all the steps that preceded the selection of the order can be understood better. Upon completion of the preparation of the order at the store level, it is forwarded to the warehouse in any one of many ways: by a delivery truck driver, by mail, at a drop-off point by a store employee, by telephone, or transmitted by telex or tape.

Orders are made on a variety of forms: a pre-printed order form, an adding machine tape on which the item line number and quantity needed are printed, a mark sensing card used with an electrographic pencil, a direct teletyped order, and a tape-transmitted order. With the advent of the use of scanners, their monitors may be used for inventory control; and as an item is sold, the monitor places the order to replace the merchandise sold.

Modular or standing orders may be a part of the ordering process (usually used by chains with stores doing a high volume). Firms using modular orders automatically send the merchandise called for on the standing order (usually fast-moving merchandise) to the retail units, unless changes are made by the individual retail outlets. Modular orders are usually adjusted at fixed intervals by the retail units. The modular order is based on the theory that 80 percent of the tonnage comes from 20 percent of the variety.

Modular orders serve several purposes:

1. The order clerks are not required to spend hours preparing orders.
2. The warehouse knows what the standardized needs are for those stores on the program.
3. Billing time is saved.
4. The modular order can be prepared on a time fill-in basis when the center has a slack period.

Therefore, the adoption of modular ordering can help reduce operating costs.

Data processing systems used at distribution centers maintain inventory records and convert store orders into store invoices, listing the items according to the selection line layout.

Operators of manual-selection food distribution centers recognize that efficient operation requires the store invoice to list items according to selection line sequence so as to permit order pickers to assemble each order in sequence by moving only forward along the selection line.

Even in manual-selection warehouses, the computer has cut out wasted motion and time from the selection operation. When the order is received from the store, it is put into the computer which bills for those items that can be filled and places scratches on back order. An order slip is also printed and tells the order selector just what to pick, where, and just how long it should take. Even the sequence of selection is predetermined so that heavy merchandise is at the bottom of each pallet and lighter goods on top. The exact number of steps each selector must take and time for the selection of each order is also on the slip. Most orders are broken up by aisles, so that no order selector moves out of his or her aisle. The various portions of the order from the different selector aisles are then assembled at the front of the warehouse and combined for shipment.

Most data processing systems use slot number selection. Nonautomated control systems select by description, which requires reading the item name, description, size, etc., in order to pick the correct items. Selecting by number and in sequence is faster and more accurate—reading numbers is easier and faster than reading item names, descriptions, and sizes. (However, in addition to slot number, most computers cross-reference item and size.) Each slot number is marked on the floor, bin, shelf, or other convenient place. Order pickers simply select the required number of cases from each slot. The amount of effort is small, since the reading is reduced to numbers instead of long descriptions. The order pickers select the items ordered case-by-case.

Case Sticker Selection Process

Simultaneous with the preparation of the invoice by the data processing department, gummed-back case stickers are printed, corresponding with each case of merchandise invoiced out to the store. These stickers are mounted on glassine sheets. As the order picker makes the rounds of the selection area and as merchandise is selected, a sticker is removed from the sheet and affixed to the case. If stickers remain on the sheet after all items have been selected, there is some kind of discrepancy in selection or inventory, and it must be "checked out."

The case-sticker selection process is most advantageous, serving the following purposes for the distribution center:

- Provides a method of checking the selector
- Serves as an inventory check
- Assists the checker on the dock.

For the store, the advantages of the sticker process include the following:

- Provides information about pack and size as well as suggested retail price, cost, date of invoice, inventory and stock rotation control, and store number
- Serves as a check for label and selection accuracy
- Verifies proper delivery to the proper store
- Provides information for cost/inventory control.

Materials Handling Equipment Used in Order Assembly

Since the grocery business is a tonnage operation, order picking requires the efficient use of materials handling equipment. The equipment used in order assembly and to bring merchandise to the loading or shipping dock may vary from hand-pulled, four-wheel trucks, to automatically controlled tractor units, to single or double pallet jacks.

When tractors are used, a pallet will be placed on the trailer deck before product selection is started. When the trailer is brought up to the loading dock, a forklift can lift the pallet and bring it into the truck, thus saving manual loading. When using the tractor-trailer system, the number of trailers "tugged" should be kept to a reasonable number. Too long a train causes the selector to waste too much time walking from the inventory to the tractor in order to move the train.

An automatic, electronic, remote-control device may be used, however. This device, worn on the belt of the selector/operator, allows the use of a longer train because the selector need not walk to the front of the train to move it. Control is effective fifty feet from the truck. One disadvantage of this is that the operation can be disrupted or the unit misdirected by electromagnetic interference, such as that caused by an airplane flying close to the center.

Another type of materials handling equipment is the tow line. The two basic types are the selection area tow line and the perimeter tow line. The tow lines may be either overhead chains or in-floor conveyors called towveyors, or sometimes, draglines.

Selection area tow lines are used to overcome the disadvantage of hauling loads from the assembly area to the shipping dock and back again. The tow line acts as the prime mover for the trailers attached to them. It is installed and routed through the distribution center and along the entire stock selection area.

The major disadvantages of using the selection area tow line with four-wheel trucks are:

1. Its speed is geared to the average worker and, therefore, sets the pace for all selectors.
2. Being a permanent installation, it forces a comparatively inflexible assembly area layout.

The tow line speed is controllable, but changes in the speed of selection may be the cause of worker objection.

The perimeter tow line is actually a modification of the selection area tow line. The basic difference is that the perimeter tow line does not follow a route through the assembly area, but, rather, it travels around the perimeter of the stock selection area. Four-wheel trailers are manually taken from the tow line and moved along the racks, bins, and pallets for order selection. The loaded trailers are then reattached to the tow line and pulled to the shipping dock.

The perimeter tow line has one principal advantage over the selection area system; that is, the picker's rate of selection is not geared to the speed of the tow line. However, a few union contracts require the selector to ride the loaded truck to the dock. One further disadvantage is the possible breakdown of the line. When this happens, production can drop as much as 50 percent.

Using a towveyor reduces selection-line travel time as the selector stays in an assigned area (with the Ramlose system, however, selectors are assigned to different areas as needed). The towveyor reduces delay and confusion on the shipping dock, since the selectors do not bring the trailers to the dock. Towveyors can pull a large number of trailers, depending on the length of the tow line; thus, all distribution center personnel engaged in moving merchandise can use the system at the same time.

Loaded vehicles are identified by the use of a blackboard, mounted on the frame, on which is written the store number, order number, or dock number; or by marking the merchandise itself with this information. Usually the total piece count is also included. Stock placed on the selection line conforms to the order blank or invoice, giving continuity to the selection process.

One other widely used piece of equipment is the pallet jack, which is made to handle either one or two pallets placed alongside each other. This equipment is battery operated. The forks are inserted into the pallet openings. The operator-selector loads the cases selected onto the pallet or pallets, and upon completion of the selection, brings the merchandise up to the bay indicated for loading. A disadvantage of the double pallet jack is the greater space needed for a turning radius. If, however, this does not pose a problem, the double pallet can cut the time consumed by the selector in making trips to the dispatch point and the shipping bay.

For mom-and-pop operations or convenience stores, where the orders are comparatively small, many warehouses use carts for loading orders. Deliveries are made on these loaded carts, and a pickup of the empty carts that were left at the last delivery is also made. Carts are fast and easy to load and save the driver unloading time.

After the merchandise is delivered to the loading dock, the order is checked. Companies use piece count or individual-item check.

SHIPPING

Shipping is another output operation of the distribution center. It is the responsibility of the dispatcher in cooperation with the platform foreman. Shipping begins when the goods constituting the order reach the shipping area, and ends when the merchandise is placed on the truck for delivery. The shipping operation is one in which the innovative use of equipment and work methods pay dividends. This step must be integrated with the selection process.

Shipping docks at the distribution center are usually wide enough to accommodate a number of trucks, thus making it possible to load more than one truck at a time. (Some centers have individual doors opening onto a common platform.)

The attainment of a solid load is of vital importance to loading the truck. Slipping and sliding must be reduced to a minimum in order to prevent damage to merchandise. The width of the truck usually allows for two pallets to be placed alongside each other. The merchandise on each pallet is bound together by tape or straps to avoid falling or shifting. Many wholesalers and retailers place plywood sheets between rows of pallets across the width of the truck to keep loads from shifting back to front.

Although few wholesalers or chain warehouses have started to use it yet, a number of manufacturers have experimented with inflatable air bags to solidify loads. Using this system, the pallets are placed side by side against one wall of the truck. After the pallets are all in place, an air bag on the other wall (or a series of

A

B

C

D

E

F

The story of an automated warehousing system in the supermarket field is shown step-by-step on this and the facing page. The scene is the Alpha Beta Warehouse, Los Angeles, and the story unfolds, in sequence, beginning on the opposite page. **A:** You are looking at the receiving dock. Trucks unload at each of the open bays. The woman at right is writing up incoming merchandise, while workmen help with the unloading. **B:** Incoming merchandise, placed on low mobile cart, runs on track past control booth which determines where goods should be directed in warehouse. **C:** Closeup of merchandise on low mobile cart being steered in proper direction by computer-controlled diverting arm at left. **D:** Carts move merchandise up to the storage racks area. Note mention on signage of "turret trucks" which will continue storage operation on tracks between each storage unit. **E:** Turret truck with forklift capability takes merchandise to appropriate location along track and lifts merchandise onto correct shelf. This primary storage area will be used to fill orders from participating retail units. **F:** A supplementary storage area where materials that are not immediately required can be stored somewhat less formally than the main storage area. Wide aisles allow movement of heavy equipment. **G:** In a storage area containing smaller merchandise units, the job of putting a shipment together begins. The order clerk places the required merchandise into a bin in the aisle; then the completed selection goes on conveyor belt at right. **H:** The conveyor belt running down the center will carry full cases needed to fill an order. Order clerks go down the line placing needed cases on the belt. **I:** Merchandise for shipment comes down the chute and winds around the carousel. At right are completed loads. In rear are loading docks where trucks will take scheduled shipments. **J:** The final step before the trucks begin to roll. Worker at left is wheeling a cart containing a load of full-case merchandise into the rear of a truck. The other worker has just deposited a palletized load on the truck. Another part of the shipment, merchandise in bins on the cart at right, is awaiting transfer onto the truck. All of this is a daily behind-the-scenes occurrence essential to the sound functioning of the nation's supermarkets.

Photo courtesy of Harris-Teeter Super Markets, Inc., Charlotte, North Carolina.

Truck containers, temporarily without cabs or wheels, are lined up at the truck dock of the Perishables Distribution Center, Indian Trail, North Carolina. Merchandise is loaded and unloaded directly onto the enclosed platform. This center services the Harris-Teeter Super Market chain.

air bags, one pallet wide) is filled. When the truck arrives at its destination, the inflated air bag or bags are deflated as needed and no longer hold the load firmly in place. The bags are reusable, and those that have not been deflated tend to hold the unloaded portion of the truck locked into place.

An important consideration in loading a truck for shipment is compliance with maximum weight regulations which vary from state to state. If the load is overweight and is intercepted en route, it may be subject to costly penalties.

INVENTORY CONTROL

Inventory control is a very important factor in the operation of the distribution center. It is a two-pronged tool and should be thought of in terms of:

- Dollar control
- Item merchandise control.

Dollar Control. Dollar control is the ability to manage the inventory through a number of merchandise turns expressed in dollars. The cost of money today dictates that an operation, to make a greater profit at a lower cost, must make an effort to turn the inventory a greater number of times each year. The chief financial officer views the inventory as dollars, not items.

Item Merchandise Control. This is an area governed by merchandisers and buyers whose objectives are to keep the out-of-stocks to a minimum and to prevent overstocks. If these two objectives are realized, turnover will increase, space problems will decrease, and the financial officer will be satisfied with the profits resulting from the turns.

One of the best indicators of efficiency is the rate of stock turn. Control of out-of-stock is an important sales problem; customers expect to be able to buy the items they want. Stock turn (defined as the number of times that the inventory turns over—comes into and out of the warehouse—for a given period) can be computed on the basis of cost, retail price, or physical units. All computations, however, must be on the same basis. Computations for an annual rate of stock turn are as follows:

$$\frac{\text{Sales at cost}}{\text{Average inventory at cost}} = \frac{\text{Annual rate of}}{\text{stock turn}}$$

$$\frac{\text{Sales at retail price}}{\text{Average inventory at selling price}} = \frac{\text{Annual rate of}}{\text{stock turn}}$$

$$\frac{\text{Sales in physical units}}{\text{Average inventory in physical units}} = \frac{\text{Annual rate of}}{\text{stock turn}}$$

$$\text{Average inventory} = \frac{\text{Opening inventory + Closing inventory}}{2}$$

If *semiannual* physical inventories are taken, the computation is as follows:

$$\text{Average inventory} = \frac{\text{Opening inventory + Midyear inventory + Closing inventory}}{3}$$

If a *quarterly* inventory rate is desired, it may be computed in the following manner and then adjusted to the annual rate:

$$\frac{\text{Sales at cost (last 3 mos.)}}{\text{Avg. inventory at cost (last 3 mos.)}} = \frac{\text{Quarterly}}{\text{stock turn rate}}$$

$$\text{Quarterly stock turn rate} \times 4 = \frac{\text{Annual stock}}{\text{turn rate}}$$

"Keeping an eye" on inventory has become simplified with the aid of data processing. Electronic data processing equipment, through its memory units, carries a perpetual inventory and issues a sophisticated report indicating inventory on hand, merchandise on order, periodic turnover, cost, extended value, total value of inventory, and as much other data as required and programmed, as often as needed. Programs can be prepared, too, for advising buyers when an item is below the danger level of "out-of-stock."

A periodic physical count, however, must be made of total inventory. This should be done to adjust for damaged merchandise, mis-selections, improper input, pilferage, and shrinkage control.

It might appear on the surface that the most efficient warehouse is one in which there is no scratch rate. This is not so. Any warehouse that has no scratch rate has too much inventory of slow movers and, possibly, of faster moving merchandise.

Before the dollar crunch of the late 1970's and early 1980, many warehouses operated at an optimum rate of 95 to 97 percent service rate (which translates to a 3 to 5 percent scratch rate) and about twenty to twenty-six turns a year. However, as the cost of money rose to 20 to 25 percent, many firms reduced inventories as deeply as they could. This caused not only the number of stock turns to rise, but also the scratch rate. The rule of thumb at the level of about twenty-five turns a year is a 1 percent greater scratch rate for every additional stock turn.

Where a chain or wholesaler is dealing with a high-volume store that gets three to five deliveries a week, a scratch from one delivery to the next may not be as serious as in a case where delivery is only weekly or less frequent. A number of wholesalers, when they were forced to lower the service rate, advise their customers so that they can order slow movers further in advance and keep somewhat larger inventories at the store level.

TRANSPORTATION

The marketing system in a mass economy is built upon an efficient and effective transportation system. Transportation must be efficient so that the product for which the consumer came to the store is available. Of the many dollars spent by the average family for the indirect cost of distribution, transportation is one of the major expenses. Transportation from the distribution center to the store may be handled by company-owned and/or company-operated trucks, privately owned and/or privately operated trucks, or contract carriers.

Owing to the great variety of operating conditions in various sections of the country, there is little uniformity in the organization of the transportation segment of the distribution center. Even in the same area of the country, great variation is found in the size of equipment, number and size of stores, etc. However, the functions performed are substantially the same. The principal requirements of transportation to stores are speed of service, regular and dependable schedules, merchandise protection, and safe and efficient handling. These functions must be performed effectively and at a minimum cost in order to keep the stores competitive.

The importance of merchandise deliveries cannot be overstated. The retail food industry owes its success to volume selling and high turnover. No profit is made in retailing until merchandise reaches the store—the only place the cash register rings. It is the function of the distribution center and the delivery system to service the stores—and service them well.

Orders are assembled and dispatched to each store according to an established weekly delivery schedule. Based on volume and need, a large store receives as many trailer deliveries during the week as may be necessary, while a small store may receive only one weekly delivery. Usually, the distribution center plans full truck or trailer loads for each delivery in order to keep distribution center and delivery expenses at a minimum. Centers servicing small towns pool the deliveries to several stores so as to use the delivery equipment to capacity for at least part of the trip.

Trucks carrying perishable items pool store orders so as to provide more frequent deliveries to assure freshness. Many companies utilize a program of night selection and delivery of merchandise, especially of perishables, and more particularly, produce, thereby permitting more effective utilization of delivery equipment, lowering fixed costs per ton moved, and supplying the stores with fresh merchandise from the day's business. In areas where distances from warehouses are great, combination (compartmentalized) trucks are frequently used. Dry groceries, dairy, meat, and even frozen goods are delivered on the same truck.

The drop-trailer method of delivery is used primarily for dry groceries. With this method, loaded trailers are dropped at the stores, and the empty trailer left on the previous run is picked up, thereby giving the store time to unload the merchandise as it is needed. The trailer serves as a storage facility until the merchandise can be stocked on the shelves. All operators make every effort to obtain the maximum legal payload for each delivery unit. Backhauls are used as frequently as possible, bringing merchandise back to the center and resulting in some form of allowance on trucking costs.

The backhaul permits a truck that is making retail deliveries outbound to pick up merchandise from the manufacturer's depot on his return to the warehouse. An allowance is made from the cost of the delivered price of the merchandise. If the allowance is too small or no allowance is granted, the backhaul is prohibitive. If the backhaul is "cost-justified," it then becomes profitable for the truck to pick up the merchandise.

It was not until the middle of 1980 that cost-justified backhaul was legally instituted. Before that, it lay in a shadowy legal area. The law permitted an FOB system or a delivered-price system, and through various FTC rulings, it was (under some interpretations) deemed illegal to give a cost-justified backhaul allowance, since the allowances were based on distance and time and were not the same for all backhauls.

People and Transportation

The people involved in transportation are the traffic manager, dispatchers, "lumpers" (contract unloaders), maintenance crew, drivers, and helpers. With proper direction exercised by the traffic manager and dispatcher, with safety controls, accident prevention, customer service and relations, and good union-management relations, the transportation area can be an efficient and effective system.

Methods of Allocating Delivery Expense

When discussing the methods of allocating delivery expenses, a distinction must be made between two types of operation: a chain headquarters servicing its stores, and a wholesale distribution center servicing its customers.

The delivery expense allocation by a chain headquarters depends on the accouting philosophy of the organization; there are chains that prefer to make the headquarters a profit center and charge their stores as if they were customers; and there are chains that give every consideration to the individual store, charging it the actual adjusted cost of transportation and warehousing.

As in the case of a chain operation, economic necessity and accounting principles must govern the allocation of delivery expense by a wholesale distribution center to stores. The method used to allocate delivery expense depends on the nature and organization of the wholesale distribution center. It is either: (1) owned by a number of members, independent of each other (as in a cooperative), each of whom is not responsible for the expenses of the other members, but is expected to pay an equitable share of the center's expenses; or (2) owned by a wholesale food distributor which is supplying voluntary, small chain or unaffiliated independents.

Wholesale Distribution Center. Because of these distinctions between the chain headquarters operation and the wholesale distribution center, each has a different basis for allocating transportation charges. The wholesale distribution center may use either one or a combination of several ways of allocating these costs:

1. *Percentage of purchases*—in many instances, a composite percentage, including warehousing and administration costs.
2. *Volume/percentage*—the larger the volume per load, the less the charge (on a steady basis).
3. *Distance of haul*—the farther away from the distribution center, the higher the charge (as explained on the next page in the discussion of the ton-mile method).
4. *Fixed charge* for use of trailer, driver, etc.—an established price regardless of dollar value of load.
5. *"Public carrier" charge* based on formal rates of the Interstate Commerce Commission (ICC), when deliveries are made in outlying districts.

Chain Organization. The distribution center of a chain organization allocates delivery expense differently. At the end of each accounting period, each retail unit is usually provided with a store operating statement informing the store managers as to the distribution of the gross profit realized by each individual store for the period. Usually near the bottom of this statement are found the words, "transportation and warehousing," the figures for which are expressed in dollars and as a percentage of total sales. This is an allocated amount, since calculating the exact share of center costs is not possible.

Food chains have several different methods of allocating delivery expense among the individual store units. The three most common methods are:

1. *Percentage of sales.*
2. *Mileage by hundred-weight* or *ton-mile method.*
3. *Overall operating expense*, in which the company does not attempt to break down the delivery costs on an individual store or departmental basis.

The percentage-of-sales method is easy to apply and justify. Basically, it is the prorating of distribution center and transportation expense to each store serviced by the center. The sales for the center for an accounting period by department—grocery, meat, and produce—are divided by the total sales. The resulting percentages are then multiplied by departmental distribution center and transportation expense, and this amount is charged to the store. This method of allocation is simple and particularly applicable to a situation where the distances from the distribution center to the stores are relatively uniform. A close correlation exists between the amount of merchandise delivered to each retail outlet and the sales of that outlet.

The second and more frequent method used by food chains for allocating delivery expenses—the ton-mile method—consists of two basic types: straight ton-mile and ton-mile by zone.

Under the straight ton-mile method, the transportation cost applied to each store is based upon the distance from the point of shipment to the receiving retail store. In general, this cost includes either the fixed rate of the contract carrier, or, if delivery is made by a company-owned truck, an amount sufficient to cover the driver's salary, truck-operating expenses, depreciation, taxes, and insurance. Each of these factors is taken into consideration and a rate set, which is sufficiently high to cover expenses without showing a profit, since service to stores is not a profit-making function. In practice, a per hundredweight charge, which is enough to cover all elements of the delivery expense, is used. This rate per hundredweight is then multiplied by the number of miles hauled, and the resultant figure is the amount charged to the store. Where special equipment is required, e.g., refrigerated vehicles, the rate is usually higher.

When the straight ton-mile method is used, accurate records of the shipments to each store must be kept so that each store is charged for the tonnage delivered. The data processing system records the weight of each item, and the total weight of the invoiced merchandise is calculated. The rate per hundredweight for the distance involved is then applied to determine the charge for each delivery. At the end of each accounting period, these charges are totaled and are debited to the store's operation for that period.

A variation of the ton-mile method is to use zones. Zones are established by drawing concentric circles on area maps at predetermined distances from the distribution center. For example, all stores inside a circle having a five-mile radius are in zone one; the next zone consists of all stores between five and ten miles from the distribution center, and so on. As the distance from the warehouse increases, the zones usually become larger. For example, stores in zones fifty miles or more from the warehouse could be in zone ten which is fifteen miles wide, whereas zone one, closest to the warehouse, may be only five miles wide. All stores within a given zone pay the same rate per hundredweight for delivery.

The last method of "allocating" distribution center and transportation expense is not to allocate costs at all. Delivery expense is incorporated into overall operating expenses, and no attempt is made to allocate costs to individual stores. It should not be inferred that this is true of all store expenses. Generally, the primary interest in the store's operation lies in the operating gain; that is, the amount remaining after wages, variable expenses, and fixed expenses have been subtracted from total store gross profit. These expenses usually can be attributed directly to the store and are controlled by store management. Since transportation and distribution center expenses cannot be regulated by the store manager, company executives do not concern themselves with the amount charged to individual stores.

Store managers are ranked and rated, at least in part, and often get bonuses based on the bottom line of the store operating statement. Therefore, many store managers, as well as other company executives, believe that only expenses over which the store manager exercises control should be included in the operating statement.

The store manager assigned to a store one hundred miles from the distribution center and in the same selling price zone as store managers assigned to stores closer to the center argues logically that he or she does not control location and should not be required to pay higher charges for delivery. In other words, it is logical that stores using the same retail prices should be charged the same amount for merchandise in the store, or the operating profit should not be a factor in store and store manager comparisons. If all stores were charged the same rate for delivery, such as the same percentage of sales, or if delivery expenses were not allocated to individual stores, management could use operating profit to evaluate stores and store managers. In companies using some form of ton-mile charge for delivery without changing retail prices as the charges increase, management should not penalize store managers.

Delivery Equipment

In order to deliver products properly, the center must have the necessary equipment; whether it be company-owned, leased or contract carrier. The equipment may range from a two-axle truck to a forty-five-foot trailer. Each mode of rental or ownership has its advantages and disadvantages. All of this equipment must be properly maintained and in good condition in order to give the stores proper service.

FOOD DISTRIBUTION
CENTER OPERATING EFFICIENCY

Since center operation is an important part of the distribution process, ways of measuring and controlling center costs are needed. Adequate expense records showing comparative operation figures are desirable. Since labor accounts for more than 50 percent of these costs, center cost-control programs are primarily designed to measure operating efficiency and cost of labor.

Two methods of measuring distribution are tons per man-hour and cases handled per man-hour. Both methods are computed basically by figuring "incoming" plus "outgoing" ("throughput") divided by the number of man-hours worked.

In addition to these productivity measures, control of the accident frequency rate and the number of disabling injuries per million man-hours worked (upon which insurance rates are based) must be calculated. Absenteeism, labor turnover, and damage are other factors to be considered. Also, the adoption of modular ordering (standing orders) is practical and can help reduce operating costs. (See page 217 for a discussion of modular ordering.)

NONFOODS

Many supermarket operators use the services of a rack jobber to supply and stock nonfood items. Rack jobbers service the nonfoods which they supply. Their service includes pricing, rotating of stock, changing

items, removing of unusable merchandise, etc. Their margin covers the cost of this service.

Rack jobbing, however, is declining as a factor in the supermarket industry as chains and wholesalers either buy rack-jobber firms and incorporate them into their normal operations or just assume the functions themselves. As the volume and variety of nonfood items increases, the increased margin that can be obtained by buying direct through the distribution center has been responsible for the elimination of the rack jobber by many chains and group operators. Increasingly, distribution centers are handling more nonfood items. Since it is becoming increasingly important for nonfoods to be handled by knowledgeable people, distribution centers are hiring specialists to buy and merchandise these products.

The selling price of many of these nonfood items is relatively high, and they are generally stored in a specific area of the distribution center, along with other small, high-unit-value nonfood items, such as cigarettes. Since many high-value items sell in limited quantity, less than case lots are shipped to stores. Therefore, the area may be referred to as the small-goods, broken package or repack room. It is enclosed, kept under close supervision, and locked when not in use. The area is set up as a selection line, with provisions for selection by retail units or case units. Delivery to the stores is by special container. These items are invoiced separately and are carefully checked at the store.

The repack room is designed with shelves and bins to hold cases and bulk quantities. Some centers either print retail price tickets to be included with each shipment or price-mark each unit. In many instances, returnable shipping containers are used to ship store orders as a unit. These containers are almost always sealed when sent to the loading dock for delivery to the stores. They are generally marked in some way as master cases.

A small-goods operation is absolutely necessary to supply less than case lots of low-turnover, high-value items to the retail units. Better inventory control and less investment in merchandise, both at the center and the store, are achieved by permitting orders by individual units. Pilferage is reduced by direct shelf-stocking from the delivery container and by carrying no reserve stock at store level.

Tax stamping of cigarette packages is another operation usually conducted in the small-goods room. This process is performed by automatic machines. The meter is used in much the same manner as a postage meter; it is refilled by the authorizing agent, paid by the center, and charged to the retailer. The retailer then passes on the charge to the consumer.

Another question confronting distribution center operators is which is most economical: pricing of nonfoods at the center or at store level. Operators agree that price changes are costly; therefore, central price marking is profitable only on items that are price stable.

FROZEN FOODS

The variety, inventory, and sales of frozen foods have grown phenomenally. Some industry people forecast that they will account for 10 percent of supermarket sales in the next few years.

The principle components of a frozen-foods distribution center include: storage space, order-assembly room, and order-holding space. Special equipment and handling is required to maintain the quality of frozen-food items; therefore, storage/ order-assembly space and order-holding rooms are held at or near 0°F. Order-holding space is needed for holding assembled orders before they are loaded onto delivery trucks. Of course, space for holding orders is unnecessary if orders are loaded from the order assembly line directly onto refrigerated delivery trucks.

Controlled-temperature order-assembly rooms are needed to maintain frozen-food quality. Employees at both the distribution center and at store level must understand the importance of continuous temperature control. Bacteria are merely kept inactive by freezing and become more active as temperatures increase above 0°F. Strict temperature control at all times is essential. Regulatory agencies monitor frozen foods intended for sale in order to protect consumers against products that may have been thawed and refrozen.

Many operators rent freezer storage space from public refrigeration plants. Others feel that there are cost advantages to handling frozen foods in company-owned distribution centers instead of contracting for distribution. There are, of course, advantages and disadvantages to both handling methods. In addition to cost savings, the operator must weigh availability and quick accessibility of product, location of contract distributor, space, cost of equipment, and so forth. Another consideration is working conditions; personnel working in facilities where temperatures are maintained at levels below 0°F. must be properly clothed in insulated garments and shoes, and must be given breaks at frequent intervals.

PRODUCE

The perishability of produce poses problems for the distribution center, such as quality inspection and control and temperature and humidity control.

The receiving function of the produce distribution center is a two-fold operation: inspection and

Photo courtesy of Harris-Teeter Super Markets, Inc., Charlotte, North Carolina.

In the frozen foods room of Harris-Teeter's Perishables Distribution Center at Indian Trail, North Carolina, temperature control is kept at or near 0° F. Note the forklift operator's winter gear.

A produce distribution center inspector examines fruit as it comes around on a carousel after it has been automatically wrapped. He then prepares the packaged produce for shipment to the supermarket. The maintenance of temperature and humidity control is a central requirement at a produce center.

checking. High-volume staples, depending on geography and speed of transportation, may be shipped by rail or truck from the growing areas. Locally grown produce and slow movers are transported by truck from the produce terminal or commission house. Highly perishable items can be received and stored easily with modern materials handling equipment. Frames built on pallets provide a means of storing and transporting hard-to-handle items, such as watermelons. Many cartoned or boxed produce items can be palletized.

Inspection of produce on arrival at the center is the function of the produce inspector. If a company is to protect its investment and give customers the highest possible quality, every effort must be made to accept and receive only quality merchandise.

Probably the most important factors contributing to the deterioration of fruits and vegetables are respiration and decay. In the process of respiration, oxygen is taken in, it combines with sugar, and gives off heat. This is a continuing process, the higher the outside temperature, the greater the respiration rate and the likelihood of spoilage. For every 18°F. rise in temperature between 32 and 80°F., respiration is doubled or tripled.

Proper refrigeration or icing and ventilation are the best-known methods of slowing down respiration. Thus, the produce inspector must continually check the temperature. In warm weather, the produce inspector checks rail cars for temperature and the amount of ice in the bunkers upon delivery. Very cold weather necessitates the use of heaters.

The produce inspector must also check for the presence of decay. This is done either by selecting random samples or by thoroughly inspecting every item in the case or carton. Normally, maximum decay percentages are established and anything over that must be reported to U.S. Department of Agriculture inspectors before merchandise can be returned. Three percent decay on citrus and one percent on potatoes are two examples of maximum decay percentages in use. Finally, the produce inspector should inspect the produce for in-transit damage.

As with all perishables, temperature control is considered most important. However, with produce quality control, there is another factor: humidity control. Ideal temperature and humidity vary with each item. Ideally, the assembly area should be an air-conditioned room. Because constant changes in temperature results in a deterioration of quality, the ideal distribution program is to deliver bulky staples, nicknamed "hardware," during the early part of the week, in addition to regular needs. The logic for this is that more perishables are sold toward the weekend; it, therefore, frees the distribution process to better handle the merchandise moving into the stores for weekend business. Order assembly is generally done during the night into the early morning hours.

MEAT

Meat is frequently supplied by packers or meat wholesalers, although many companies feel that the distribution of fresh meat through the center provides better quality and quantity control. Volume is an important factor in determining if meat is to be handled at the food distribution center.

Meat order assembly operations are, in many respects, similar to the produce operation. Air conditioning, inspection, fast turnover, cleanliness, and sanitary conditions are the prime considerations for successful meat distribution. U.S. Department of Agriculture inspectors monitor and enforce pure food standards, freshness, sanitation, and grading of all meats shipped interstate. Sanitation is also monitored by state and local authorities.

With assembly-line operations, the centers are broken down into product groupings. Orders taken by the afternoon of one day are generally delivered the following day. The order pickers select the items, verify quantity ordered, record the weights, and place the merchandise in delivery containers. Boxed meat is shipped in boxes in primal cuts, deboned and defatted. Each box weighs from forty to seventy pounds; boxes stack and handle easily.

SAFETY PROGRAMS

Modern management recognizes that a well-organized accident prevention program not only saves in insurance payments, but also saves by increasing efficiency. A continuous safety program is needed to prevent injury to personnel and to decrease property damage. Accidents are costly in terms of money and lost production.

Approximately 80 percent of all accidents can be eliminated by providing workers with an accident prevention education program. Physical layout, adequate lighting, use of color, safety devices, etc., are designed to reduce accidents and provide safe working conditions. All employees must understand the basic fundamentals of safety for themselves as well as for others.

A good safety record is achieved by using safe work methods and procedures. A well-planned safety program should include the following:

- Periodic physical examination of all employees (health insurance covers costs, but does not prevent accidents caused by physical limitations)
- Keeping aisles clear
- Safe traffic rules, strictly enforced
- Orderliness of work and storage areas
- Cleanliness of floors
- Ventilation adequate for healthful working conditions
- Authorized and trained personnel for all jobs

- Daily inspection and prompt maintenance of all equipment
- Safe loading and stacking according to specifications
- Proper maintenance of building
- Reporting and investigating accidents; remedial action should be taken after each accident
- Confining smoking to specific areas and providing fireproof containers for matches and cigarettes.

An important factor in reducing accidents is the recognition that the responsibility for any accident is, in part, an individual problem related to mental outlook. Attitudes regarding safety can be controlled through education and well-planned safety program.

The Occupational Safety and Health Act (OSHA) was passed in 1970. The purpose of this law is to protect labor and prevent hazardous conditions which could expose personnel to injuries and fatalities. Violations can result in substantial fines. By following the procedures listed above, as well as OSHA guidelines, the likelihood of accidents can be minimized.

A fire-fighting plan is also essential. In one plant, the general warehouse foreman was designated a fire chief and was empowered to set up fire drills and establish a fire fighting system. The warehouse was a large, one-story operation, and to make his daily inspections, the company equipped him with an electric-powered motor scooter. Another company uses a jeep as its fire engine. It is equipped with a hose and other fire-fighting equipment.

Many companies have installed automatic relay signal equipment and automatic sprinkler systems. Sprinkler systems are required by law in many states as well as by most insurance companies. All employees should know what to do in case of a fire—sounding the alarm and calling for help first, then proceeding to keep the damage at a minimum. Trying to put out the fire alone before summoning help may result in even heavier damage.

HOUSEKEEPING

Good housekeeping is not only a function of the retailer in the store, but is also essential in the warehouse. The OSHA rules on warehouses make sanitation rules compliance the direct responsibility of the chief executive officer of the company. There is no allowance for delegation of responsibility.

A number of years ago, the head of American Stores was given a jail term because of a sanitation violation in one of that firm's Acme warehouses. The case went all the way to the U.S. Supreme Court before the sentence was rescinded. What kept the sentence from being enforced was the fact that evidence was shown that proper action had been instituted by that executive to guarantee corrections of the existing problems. However, the law is clear, and unless evidence is presented that shows sound and realistic self-policing activity, monitored on a regular basis by the chief executive officer, her or she is liable to a jail sentence, should any company be found to have violated the sanitation code.

Several other warehouses have been closed and hundreds of thousands of dollars worth of merchandise confiscated because of various violations. Almost all warehouses today use a black-light inspection of all products that come into the warehouse in paper or cardboard primary containers.

Under the black light, evidence of any bird or rodent soiling or infestation of the product becomes evident, and that carload or truckload of product is rejected. Unless each warehouse uses this procedure, the few warehouses that do not eventually will receive all of the rejected merchandise, if the processor is trying to avoid taking the loss of the value of the product. However, the loss of the product is much less of a problem to a retailer than a newspaper story carrying news of confiscation of a firm's product or of the closing of a warehouse because of sanitation violations.

An insect and rodent infestation, which often enters the warehouse with a load of product, may be more common, but birds in the warehouse are another difficult-to-correct problem, once they get into the building. Grocery warehouses tend to be huge structures with ceilings ranging anywhere between twenty-five and one hundred feet high. When doors are opened to admit trucks and/or rail cars, birds often fly in and then have difficulties in finding their way out. Such birds attempt to build nests and live in the warehouse, unless strong, active efforts are made to eliminate them.

FUTURE IMPROVEMENTS

Over the years, the cost of operating a distribution center has outstripped profit. Labor costs have risen out of proportion to productivity. The net result is that management has been looking for ways to solve the problem of improving its profit picture. In order to accomplish this, distribution centers have been undergoing change. Efforts made to automate warehouses have not been overly successful. However, mechanization has been expanded over the years. In order to bridge the gap between rising costs and declining profits, the need for improvements is apparent in order to continue the delivery of food at reasonable cost.

Photo courtesy of Harris-Teeter Super Markets, Inc.,
Charlotte, North Carolina.

Thanks to modern electronics, the giant-size distribution center can maintain tighter security and control than ever before. Here, a security officer surveys the screens that give him a birds-eye view of the entire warehousing area.

27

CONSUMERISM AND REGULATORY AGENCIES

WHAT IS CONSUMERISM?

Consumerism is often misunderstood; it can certainly mean many things to many people. Some food retailers who do not understand it, just wish it would go away; they still remember the meat boycotts of the 1960's and 1970's and that is what consumerism means to them. However, it is vital for the food retailer to understand the true meaning and scope of consumerism.

Consumerism may be defined as "the promotion of consumers' interests." Food retailers who have successfully dealt with consumerism, whether they are aware of it or not, have substituted the word "customer" for "consumer" in this definition, so that it now reads: "Consumerism is the promotion of the *customers'* interests."

Consumer/customer satisfaction has been the keystone of every successful food retailer's operation since the beginning of mass grocery merchandising. Considering the low profit margin of the industry on the whole, each store is dependent on high volume to stay in business. To generate this volume, the supermarket must attract and keep customers by means of a clean and bright store, competitive prices, a wide variety of fresh products conveniently displayed, and courteous help.

Even though the majority of food retailers understands that customer satisfaction is the most basic and certainly the most preferable type of consumerism, the industry has been confronted with another aspect of this concept—the rise of an organized consumer movement in the late 1960's.

An underlying tenet of the consumer movement is that many of its members are unwilling to believe that any aspect of American business can ever be dedicated to satisfying the needs of the consumer. They believe that the consumer must be "protected" by laws and regulations that will force the food industry, among others, "to do what is right."

The consumer movement is not easy to define; it consists of many groups and a variety of principles However, for our purposes, the consumer movement can be broken down into several entities. The first would be the large consumer advocacy groups that are broadly based, have a permanent staff, and are headed by a consumer advocate, such as Ralph Nader. These groups are usually national and often address a variety of issues.

In addition to these larger national groups, there are smaller, local consumer groups that can consist of anywhere from two or three area residents to several dozen people. They are flexible enough to expand their membership for organized letter-writing campaigns, telephone calls, boycotts, etc. This type of consumer group will often perceive a consumer need and lobby to have this need satisfied by legislation.

Depending on their membership, they may have little real knowledge of supermarket operations, tending to seize on a solitary instance or circumstance that they believe needs correction. Their efforts often result in city or county legislation that can be troublesome for supermarket companies that operate in several jurisdictions. For instance, part of a consumer code enacted in Westchester County in New York State mandates certain sizes of type on window signs. Chains that do business in surrounding areas as well as Westchester have had to redesign their window signs for the entire chain even though these requirements are not in force outside the county.

However, community consumer groups of this type present a splendid opportunity for the food retailer to present industry's side of the story. An effort should be made to identify the group's members and invite them to become members of a consumer advisory board responsible for meeting with store management and giving it input on local consumer concerns. In turn, store management can educate these consumers about supermarket operations. In many cases, efforts of this nature will avoid unnecessary regulation.

The *individual* consumer should not be discounted; he or she can be a very vocal part of the consumer movement. A letter to the editor of the local newpaper or an appeal to a state legislator from a disgruntled customer can start a chain of events that can result in "corrective" legislation. For example, in one such incident, a customer received an unsatisfactory answer from a supermarket manager about the store's pricing policy. As a result of this occurrence, he petitioned his state representative to actively support a repricing ban. It took quite a bit of effort by the chain's management and the state retailers' association to convince the lawmaker that the legislation was uncalled for and would only cost the consumer more in the long run.

On the whole, consumerism has made industry more aware of the public's demands. Many in the food industry have questioned its value. Although some government regulation is necessary, consumers make a choice every time they shop in a supermarket; customers will generally shop where they get what they want, and that is one of the best, most direct forms of consumerism.

REASONS FOR THE
GROWTH OF CONSUMERISM

A number of conditions laid the basis for the growth of the consumer movement in the 1960's. One important factor was the general decline in public confidence in big business and government.

Another factor is the inflationary spiral which has continually raised the price of consumer goods and services in recent years. Although inflation has adversely affected the prices of most consumer items, the very accessibility of the supermarket makes it a convenient target for discontented consumers who are distressed about higher prices. The purchase of automobiles and clothing can be deferred until prices relax or more cash is available. However, food is a necessity, and its purchase cannot be put off. In addition, the price increases of items that are not purchased on a regular basis, such as clothing and automobiles, are not noticed as easily. Consumers are confronted by higher food prices on a very regular basis—at least weekly—so that even a small increase is noted and questioned. Not completely understanding why food prices have risen, many consumers think that supermarkets are reaping huge profits as a result of higher food prices.

Unfortunately, lawmakers have helped fuel these attitudes. Besieged themselves by a lack of public confidence, they have set about to seize issues that they perceive to be popular with their constituents. Thus, consumer issues have become the "in" thing, and, as a result, there is a growing tendency for the food industry to be saturated with regulations. Frustrated supermarket operators have tried to comply with thousands of laws and regulations that overlap and may vary from community to community. The added cost that has resulted from all this legislation has been felt at all stages of the food production and distribution chain, and ultimately, by the consumer.

The consumer movement has shown signs of slowing up during the past several years. Government reports have included more information on the reasons why food prices are going up. Food retailers are making greater efforts to open up lines of communication with consumers and consumer advocacy groups. In turn, many of these consumer groups have shown more willingness to work hand-in-hand with supermarket operators to work out problems and secure voluntary solutions without government intervention.

It would be well for food retailers to remember that even though there are slowdowns in the activist consumer movement from time to time, it should always be ready to deal with new issues and consumer concerns. Any further price increases over the coming years very likely will result in renewed and intense consumerism that food retailers must be prepared to meet.

THE CONSUMER OPPORTUNITY

The food retailing industry, above all others, has a vast potential for communicating with the consumer. No other industry is in such close and direct contact with its customers on such a regular basis.

This situation presents both an opportunity and a challenge. The very accessibility of food retailers makes them an easy target for consumer complaints. Supermarkets are the last stop in the food distribution chain and can be blamed for everything from a shortage of lettuce to higher beef prices.

But this very same accessibility presents a golden opportunity for supermarket operators to effectively communicate with consumers. If a store is short on lettuce and no attempt is make to tell the consumer why, he or she can assume that the store is managed poorly. Why not put up a sign in the produce department to tell the consumer that lettuce is in short supply because of weather conditions? Why not tell produce clerks to suggest that consumers purchase an alternate salad green, such as escarole? This is customer service and, after all, that is what consumer affairs are really about.

The most important thing to remember is that any consumer affairs program should start with the company's total commitment to customer service. The efforts of even the largest staff devoted solely to consumer affairs will prove fruitless unless every single employee in the company shares this commitment. Once this commitment has been made, then there are many different ways to implement effective consumer relations.

IMPROVING CONSUMER RELATIONS

Since the onset of the consumer movement, more and more food retailers have set up some sort of formal mechanism to improve consumer relations. The Food Marketing Institute, which is the national trade association for the supermarket industry, has a Consumer Affairs Council comprised of a series of working task forces. These groups provide consumer affairs input to program development as well as policy information in these areas. The steering committee for the Council consists of fifteen members who are representatives of FMI's overall membership. Some of these task forces deal with on-going issues; whereas others only consider those consumer issues that are particularly important at the moment.

State trade associations, such as the New York State Food Merchants Association, have started programs to coordinate the consumer activities of their member stores, to assist the smaller members who do not have a consumer affairs capability, and to conduct consumer education sessions.

Some of the consumer programs have included the formation of consumer panels or boards at individual chains. Other food retailers have met with consumer advocates on a regular basis. Many chains distribute information to help consumers understand their operations. Most distribute leaflets and bag stuffers with nutritional information and recipes.

There are many supermarket companies that have a regular policy of conducting consumer outreach programs in which a store executive or consumer affairs director visits local community groups to talk about food issues and educate consumers about the industry. This is also an excellent way to discover the general public's attitudes or misconceptions about food matters. Having this kind of information is of help to the food retailer in better serving his customers.

However, the results of a recent survey of food retailers have disclosed that more intensive efforts must be mounted to satisfy consumer demands that may arise in the future. According to this survey, only 17 percent of the responding stores have an employee whose sole duty is the area of consumer affairs: 8 percent have no formal mechanism at all; 44 percent have a consumer affairs department, but 60 percent have an employee who handles consumer affairs in addition to other duties.

Consumer relations should be an actively positive effort, but this is not usually the case. The same survey, cited above, showed that, in most companies, consumer activities are very heavily directed to answering complaints. The survey also disclosed that the most frequently voiced consumer complaints are against the product itself.

It is also important that store personnel be instructed and motivated to have a good attitude toward customers. This is not always easy in today's business climate, in a field that deals so closely with so many people of varying dispositions and temperaments. The simple fact remains, however, that customers are necessary to keep food retailers in business. A rude or indifferent clerk, too many items out of stock, and a messy store will turn customers away. If enough leave to shop at the competition, the answer is clear. The food store that does not realize that everyone, from top management on down, should be dedicated to satisfying the customer, may soon be out of business.

Companies that have the budget for a full-time executive, whose sole responsibility is consumer affairs, possess the ideal conditions by which to educate consumers, train store personnel, maintain contact with the local community, develop consumer advisory boards, give management input on consumer trends, and do a host of other things in the performance of customer services and the creation of a positive store image.

However, the low profit margins so widespread in the food industry leave little part of the operating budget that can be used for consumer affairs and public relations. Although the results of these activities cannot be measured strictly in terms of dollars, total neglect of consumer affairs can cause customer dissatisfaction and excessive regulatory intervention.

Photo courtesy of Giant Food Inc.

Supermarkets have made increasing efforts to improve communications with their customers. One such effort, hanging from the ceiling of this store, lists a "Consumer Bill of Rights." Included are: the right to service, to be informed, to choose, to be heard, to redress, and to safety.

Many of the activities conducted by the consumer affairs departments of the larger food retailers, can be borrowed outright or adapted by chains and single-store operators who do not have this capability. An individual store operator can be just as effective in speaking to large community groups about the food industry as the representative of a large chain. Nutritional information and food shopping tips are just as helpful to the consumer whether they are printed on expensive glossy stock or copied on a duplicating machine.

Many food retailers who do not have the luxury of enough operating capital to have a structured consumer affairs department have found that some common sense and innovation can go a long way to promote effective customer relations. The following are some ideas that every food retailer might apply to his or her consumer affairs efforts.

Everything possible should be done, from an operations standpoint, to reduce consumer complaints. Practices, such as stock rotation to insure a fresh product, clean and uncluttered aisles, prices well-indicated, etc., may seem quite basic, but are sometimes neglected, giving the customer a poor image of the store. Even the most ambitious consumer affairs program will fail, if there are deficiencies in these areas.

A food store with good housekeeping methods on an ongoing basis might still be the object of organized consumer demands, but is less likely to be singled out by an individual consumer who is dissatisfied. The less time spent on answering direct consumer complaints about stale produce or unsanitary conditions, the greater the effort that can be expended on positive

consumer projects. Sloppy housekeeping is a red flag that says "We don't care!" to both consumers and government officials.

It is also well to remember that many government agencies act on direct consumer complaints by visiting the store in addition to their regularly scheduled inspections. Even if no violation is discovered, such occasions may cause a disruption of business and be unsettling to any customers shopping at the time.

Wherever possible, a *uniform* company policy should prevail, and all employees should be aware of it and observe it. It also helps to post signs or have a leaflet describing the store's policy on rainchecks, refund policies, etc. In some jurisdictions, such matters may be regulated by law. In any event, all should be aware of store policies so that consumers will not be confused or misled. If it is the supermarket's policy not to accept returns without the register tape, for example, then this fact should be made known.

There may be exceptions to a uniform company policy, however; a typical example is a large supermarket chain that operates over a wide area with varying price structures from community to community. This situation may cause consumer complaints. Store personnel should be given a simple and direct answer that would explain why the price differences exist—higher rents in the area, for example.

Food store operators will fare better if they are not defensive during any confrontations they may have with individual consumers or with an organized consumer movement. The food merchant, even when faced with an unreasonable situation, should keep a cool head and think of ways to turn such situations around to his advantage.

Several years ago, during the height of the consumer boycotts, an upstate New York food retailer learned that his store was to be the location of a press conference called by a local consumer advocate to air complaints about the high cost of beef. This farsighted merchant put out coffee and doughnuts for the agitated consumers and the press people. As a result, he received very favorable press coverage and had a better opportunity to explain why beef prices had risen.

There are many sources of consumer information that food retailers can use to educate and inform their customers. Food store suppliers will often have leaflets and flyers available that contain recipes, food shopping tips, and nutritional information. Even if an individual retailer does not have the capability to produce his or her own consumer materials, the distribution of these manufacturers' pamphlets can be an important customer service.

Trade associations can be very helpful to food retailers in their consumer affairs efforts. Such groups

Soliciting patron views is one technique used by supermarkets to win consumer approval. Here, at Pantry Pride, a "club hostess" offers membership applications, brochures, and other publications. One sign urges: "Make your views felt."

can supply research and information about consumer issues and, through seminars and meetings, educate members about consumerism.

Before starting any consumer affairs program, the food retailer should take a close, hard look at the community, the customers, and the store's own operation, and then, tailor the program accordingly. A consumer advisory board could be very successful in a suburban area where the residents might be willing to devote their time and effort to serving on the board. However, it probably would be less successful in a large city where the residents are more accustomed to anonymity. Learning consumer concerns in large cities probably could be better accomplished with in-store questionnaires that the customer could complete at his or her convenience.

There is really no set formula for handling consumer affairs effectively. The innovative food retailer who is truly committed to customer service will be able to develop an ongoing consumer affairs effort that will be worthwhile for himself and his customers. In no way, should any consumer affairs program be a slick public relations effort to cover up sloppy operations or inefficient management. Nor should a con-

sumer affairs program be activated only when restrictive legislation is proposed or an organized consumer protest is imminent.

The more progressive and successful companies have found a simple formula: Lead, do not follow the consumer.

A number of years ago, when meat prices were high and consumers were fuming about the prices, Giant Foods, Landover, Maryland, took full-page ads in their trading areas around the nation's capital headed "DON'T BUY MEAT." The ad went on to advise consumers about meat substitutes available at the store. The ad also pointed out that if consumers did not buy as much meat as in the past, the supply-demand factors would fall into a consumer-favorable posture. After taking the complete consumer position, Giant then stated that for those consumers who still insisted on the right to buy meat, the store would continue to carry it.

In the past few years, a number of regional chains have taken similar ads about lettuce, when it was in short supply and prices were high. Some chains have even refused to stock the item during those periods.

On another front, Pathmark led the fight to permit the substitution of generic drugs for branded items and thus reduce the prices of prescriptions. Pathmark also was the firm that went into court and fought the light-bulb manufacturers on price fixing. In both cases, the firm came out "the champion of the consumer."

Giant and Pathmark are just two examples of chains that have convinced the consumer that their goals are common ones. When a firm achieves such an image, it becomes the leader in the area. But, it need not just be the large regional chains that set such a consumer-oriented pace. Smaller groups can accomplish similar patterns and receive the goodwill of the consumer.

Several years ago, the woman president of a small Alabama group of Piggly Wiggly (franchise group) stores went onto the firm's weekly radio program and said, "I have seen the produce that our stores are prepared to sell this coming week. I wouldn't buy it personally, and I'm advising all our customers not to buy produce in our stores this week. I'll do everything in my power to correct this unfortunate situation by next week."

On a smaller scale, a number of independent companies have used hand-printed signs advising consumers not to buy certain produce or meat items because of what they consider poor quality or high prices. When the Bing cherry crop was hard hit by last-minute rains in 1980, a number of East Coast chains refused to handle the product which was selling as high as $1.50 to $2.00 a pound, and quality was poor.

Enlightening customers is the role played by these posters over the meat case. Each poster indicates cut locations for a particular animal, and the types of preparation deemed suitable.

Others put signs up on the reduced-size displays of cherries, advising customers not to buy.

Just one word of caution: The consumer wants to know not just "What have you done for me?" but also, "What have you done for me lately?" Therefore, no firm can rest on past accomplishments for very long, but must strive to keep the pro-consumerist image bright and current.

REGULATORY AGENCIES

Like other industries, the food industry, with special emphasis on the supermarket, is subject to government regulation in many areas. However, because food is so important to the health and nutrition of its people, more of these governmental agencies are involved in policing and directing the food industry than any other business area.

There are many agencies involved in the industry's regulation which play an important, but relatively *indirect* role in the ultimate destiny and behavior of the manufacturer, wholesaler, retailer, or any other segment of the food business. These agencies include (not necessarily in the order of their importance):

- Federal Communications Commission (FCC)
- Interstate Commerce Commission (ICC)
- Securities and Exchange Commission (SEC)
- Occupational Safety and Health Administration (OSHA).

In addition, there are those agencies that play a *direct* and leading role in the promulgation and enforcement of rules and regulations that are the result of consumer requests and that directly relate to the well-being of the public. Needless to say, these agencies are in every strata of government—federal, state, and municipal—all having their varying effects on the food industry, in some instances interlocking and/or overlapping.

Federal Agencies

Federal Trade Commission (FTC). Among the important functions of the FTC is the regulation of insufficient quantities of advertised specials, "rain checks," games and other promotions, price comparison advertising, etc. The FTC also sees to it that all deals and allowances are equitable and available to all. It is the function of the Consumer Protection Bureau to police advertising and to curtail the advertising that it judges to be detrimental to the consumer.

Department of Agriculture (USDA). The U.S. Department of Agriculture has many, varied func-

tions. The earliest step in the food cycle is the crop forecast, made periodically from the time of planting right up until the time of the last harvest. Buyers for supermarkets and manufacturing processors use these forecasts in order to plan for their operations.

The USDA also does considerable research along a number of fronts, starting with helping develop seed, fertilizer, and other pre-planting procedures through the planting, maintenance, and harvesting of crops—even post-harvest techniques that will bring a larger and better crop to the market.

The U.S. Department of Agriculture also sets the standard for the grading of agricultural products by which the buying public can ascertain the grade, and simultaneously the quality, of the produce purchased (i.e., eggs graded "A" or other grades; canned or frozen fruit or vegetables marked "Fancy" or other grades; meat graded "Choice" or other grades, etc.). These grades can also serve as a guide or standard by which the distributor buys the produce as well as the price to be paid. The fact that a product is ungraded, however, is no indication of inferior quality. It merely means that the product was not inspected for grading purposes. There are products that must be inspected for cleanliness and/or health conformance in accordance with health codes and that can be marked "Inspected" without a grading connotation.

Depending on the Administration and its Secretary of Agriculture, one function of the USDA has been quite controversial—distributive functions. Various departments within the USDA work with transportation, economics, and other areas that deal with the crop after it leaves the farm. Some Secretaries of Agriculture have been firmly opposed to such activities of the department, while others have fostered it. Still others have changed their positions after assuming the post (e.g., Earl Butz and Bob Bergland).

The argument against post-harvest research, perhaps over-simplified, states: The function of the U.S. Department of Agriculture is to help the farmer until the crop leaves the field. It then is no longer the responsibility of the USDA. Those who support this position may not necessarily oppose research beyond the harvest stage; they feel it should fall under the aegis of some other agency and is not a function of the Department of Agriculture.

The other school of thought is that the function of the USDA is to get the crop to the consumer in the best and most plentiful method possible. They point out the astounding statistic that 40 percent to 60 percent (depending on which of the surveys is accepted, but a huge figure in either case) of the crop that is harvested never is consumed. This tremendous waste is the result of a huge number of factors, from improper packing, to transportation, to wasteful manufacturing, storing and handling practices.

Those who oppose spending USDA funds on distributive research to solve some of the problems feel that individual companies should pay for this research. The other side says that food processors, wholesalers, and retailers are not in a position to do so. Thus, a large food manufacturer might spend on research, but only for what might directly affect him. The smaller manufacturer has no such capability. The same holds true for wholesalers and retailers.

There are also gray areas involving transportation, packaging, and other factors that would affect everyone, yet "fall between the cracks" of the compartmentalized food industry. On several occasions, efforts have been made to place the post-harvest research function into some part of the U.S. Department of Commerce. But, to date, all such efforts have failed. The waste rate in the food field is still a world disgrace.

Among the benefits that have been derived from such post-harvest research (for the farmer and all the way to the consumer) in the past twenty-five years have been:

- Extending the selling season (and thus utilizing larger crops) of various farm items. (Navel oranges, for example, used to have about a six-week season; apples had about a three-month selling season. With the help of controlled temperature and humidity for storage, navel oranges now are found in stores from November until about June. Apples have become an all-year fruit.)
- Methods of stacking produce in transit to permit circulation of cold air, thus doubling and tripling shelf life
- Packing materials and cartons that eliminate much bruising and damage to fruits and vegetables
- Cooling equipment that preserves crops in transit
- Methods of handling and storing that eliminate much of the old methods which created much more damage.

The above are just a few of the ways such marketing research has helped the entire food chain.

The question really resolves itself around: Does the responsibility of the U.S. Department of Agriculture end with the harvest or with the delivery of the product to the consumer? If the former, then whose function is it to bring the product from the field to the consumer with an eye toward eliminating such tremendous waste?

Food and Drug Administration (FDA). The Food and Drug Administration of the Department of Health and Human Services has among its functions the responsibilities of proper labeling for contents, nutritive values, and cautions, if any, of foods, medicines, etc. Of course, they perform the task of advising and educating consumers as another of their functions.

The FDA also has responsibility for product recalls and inspections that involve improper packing which could cause illness and other health and safety hazards to the user or handler of the product. New methods of packaging, new products in the health field, and other products that could pose a potential danger if not tested before being made available for public use, also must be approved by the FDA before being sold to the public.

A considerable amount of business displeasure has been voiced over the years concerning the restrictive practices of the FDA and the considerable delays before products can be marketed. In spite of the complaints, it is because of the FDA that arsenic no longer is used to preserve dried fruits or that potential carcinogens are no longer used in a host of consumer products. Because of the FDA, there is virtually no case of sand being mixed with sugar, or filler products of much less nominal or nutritional value being substituted in manufactured products without at least being listed on the product label.

Consumer Affairs Advisor to the President. This is not an agency, but rather an office without portfolio; and is, in the true sense of the word, an advisor who serves as a liaison between the President and the nation's consumers and agencies.

Over the past decade, a number of efforts have been made to raise the President's consumer affairs advisor to the status of Cabinet officer. The strong opposition of many businesses, including most of the food industry, has prevented this to date, but the outlook for such status in the next decade is fairly bright, according to most Washington experts.

State Agencies

State Departments of Agriculture. Depending on the governmental structure of the state in which it is found, the state department of agriculture has various subdivisions that basically perform the following functions:

- Sets up state standards and grades for agricultural products (not to supercede federal standards)
- Promulgates regulations that apply to consumer needs and demands in the state as well as policing of state consumer affairs regulations
- Promulgates state sanitation regulations and policing of state sanitation laws and regulations
- Issues licenses to various food establishments.

FIGURE 25
UNIT PRICING

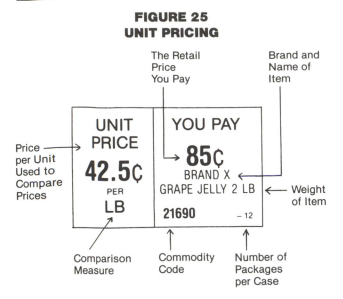

Unit pricing laws have been passed in many states, requiring supermarkets to indicate clearly an item's cost for a usual measure, such as ounces or pounds. As indicated in this example, if you are paying 85¢ for two pounds of grape jelly, then your unit price is 42.5¢ per pound.

Municipal Agencies

Department of Consumer Affairs. Throughout the country, in many communities, there are local consumer affairs agencies whose function it is to answer the multitude of consumer complaints in addition to normal routine inspections of places of business. Their duties, as they apply to the food business, include:

- Unit pricing regulation and enforcement
- Inspection for short weight in packaging of manufacturer and store
- Weights and measures inspection (scales)
- Failure on the part of the retailer to comply with his or her advertising program (e.g., improper pricing or improper checking out of advertised products; not having advertised product available for purchase, etc.)
- Mislabeling of products, such as calling a meat product by a name or primal cut other than it actually is
- Selling of outdated merchandise.

Local Department of Health. Local departments of health are usually responsible for the following:

- Promulgation of health and cleanliness regulations pertinent to food-handling establishments and their personnel (e.g., no smoking in food establishments, no dogs or animals permitted in food stores, etc.)
- Enforcement of these regulations
- Routine inspections—proper handling, cleanliness of stores and personnel
- Licensing of premises or employees where required.

Federal, state and local government agencies have cooperated in the preparation, maintenance and enforcement of various programs. For example, a sanitation program has been developed and prepared by several federal agencies (FDA, OSHA, etc.). It generally is being adopted by state and local agencies that get federal funding assistance; enforcement, however, is maintained on the local level.

THE FUTURE OF CONSUMERISM

Consumerism is indeed a way of life today, and it must be recognized that the food store, being the most widely used, the most frequently visited, the most visible, and having a most profound effect on the well-being of the consumer, must be in the forefront of the consumer focus. Also, for these same reasons, those government agencies, whose duties are the promulgation and enforcement of consumer protection laws and regulations, have been called upon to assist the consumer in this effort.

No one can predict what turns consumerism will take in the future. As has happened in the past, a sharp increase in the inflation rate will induce consumer discontent. Some of this discontent will result in renewed attacks on the food industry. For this reason, consumer affairs programs will become increasingly important for all food retailers in the future.

Of special value will be consumer affairs efforts that will educate and inform the consumer about the food distribution chain. In some industries, consumers are being drawn into the decision-making process. Those food retailers who have already started consumer advisory boards have recognized this new trend in consumerism. But whatever trends may emerge in the coming years, the food retailer who has made the basic and total commitment to customer service will have the most effective consumer affairs program.

28

One of the chief objectives of management is an attempt to achieve an effective and efficient organization. This involves an increase in productivity while maintaining or decreasing costs. Required to achieve this is a systematic approach by both executive management and individual store managers as well as the cooperation of management subordinates, i.e., assistant managers, department managers, etc.

Successful stores accomplish this goal through the use of an efficiency checklist which allows people to work more effectively in performing their duties and operating their section, department, store, or organization. This involves planning all the necessary activities performed within a specific time frame, i.e., morning, afternoon, day, week, etc. Many of these activities and tasks are repeated each day, e.g., the grocery manager checks the shelves. All necessary activities may be listed in a checklist form (and duplicated or printed) so that performance of the activity may be verified and standards maintained. In this way, there is less chance of forgetting or varying an established and necessary activity.

A checklist also can serve as a control for the manager or supervisor when he or she is monitoring store activities. Management, at the store level, may prepare checklists for each of the areas of responsibility.

Management should be thoroughly familiar with the following pointers for more efficient operations:

Work Methods and Standards. Work standards should be set according to the work methods used. The best way to do each job under existing conditions should be established; and, then, employees should be trained in the use of the established procedure.

Most workers, untrained and left to devise their own work methods, perform their tasks in a slow, more laborious way. Efficient performance is the result of training. Proper training produces good work habits which yield more positive morale. This serves as an added incentive affecting proper work flow.

An effective manager must also avoid overstaffing in a specific activity or a department, since this leads to a decrease in efficiency and profitability.

Assign responsibility and work to the lowest level possible. For example, using a store manager as a bagger is "expensive" bagging.

Labor efficiency is achieved by each worker knowing the work schedule, duties, and the performance or production standards for the job. The duties of a job may vary from store to store and from area to area, but once established, should be properly communicated to personnel.

Work schedules should be planned to provide enough workers to do the job without lost time. For example, delivery truck unloading, when trailers are not dropped, must be done promptly and efficiently. This requires an adequate labor force at the time of arrival. If the truck is late, many hours of labor may be lost unless other work is planned. The store manager should plan work to be done while waiting for the next job.

The important factor is that workers know work schedules, job priorities, and standards of performance.

Labor Turnover. The cost of training new employees varies with the degree of skill required. Training requires a trainer; also, the productivity of the beginner is relatively low. Both of these factors increase operating costs. Employee selection and personnel policies affect the rate of turnover. A high employee turnover rate indicates that an overhaul of policies and procedures is needed. Sometimes, this can be attributed to the difficulty of the work, low-level job entry or nonmotivated part-time employees, or the manner in which the job is portrayed by the personnel department or trainer.

Store Employees and Store Image. Supermarkets tend to be very similar in appearance, layout, and design. There is some element of difference, however, to customers who prefer one particular store over another. In such cases, a more favorable image has been created by the store. This image is, to a considerable extent, created by the store employees. The store and department managers, the clerks, stockers, checkers, and baggers create the shopping atmosphere—friendly and attracting, or cold and repellent.

Supermarket managers and supervisors should check employee attitudes and design informational and training programs to develop favorable attitudes which will be conveyed to shoppers through actions and words. The friendly store attracts shoppers.

Employee Selection. The quality of people hired to work in a store and the training provided are important factors in terms of customer relations. Labor turnover is costly, since training is expensive and the productivity of beginners is relatively low. The time and money spent in selecting the best available employees is well worth the effort. The use of professionals and consultants to test and screen applicants is especially useful, if satisfactory people are to be selected.

Well-selected and trained employees radiate their feelings to shoppers. Also, fair wages and working conditions are needed to maintain a satisfied labor force. Money spent on personnel is an important factor in image building.

Incentive Plans. Incentive plans are established in order to share with the worker the gains of increased productivity. The basic plan must be scientifically developed and not altered capriciously. The plan should put continuous and firm pressure on workers to perform efficiently. In many instances, pay scales are determined by negotiation between labor and management.

Teamwork Pay Schedule. A variation of the usual incentive pay plan is a teamwork pay schedule. A base pay schedule is used with a base rate of pay for each job classification. For each one dollar increase in the store sales per man-hour, maintained for four out of five weeks, the employees are moved to the next pay step. This type of pay plan requires educating employees on how to work better as a team and keeping them posted on the progress the store is making. The base is sales, which means increased profits as the sales per man-hour increase. Sharing this increase with the employees provides an excellent incentive. Where unions are concerned, however, agreement to a teamwork pay schedule must be reached beforehand.

Suggestion System. Employee suggestions for methods of improving operations are of great value to a manager. All suggestions should be discussed with the submitting employee. A suggestion system keeps all employees alert for better ways of accomplishing jobs. It also allows for greater participation on the part of the employees, making them feel part of the organization in assisting the company in reaching its goals. Suggestions that are implemented should be posted with acknowledgment and recognition for the person submitting it. Some industrial psychologists strongly recommend this suggestion program for employees, naming it management by participation. Wherever this program has been properly implemented, it has been successful.

Inventory Standards. Two facets to inventory standards are providing adequate shelf stock for maximum sales and, at the same time, minimizing capital invested in merchandise. Both facets must be controlled. Sales are increased by minimizing stock-outs; interest costs increase as more capital is required to finance store inventories. Each operator should devise a satisfactory control system, and a checklist. Stock-outs can be controlled by number or by percentage of total stock, such as the 4 percent out-of-stock considered normal. However, the items themselves are more important than the number.

Inventory control can be measured by total dollar value in relation to sales. Normal average store inventory should be established.

Ordering Controls. Ordering is a vital function; it is important in terms of maintaining adequate stock without overstocking, as well as the cost of making out the order.

Ordering cycles vary (based on velocity, lag time, perishability, source, and method of delivery) and ordering procedures differ from store to store. For most stores, the basis for ordering is projection of velocity and capacity of shelf-space; each item has its own standards.

Errors and mistakes in estimating weekly movement, especially on sale items, require procedures for fill-in ordering. Fill-in orders must be controlled; they are expensive to place, more difficult to handle in the distribution center, and very expensive to deliver. Therefore, few firms permit fill-in orders. It would be easy for store managers to become dependent on fill-in deliveries if it were not for the penalties attached. Penalties that reflect a reduced store operating profit often act as an effective control on fill-in ordering.

Effective ordering is achieved by delegating the responsibility by area to employees. Each employee becomes an "expert" for his or her section and, thus, becomes efficient in the performance of routine ordering, developing good judgment relative to estimating movement.

Control of Supplies. The cost of supplies does not appear to be large, but can easily affect store operating profit. The ordering and control of supplies determines the amount of capital required to finance the inventory as well as the risk of loss through damage or loss of equipment.

The use of proper supplies is an important cost factor. For example, using more film and a larger tray than necessary for wrapping meat or produce may be insignificant on a per-item basis, but in terms of 10,000 packages becomes important. Also, the use of supplies, such as floor waxes or cleaners, from shelf stock is expensive; commercial cleaners purchased in bulk quantities, such as drums, are not only cheaper, but more satisfactory for industrial uses. The use of shelf merchandise as supplies must be limited to items not available in commercial units, and must be recorded as an expense—not as inventory shrinkage.

Expense Control. Expenses reduce store operating profit and must be controlled. All expenses that are subject to control at the store level are the responsibility of the store manager. Some expenses, such as rent and other allocated costs, are fixed; others, such as wages, electricity, water, etc., are variable and controllable, within limits, by the store manager.

A realistic approach to payroll control is important. A scale indicating the rate of pay for each job title with allowances for merit, longevity, and for variations in operating situations is such an approach. Therefore, one scale for a chain or group of stores is not satisfactory unless a correction factor is determined for each store.

Expenses can be kept to a minimum by the store manager's constant surveillance. For example, controlling the use of lights and turning off those that are not needed is the type of expense control a manager must exercise. Energy costs are of utmost importance; therefore, checking thermostats on equipment and the regulation of heat has become a prime concern.

Utility Rates. Check the various rate schedules, and meter for the best service at the lowest rate. Whenever the demand on the utilities increases with the installation of additional equipment, recheck the rate schedule for the best rates. Utility charges are based on demand and kilowatts used. Learning how to use power properly is an effective control.

Duplicating and Printing. Check on the use of data processing equipment to prepare materials sent to stores. Some materials sent to stores may be reproduced by photo offset or a similar process that may be less expensive. Be alert for better, faster and less expensive reproduction processes.

Insurance Costs. Reduce premium rates by keeping claims to a minimum. Use a safety and fire prevention program. Also, a safety program for customers avoids the loss of goodwill caused by accidents. An alert manager reduces accident rates by constantly maintaining a clean, clear store. To avoid the risk of robbery or internal theft, a system that keeps on hand a minimum amount of cash should be instituted.

Internal Audits. Use internal audits to check the efficiency of each store. For example, store audits should include a check on the accuracy of prices as marked on the merchandise. Also, expense items should be reviewed by auditors.

Materials Handling. The food store operates a tonnage business. Handling tonnage requires efficient materials-handling equipment. The equipment and procedures should be reviewed periodically to determine whether the greatest possible efficiency is being achieved.

Front-End Control. Control of cash, stamps, and coupons at the checkstands is a direct responsibility of the store manager. These items should be controlled and audited.

A continual control of checker accuracy is essential in order to maintain a favorable customer image and proper cash control. The manager and head cashier are responsible for the performance of checkstand personnel. Complaints as well as overrings and shorts should be checked. Also, the general attitude of checkstand personnel toward customers must constantly be observed.

If gift or premium redemption stamps are given, they must be offered to all customers and not just when the customer makes a request. Provisions must be made to handle them efficiently. Large denomination stamps and/or a stamp dispenser speeds up checkstand traffic flow.

Store coupons should be a standard size in order to facilitate handling, counting, and storing. A clear statement of the value of each coupon is needed to assure accurate redemption.

Security Control. A major factor in store control is pilferage by customers, delivery personnel, and employees. Security rules and procedures to follow should be established and communicated to all employees. Security factors to be included are:

- Controlling all delivery entrances (back doors)
- Checking all delivery personnel on each trip into and out of the store
- Auditing all drop shipments for quantity, quality, etc.
- Controlling employee buying procedures and checking on items taken out of the store
- Regulating employee food consumption in the store
- Instituting customer pilferage control, etc.

Net profit averages about 1 percent of sales. It can be decreased, and even eliminated, by pilferage; or net profit can be increased by security control. Therefore, it is imperative that the store manager establish and maintain adequate security control.

Distribution Center Deliveries. When the retail and wholesale units are under the same ownership, time and money are saved by keeping actual item checks on delivered merchandise to a minimum. Spot checks on selectors and on store deliveries are often adequate to keep workers efficient. Trouble spots should receive full checks and audits. Also, check by item or weight all incoming merchandise delivered by vendor representatives.

All drivers should be on a schedule, and all deviations from the established timing, reported and explained in writing. A recording speedometer and clock record is necessary in order to keep drivers on schedule. All reports should be investigated and the disposition reported, through channels, to the driver. Auditing of driver performance helps keep records honest and accurate.

Dropping trailers saves the time of the driver and the tractor unit. Also, the store unloading schedule and delivery time need not match exactly and should result in less lost time.

Schedule Deliveries. The store manager should schedule all deliveries to the store, including those from the distribution center and direct shipments. Proper scheduling saves time and assures proper auditing of all deliveries. In addition, supplier relations will be better. An even work flow can be effected by assigning the proper number of employees.

Audit All "Paid-Outs." To avoid paying refunds out of store operating profit, specific procedures must be established and followed. To assure accuracy, audits must be made at frequent and irregular intervals. Included in paid-outs are: bottle refunds, coupon redemptions, cash register voids, trading stamps, merchandise refunds, etc.

Owning vs. Leasing. Review the owning versus leasing situation whenever interest rates change and tax laws are revised. The depreciation allowed by tax laws may be a deciding factor. Cheap borrowed capital and large depreciation allowances make owning profitable, while the reverse makes leasing advantageous.

Packaging. Whenever possible, automatic or semiautomatic equipment should be used to package merchandise. Central wrapping may be necessary when using automated equipment.

Communications. Communications are necessary only when the information is relevant and usable. A periodic review of the forms used and their distribution is essential.

The number of forms used in most companies is far in excess of needs. Too many copies are mailed and filed, taking needed space and valuable time. Many forms can be eliminated, but the information must still reach all parties concerned.

Paperwork. The use of data processing and other automatic equipment at the central office is cheaper than hand work at store level. Management should plan to do paper work at the most efficient point.

Maintenance. Preventive maintenance keeps equipment in service longer and reduces the cost of repairs. Shutdowns of temperature-control equipment increase costs resulting from damaged or unsalable merchandise, as well as the added labor cost involved in removing the item and replacing it with salable merchandise.

Cleanliness, as well as preventative maintenance on equipment, will reduce repair and replacement costs. A prepared checklist must be checked each day to ensure tighter control by supervisors.

Too many stores use a feather duster which merely shifts dust around. Dust should be removed with damp cloths.

Salvage Control. Compactors and tanks for waste disposal are two convenient devices, but both can consume materials that can be converted into money. All employees should know which items are to be salvaged and how it is done.

Frequently, it is easier for an employee trimming produce to drop the entire item into the disposal unit than to trim it. Similarly, in the meat department, it is easier to drop items in the bone or tallow barrel than to trim them completely. Paper, cardboard, and twine are all salvageable and can be returned to the distribution center on delivery trucks at little or no direct cost.

Control is exercised by comparing the values of the tallow, bones, paper, etc., credited to each store. Stores out-of-line with the established averages need checking. Store managers should know the average expected for their stores as a means of exercising control. The salvage of damaged merchandise in order to get the best return possible is a store manager's responsibility.

Waste Products. The alert supermarket manager devises ways and means to convert "waste" products into money. For example, a store manager converted suet into birdseed cake. By mixing one pound of birdseed with two pounds of fat, the selling price of each item separately was increased considerably. Be alert to other opportunities to convert "waste" into profit.

Sales Promotions. Signs, buttons, bag stuffers, and the proper coordination of all advertising is essential for a successful store. Especially important, but often overlooked, are the suggestions made to customers by personnel in the produce, meat or other departments, informing them of specials. The impression made by these employees will provide a more favorable image of the entire store.

Check Cashing. Make friends with people in the trading areas, especially newcomers, by issuing personalized check-cashing identification cards. These cards, sent to people with established, adequate financial ratings and inviting them to visit the supermarket and use the free check-cashing service, should attract many good customers. A control must be maintained on all checks that are presented to be cashed.

Promote Customer Benefits. Any changes made for greater customer service and satisfaction should be merchandised. That is, tell the customers about the change and explain the benefits. For example, after changing to heavier weight kraft bags, company advertisements should inform customers of the improvement.

Community Relations. A successful retail outlet must be a part of, and accepted by, the community. The store manager should become involved as a leader in community-relations programs. The support of all employees should be enlisted. Participation in community activities, through service clubs, boys' clubs, athletic programs, church groups, etc., is an important factor in creating a favorable store image and building sales. A scholarship program in the local high school creates a favorable image in the minds of future customers and builds future sales.

Services to groups, such as lending large coffee-makers for meetings, is a service appreciated by many groups. Helping to raise funds by offering store facilities and participation of employees creates a good-neighbor feeling. The increased goodwill generated by such programs should be reflected in sales. Be sure to promote these goodwill programs.

New Methods. Competitive pressures force each operator to continually search for more efficient methods. Not all the new methods available, however, are more efficient for all operators. A procedure must be evaluated in relation to each situation; the operator must decide the effectiveness of any procedure in terms of his or her own equipment, personnel, etc.

New ideas, methods, and procedures should be tested, evaluated, and instituted in stores where there is sufficient indication that greater efficiency is possible. Decisions to use or not to use them should be based on facts.

Advance Dating   Setting the date of delivery on a bill after the merchandise is delivered, thus permitting extra time to pay and discount payment. This is rarely done with food items sold to the chain or wholesaler and is more common with general merchandise items.

Air Curtain   A stream of air used as a barrier to prevent heat or cold loss to the surrounding area. Used over some refrigerated or freezer cases to keep in cold. Also used between some back rooms and dairy display cases that can be fed from behind the case.

Air Door   A stream of air at the entrance or exit to the store which serves as a barrier to help retain heat or cool air from diluting the desired temperature by mixing with the air outside the store. Not totally effective or as effective as a solid door, but does accomplish the feeling that there is no physical barrier to entering the store.

Anticipation   (of bills) Paying for merchandise in advance of the due date so that a discount can be taken in addition to whatever discount terms are normally given.

Appetizer Department   Usually called *deli* (q.v.) or *delicatessen*. Generally, the service version of such. Also called *appy*.

Appy   See *appetizer department; deli.*

Aseptic Packaging   Process for packaging perishable fluids, such as milk or fruit juices, which eliminates the need for refrigerating or freezing and creates a shelf life of six months to a year. When package is opened or punctured in any way, however, product must be treated like fresh milk, for example, and refrigerated. Process entails packaging "in a sea of the product" in sterile surroundings. The package is then sealed with an antibacterial product and is air and water tight. Also, such products are sometimes known as sterilized or sterile milk, juice, etc.

Back Order   Transferring an order from current to a future delivery by a manufacturer, chain or wholesale warehouse because the product is not in stock.

Back Room   Nonselling area of a store where merchandise is stored or prepared for placement onto the selling floor.

Backhaul   Method of moving merchandise from the manufacturer's depot to the chain or wholesaler warehouse using the wholesaler or chain's own trucks. On the "front" end of the haul, the truck is delivering to stores. Rather than return empty to the warehouse, it is more efficient for the truck to go to the manufacturer depot in that area and pick up goods bound for that warehouse; otherwise these goods would be shipped by another truck which would then return to the manufacturer's depot empty. Considerable saving of fuel and money is available through this system, and it can cut the price of groceries to the ultimate consumer.

Bag   Paper container. Known in some areas as a *sack*.

Bagger   Person at the checkstand who packs groceries into bags or boxes after the item has been scanned or rung up at the register. Many box stores have eliminated baggers and have customers do their own bagging. In some stores, baggers also carry orders out to vehicles of the shoppers. Some scanning operations are set up so that the checker pulls the item over the scanner and then deposits the item directly into the bag or box.

Bakeoff   An in-store operation that has a store employee place frozen and prepared bakery items into a store oven and finish the product. Such personnel also may ice cakes, etc. Thus, a semi-skilled person can prepare freshly baked goods for sale in the store. See also *scratch bakery*.

Big-Ticket Item   A higher than normally priced item for the supermarket. Thus, a wristwatch or five-pound package of steak or canned ham would be a big-ticket item. Most such items are meat department, general merchandise or HABA (qq.v.) merchandise.

Blister Pack   A package in which an item of merchandise is enveloped by a plastic sheath and attached to a piece of cardboard which generally describes the attached item. The process makes for easier display and storage and has the advantage of making small items less susceptible to theft.

Bloom   Originally a term used with meat which described the fresh, red look of fresh meat. The "bloom" disappears as the product ages. Today used also for vegetables and fruits to describe freshness and the look of freshness.

Bodega Small, generally family-run grocery store in a Spanish-speaking neighborhood.

Box Cartons in which merchandise is shipped. When emptied, is often used and even preferred by customers for packing grocery orders.

Box Boy, Box Girl Synonym for *bagger* or *carry-out boy, carry-out girl* (qq.v.).

Box Store Either a limited assortment or warehouse store in which the merchandise is offered to the customer in the original shipping container which is cut open. Most such stores do not provide bags for the customers, and the shipping containers (boxes) are provided for the customers to take their orders out of the store.

Boxed Beef System of cutting meat into primal cuts at the slaughterhouse so that waste bone and fat are not shipped to the store with the carcass. Also, such waste brings a higher price when created in a U.S.D.A. supervised plant, which most stores cannot afford. This system has replaced the carcass (q.v.) beef system almost totally, whether the boxing (placing the primal cuts in a carton) is done at the slaughterhouse or a company-owned, central cutting facility. Boxing is spreading to products other than beef.

Breaking (meat, beef or carcasses) Cutting carcasses of animals into primal cuts.

Broker Agent or sales force for a manufacturer or processor of food who acts for his client in dealing with the chain or wholesaler and stores in the brokerage territory. Never has physical possession of merchandise between the manufacturer and warehouse.

Bulk Produce Large quantity display of produce from which customer is permitted to select individual items and quantities desired from total supply of merchandise.

Carcass Sides or quarters of animals (most often beef) from which bones and fat must be eliminated and which must be "broken" into primal, subprimal and store cuts.

Carry-Out Taking packed order from checkout area after payment to the vehicle of the customer. A service provided by many retailers in Midwest, South, and Southwest more often than in other parts of the nation.

Carry-Out Boy, Carry-Out Girl Person who performs the carry-out service. See also *carry-out*.

Chain Firm that owns a group of stores. Often a firm that owns six or more stores. Some sources differentiate a chain from an independent by the number of stores owned; varying separation points are used, with the numbers ranging to eight, ten or twelve stores. Sales of the group often are used as the break point between an independent and a chain. When an independent owns more than one store and falls somewhere below the definition point for a chain in the particular definer's terminology, often that firm is referred to as an *independent chain*. Some purists consider this an anachronism, however.

Checker Cashier who rings up a purchase on a cash register, or scans the purchase, and takes payment from the customer.

Checkout To pay for and bag or box the purchase. (When used as a noun, generally the pay-bagging operation.)

Checkout Counter See *checkstand*.

Checkstand The table or platform where the cash register is located and where the purchase is paid for.

Cherry Picker Warehouse piece of equipment that helps select merchandise from elevated locations.

Cherry Picking Buying only specials, often loss leaders (q.v.), at the store.

COD Cash (or instrument of payment) on delivery of merchandise. Term of delivery of merchandise where credit is not sought or established and/or where the seller does not wish to extend credit terms.

Coffin Case Freezer box in which merchandise is top-loaded and removed. So-called because its general shape is long and thin and suggestive of the shape of a coffin.

Combination Store Originally a "wedding" of a complete supermarket and a full-line drug and sundries operation. Such stores originally contained 55,000 or more square feet. However, as variations were created, the definitions became more loose so that now any store that carries 30 percent or more of general merchandise and HABA(qq.v.), whether it has a pharmacy or not, can be called a combination store. The variations have brought its meaning to be almost synonymous with the term *superstore*. See also *superstore*.

Confined Label Brands of merchandise that are available only to retailers or wholesalers who subscribe to the group that controls the label.

Continuity Promotion of the sale of a series of related items over a long period of time, such as dishes, flatware, glassware, book sets and encyclopedia, record sets, etc. Usually, a specially priced first item and then a somewhat higher price for the ensuing items of the series, a different item being sold each week. The object of the promotion is to bring the customer into the store for a number of consecutive weeks in the hopes of making him or her a regular customer.

Controlled Label Brand of merchandise available only to a subscribing retailer or wholesaler in an area, but not an open, nationally branded item.

Convenience Store A grocery store that sells a limited number of high-demand items. The store is generally small, open long hours, priced higher than a supermarket, and often used as a convenience by the customer who does not want to spend the time and effort entailed in a trip to the supermarket. In recent years, such stores have shifted more and more of their operations to the sale of fast and prepared foods and gasoline and have cut down considerably on the grocery items carried.

Co-op A wholesale operation where the customers band together and jointly own the warehouse facility. Such an enterprise generally charges the normal wholesaler upcharge (q.v.), but periodically returns to the members in the form of rebates all surplus funds or increases in the members' equity in the co-op as it increases inventories or adds facilities. Synonym for *cooperative*.

Cooperative See *co-op*.

Cost-Justified Backhaul A backhaul arrangement where the allowance to the entity picking up the merchandise is the actual cost that the supplier would have to pay to make the delivery. See also *backhaul*.

Coupon A printed offer to supply an item or items of merchandise at some reduced price or even free. The offer can be made by the manufacturer (*manufacturer's coupon*, in which case an allowance for handling is made to the retailer for each coupon handled). It can also be a retailer-sponsored offer (*store* or *retailer coupon*). In either case, it is a promotional device to get the customer to try or continue the product or to get the customer into the store. In recent years, many retailers have been using a promotional device of doubling or even tripling the manufacturer's inducement price on the coupon.

Courtesy Counter That area of the store where a host of services for the customer are performed, i.e., accepting returned merchandise, accepting bottle returns, verifying or cashing checks, selling tobacco products and other high-ticket general merchandise which require personal handling, pilfer protection, etc.

Cut Carton Method of selling in which the original shipping container is opened and merchandise sold from the container rather than being placed onto shelves and gondolas and individually packed out.

Dairy Department Section of store responsible for milk, eggs, cheeses, refrigerated dough, butter, oleo, bacon and other packaged meats, and all such related products.

Dating Extra period of credit, determined by the date put on a bill other than the actual delivery date.

Dead Load A shipment on truck or rail in which merchandise is hand-stacked in the vehicle without unitized loading, using slip sheets or pallets to make loading or unloading faster and more efficient.

Deadheading Truck returning to the warehouse or going out on a trip without a load of merchandise.

Deli Actual merchandise or department. Smoked or prepared meats, salads, cheeses, specialty items, sandwiches, and often complete takeout meals can be purchased in the deli department. Depending on the region of the country and the ethnic composition of the clientele, a variety of specialty and prepared foods in bulk or by specific weight and number is sold here. Also called *delicatessen*.

Delicatessen See *deli*.

Demand Item Also known as *high-volume item*, is one of the universally desired items sold in the food store (e.g., milk, eggs, bread, sugar, potatoes, etc.).

Direct Store Delivery Items delivered to a store that bypass the normal warehouse because of freshness, bulk, or simply tradition. Such items include soda pop, many branded breads and packaged cakes, cookies, potato chips, milk and other dairy items.

Disappearance Difference between actual inventory and that which should be in stock.

Discount A price lower than normal. Allowance often offered a buyer for prompt payment, quantity buying, or some special reason.

Discount Supermarket Supermarket that sells merchandise at prices under conventional supermarket prices in the trading area.

Distribution Center See *warehouse*.

District Manager Chain supervisor who is in charge of a given region and is a liaison and supervisory link between headquarters and store.

Door Freezer Case A frozen foods case that has doors on its face. Such cases have become more popular with the advent of high energy costs. Many retailers feel, however, that such cases inhibit impulse sales.

Double Coupon Allowing double the face value for a manufacturer's coupon. See also *coupon*.

Dry Grocery Products handled in the grocery department, generally prepackaged in cans, bottles, jars, cartons, or bags.

Dump Display Merchandise offered in a mass, jumbled array for sale rather than neatly packed out.

ECR Electronic cash register.

EDP Electronic data processing.

EOM End of month. Generally, in regard to payment or discount terms.

ESOP Employee stock option program.

Expiration Date   Last date on which perishable merchandise may be sold.

Extra Dating   Additional time in which to pay bills.

Facings   Number of items of a product along the front of a gondola (e.g., three facings would have three items, five facings would have five items, etc.).

Fast Mover   Merchandise that sells rapidly. High-demand item. See also *demand item*.

Flip Board   Simple, hinged device that facilitates price marking the bottom layer of merchandise in the shipping carton.

FOB   Free on board. Generally followed by a location, indicating at which point the merchandise becomes the responsibility of the buyer from the standpoint of transportation, insurance, and possession.

Fore Quarters   Front quarters of carcass of meat.

Forklift Truck   Device used for lifting and moving pallets and palletized loads. With special attachments can also handle slip-sheeted loads.

Front End   That portion of store where merchandise is checked, paid for, and bagged or boxed.

Fronthaul   The beginning portion (in which store deliveries usually are made) of the trip which is concluded with a backhaul. See also *backhaul*.

General Merchandise   Nonfood items beyond those few that are generally considered grocery items (e.g., candles, matches, shoe polish and laces, clothespins and lines, etc.). Such merchandise can include everything from apparel through hardware items, stationery supplies, etc. Some firms include drugs and HABA items as part of general merchandise, while others break them out as a separate department.

Generated Label   See *secondary label*.

Generics   Products that do not carry a brand name on the package, but are identified only by the type of goods contained. Usually a very simple label, with acceptable, but lowest grade or quality of merchandise (although generally just as nutritious as better grades) and the lowest priced items in the category.

Gondola   Fixture containing shelves (usually adjustable) on which merchandise is placed for selling.

Grazing   The eating of products in the store by shoppers or employees without paying for them.

Grocery Item   Any merchandise sold in grocery department. See also *dry grocery*.

Gross Margin   Difference between cost and selling price.

HABA   Health and beauty aids.

Hanging Beef   System by which carcass beef was delivered to stores and entailed "breaking" carcasses into primal and store cuts in the store itself. Some hanging beef is still delivered to some central meat-cutting facilities, but rarely ever delivered to stores.

Hardware   (produce) Staple produce items, such as potatoes, onions, beets, and even apples and oranges.

High-Volume Item   See *demand item*.

High-Volume Store   Store that has large sales turnover. The actual dollar or tonnage figure for such a store would be determined by the type of store and its location. In some regions, a supermarket that does $150,000 a week is considered high-volume, whereas in some highly populated areas of the East, $300,000 a week might just about qualify. A high-volume convenience store might do $40,000 a week, and a high-volume limited-assortment store might do $100,000 a week. Again, area and local standards set the pace.

Hind Quarters   Rear quarters of a carcass.

Hollow Pallet   A pallet of merchandise that has one or more cases missing from the interior and loaded so that it looks as if it contains more merchandise than it actually does. Some warehouses weigh pallets randomly to check and try to stem this thievery.

House Brands   All private or confined labels (qq.v.).

Hypermarket   Large store containing several hundred thousand square feet and usually selling almost a full line of a department-store assortment of goods in addition to a supermarket variety of foods. Generally thought of as originating in France (*hypermarche*), but actually the French version is similar to stores that were already in operation in the United States.

Impulse Item   Merchandise that is the opposite of a demand item (q.v.). Generally, a high-profit item and which, because of location and display, the retailer hopes will be purchased even though it may not be on the shopping list.

In-and-Out   Generally fast-turnover, general-merchandise items that are stocked once and when sold are not repurchased. Often special deal items.

Independent   Retailer who owns one or more stores, but fewer than the number that would raise him to the chain category. See also *chain*.

Integrated Merchandising   Placing related merchandise together. Usually refers to placing general merchandise near related grocery items (e.g., coffee makers, filters, mugs, etc., near the coffee). See also *segregated merchandising*.

Item Pricing   Stamping or affixing the price of the item on each container of merchandise.

Leader   Item that will attract customers into store, often because of advertised price. Can also be a promotion with a similar aim.

Limited-Assortment Store Store that has a small number of items (generally no more than 1,000–1,200, although often limited to 400–800). Originally, such stores had only grocery items, but most stores have added various perishables.

Load-Limit Line Point beyond which no frozen foods should be put into a freezer case. Beyond that point the product will not be protected and will thaw. Also, stocking beyond the load-limit line lowers the efficiency of the rest of the freezer-case operation.

Loss Leader Item sold at a loss to attract customers to the store in hope that customers will buy other items. See also *leader*.

Lumper Independent contract loader or unloader who for a fee will help a driver unload a truck at a warehouse. (Obligation of driver is to deliver merchandise onto warehouse dock. Use of lumpers eliminates the need for more than just a driver on the transportation portion of the delivery.)

Ma & Pa Store See *mom & pop store*.

Manufacturer's Coupon Coupon issued by the manufacturer as an inducement to the consumer (usually by cents-off a regular price) to buy a product. Retailer is given a handling allowance plus the cents-off for handling the coupon. See also *coupon*.

Manufacturer's Representative Either directly employed salesperson or broker who represents a manufacturer to the chain or wholesaler.

Margin Difference between cost and selling price.

Markdown Reduction from original selling price.

Markup Amount added to cost to arrive at selling price.

Meat Beef, pork, lamb, and poultry sold in supermarket.

Meat Workroom Area in which butchers "break" primal cuts of meat into store cuts and perform other preparatory work to make meat products ready for sale.

MIS Management Information Services.

Modular Packaging System in which secondary packages are integrated so that all three dimensions are modules of a constant. Thus, all dimensions would have to be 1, 2, 4, 8, etc., or 1, ½, ¼, ⅛ of the base module. All packages, therefore, would interlock and make for a solid, unitized load on a pallet, thereby reducing damage to product in transit.

Mom & Pop Store Small grocery, generally operated by a family catering to neighborhood trade, extending credit. Also called *ma & pa store*.

Multideck Case Refrigerator or freezer that has as many as five shelf levels.

Out-of-Stocks Merchandise normally carried in a store or warehouse which is not at present in inventory, but which will be put back on sale when the product becomes available. Also called *outs; scratches* (q.v.); *shorts*.

Outs See *out-of-stocks; scratches*.

Overring Amount entered on the cash register which is in excess of the correct amount of the purchase.

Pack Date Date on which an item was packaged, canned, etc. Placed on package for reference or to indicate when item might lose freshness.

Pack Out To place merchandise on shelves of gondolas or in other display and/or selling areas.

Packer Label Label on merchandise that generally is not a national brand and not one of the private labels (q.v.) or house brands (q.v.) of the retailer. Most often a low-priced promotional product.

Pallet Platform, generally of wood (but also made of aluminum and, on occasion, of other material) on which merchandise is stacked to create a unitized load. See also *standard pallet*.

Pallet Exchange System for taking empty pallets as replacement for loaded ones which are left with merchandise.

Pallet Jack Device for lifting and moving pallets.

Perishables All food products that tend to deteriorate and spoil rapidly and generally need some artificial means, such as cold, to slow the deterioration of product.

Plan-o-Gram Layout for stocking merchandise on shelves or in cases, telling stock clerks just where and how much of each product to put on display.

POP Point-of-purchase. In supermarkets, generally the checkstand area.

POS Point-of-sale. In supermarkets, also generally the checkout area.

Prepackaging Putting merchandise into containers and other forms of packaging prior to offering for sale.

Prepricing Putting price onto item at warehouse or manufacturing plant. Rarely done for foods. Most common in general merchandise.

Price File The computer memory bank that matches the store prices to the Universal Product Code indication of what the product is. This is the key to making UPC and scanning work in the store. See also *UPC, scanner*.

Price Leader Item of merchandise so priced as to attract a customer into the store. See also *leader*.

Primal Cut Large portions of meat, running 20 to 40 pounds, which need final trimming and cutting to become store cuts, which will be offered for sale.

Private Label Brand of merchandise owned by the retailers and available only in that retailer's stores. Can be a wholesaler label available only in the stores of that wholesaler's customers. See also *confined label*.

Produce   Fruits and vegetables.

Pull Date   Date on package on which item should be removed from sale because of probable loss of freshness.

Push-Pull   Device for grabbing the lip of a slip sheet so that it can be pulled onto a forklift or slave pallet for moving or storing a slip-sheeted unitized load.

Quality Assurance Date   Last date of sale on which the manufacturer will assure freshness and quality of merchandise.

Quality Control Circles   System of involving employees in decision making on operational and other efforts of firm.

Quarters of Beef   One of four approximately equal portions of the carcass (q.v.). One of either two hind or fore quarters (qq.v.).

Retail Cut   See *store cut.*

Retailer Coupon   See *store coupon.*

Retort Pouch   Layered, laminated, aluminum-plastic package that is air- and watertight and will preserve perishable items as long as a can without the need for refrigeration or freezing.

ROG   Receipt of goods. Date from which credit terms begin, if so specified.

Sack   See *bag.*

Scanner   Device using laser beam which reads a code and transmits a signal which when identified by a programmed computer will call up price and description of item for checking out goods by electronic cash register.

Scratch Bakery   Bakery in store which mixes and prepares all products from raw ingredients, and then bakes and otherwise prepares them for sale.

Scratches   Undeliverable portions of store orders at the warehouse levels. Generally placed on back order, unless otherwise instructed. See also *out-of-stocks.*

Secondary Label   Also known as *generated label.* Generally a low-end house brand used by many firms as an alternative to generic labels. See also *generics.*

Segregated Merchandising   Confining general merchandise to a separate section of the store rather than putting such items near related food items. See also *integrated merchandising.*

Self-Service Department   Area where customer serves self with prepackaged items such as in deli or bakery. As opposed to *service departments,* where orders are filled on request.

Service Deli   Delicatessen where orders are filled on request rather than having merchandise prepacked.

Service Rate   The percentage of an order filled by the warehouse. Consists of the order minus the scratches. If a warehouse scratches 5 percent of the order (cannot fill 5 percent because of out-of-stocks) it has a 95 percent service rate.

Shelf Diagram   Plan for how many facings and how much of any item to place on shelves and where. See also *facings.*

Shelf Life   The length of time that a product can be held without deteriorating.

Shelf Talker   Small sign placed on the lip of a shelf, generally sticking out into the aisle, used to attract attention to the item alongside which it is placed.

Shorts   See *scratches; out-of-stocks.*

Shrink   Difference between what should be in inventory and what actually is. Some of this is accounted for by waste, breakage, spoilage, theft, grazing (q.v.), etc.

Sides   (of beef) Half a carcass.

Slave Pallet   Pallet or sheet of plywood onto which a slip-sheeted load or a smaller pallet is put for uniform storage. If slave pallet is smaller than pallet it replaces, it must be hand loaded.

Slip Sheet   Cardboard base for load of product which replaces pallets and acts as base for unitized load.

Slot   Space in a warehouse where a unitized quantity of merchandise is stored.

Slotting   Determining where merchandise being put into or taken out of stock should be placed or taken from.

Slow Mover   Merchandise that does not turn over as rapidly as average.

Special   Lower than normal price for an item used to attract customers.

Spot Terms   Requiring payment before delivery of merchandise.

Standard Pallet   By agreement, 48 inch × 40 inch platform for storing goods and unitizing load.

Sterile Milk, Sterilized Milk   Aseptically packaged fluid that does not require refrigeration until the package is opened. Also *sterile juice, sterilized juice.*

Stock Boy, Stock Girl   Person who packs out merchandise.

Stock Turn   See *turns.*

Stockout   Merchandise missing from the shelves or selling area of a store.

Store Coupon   Coupon for cents-off or free item issued by a retailer. Also called *retailer coupon.* See also *coupon.*

Store Cut   Meat ready for display and sale at the store level. Also called *retail cut.*

Subprimal Cut   Cut of meat smaller than a primal cut. See also *primal cut.*

Supermarket   Place where groceries are sold. Generally, one that does a volume of $2 million or more a year, has all basic departments, and has 7,000 square feet or more of selling space. Given these criteria, a store falling short for any one item will still be considered a supermarket.

Superstore Large supermarket that generally handles large amount of general merchandise. At one time, criteria called for a minimum of 55,000 square feet. However, stores of 35,000 square feet and up can still be superstores, depending on volume and how much general merchandise is carried. See also *supermarket.*

Tape Generally refers to cash-register paper on which an itemized account of the checked-out order is made and totaled.

Throughput Combined shipping and receiving at warehouse. Total volume handled at checkstand. Generally, total volume handled in an operation in a single shift or day (even figured monthly or annually in some cases).

Top-Loading Placing paper and other lightweight items on top of the pallets in a truck to make use of otherwise empty space.

Trimming Removing excess vegetation, fat, or bones from meat, lettuce, etc.

Triple Coupon Allowing shopper three times the face value of a manufacturer's cents-off coupon. See also *coupon; manufacturer's coupon.*

Tugger Tractor for hauling pallets or carts through a warehouse as they are being loaded by order selectors.

Turns Number of times a product is completely turned over in a store or warehouse. Theoretically, this would mean the average amount of a product that would have to be completely sold to make one turn. A well-run warehouse should never be out of stock on any item, and a turn is just a mathematical measuring tool.

Underring Amount entered on the cash register

which is less than the correct amount of the purchase.

Unit Price Price per measure—ounces, pounds, gallons, quarts, units. Since many items come in fractions of a unit, this permits the shopper to know the cost for each unit for comparison purposes.

Unitized Load Full amount on a pallet or slip sheet. Often held together by a film overwrap, banding of some sort, or in some way held together to keep the integrity of that quantity through normal shipping hazards.

Universal Price Code See *UPC.*

UPC Universal Price Code. Bar symbols for identifying item and price by a scanner. See also *scanner.*

Upcharge Amount, usually a percentage, added to the price of goods by a wholesaler to pay his fee for storage, shipping, etc.

Upright Case Refrigerated or freezer case that has a number of shelves and is considerably taller than coffin (q.v.) or reach-in cases.

Volume Synonym for sales.

Voluntary Group of independent supermarkets carrying a common banner (or name) sponsored by a regular wholesaler.

Warehouse Place where merchandise for a supermarket is stored and assembled for the supermarket orders.

Warehouse Store Supermarket that generally sells a reduced number of items at discounted prices. Eliminates many of the normal services and labors performed by the conventional supermarket in order to reduce costs and, thus, the prices charged.

Waste That portion of produce or meat that must be discarded because it is unsalable (e.g., some fat, bones, excess vegetation, spoilage).

Wrapper Meat department person who weighs, packages, and wraps the cut meat for placement into the selling cases.

SELECTED BIBLIOGRAPHY

BOOKS

Albanese, Robert. *Managing Toward Accountability for Performance*. Homewood, Ill.: Richard D. Irwin Inc., 1978.

Applebaum, William. *Guide to Store Locations Research: With Emphasis on Supermarkets*. Reading, Mass.: Addison-Wesley Publishing Co., Inc., 1968.

Baer, Walter E. *Operating Managers' Labor Relations*. Dubuque, Iowa: Kendall/Hunt Publishing Co., 1977.

Baker, Stephen. *Systematic Approach to Advertising Creativity*. New York: McGraw-Hill Inc., 1979.

Batten, J.D. *Beyond Management by Objectives*. New York: American Management Association, 1980.

Beckman, Theodore N. and Herman C. Nolan. *Chain Store Problems: A Critical Analysis*. New York: Arno Press Inc., 1976.

Belden, Donald L. *The Role of the Buyer in Mass Merchandising*. New York: Lebhar-Friedman Books, 1971.

Bell, J.N. *Merchants and Merchandise*. New York: St. Martin's Press Inc., 1977.

Berliner, William M. *Managerial and Supervisory Practice*. Homewood, Ill.: Richard D. Irwin Inc., 1979.

Bohlinger, Maryanne S. *Merchandise Buying Principles and Applications*. Dubuque, Iowa: Wm. C. Brown Co., Publishers, 1977.

Bolen, William H. *Contemporary Retailing*. Englewood Cliffs, N.J.: Prentice-Hall, Inc., 1978.

Borden, Jr., Neil H. *Acceptance of New Food Products by Supermarkets*. New York: Fairchild Publications, 1969.

Britt, Stewart H. *Psychological Principles of Marketing and Consumer Behavior*. Lexington, Mass.: Lexington Books, 1978.

Burack, Elmer. *Personnel Management: A Human Resource Systems Approach*. St. Paul, Minn.: West Publishing Co., 1977.

Burke, John D. *Advertising in the Marketplace*. New York: McGraw-Hill Inc., 1973.

Buskirk, Richard H. *Business and Administrative Policy*. New York: John Wiley & Sons, Inc., 1977.

Buskirk, Richard H. *Handbook of Managerial Tactics*. Boston: CBI Publishing Co., Inc., 1976.

Caples, John. *Tested Advertising Methods*. Englewood Cliffs, N.J.: Prentice-Hall, Inc., 1974.

Caplow, Theodore. *How to Run Any Organization*. New York: Holt, Rinehart & Winston, 1976.

Chambers, Raymond L. *The Buyer's Handbook: Guide to Defensive Shopping*. Englewood Cliffs, N.J.: Prentice-Hall, Inc., 1976.

Comer, James M. *Sales Management*. Santa Monica, Calif.: Goodyear Publishing Co., Inc., 1977.

Creasy, Donna N. *Food Careers*. Englewood Cliffs, N.J.: Prentice-Hall, Inc., 1977 (Home Economics Careers Series).

Cross, Jennifer. *The Supermarket Trap—The Consumer and the Food Industry*. Bloomington: Indiana University Press, 1976.

Cushman, Ronald A. and Willard R. Daggett. *Supermarket Merchandising*. New York: Fairchild Publications, 1976 (Co-operative Education Workbook Series).

Darrah, L.B. *Food Marketing*. New York: John Wiley & Sons, Inc., 1971.

Davidson, W.R., et al. *Retailing Management*. New York: John Wiley & Sons, Inc., 1975.

Davis, Keith. *The Dynamics of Organizational Behavior*. New York: McGraw-Hill Inc., 1977.

Daykin, Leonard, editor. *Outstanding New Supermarkets*. New York: Progressive Grocer, 1969.

DeLozier, M. Wayne. *The Marketing Communications Process*. New York: McGraw-Hill Inc., 1976.

Dirksen, Charles J. and Arthur Kroeger. *Advertising Principles and Problems*. Homewood, Ill.: Richard D. Irwin, Inc., 1977.

Duckham, A.N. *Food Production and Consumption*. New York: American Elsevier Publishers, 1977.

Edison, Judith and Kenneth Mills. *Checker-Cashier.* Cincinnati: South-Western Publishing Co., 1969 (Distributive Education Series).

Engel, James F. *Promotional Strategy.* Homewood, Ill.: Richard D. Irwin, Inc., 1977.

Food and Beverage Industries: A Bibliography and Guidebook. Detroit: Gale Research Co., 1970 (Management Information Guide Series).

Food Care and Food Storage. Boston: CBI Publishing Co., Inc., 1974 (Foodservice Career Education Series).

Fulmer, Robert M. *Management and Organization.* New York: Harper & Row, Publishers, Inc., 1980.

Gentile, Richard J. *Retail Advertising: A Management Approach.* New York: Lebhar-Friedman Books, 1976.

Gentile, Richard J. and Anne Gentile. *Retailing Strategy.* New York: Lebhar-Friedman Books, 1978.

Gillespie, Karen and Joseph Hecht. *Retail Business Management.* New York: McGraw-Hill Inc., 1977.

Goldbeck, Nikki and David Goldbeck. *The Supermarket Handbook.* New York: New American Library, 1976.

Grocery Retailing in the Eighties. New York: Progressive Grocer, 1980.

Guirdham, M. *Marketing: The Management of Distribution Channels.* Elmsford, N.Y.: Pergamon Press, Inc., 1972.

Halsey, George. *Policy Making.* New York: Harper & Row, Publishers, Inc., 1976.

Harrell, Gilbert D., et al. *Universal Product Code: Price Removal and Consumer Behavior in Supermarkets.* East Lansing: Michigan State University, Graduate School of Business Administration, 1976.

Harwell, Edward M. *Personnel Management and Training.* New York: Lebhar-Friedman Books, 1969.

Hass, Harold M. *Social and Economic Aspects of the Chain Store Movement.* New York: Arno Press Inc., 1979 (Small Business Enterprise in America Series).

Hayward, George S. and Glen York. *Food Store Distributor: A Retail Sales Guide.* New York: Lebhar-Friedman Books, 1977.

Hicks, Herbert G. *Business: An Involvement Approach.* New York: McGraw-Hill Inc., 1976.

Hightower, Jim. *Eat Your Heart Out: How Food Profiteers Victimize the Consumer.* New York: Random House, Inc., 1976.

Hirshleifer, Jack. *Price Theory and Applications.* Englewood Cliffs, N.J.: Prentice-Hall, Inc., 1980.

Ignizio, James P., et al. *Operations Research in Decision Making.* New York: Crane, Russak & Co., Inc., 1975.

Jugenheimer, Donald W. and Gordon White. *Basic Advertising.* Columbus, Ohio: Grid Inc., 1980.

Kane, Bernard J. *A Systematic Guide to Supermarket Location Analysis.* New York: Fairchild Publications, 1967.

Kerby, J.K. *Consumer Behavior: Conceptual Foundations.* New York: Technical Publishing, 1975.

Keyes, Ruth A. and Ronald A. Cushman. *Essentials of Retailing.* New York: Fairchild Publications, 1977.

Lage, G. *Price System and Resource Allocation: A Book of Problems.* New York: Holt, Rinehart & Winston, Inc., 1976.

Laine, Steven and Iris Laine. *Promotion in Food Service.* New York: McGraw-Hill Inc., 1972.

Leed, Theodore W. and Gene A. German. *Food Merchandising: Principles and Practices.* New York: Lebhar-Friedman Books, 1979.

Lerner, Mark. *Careers in a Supermarket.* Minneapolis: Lerner Publications Co., 1977 (Early Career Book Series).

Lion, Edgar. *Shopping Centers.* New York: John Wiley & Sons, Inc., 1976.

Luck, David J. *Marketing Research.* Englewood Cliffs, N.J.: Prentice-Hall, Inc., 1978.

Lynch, R.L. and Richard L. Lunch, editors. *Food Marketing.* New York: McGraw-Hill Inc., 1979 (Career Competencies in Marketing Series).

Macmillan, N. *The New Marketing.* Englewood Cliffs, N.J.: Prentice-Hall, Inc., 1976.

Malickson, David and John Nasar. *Advertising: How to Write the Kind that Works.* New York: Charles Scribner's Sons, 1977.

Mallowe, Jr., Charles A. and Daniel J. McLaughlin. *Food Marketing and Distribution: Selected Readings.* New York: Lebhar-Friedman Books, 1971.

Mansfield, Edwin, editor. *Managerial Economics and Operations Research.* New York: W.W. Norton & Co., Inc., 1980.

Marion, Bruce W., et al. *The Food Retailing Industry: Market Structure, Profits and Prices.* New York: Praeger Publishers, 1979.

Massie, Joseph L. and John Douglas. *Managing: A Contemporary Introduction.* Englewood Cliffs, N.J.: Prentice-Hall, Inc., 1977.

Maude, B. *Communications at Work.* Brooklyn: Beekman Publishers, Inc., 1977.

McGabe, Bernard and John P. Marchak, editors. *Supermarket Cashier*. St. Paul, Minn.: Changing Times Education Service, 1976.

Melcher, Arlyn J. *Structure and Process of Organization: A Systems Approach*. Englewood Cliffs, N.J.: Prentice-Hall, Inc., 1976.

Mitchell, Joan. *Price Determination and Price Policy*. Winchester, Mass.: Allen & Unwin, Inc., 1977 (Economics and Society Series).

Monsen, Joseph. *Business and Changing Environment*. New York: McGraw-Hill Inc., 1976.

Montgomery, Douglas and Lynwood A. Johnson. *Forecasting and Time Series Analysis*. New York: McGraw-Hill Inc., 1976.

Newman, Bernard H. and Mary E. Oliverio. *Business Communications: A Managerial Approach*. New York: Monongahela Publishing Co., Inc., 1976.

Oats, James F. *Business and Social Change: Looks to the Future*. New York: McGraw-Hill Inc., 1978.

Oxenfeldt, Alfred R. *Pricing Strategies*. New York: American Management Association, Inc., 1975.

Peak, Hugh S. and Ellen Peak. *Supermarket Merchandising and Management*. Englewood Cliffs, N.J.: Prentice-Hall, Inc., 1977.

Pintel, Gerald and Jay Diamond. *Retailing*. Englewood Cliffs, N.J.: Prentice-Hall, Inc., 1977.

Reeser, Clayton and Marvin Loper. *The Key to Organizational Effectiveness*. Glenview, Ill.: Scott, Foresman & Company, 1978.

Reichard, Robert S. *Practical Techniques of Sales Forecasting*. New York: McGraw-Hill Inc., 1976.

Richey, Jim. *Supermarket Language: A Survival Vocabulary*. Hayward, Calif.: Janus Book Publishers, 1978.

Rishoi, Don C. *Food Store Sanitation*. New York: Lebhar-Friedman Books, 1976.

Robin, Donald. *Marketing*. New York: Harper & Row, Publishers, Inc., 1978.

Roman, Kenneth and Jane Maas. *How to Advertise*. New York: St. Martin's Press, 1977.

Rosenberg, Robert and William G. Ott. *Business and the Law*. New York: McGraw-Hill Inc., 1976.

Roy, Robert H. *The Cultures of Management*. Baltimore: Johns Hopkins University Press, 1977.

Rue, Leslie W. and Lloyd L. Byars. *Management Theory and Application*. Homewood, Ill.: Richard D. Irwin, Inc., 1977.

Sandage, Charles H. *Advertising Theory and Practice*. Homewood, Ill.: Richard D. Irwin, Inc., 1979.

Sanford, Aubrey. *Communication Behavior in Organizations*. Columbus, Ohio: Charles E. Merrill Publishing Co., 1976.

Schaleben-Lewis, Joy. *Careers in a Supermarket*. Milwaukee: Raintree Publications, Inc., 1977.

Schewe, Charles D. and Reuben Smith. *Marketing Concepts and Applications*. New York: McGraw-Hill Inc., 1980.

Schwarz, Ted. *The Successful Promoter*. Chicago: H. Regnery Co., 1976.

Seltz, David. *Food Service Marketing and Promotion*. New York: Lebhar-Friedman Books, 1977.

Shaffer, Harold and Herbert Greenwald. *Independent Retailing*. Englewood Cliffs, N.J.: Prentice-Hall, Inc., 1976.

Shapiro, Steven L. *Supervision: An Introduction to Business Management*. New York: Fairchild Publications, 1978.

Simmons, James. *The Changing Pattern of Retail Locations*. Chicago: University of Chicago Press, 1977.

SN Distribution Study of Grocery Store Sales. New York: Fairchild Publications (published annually).

Stanley, Richard E. *Promotion: Advertising, Publicity, Personal Selling, Sales Promotion*. Englewood Cliffs, N.J.: Prentice-Hall, Inc., 1977.

Stanton, William J. *Fundamentals of Marketing*. New York: McGraw-Hill Inc., 1978.

Staudt, Thomas A. *A Managerial Introduction to Marketing*. Englewood Cliffs, N.J.: Prentice-Hall, Inc., 1976.

Stern, Lewis W. and Adel I. El-Ansary. *Marketing Channels*. Englewood Cliffs, N.J.: Prentice-Hall, Inc., 1977.

Supermarkets: Fifty Years of Progress. New York: Progressive Grocer, n.d.

Tarzian, Lucy, editor. *Progressive Grocers Marketing Guidebook*. New York: Progressive Grocer (published annually).

Taylor, R.J. *Food Additives*. New York: John Wiley & Sons, Inc., 1980 (Institution of Environmental Sciences Series).

Uris, Auren. *The Executive Deskbook*. New York: Van Nostrand Reinhold Co., 1976.

U.S. National Commission on Food Marketing. *Food from Farmer to Consumer*. New York: Arno Press, 1976 (reprint of 1966 edition).

Uyterhoeven, Hugo E.R., Robert W. Ackerman and John W. Rosenblum. *Strategy and Organization*. Homewood, Ill.: Richard D. Irwin, Inc., 1977.

Vernon, Jr., Ivan and Charles Lamb. *Pricing Functions: A Pragmatic Approach.* Lexington, Mass.: Lexington Books, 1976.

Wagner, Raynor. *A Survey of Business Conservation of Building of Neighborhoods.* Easton, Pa.: Hive Publishing Co., 1978.

Walker, John E. *Public Relations: A Team Effort.* Midland, Mich.: Pendell Publishing Company, 1976.

Weber, John A. *Growth Opportunity Analysis.* Reston, Va.: Reston Publishing Co., 1976.

Wells, Walter. *Communication in Business.* Belmont, Calif.: Wadsworth Publishing Co., 1977.

Wingate, John Williams. *Retail Merchandise Management.* Englewood Cliffs, N.J.: Prentice-Hall, Inc., 1980.

PERIODICALS

Abaganale, F. "Tips for Cancelling Your Bad Check Losses." *Progressive Grocer,* June 1980.

Aders, Robert O. and Roger L. Jenkins. "Outlook for the Retail Food Industry." *Survey of Business,* Summer 1980.

Applebaum, William, "Can Store Location Be a Science?" *Economic Geography,* July 1975.

Arthur, D. "Guidelines for Effective Delegation." *Supermarket Management,* October 1979.

"At Last, Front-End Technology Comes of Age." *Chain Store Age Executive,* August 1979.

Azzarone, Stephanie. "Here Are Six Ways to Hike Dairy Biz 10–15%." *Supermarketing,* July 1976.

Azzarone, Stephanie. "Warehouse or Wholesaler—Food Chains Disagree on Best Distribution System." *Supermarketing,* February 1977.

Balding, L.A. "Beating the Bushes for New Store Locations." *Stores,* October 1980.

Bartz, D. "Six Direct Vendor Delivery Guidelines, Tighten Store Security, Prevent Lost Profits." *Supermarketing,* January 1979.

Bloom, Derek. "The Renaissance of Retail Auditing." *Journal of Advertising Research,* June 1980.

Burck, Charles G. "Plain Labels Challenge the Supermarket Establishment." *Fortune,* March 26, 1979.

Burkhooder, R. C. and L. M. Kinomoto. "How to Decide Who Needs What Kind of Training." *Supervision,* Spring 1979.

"Cashiers Get 'in the Swim' with Slot Scanners." *Computerworld,* April 23, 1979.

"Chains' New Sanitation Push." *Chain Store Age Executive,* July 1977.

"Chains Struggle with Government." *Chain Store Age Executive,* October 1976.

"Changing Consumer Lifestyles Hike Publications Sales." *Supermarketing,* March 1979.

Cooper, Ann. "Packaging—The Shape of Things to Come." *Marketing* (London), March 1980.

"Cosmetics: A Star Is Born." *Progressive Grocer,* August 1979.

Covell, R. "What Motivates Shoppers to Buy Meat in Your Stores?" *Supermarketing,* December 1976.

Dietrich, R. D. "Woo the Working Woman or She'll Leave You." *Progressive Grocer,* November 1977.

Dumas, L.S. "Demand for Microwave-Ovenable Goods Heating Up: Should Supermarkets Revamp Merchandising Program?" *Supermarketing,* May 1978.

Dyer, L.W. "Frozen Product Movement." *Quick Frozen Foods,* May 1978.

Dyer, L.W. "There's No Place Like a Supermarket for Holiday Merchandising Ideas." *Progressive Grocer,* October 1979.

Dyer, L.W. "Tool Up for More Effective Merchandising." *Progressive Grocer,* January 1979.

Dyer, L.W. "Twenty-one Smart Ideas to Boost Back-to-School Sales." *Progressive Grocer,* August 1979.

"Equipment Manufacturers." *Progressive Grocer,* December 1979.

Farrant, A. W. "Absenteeism, How to Lower It." *Supervision,* Spring 1978.

Farrell, Jack W. "Better Equipment Utilization: Key to Supermarket Service." *Traffic Management,* November 1978.

Fensholt, Carol. "Consumer Affairs Breaking New Ground." *Supermarketing,* April 1978.

Fensholt, Carol. "How Do Employees Steal? Ex-thief Knows 450 Ways." *Supermarket Business,* July 1980.

Fensholt, Carol. "Supermarkets' New Complexity Makes Formal Training Vital." *Supermarketing,* July 1979.

Fensholt, Carol. "Wholesalers Mount New Productivity Programs." *Supermarketing,* October 1978.

Ferguson, Jr., Carl E., J. Barry Mason, and J.B. Wilkinson. "Estimating Consumer Losses from Unavailable Advertised Grocery Specials." *Journal of Consumer Affairs,* Winter 1979.

"Fifteen-Hour Day in the Life of a Field Man." *Progressive Grocer,* Spring 1978.

Forrester, J. "Good Design Is Key Factor to Food Prep Room Sanitation." *Supermarket Business,* December 1979.

"Frozen Product Movement." *Quick Frozen Foods,* May 1978.

"Frozens: New Life from Changing Lifestyles." *Progressive Grocer,* November 1978.

Gage, Theodore J. "Carting the Supermarket into the '80's." *Advertising Age,* April 21, 1980.

"General Merchandise '81." *Supermarket News,* Section 2, January 12, 1981.

Golding, M. S. "Walking the Supervisory Tightrope between Management and Labor." *Supermarket Management,* December 1979.

Goodrich, Jonathan N. and Jo Ann Hoffman. "Warehouse Retailing: The Trend of the Future?" *Business Horizons,* April 1979.

Grimes, A. "Dairy Department Management Still a Problem: Needed Training, Proper Space/Profit Allocation." *Supermarketing,* January 1979.

"The Growth Years 1952–1977." *Supermarket News,* Section 2, October 24, 1977.

Harris, Brian F. and Michael K. Mills. "The Impact of Item Price Removal on Grocery Shopping Behavior." *Journal of Retailing,* Winter 1980.

Harris, C. "Consumers Want Guidance, Openness and They Switch Stores to Get It." *Supermarket Business,* Fall 1980.

Haynes, Joel B. and Clifford J. Elliott. "Supermarket Selection Criteria: A Comparison of Managers and Customers." *Baylor Business Studies,* May/June/July 1980.

Helm, D.F. and S. M. Wood. "Cosmetics Try New Setting." *Advertising Age,* February 1979.

Herring, James P. "Management Today—A Retailer's View." *Michigan Business Review,* March 1979.

Hough, L. J. "Are Grocery Promotions Loved or Hated?" *Advertising Age,* April 1978.

"How to Evaluate Downtown Development." *Stores,* February 1980.

"How to Turn P-O-P into Sales Dollars." *Progressive Grocer,* June 1977.

Howard, Grover A. "Future Shock in the Supermarket—A Guide to the Process of Technological Modernization." *The Futurist,* June 1975.

Howe, W. C. "People-Planning." *Supervision,* December 1977.

Hutt, Michael D. "The Retail Buying Committee: A Look at Cohesiveness and Leadership." *Journal of Retailing,* Winter 1979.

Jordan, R. B. "Planning, Organizing and Conducting the Annual Physical Inventory." *Management Accounting,* August 1977.

Krueger A. and B. P. Smith. "Eighty Promo Ideas Help Launch '80 with Sales Bang." *Supermarket Business,* December 1979.

Langrehr, Frederick W. and Richard K. Robinson. "Shoppers' Reactions to Supermarket Price Scanning and Shopper Price Marking." *Journal of Consumer Affairs,* Winter 1979.

Linsen, M. A. "Bagging Basics: Send Her Home Happy." *Progressive Grocer,* May 1978.

Linsen, M. A. "How to Conduct Successful and Lawful Job Interviews." *Progressive Grocer,* June 1979.

"Lively Arts of Advertising and Promotion." *Progressive Grocer,* September 1978.

Lynch, Clifford F. "A Market-Oriented Perspective on Physical Distribution." *Survey of Business,* Spring 1980.

Machiaverna, A. "Here's How Five Chains Approach Meat Training." *Supermarketing,* December 1977.

"Manufacturer Relations—Wanted Merchandising & Promotional Help." *Progressive Grocer,* April 1980.

"Market Profiles '80." *Supermarket News,* Section 2, August 18, 1980.

Martin, S. "Is the Supermarket Outmoded?" *Quick Frozen Foods,* March 1979.

Martin, S. "Retail or Food Service? A Balancing Act." *Quick Frozen Foods,* May 1980.

Marton, E. F. "Undercover Team Can Cut Internal Theft." *Supermarket Business,* March 1980.

Mason, J. Barry and Morris L. Mayer. "Retail Merchandise Information Systems for the 1980's." *Journal of Retailing,* Spring 1980.

Milford, W. J. "Developing New Supervisory Techniques." *Supervision,* August 1977.

Miller, R. L. "What the Supervisor Should Know about Handling Employee Complaints." *Supermarket Management,* February 1978.

"Money Management Moves to Retail Forefront." *Chain Store Age Executive,* February 1980.

Mottus, Allan G. "Tight Economy Leaves No Place for Clones." *Product Marketing,* April 1979.

Murphy, P. E. "Effect of Social Class on Brand and Price Consciousness for Supermarket Products." *Retailing,* Summer 1978.

"No-Frills Food: New Power for the Supermarkets." *Business Week,* March 23, 1981.

"Non-Foods."*Progressive Grocer*, April 1980.

"Nonfoods Are Breaking New Ground Slowly." *Progressive Grocer*, September 1980.

"Non-Foods Get More Attention." *Chain Store Age*, September 1978.

O'Neill, R. E. "Cheese/Deli Report: Satisfying that Craving for Profit."*Progressive Grocer*, June 1979.

O'Neill, R. E. "Closeup Look on How Individual Brands Perform in Sales and Profits." *Progressive Grocer*," October 1976.

O'Neill, R. E. "Is the Meat Department Slipping?" *Progressive Grocer*, March 1980.

Pagliaro, J. L. "Specific Price Strategy Is Vital on Today's Marketing Battlefield." *Supermarket Business*, August 1980.

Partch, K. "Warehouse Stores Challenge Supermarkets." *Advertising Age*, October 30, 1978.

"Putting Energy into Energy Management." *Chain Store Age Executive*, August 1980.

Radler, L. "Mayfair's Dairy Philosophy: Quality Eggs, Yogurt Section Draw Shoppers but Backbone Is Attention to Merchandise Basis." *Supermarket Business*, August 1980.

Rauch, H. S. "What Is Computerism Doing to Buyer/Salesman Relationship?" *Supermarketing*, June 1979.

"Retailers Find Ways Other Than Technology to Cope with Shoplifting and Employee Theft." *Merchandising*, July 1980.

"Retailers Value Service Merchandiser Skill, but Worry About Loss of Department Control." *Supermarket Business*, December 1979.

"Retailing Guide to Purchase Order Management." *CPA Journal*, April 1980.

Riesz, P. C. "Price Quality Correlations for Packaged Food Products." *Consumer Affairs*, Winter 1979.

"Scanning Systems to the Forefront." *Chain Store Age Executive*, August 1980.

"Seeking Sanitation Gains." *Chain Store Age Executive*, November 1977.

Selitzer, R. "Cooperation with Suppliers Saves 20% in Costs." *Supermarketing*, May 1978.

Shulman, Richard E. "Determining Warehouse Space, Evaluating Manufacturer Deals Are Functions to be Handled by In-House Computers." *Supermarketing*, January 1978.

"Sixth Sense for Site Selection." *Progressive Grocer*, September 1980.

Snyder, G. H. "Frozen Foods: Facing up to the '80's." *Progressive Grocer*, November 1979.

Snyder, G. H. "General Merchandise: Can Its Sales Share Double in the '80's?" *Progressive Grocer*, January 1980.

Snyder, G. H. "General Merchandise: Fifteen Do's and Don't's for Coping with Promotional Leftovers." *Progressive Grocer*, March 1978.

Snyder, G. H. "Irresistible Force Rolls On: General Merchandise." *Progressive Grocer*, January 1979.

Snyder, G. H. "Selling at the Checkout Adapts to Age of the Scanner." *Progressive Grocer*," March 1979.

"Speeding Supermarket Checkout." *Data Processor*, September 1978.

"Spotlight on Frozen Foods." *Supermarketing*, May 1977.

Stanley, Thomas J. and Murphy A. Sewall. "Predicting Supermarket Trade: Implications for Marketing Management." *Journal of Retailing*, Summer 1978.

"Store Formats in the 1980's: A Study of Innovations and Productivity." *Supermarket News*, Section 2, October 20, 1980.

"Store Location Research—A Survey by Retailing Chains." *Journal of Retailing*, May 1974.

"Supermarket Frozen Foods Departments Continue to Grow." *Quick Frozen Foods*, November 1978.

"Supermarket Scanners Take Hold." *Business Week*, April 23, 1979.

"Supermarketing Spotlight on Dairy," *Supermarketing*, August 1978.

"Supermarkets and Wholesalers." *Forbes*, January 8, 1979.

"Supermarkets in the 1980's." *Supermarket News*, Section 2, October 15, 1979.

"Supermarkets Seeking New Items to Buck Restaurants." *Advertising Age*, November 22, 1976.

Tomlinson, Wayne E. "Strip-Style Shopping Centers: Problems and Opportunities." *Journal of Property Management*, November/December 1979.

"Trying to Get the Jump on Theft." *Chain Store Age Executive*, August 1980.

Vinson, W. D. and D. F. Heang. "Is Quality Out of Control?" *Harvard Business Review*, November 1977.

Wallace, M. J. "Toiletries Carve a Food Store Niche." *Advertising Age*, February 1979.

Walzer, E.B. "Independents Thrive with Wholesaler Help." *Progressive Grocer*, September 1978.

Walzer, E. B. "Selected by Nationwide Poll: 141 Outstanding Independents." *Progressive Grocer*, March 1980.

Ward, Paul J. "A Supermarket Where 'Display Means Sales.'" *PNPA Press*, July/August 1977.

Waschler, J. "Grocery Retailers Must Upgrade Customer Relations, P. R. Efforts." *Supermarketing*, December 1977.

Weinstein, Mike. "Mechanization: Distribution Labor Costs Cut." *Chain Store Age Executive*, June 1979.

Williams, H. E. "New Era for Quality Control." *Management World*, August 1978.

FOOD ASSOCIATIONS

American Bakers Association
2020 "K" Street, N.W.
Washington, D.C. 20006

American Beekeeping Federation
13637 N.W., 39th Avenue
Gainesville, Florida 32601

American Dairy Association, Inc.
6300 N. River Road
Rosemont, Illinois 60018

The American Dietetic Association
430 North Michigan Avenue
Chicago, Illinois 60611

American Dry Milk Institute, Inc.
130 North Franklin Street
Chicago, Illinois 60606

American Frozen Food Institute
1700 Old Meadow Road
McLean, Virginia 22102

American Meat Institute
1600 Wilson Boulevard
Arlington, Virginia 22209

American Spice Trade Association
P.O. Box 1267
Englewood Cliffs, New Jersey 07632

The Association for Dressings & Sauces
c/o Robert Kellen & Co.
64 Perimeter Center, E., Suite 790
Atlanta, Georgia 30346

Biscuit and Cracker Distributors Assoc.
111 E. Wacker Drive
Chicago, Illinois 60601

California Dried Fruit Export Association
P.O. Box 270A
303 Brokaw Road
Santa Clara, California 95052

California Rice Export Association
P.O. Box 958
901 South River Road
West Sacramento, California 95691

Canned and Cooked Meat Importers Association
888 17th Street, N.W.
Washington, D.C. 20005

Cereal Institute, Inc.
1111 Plaza Drive
Schaumburg, Illinois 60195

Cooperative Food Distributors of America
1800 "M" Street, N.W.
Washington, D.C. 20036

Fibre Box Association
224 South Michigan Avenue
Chicago, Illinois 60604

Food Marketing Institute
1750 "K" Street, N.W.
Washington, D.C. 20006

Food Processing Machinery & Supplies Association
1828 "L" Street, N.W.
Washington, D.C. 20036

Frozen Food Association of New England
77 Great Road
Acton, Massachusetts 01720

Frozen Potato Products Institute
c/o Smith, Bucklin & Associates
111 East Wacker Drive
Chicago, Illinois 60601

General Merchandise Distributors Council
5250 Far Hills Avenue, Suite 221
Dayton, Ohio 45429

Grocery Manufacturers of America
3217 "K" Street, N.W.
Washington, D.C. 20005

International Association of Ice Cream Manufacturers & Milk Industry Foundation
1105 Barr Building
910 17th Street
Washington, D.C. 20006

International Council of Shopping Centers
665 Fifth Avenue
New York, New York 10022

International Jelly and Preserve Association
64 Perimeter Center East, Suite 790
Atlanta, Georgia 30346

Miller's National Federation
1776 F Street, N.W.
Washington, D.C. 20006

National-American Wholesale Grocers' Association
51 Madison Avenue
New York, New York 10010

National Association of Convenience Stores
5205 Leesburg Turnpike, Suite 305
Falls Church, Virginia 22041

National Association of Concessionaires
35 E. Wacker Drive, Suite 1840
Chicago, Illinois 60601

National Association of Greenhouse
  Vegetable Growers
R. A. Gall Building B7
6500 Peal Road
Cleveland, Ohio 44130

National Association of Margarine Manufacturers
1725 "K" Street, N.W.
Washington, D.C. 20006

National Association of Meat Purveyors
252 West Ina Road
Tucson, Arizona 85704

National Association of Retail Grocers of U.S.
11800 Sunrise Valley Drive
Reston, Virginia 22091

National Association of Service Merchandising
805 Merchandise Mart
Chicago, Illinois 60654

National Association for the
  Specialty Food Trade, Inc.
1270 Avenue of the Americas
New York, New York 10019

National Association of Tobacco Distributors
58 East 79th Street
New York, New York 10021

National Broiler Council
1155 15th Street, N.W.
Washington, D.C. 20005

National Candy Wholesalers Assoc., Inc.
1430 "K" Street, N.W.
Washington, D.C. 20005

National Cheese Institute, Inc./
  American Butter Institute
110 North Franklin Street
Chicago, Illinois 60606

National Coffee Association of the U.S.A.
120 Wall Street
New York, New York 10005

National Confectioners' Assoc. of the U.S.
5101 Wisconsin Avenue, N.W.
Washington, D.C. 20016

National Corn Growers Association
815 Office Park Road
Des Moines, Iowa 50265

National Dairy Council
6300 N. River Road
Rosemont, Illinois 60018

National Dry Bean Council, Inc.
Shields, Inc.
Box 472
Buhl, Idaho 83316

National Fisheries Institute
1101 Connecticut Avenue, N.W.
Washington, D.C. 20006

National Food Brokers Association
The NFBA Building
1916 "M" Street, N.W.
Washington, D.C. 20036

National Frozen Foods Association
P.O. Box 398
Hershey, Pennsylvania 17033

National Frozen Pizza Institute
1700 Old Meadow Road, Suite 100
McLean, Virginia 22102

National Honey Packers and Dealers Association
1515 5th Street
Snohomish, Washington 98290

National Independent Poultry and
  Food Distributors Association
4801 North State Street, Suite 116
Jackson, Mississippi 39206

National Kraut Packers Association, Inc.
108½ East Main Street
St. Charles, Illinois 60174

National Live Stock & Meat Board
444 N. Michigan Avenue
Chicago, Illinois 60611

National Macaroni Manufacturers' Association
19 South Bothwell Street
Palatine, Illinois 60067

National Meat Canners Association
P.O. Box 3556
Washington, D.C. 20007

National Paper Box Association
231 Kings Highway East
Haddonfield, New Jersey 08033

National Peanut Council
1000 16th Street, N.W., Suite 506
Washington, D.C. 20036

National Prepared Frozen Food Processors Assoc.
Box 594
Valley Stream, New York 11580

National Red Cherry Institute
415 West Grand River Avenue
East Lansing, Michigan 48823

National Soft Drink Association
1101 16th Street, N.W.
Washington, D.C. 20036

National Sugar Brokers Association, Inc.
One World Trade Center, Suite 5011
New York, New York 10048

National Turkey Federation
Reston International Center
11800 Sunrise Valley Drive
Reston, Virginia 22091

Natural Food Associates
Box 210
Atlanta, Texas 75551

New York Coffee and Sugar Exchange, Inc.
4 World Trade Center, S.E.
New York, New York 10048

Packaging Institute
342 Madison Avenue
New York, New York 10017

Paperboard Packaging Council
1800 "K" Street, N.W., Suite 600
Washington, D.C. 20006

Peanut Butter Manufacturers and
    Nut Salters Association
5101 Wisconsin Avenue
Washington, D.C. 20016

Pet Food Institute
1101 Connecticut Avenue, N.W.
Washington, D.C. 20006

Pickle Packers International, Inc.
P.O. Box 31
St. Charles, Illinois 60174

The Popcorn Institute
One Illinois Center, 111 East Wacker Dr.
Chicago, Illinois 60601

The Potato Association of America
114 Deering Hall
University of Maine
Orono, Maine 04473

Potato Chip/Snack Food Association
One Skyline Place, Suite 202
5205 Leesburg Pike
Baileys Crossroads, Virginia 22041

Poultry & Egg Institute of America
1815 N. Lynn Street
Arlington, Virginia 22209

Processed Apples Institute, Inc.
64 Perimeter Center East
Atlanta, Georgia 30346

Produce Marketing Association
700 Barksdale Road, Suite 6
Newark, Delaware 19711

The Rice Millers Association
2001 Jefferson Davis Highway
Arlington, Virginia 22202

Shellfish Institute of North America
212 Washington Avenue, Suite 9
Baltimore, Maryland 21204

The Sugar Association, Inc.
1511 "K" Street, N.W.
Washington, D.C. 20005

Tuna Research Foundation
1101 17th Street, N.W., Suite 607
Washington, D.C. 20036

United Dairy Industry Association
6300 N. River Road
Rosemont, Illinois 60018

United States Council for Special Foods
64 Perimeter Center East, Suite 790
Atlanta, Georgia 30346

United States National Fruit Export Council
1133 20th Street, N.W.
Washington, D.C. 20036

Vanilla Bean Association of America
35-02 48th Avenue
Long Island City, New York 11101

The Vinegar Institute
c/o Robert Kellen & Company
64 Perimeter Center, East
Atlanta, Georgia 30346

Western States Meat Packers Association, Inc.
88 First Street
San Francisco, California 94105

Wheat Flour Institute
1776 F Street, N.W.
Washington, D.C. 20006

The Wine Institute
165 Post Street
San Francisco, California 94108